Lecture Notes in Artificial 1

Subseries of Lecture Notes in Comput

Edited by J. G. Carbonell and J. Siekma....

Lecture Notes in Computer Science

Edited by G. Goos, J. Hartmanis and J. van Leeuwen

T0230090

Springer
Berlin
Heidelberg
New York
Barcelona
Hong Kong
London
Milan
Paris
Tokyo

Barbara Dunin-Kęplicz   Edward Nawarecki (Eds.)

From Theory to Practice in Multi-Agent Systems

Second International Workshop of Central and Eastern
Europe on Multi-Agent Systems, CEEMAS 2001
Cracow, Poland, September 26-29, 2001
Revised Papers

 Springer

Series Editors

Jaime G. Carbonell,Carnegie Mellon University, Pittsburgh, PA, USA
Jörg Siekmann, University of Saarland, Saarbrücken, Germany

Volume Editors

Barbara Dunin-Kęplicz
Warsaw University
Institute of Informatics
ul. Banacha 2, 02-097 Warsaw, Poland
E-mail: keplicz@mimuw.edu.pl

Edward Nawarecki
University of Mining and Metallurgy
Department of Computer Science
al. Mickiewicza 30, 30-059 Krakow, Poland
E-mail: nawar@agh.edu.pl

Cataloging-in-Publication Data applied for

Die Deutsche Bibliothek - CIP-Einheitsaufnahme

From theory to practice in multi-agent systems : revised papers / Second
International Workshop of Central and Eastern Europe on Multi-Agent Systems,
CEEMAS 2001, Cracow, Polland, September 26 - 29, 2001. Barbara Dunin-Keplicz
;
Edward Nawarecki (ed.). - Berlin ; Heidelberg ; New York ; Barcelona ; Hong Kong ;
London ; Milan ; Paris ; Tokyo : Springer, 2002
    (Lecture notes in computer science ; Vol. 2296 : Lecture notes
    in artificial intelligence)
    ISBN 3-540-43370-8

CR Subject Classification (1998): I.2.11, C.2.4, D.2, H.5.3, I.2

ISSN 0302-9743
ISBN 3-540-43370-8 Springer-Verlag Berlin Heidelberg New York

Springer-Verlag Berlin Heidelberg New York
a member of BertelsmannSpringer Science+Business Media GmbH

http://www.springer.de

© Springer-Verlag Berlin Heidelberg 2002
Printed in Germany

Typesetting: Camera-ready by author, data conversion by PTP-Berlin, Stefan Sossna
Printed on acid-free paper   SPIN 10846424   06/3142   5 4 3 2 1 0

Preface

This volume contains the papers selected for presentation at CEEMAS 2001. The workshop was the fourth in a series of international conferences devoted to autonomous agents and multi-agent systems organized in Central-Eastern Europe. Its predecessors were CEEMAS'99 and DAIMAS'97, which took place in St. Petersburg, Russia, as well as DIMAS'95, which took place in Cracow, Poland.

Organizers of all these events made efforts to make them wide-open to participants from all over the world. This would have been impossible without some help from friendly centers in the Czech Republic, England, France, Japan, and The Netherlands.

DIMAS'95 featured papers from 15 countries, while CEEMAS'99 from 18 countries. A total of 61 papers were submitted to CEEMAS 2001 from 17 countries. Out of these papers, 31 were selected for regular presentation, while 14 were qualified as posters.

The motto of the meeting was "Diversity is the core of multi-agent systems". This variety of subjects was clearly visible in the CEEMAS 2001 program, addressing the following major areas of multi-agent systems:

- Organizations and social aspects of multi-agent systems
- Agent and multi-agent system architectures, models, and formalisms
- Communication languages, protocols, and negotiation
- Applications of multi-agent systems
- Agent and multi-agent development tools
- Theoretical foundations of Distributed AI
- Learning in multi-agent systems

The richness of workshop subjects was ensured thanks to the CEEMAS 2001 contributing authors as well as the keynote speakers. We would like to thank Jeffrey Bradshaw (University of West Florida, USA), Toru Ishida (Kyoto University, Japan), Nick Jennings (University of Southampton, UK), Andrzej Skowron (Warsaw University, Poland), and Krzysztof Zieliński (University of Mining and Metallurgy, Poland) for presenting invited talks announcing the most recent trends in multi-agent technology.

Special thanks are due to the members of the Program Committee, aided by auxiliary reviewers, for their professionalism and guidance in the process of selecting papers for the workshop.

Nothing would have been possible without the initiative and dedication of the Organizing Committee at the University of Mining and Metallurgy and the Jagiellonian University.

Finally, we would like to acknowledge the role of the workshop sponsors: the Rectors of the University of Mining and Metallurgy and the Jagiellonian University, as well as AgentLink.

January 2002   Barbara Dunin-Kęplicz
                                                               Edward Nawarecki

CEEMAS 2001

Second International Workshop of Central and Eastern Europe on Multi-Agent Systems, Cracow, Poland, 26–29 September 2001

Under the auspices of

JM Rectors of the University of Mining and Metallurgy and Jagiellonian University

Chairpersons

Edward Nawarecki (Poland) *chair*
Barbara Dunin-Kęplicz (Poland) *program co-chair*
Yves Demazeau (France) *co-chair*
Vladimir Gorodetski (Russia) *co-chair*

Program Committee

Stanis law Ambroszkiewicz (Poland)
Magnus Boman (Sweden)
Hans-Dieter Burkhard (Germany)
Cristiano Castelfranchi (Italy)
Krzysztof Cetnarowicz (Poland)
Pierre Deschizeaux (France)
Grzegorz Dobrowolski (Poland)
Aldo Dragoni (Italy)
Love Ekenberg (Sweden)
Mariusz Flasiński (Poland)
Adina M. Florea (Romania)
Piotr Gmytrasiewicz (USA)
Adam Grzech (Poland)
Gregory O'Hare (Ireland)
Wiebe van der Hoek (The Netherlands)
Toru Ishida (Japan)
Nick Jennings (UK)

Jean-Luc Koning (France)
Abder Koukam (France)
Vladimir Marik (Czech Republic)
Pierre Massotte (France)
Antoni Mazurkiewicz (Poland)
John W. Perram (Denmark)
Lech Polkowski (Poland)
Joel Quinqueton (France)
Leszek Rutkowski (Poland)
Robert Schaefer (Poland)
Carles Sierra (Spain)
Andrzej Skowron (Poland)
Alexander Smirnov (Russia)
Vilem Srovnal (Czech Republic)
Vadim Stefanuk (Russia)
Jozsef Vancza (Hungary)
Rineke Verbrugge (The Netherlands)

Auxiliary reviewers

Markus Hannebauer (Germany), Marek Kisiel-Dorohinicki (Poland),
Igor Kotenko (Russia), Johan Kummeneje (Sweden), Xudong Luo (UK),
Mirjam Minor (Germany), Sebastian Müller (Germany), Kay Schröter (Germany)

Sponsored by

AgentLink, European Commission's IST-funded Network of Excellence for Agent-Based Computing

Table of Contents

Invited Papers

Approximate Reasoning by Agents

Andrzej Skowron

Institute of Mathematics, Warsaw University
Banacha 2, 02-097 Warsaw, Poland
skowron@mimuw.edu.pl

Abstract. We present an approach to approximate reasoning by agents in distributed environments based on calculi of information granules. Approximate reasoning schemes are basic schemes of information granule construction. An important property of such schemes is their robustness with respect to input deviations. In distributed environments, such schemes are extended to rough neural networks that transform information granules into information granules rather than vectors of real numbers into (vectors of) real numbers. Problems of learning in rough neural networks from experimental data and background knowledge are outlined.

1 Introduction

Information granulation belongs to intensively studied topics in soft computing (see, e.g., [28], [29], [30]). One of the recently emerging approaches to deal with information granulation, called granular computing (GC), is based on information granule calculi (see, e.g., [17], [24]). The development of such calculi is important for making progress in many areas like object identification by autonomous systems (see, e.g., [2], [26]), web mining (see, e.g., [6]), spatial reasoning (see, e.g., [3]) or sensor fusion (see, e.g., [1], [13]). One of the main goals of GC is to achieve computing with words (CWW) (see, e.g., [28], [29], [30]).

Any approach to information granulation should make it possible to define complex information granules (e.g., in spatial and temporal reasoning, one should be able to determine if the situation on the road is safe on the basis of sensor measurements [26] or to classify situations in complex games like soccer [25]). These complex information granules constitute a form of information fusion. Any calculus of complex information granules should make it possible to (i) deal with vagueness of information granules, (ii) develop strategies of inducing multi-layered schemes of complex granule construction, (iii) derive robust (stable) information granule construction schemes with respect to deviations of granules from which they are constructed, and (iv) develop adaptive strategies for reconstruction of induced schemes of complex information granule synthesis. To deal with vagueness, one can adopt fuzzy set theory [27] or rough set theory [12] either separately or in combination [10]. The second requirement is related to the problem of understanding of reasoning from measurements relative to perception (see, e.g., [30]) and to concept approximation learning in layered

B. Dunin-Kęplicz and E. Nawarecki (Eds.): CEEMAS 2001, LNAI 2296, pp. 3–14, 2002.

learning [25] as well as to fusion of information from different sources (see, e.g., [28], [29], [30]). The importance of searching for approximate reasoning schemes (*AR*-schemes, for short) as schemes of new information granule construction, is stressed in rough mereology (see, e.g., [15], [16], [16], [19]). In general, this leads to hierarchical schemes of new information granule construction. This process is closely related to ideas of co-operation, negotiations and conflict resolution in multi-agent systems [5]. Among important topics studied in relation to *AR*-schemes are methods for specifying operations on information granules; in particular, AR-schemes are useful in constructing information granules from data and background knowledge, and in supplying methods for inducing these hierarchical schemes of information granule construction. One of the possible approaches is to learn such schemes using evolutionary strategies [8]. Robustness of the scheme means that any scheme produces a higher order information granule that is a clump (e.g., a set) of close information granules rather than a single information granule. Such a clump is constructed by means of the scheme from the Cartesian product of input clumps (e.g., clusters) satisfying some constraints. The input clumps are defined by deviations (up to acceptable degrees) of input information granules from standards (prototypes).

It is worthwhile to mention that modeling complex phenomena requires us to use complex information granules representing local models (perceived by local agents) that are fused. This process involves negotiations between agents [5] to resolve contradictions and conflicts in local modeling. This kind of modeling will become more and more important in solving complex real-life problems which we are unable to model using traditional analytical approaches. If the latter approaches can be applied to modeling of such problems they lead to exact models. However, the necessary assumptions used to build them in case of complex real-life problems are often cause the resulting solutions to be *too far* from reality to be accepted as solutions of such problems.

Let us also observe, using multi-agent terminology, that local agents perform operations on information granules that are *understandable* by them. Hence, granules submitted as arguments by other agents should be approximated by means of properly tuned approximation spaces creating interfaces between agents. The process of tuning of the approximation space [23], [19] parameters in *AR*-schemes corresponds to the tuning of weights in neural networks. The methods for inducing of *AR*-schemes transforming information granules into information granules developed using rough set (see, e.g., [12], [7]) and rough mereological methods in hybridization with other soft computing approaches create a core for rough neurocomputing (RNC) (see, e.g., [11], [19]). In RNC, computations are performed on information granules.

One of the basic problems concerns relationships between information granules and words (linguistic terms) in a natural language and also a possibility to use induced *AR*-schemes as schemes matching up to a satisfactory degree reasoning schemes in natural language. Further research in this direction will create strong links between RNC and CWW.

RNC aims at defining information granules using rough sets [12], [7] and rough mereology (see, e.g., [16], [16], [19]) introduced to deal with vague concepts in hybridization with other soft computing methods like neural networks [20], fuzzy sets [10], [27], [29] and evolutionary programming [11], [8]. The methods based on the above mentioned approaches can be used for constructing of more complex information granules by means of schemes analogous to neural networks.

We outline a rough neurocomputing model as a basis for granular computing.

2   Information Granules

We assume each agent ag from a given collection Ag of agents [5] is equipped with a system of information granules $S(ag)$ specifying information granules the agent ag is perceiving and the inclusion (or closeness) relations to a degree used by ag to measure the degree of inclusion (or closenees) between information granules. A formal definition of information granule system the reader can find, e.g., in [22]. Using such system $S(ag)$ the agent ag creates its representations, e.g. in the form of decision systems [12]. The construction of information granules can be quite complex.

Let us consider classifiers as examples of information granules (see Figure 1). Classifiers are important examples of information granules because they are intensively used in machine learning and pattern recognition applications.

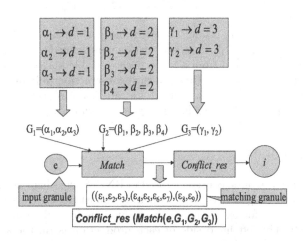

Fig. 1. An example of information granule: Classifier

First let us assume there is given a consistent decision table $DT = (U, A, d)$ with r decision values. Let E be a set of Boolean descriptors being conjunctions of elementary descriptors, i.e., expressions of the form (a, v) over attributes from $\mathcal{A} = (U, A)$ where $a \in A$ and v is a value of a.

The classifier construction from DT can be described as follows:

1. Construct granules G_j corresponding to each particular decision $j = 1, \ldots, r$ of $\mathcal{A}$ by taking a collection $\{g_{ij} : i = 1, \ldots, k_j\}$ of the left hand sides of decision rules for a given decision j for $j = 1, \cdots, r$ (in Figure 1 we have $r = 3$).
2. Construct a granule defined by a term

$$Match(e, \{G_1, \ldots, G_r\})$$

where $G_1, \ldots, G_r$ are constants and e is a variable taking values from E. Any instantiation of e defines the result of voting by all decision rules for a given object represented by e.
3. Construct a term

$$Conflict\_res(Match(e, \{G_1, \ldots, G_r\}))$$

where $Conflict\_res$ is a voting operation resolving conflicts between decision rules.

Let us observe that the decision predicted by the classifier is equal to the value of the constructed term for a particular input information granule e. We have represented a classifier construction by a term

$$Conflict\_res(Match(e, \{G_1, \ldots, G_r\}))$$

with matching and conflict resolution operations performed on information granules. Let us observe that $G_1, \ldots, G_r$ are parameters defined by the left hand sides of decision rules generated from a given decision table and e is a variable with values in E. Parameters to be tuned in such construction to induce high quality classifiers are voting strategies, matching strategies of objects against rules as well as other parameters like inclusion degrees of granules to the target granule.

3   *AR*-Schemes

AR-schemes are the basic constructs used in RNC. Such schemes can be derived from parameterized productions representing robust dependencies in data. Algorithmic methods for extracting such productions from data are discussed in [16], [21], [14]. The left hand side of each production is (in the simplest case) of the form $(st_1(ag), (\epsilon_1^{(1)}, \cdots, \epsilon_r^{(1)})), \cdots, (st_k(ag), (\epsilon_1^{(k)}, \cdots, \epsilon_r^{(k)}))$ and the right hand side is of the form $(st(ag), (\epsilon_1, \cdots, \epsilon_r)$ for some positive integers k, r.

Such production represents an information about an operation o which can be performed by the agent ag. In the production k denotes the arity of operation. The operation o represented by the production is transforming standard (prototype) input information granules $st_1(ag), \cdots, st_k(ag)$ into the standard (prototype) information granule $st(ag)$. Moreover, if input information granules

$g_1, \cdots, g_k$ are close to $st_1(ag), \cdots, st_k(ag)$ to degrees $\epsilon_j^{(1)}, \cdots, \epsilon_j^{(k)}$ then the result of the operation o on information granules $g_1, \cdots, g_k$ is close to the standard $st(ag)$ to a degree at least ϵ_j where $1 \leq j \leq k$. Standard (prototype) granules can be interpreted in different ways. In particular they can correspond to concept names in natural language.

The productions described above are basic components of a reasoning system over an agent set Ag. An important property of such productions is that they are expected to be discovered from available experimental data and background knowledge. Let us also observe that the degree structure is not necessarily restricted to reals from the interval $[0, 1]$. The inclusion degrees can have a structure of complex information granules used to represent the degree of inclusion. It is worthwhile to mention that the productions can also be interpreted as a constructive description of some operations on fuzzy sets. The methods for such constructive description are based on rough sets and Boolean reasoning (see, e.g., [7], [12]).

AR-schemes can be treated as derivations obtained by using productions from different agents. The relevant derivations generating AR-schemes satisfy so called robustness (or stability) condition. This means that at any node of derivation the inclusion (or closeness) degree of constructed granule to the prototype (standard) granule is higher than required by the production to which the result should be sent. This makes it possible to obtain a sufficient robustness condition for whole derivations. For details the reader is referred to, e.g., [17], [18]. In cases where standards are interpreted as concept names in natural language and a reasoning scheme in natural language over the standard concepts is given, the corresponding AR-scheme represents a cluster of reasoning (constructions) approximately following (by means of other information granule systems) the reasoning in natural language. In the following section, we discuss in more details the concept of standard information granules.

3.1 Standards

In this section we discuss different approaches to standard information granule definition.

Standards represented by rough sets. In the simplest case, standards can be represented by the lower approximations of concepts. The degree of inclusion of a pattern supported by objects from the set $X \subseteq U$ into the lower approximation supported by the objects from the set $Y \subseteq U$ can be measured by the ratio $|X \cap Y|/|X|$ where U is the set of objects in a given decision table (representing the training sample).

However, if the lower approximation is intended to describe the concept in an extension of the training sample U, then inductive reasoning should be used to find an approximation of this lower approximation of the concept. Such approximations can be represented, e.g., by decision rules describing the lower approximation and its complement together with a method making possible to measure matching degrees of new objects and the decision rules as well as the method for conflict resolution between decision rules voting for the new objects. In such cases the degree of inclusion of any pattern in the lower approximation has more complex structure and can be represented by two vectors of inclusion degrees of this pattern in decision rules representing the lower approximation and its complement, respectively.

Using the rough set approach, one can measure not only the degree of inclusion of a concept in the lower approximation but also the degree of inclusion of a concept in other information granules defined using rough set approach such as upper approximations, boundary regions or complements of upper approximations of concepts. In this case instead of one degree one should consider a vector of degrees. However, if the lower approximation is too small the measurements based on inclusion in the standard defined by the lower approximation can be unreliable and then it can be necessary to consider other kinds of standards which can be constructed using, e.g., rough-fuzzy approach or classifier construction methods.

Standards corresponding to rough-fuzzy sets. The presented in the previous section approach can be extended to concepts defined by fuzzy sets. We will show that the dependencies between linguistic variables can be modeled by productions. Using the rough-fuzzy approach one can search for dependencies between lower approximations of differences between relevant cuts of fuzzy sets modeling linguistic variables. The productions built along such dependencies make it possible to model dependencies between linguistic variables. Moreover, the approximate reasoning on linguistic variables can be modeled by approximate reasoning schemes (AR-schemes) derived from productions.

We are going now to describe rough-fuzzy granules. We assume if X is an information granule, e.g., a set of objects, then its upper and lower approximations with respect to any subset of attributes in a given information system or decision table is an information granule too. Let us see now how such information granules can be used to define in a constructive way fuzzy concept [27] approximations.

Let $DT = (U, A, d)$ be a decision table with the decision being the restriction to the objects from U of the fuzzy membership function $\mu : U \to [0, 1]$. Consider reals $0 < c_1 < \ldots < c_k$ where $c_i \in (0, 1]$ for $i = 1, \ldots, k$. Any c_i defines c_i-cut by $X_i = \{x \in U : \mu(x) \geq c_i\}$. Assume $X_0 = U, X_{k+1} = X_{k+2} = \emptyset$.

A *rough–fuzzy granule* (*rf–granule*, for short) corresponding to $(DT, c_1, \ldots, c_k)$ is any granule $g = (g_0, \ldots, g_k)$ such that for some $B \subseteq A$

1. $Sem_B(g_i) = (\underline{B}(X_i - X_{i+1}), \overline{B}(X_i - X_{i+1}))$ for $i = 0, \ldots, k$;
2. $\overline{B}(X_i - X_{i+1}) \subseteq (X_{i-1} - X_{i+2})$ for $i = 1, \ldots, k$.

where $\underline{B}$ and $\overline{B}$ denote the B-lower and B-upper approximation operators, respectively [12] and $Sem_B(g_i)$ denotes the semantics of g_i.

Any function $\mu^* : U \to [0, 1]$ satisfying the following conditions:

1. $\mu^*(x) = 0$ for $x \in U - \overline{B}X_1$;

2. $\mu^*(x) = 1$ for $x \in \underline{B}X_k$;
3. $\mu^*(x) = c_{i-1}$ for $x \in \underline{B}(X_{i-1} - X_i)$ and $i = 2, \ldots, k-1$;
4. $c_{i-1} < \mu^*(x) < c_i$ for $x \in (\overline{B}X_i - \underline{B}X_i)$ where $i = 1, \ldots, k$, and $c_0 = 0$;

is called a B-approximation of μ.

Assume a rule **if** α **and** β **then** γ is given where α, β, γ are linguistic variables. The aim is to develop a searching method for rough-fuzzy granules g^1, g^2, g^3 approximating to satisfactory degrees α, β, γ, respectively and at the same time making it possible to discover association rules of the form **if** α' **and** β' **then** γ' with a sufficiently large support and confidence coefficients, where α', β', γ' are some components (e.g., the lower approximations of differences between cuts of fuzzy concepts corresponding to linguistic variables) of granules g^1, g^2, g^3 (modeling linguistic variables), respectively. Searching for such patterns and rules is a complex process with many parameters to be tuned. For given linguistic rules, the relevant cuts for corresponding to them fuzzy concepts should be discovered. Next, the relevant features (attributes) should be chosen. They are used to construct approximations of differences between cuts. Moreover, relevant measures should be chosen to measure the degree of inclusion of object patterns in the constructed lower approximations. One can expect that these measures are parameterized and the relevant parameters should be discovered in the process searching for productions. Certainly, in searching for relevant parameters in this complex optimization process evolutionary techniques can be used. This quality of discovered rules can be measured as a degree to which discovered rule **if** α' **and** β' **then** γ' approximates the linguistic rule **if** α **and** β **then** γ. This can be expressed by means of such parameters like degrees of inclusion of patterns α', β', γ' in α, β, γ, their supports etc.

Let us observe that for a given linguistic rule it will be necessary to find a family of rules represented by discovered patterns which together create an information granule sufficiently close to modeled linguistic rule.

One can also search for more general information granules representing clusters of discovered rules **if** α' **and** β' **then** γ' approximating the linguistic rule **if** α **and** β **then** γ. These clustered rules can be of higher quality. Certainly, this makes it necessary to discover and tune many parameters relevant for measuring similarity or closeness of rules.

The discussed problem is of a great importance in classification of situations by autonomous systems on the basis of sensor measurements [26]. Moreover, this is one of the basic problems to be investigated for hybridization of rough and fuzzy approaches.

Standards corresponding to classifiers. For classifiers we obtain another possibility. Let us consider information granules corresponding to values of terms $Match(e, \{G_1, \cdots, G_k)\}$ for $e \in E$ [21]. Any such granule defines a probability distribution on a set of possible decisions (extended by the value corresponding to *no decision predicted*). Probability for each such value is obtained simply as a ratio of all votes for the decision value determined by this information granule and the number of objects. Some probability distributions can be chosen as standards. It means, that instead of the lower approximations one can use such probability distributions. Certainly, it can be sometimes useful to choose not one such standard but a collection of them. Now, one should decide how to measure the distances between probability distributions. Using a chosen distance measure, e.g., Euclidean, it is possible to measure a degree of closeness of classified objects e, e' using the probability distributions corresponding to them. The next steps of construction of approximate reasoning rule based on classifiers is analogous to the discussed before.

One of the most interesting case is received if standards are interpreted as concepts from natural language. In this case measures of inclusion and closeness can be based on semantic similarity and closeness relations rather than on statistical properties. Constructing such measures is a challenge. This case is strongly related to the CWW paradigm. The discovered productions can to satisfactory degree be consistent with reasoning steps performed in natural language.

4   Rough Neural Networks

We extend AR-schemes for synthesis of complex objects (or granules) developed in [17] by adding one important component. As a result we obtain granule construction schemes that can be treated as a generalization of neural network models. The main idea is that granules sent by one agent to another are not, in general, exactly understandable by the receiving agent. This is because these agents are using different languages and usually does not exist any translation (from the sender language to the receiver language) preserving exactly semantical meaning of formulas. Hence, it is necessary to construct interfaces that will make it possible to understand received granules approximately. These interfaces can be, in the simplest case, constructed on the basis of information exchanged by agents and stored in the form of decision data tables. From such tables the approximations of concepts can be constructed using the rough set approach [24]. In general, this is a complex process because a high quality approximation of concepts can be often obtained only in dialog (involving nagotiations, conflict resolutions and cooperation) among agents. In this process the approximation can be constructed gradually when dialog is progressing. In our model we assume that for any n-ary operation $o(ag)$ of an agent ag there are approximation spaces $AS_1(o(ag), in), ..., AS_n(o(ag), in)$ which will filter (approximate) the granules received by the agent for performing the operation $o(ag)$. In turn, the granule sent by the agent after performing the operation is filtered (approximated) by the approximation space $AS(o(ag), out)$. These approximation spaces are parameterized. The parameters are used to optimize the size of neighborhoods in these spaces as well as the inclusion relation. A granule approximation quality is taken as the optimization criterion. Approximation spaces attached to any operation of ag correspond to neuron weights in neural networks whereas the operation performed by the agent ag on information granules corresponds to the operation realized on vectors of real numbers by the neuron. The generalized scheme of agents is returning a granule in response to input information granules. It can be for example a cluster of elementary granules. Hence, our schemes realize much more general computations than neural networks operating on vectors of real numbers.

We call extended schemes for complex object construction *rough neural networks* (for complex object construction). The problem of deriving such schemes is closely related to perception (see, e.g., [30]). The stability of such networks corresponds to the resistance to noise of classical neural networks.

Let us observe that in our approach the deductive systems are substituted by productions systems of agents linked by approximation spaces, communication strategies and mechanism of derivation of AR-schemes. This revision of classical logical notions seems to be important for solving complex problems in distributed environments.

5   Decomposition of Information Granules

Information granule decomposition methods are important components of methods for inducing of AR-schemes from data and background knowledge. Such methods are used to extract from data, local decomposition schemes called produtions [18]. The AR-schemes are constructed by means of productions. The decomposition methods are based on searching for the parts of information granules that can be used to construct relevant higher level patterns matching up to a satisfactory degree the target granule.

One can distinguish two kinds of parts (represented, e.g., by sub-formulas or sub-terms) of AR-schemes. Parts of the first type are represented by expressions from a language, called the *domestic* language L_d, that has known semantics (consider, for example, semantics defined in a given information system [12]). Parts of the second type of AR-scheme are from a language, called *foreign* language L_f (e.g., natural language), that has semantics definable only in an approximate way (e.g., by means of patterns extracted using rough, fuzzy, rough–fuzzy or other approaches). For example, the parts of the second kind of scheme can be interpreted as soft properties of sensor measurements [2].

For a given expression e, representing a given scheme that consists of sub-expressions from L_f first it is necessary to search for relevant approximations in L_d of the foreign parts from L_f and next to derive global patterns from the whole expression after replacing the foreign parts by their approximations. This can be a multilevel process, i.e., we are facing problems of discovered pattern propagation through several domestic-foreign layers.

Productions from which AR-schemes are built can be induced from data and background knowledge by pattern extraction strategies. Let us consider some of such strategies. The first one makes it possible to search for relevant approximations of parts using the rough set approach. This means that each part from L_f can be replaced by its lower or upper approximation with respect to a set B of attributes. The approximation is constructed on the basis of relevant data table [12], [7]. With the second strategy parts from L_f are partitioned into a number of sub-parts corresponding to cuts (or the set theoretical differences between cuts) of fuzzy sets representing vague concepts and each sub-part is approximated by means of rough set methods. The third strategy is based on searching for patterns sufficiently included in foreign parts. In all cases, the extracted approximations replace foreign parts in the scheme and candidates for global patterns are derived from the scheme obtained after the replacement. Searching for relevant global patterns is a complex task because many parameters should be tuned, e.g., the set of relevant features used in approximation, relevant approximation operators, the number and distribution of objects from the universe of objects among different cuts and so on. One can use evolutionary techniques [8] in searching for (semi-) optimal patterns in the decomposition.

It has been shown that decomposition strategies can be based on rough set methods for decision rule generation and Boolean reasoning [16], [9], [24]. In particular, methods for decomposition based on background knowledge can be developed. The interested reader is referred to [21], [14].

Conclusions. We have discussed a methodology for synthesis of AR-schemes and rough neural networks. For more details the reader is referred to [16], [17], [19], [23], [24]. The reported research topics are very much related to multi-agent systems. We would like to emphasize two of them, namely:

1. *Algorithmic methods for synthesis of AR-schemes.* It was observed (see, e.g., [19]) that problems of negotiations and conflict resolutions are of great importance for synthesis of AR-schemes. The problem arises, e.g., when we are searching in a given set of agents for a granule sufficiently included or close to a given one. These agents, often working with different systems of information granules, can derive different granules and their fusion will be necessary to obtain the relevant output granule. In the fusion process, the negotiations and conflict resolutions are necessary. Much more work should be done in this direction by using the existing results on negotiations and conflict resolution. In particular, Boolean reasoning methods seem to be promising for solving such problems. Another problem is related to the size of production sets. These sets can be of large size and it is important to develop learning methods for extracting *small* candidate production sets in the process of extension of temporary derivations out of huge production sets. For solving this kind of problems, methods for clustering of productions should be developed to reduce the size of production sets. Moreover, dialog and cooperation strategies between agents can help to reduce the search space in the process of AR-scheme construction from productions.

2. *Algorithmic methods for learning in rough neural networks.* A basic problem in rough neural networks is related to selecting relevant approximation spaces and to parameter tuning. One can also look up to what extent the existing methods for classical neural methods can be used for learning in rough neural networks. However, it seems that new approach and methods for learning of rough neural networks should be developed to deal with real-life applications. In particular, it is due to the fact that high quality approximations of concepts can be often obtained only through dialog and

negotiations processes among agents in which gradually the concept approximation is constructed. Hence, for rough neural networks learning methods based on dialog, negotiations and conflict resolutions should be developed. In some cases, one can use directly rough set and Boolean reasoning methods (see, e.g., [24]). However, more advanced cases need new methods. In particular, hybrid methods based on rough and fuzzy approaches can bring new results [10].

Acknowledgements. The research has been supported by the State Committee for Scientific Research of the Republic of Poland (KBN) research grant 8 T11C 025 19 and by the Wallenberg Foundation grant.

References

1. Brooks, R.R., Iyengar, S.S. (1998): Multi-Sensor Fusion, Prentice-Hall PTR, Upper Saddle River, NJ
2. Doherty, P., Łukaszewicz, W., Skowron A., Szałas, A. (2001): Combining Rough and Crisp Knowledge in Deductive Databases (submitted)
3. Düntsch I. (Ed.)(2001): Spatial Reasoning, Fundamenta Informaticae **45**(1-2) (special issue)
4. Hirano, S., Inuiguchi, M., Tsumoto, S. (Eds.) (2001): Proc. RSTGC'01, Bulletin of International Rough Set Society **5**(1-2)
5. Huhns, M.N., Singh, M.P. (Eds.) (1998): Readings in Agents, Morgan Kaufmann, San Mateo
6. Kargupta, H., Chan, Ph. (2001): Advances in Distributed and Parallel Knowledge Discovery, AAAI Press/MIT Press, Cambridge
7. Komorowski, J., Pawlak, P., Polkowski, L., and Skowron A. (1999): Rough Sets: A Tutorial, in [10] 3–98
8. Koza, J. R. (1994): Genetic Programming II: Automatic Discovery of Reusable Programs, MIT Press, Cambridge, MA
9. Nguyen, H.S., Nguyen, S.H., Skowron, A. (1999): Decomposition of Task Specification, Proc. ISMIS'99, Lecture Notes in Artificial Intelligence **1609**, Springer-Verlag, Berlin, 310–318
10. Pal, S.K., Skowron, A. (Eds.) (1999): Rough-Fuzzy Hybridization: A New Trend in Decision Making, Springer-Verlag, Singapore
11. Pal, S.K., Pedrycz, W., Skowron, A., Swiniarski, R. (Eds.) (2001): Rough-Neuro Computing, Neurocomputing **36**, 1–262 (special issue)
12. Pawlak, Z. (1991): Rough Sets. Theoretical Aspects of Reasoning about Data, Kluwer Academic Publishers, Dordrecht
13. Peters, J.F., Ramanna, S., Skowron, A., Stepaniuk, J., Suraj, Z., Borkowsky, M. (2001): Sensor Fusion: A Rough Granular Approach, Proc. of Int. Fuzzy Systems Association World Congress (IFSA'01), Vancouver, July 2001, 1367–1371
14. Peters, J.F., Skowron, A. Stepaniuk, J. (2001): Information Granule Decomposition, Fundamenta Informaticae **47(3-4)**, 337–350
15. Polkowski, L., Skowron, A. (1996): Rough Mereology: A New Paradigm for Approximate Reasoning, International J. Approximate Reasoning **15**(4), 333–365

16. Polkowski, L., Skowron, A. (1996): Rough Mereological Approach to Knowledge-Based Distributed AI, (Eds.) J.K. Lee, J. Liebowitz, and J.M. Chae, Critical Technology, Proc. of the Third World Congress on Expert Systems, February 5-9, Seoul, Korea, Cognizant Communication Corporation, New York, 774–781
17. Polkowski, L., Skowron, A. (1999): Towards adaptive calculus of granules, in: [29] **30**, 201–227
18. Polkowski, L., Skowron, A. (1999): Grammar Systems for Distributed Synthesis of Approximate Solutions Extracted from Experience, (Eds.) Paun, G., Salomaa, A., Grammar Systems for Multiagent Systems, Gordon and Breach Science Publishers, Amsterdam, 316–333
19. Polkowski, L., Skowron, A. (2001): Rough-Neuro Computing, in: [32] (to appear)
20. Ripley, B.D. (1996): Pattern Recognition and Neural Networks, Cambridge University Press
21. Skowron, A. (2001): Toward Intelligent Systems: Calculi of Information Granules, in: [4] 9–30
22. Skowron, A. (2001): Approximate Reasoning by Agents in Distributed Environments, Proc. IAT'01 (to appear)
23. Skowron, A., Stepaniuk, J. (1996): Tolerance Approximation Spaces, Fundamenta Informaticae **27**(2-3), 245–253
24. Skowron, A., Stepaniuk, J. (2001): Information Granules: Towards Foundations of Granular Computing, International Journal of Intelligent Systems **16**(1), 57–86
25. Stone, P. (2000): Layered Learning in Multiagent Systems: A Winning Approach to Robotic Soccer, MIT Press, Cambridge
26. WITAS project web page: http://www.ida.liu.se/ext/witas/eng.html
27. Zadeh, L.A. (1965): Fuzzy Sets, Information and Control **8** 333–353
28. Zadeh, L.A. (1996): Fuzzy Logic = Computing with Words, IEEE Trans. on Fuzzy Systems **4**, 103–111
29. Zadeh, L.A., Kacprzyk, J. (Eds.) (1999): Computing with Words in Information/Intelligent Systems, Studies in Fuzziness and Soft Computing **30-31**, Physica–Verlag, Heidelberg
30. Zadeh, L.A. (2001): A New Direction in AI: Toward a Computational Theory of Perceptions, AI Magazine **22**(1), 73–84
31. Zhong, N., Skowron, A., Ohsuga, S. (Eds.) (1999): Proc. RSFDGr'99, Lecture Notes in Artificial Intelligence **1711** Springer–Verlag, Berlin
32. Ziarko, W., Yao, Y.Y. (Eds.) (2001): Proc. RSCTC'2000, Lecture Notes in Artificial Intelligence, Springer-Verlag, Berlin (to appear)

Network Services in Context of Pervasive Mobile Internet

Krzysztof Zieliński

Dept. of Computer Science, University of Mining & Metallurgy
Al. Mickiewicza 30, Cracow, Poland
tel:+48 (12) 617 39 82, fax:+48 (12) 617 39 66
kz@cs.agh.edu.pl
http://www.cs.agh.edu.pl

Abstract. The mobile Internet will be a dominating access information technology in the near future. This paper presents basic aspects of
mobile and pervasive computing with particular attention to SRW. It
focuses on evaluation of existing and forthcoming wireless technology,
middleware and service provision architectures for mobile applications
and illustration of the existing possibilities by practical examples.

1 Introduction

The mobile Internet without any doubt will be a dominating access information
technology in the near future. Very fascinating development of 3G and 4G [10]
telecommunication systems create new challenges in the area of system software
design and new services implementation. Understanding of these new systems
requirements play a very important role in proper exploitation of the full potential of rapidly developing distributed processing paradigms. This process should
be analysed in the context of the future Internet services that will be dominated
by pervasive computing systems and ad-hoc group communication [6]. The construction of such systems wouldn't be possible without constant progress in
software technology where mobile agents, component object oriented systems,
and instant messages based systems, play a most important role at the moment.

This paper focuses on evaluation of existing and forthcoming wireless technology, middleware and service provision architectures for mobile applications
and illustration of existing possibilities by practical examples.

The paper presents basic aspects of mobile and pervasive computing with
particular attention to SRW (Short Range Wireless) networks [3]. Comparison of
spatial capacity of several short-range wireless technologies are briefly discussed.
A new UMB (Utralwideband) technology prospect and its influence on pervasive
computing scenarios in the next few years is analysed.

In light of new technological advances, established middleware architecture
elements merit reconsideration [2]. It is clear that particular attention should be
put on mobile code and mobile agents, disconnected operation, adaptive applications and ad-hoc organisation. In this context Jini, Jiro and Jaxta technology
have been briefly described.

B. Dunin-Kęplicz and E. Nawarecki (Eds.): CEEMAS 2001, LNAI 2296, pp. 15–25, 2002.

The available communication scenarios are presented and areas of their application have been shown. These investigations have been illustrated by the results of experimental study of multimedia streaming over Bluetooth [9,11,12]. This research has been performed as a part of 6winit Project in the Department of Computer Science at UMM.

The multimedia streaming QoS study could be seen as a first stage of a larger project that is dedicated to mobile teleconferencing systems design and implementation. This system has been designed having Jini and Jiro [1,2,5] communication and management services in mind. The architecture of this system is characterised and its activity illustrated. The potential of code mobility and its influence on the system self-configuration features and maintenance are considered in detail. The advantages of using Jini and Jiro are pointed out. The paper is finished with conclusions.

2   Short Range Wireless Networks

Short Range Wireless Networks [3] are a complementary class of emerging technologies meant primarily for indoor use over very short distances. SRW links offer peak speeds of tens or even hundreds of megabits per second, at very low cost and with very low power, to many closely spaced users. In its base set of applications, SWR technologies provide cableless connections among the portable devices people wear and carry daily, including cell phones, headsets, PDAs, laptop computers, etc.

A fundamental concept behind SRW systems, especially personal area network (PAN) systems, asserts that any time two SWR-equipped devices get within 10 meters of one another they can form, either automatically or under user control, a spontaneous, just-in-time, disposable connection for whatever purpose is at hand. From the user perspective, these purposes fall into three broad categories [3]:

1. Leveraging device synergies - spontaneous, synergistic connections help solve the human-interface problems that arise from stuffing more and more complexity into small packages.
2. Grouping Internet users efficiently - SWR offers data connections at much higher speeds, for more users, with far longer battery life than possible with cellular-based systems.
3. Making queues obsolete - customers could serve themselves without waiting if they could obtain secure access to the system via handheld devices.

Emerging SRW standards and technologies such as IEEE 802.11b, Bluetooth, and IEEE 802.11a, vary in their spatial capacities, defined as bits per second per square meter.

Traditional wireless systems operate within the confines of a narrow band of frequencies assigned by government regulatory authorities. Ultrawideband (UWB) occupy a broad spectrum of frequencies, typically 1.5 to 4 GHz wide, that cover many already-assigned frequency bands in the 1 to 6 GHz range.

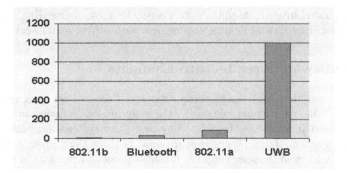

Fig. 1. Comparison of spatial capacity of several short-range wireless technologies

UWB purports to occupy these frequencies without causing undue interference. It does so by emitting a power as low as incidental radiation. Systems based on this emerging technology operate with a speed of 50 Mbps at a range of 10 meters. At least six such systems could operate within the same 10-meter-radius circle and experience only minimal degradation. The projected spatial capacity for such a system would be more than 1000 Kbps. It would create a new tremendous impact on pervasive mobile Internet services development. The comparison of spatial capacity of several short-range wireless technologies are depicted in Fig.1.

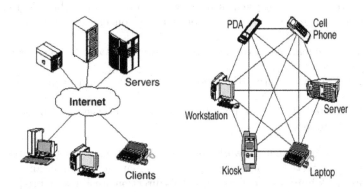

Fig. 2. Web based-computing vs. Peer-to-Peer computing

Short-range wireless networks would, without any doubt, offer the highest band-width at lowest power levels, in the most crowded spaces, for most users. The development of SRW systems will stimulate a transition, depicted in Fig.2, from Web-based Internet computing to Peer-to-Peer communicating systems. It requires new scalable and flexible service provision software architectures.

3   Middleware Architecture Elements

It is very clear that Web-based computing and Peer-to-Peer systems complement each other and would coexist in the near future. Software architectures for Web-based Internet are dominated by multi-tier systems exploiting Java 2 Enterprise Edition. J2EE [5] systems are built of three tiers: presentation - implemented with web browser support, business processes run within web server or application server environments, and databases.

The most advanced component of this architecture is EJB (Enterprise Java Bean)[5] application server. The container equips application components with services such as: transaction, security, and persistence, that play a crucial role in distributed environments. The localisation of components is typically performed with support of the JNDI interface and inter-component communication is performed using RMI or CORBA. The interactions between a user browser and an application follows a request-reply schema, and is typically performed with the HTTP protocol.

The discussed Web based architecture has same disadvantages in the context of network computing and small mobile devices used for service access. The most evident are:

1. The architecture is rather strongly dedicated to data access systems and does not support distributed computing where groups of devices cooperate with each other, performing the same application.
2. The thin client approach is not always suitable for mobile devices where specialised applications should be installed on end-user terminals to face connectivity problems.
3. HTTP implemented over TCP is not always suitable for client-server communication.
4. tandard browsers are rather too resource consuming to run on very simple PDAs or Pocket PCs.
5. The limited display of portable devices makes the data presentation in HTML impossible.

It is very clear that network computing over the Internet requires a more powerful architecture that is scalable, easy to manage and maintain. The J2EE software stack important extensions in this direction are Jini and Jiro [1,2,5]. Jini offers service a support model perfectly compatible with network computing and mobile system applications requirements. The key component of this architecture is the Lookup Service server that is a repository of registered service descriptions and client interfaces - proxies to these services. The end-user device localises the Lookup Server, chooses one of the registered services it is interested in, and downloads the suitable service access interface. The only limitation is that the proxy code must be written in Java to be dynamically loaded. The server side could be implemented in any language. Also, the communication protocol between the client service access interface and the server could be anything.

The Jini architecture is consistent with SUN Microsystems JWE (Java Wireless Environment) and JME (Java Micro Edition) efforts, which put Java as the most promising language for mobile devices programming.

A further extension of the Jini environment is Jiro technology which provides important management services such as: Security Service, Event Service, Scheduling Service, and Log Service. It also implements so called Dynamic System Model (DSM) that makes deployment and processing of applications a lot easier than with Jini. DSM provides: Remote Instantiation, and Remote Static Method Invocation as an alternative to Jini's existing Remote Method Invocation. These mechanisms make a programming with Jiro much more user-friendly than in Jini.

Finally SUN's newest Java technology Jaxta addresses the requirements of ad-hoc secure group communication. Jxta is an open computing platform designed for Peer-to-Peer computing and standardises in peer behaviour how they: discover each other on the net, advertise network resources, communicate with each other and cooperate to form secure peer groups. Jaxta works as a technology architecture, uses a small number of protocols which are easy to implement and to integrate with existing applications. It is also language and protocol independent, and the existing implementation fits into almost all devices that are net-enabled. The layered architecture of Jaxta is depicted in Fig. 3.

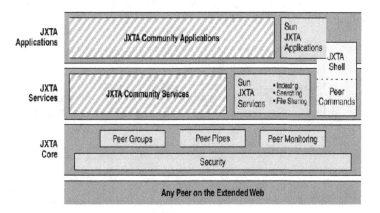

Fig. 3. Layers of Jaxta

Jaxta Core provides: Security, Peer Groups, Peer Pipes and Peer Monitoring. Security supports a simple crypto-library, an authentication framework modelled after PAM, a password based login scheme, and access control mechanisms. It also supports transport security that is modelled after SSL/TSL.

Peer Groups provide services such as: Discover Service, Access Service, Membership Service, Pipe Servce, Resolver Service. Peer Pipes organises communication which in existing implementations is asynchronous, unidirectional, and unreliable.

Peer Monitoring supports the capability to closely keep track of peer status, its activity, resource usage traffic metering and bandwidth balancing.

Jaxta without any doubt creates a very powerful framework for mobile ad-hoc Peer-to-Peer computing. It still requires validation and wider acceptance by industry. In this situation we decided to limit our experimental applications implementation to Jini and Jiro environment. It is also consistent with the current stage of development of SRW networks.

4   Multimedia Streaming over Bluetooth

Multimedia streaming over SWR is one of the most interesting mobile applications. The WLAN technology provides enough bandwidth to ensure proper QoS even for high quality video. The open question is PAN capability for multimedia streaming. Bluetooth (IEEE 802.15) is a typical representative of technology for PANs providing data transmission limited to a few meters and theoretical throughput of 1Mbps. WLAN and PAN technologies complement each other offering solutions of compromise between cost, flexibility and throughput.

Multimedia stream transmission over Bluetooth link [13] has been tested [4] with configuration depicted in Fig.4.

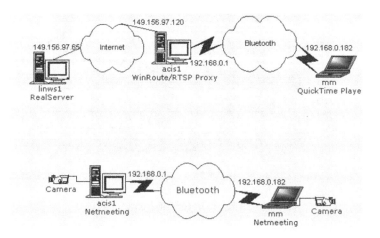

Fig. 4. Audio/Video streaming Bluetooth testing configuration

The top configuration is used for video streaming from video servers and the bottom corresponds to a videoconferencing scenario. Audio/Video streams encoding formats, programs, and video conferencing tools under test have been collected in Table 1. They have been chosen to cover the most popular tools and encoding standard used today for multimedia streaming over the Internet.

Table 1. A/V streaming tools and standards

Compression standard	MPEG-1 MPEG-4 RealAudio/Video H.263
Programs	RealPlayer & Server Quick Time Player Darwin Streaming Server
Videoconferencing Tools	VIC/RAT, Netmeeting
Protocols	RTP, PNM

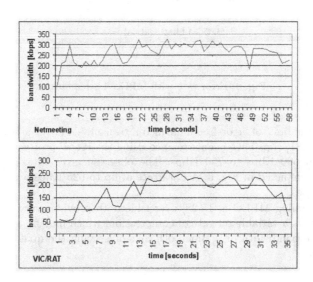

Fig. 5. Video streaming bandwidth during Netmeeting and VIC/RAT sessions

There was no problem with streaming H.263 [18,20] video and audio. These streams did not suffer any additional degradation when they were transmitted over a wireless Bluetooth link and achieved bandwidth which was very stable and high enough. The required bandwidth during Netmeeting and VIC/RAT [22] videoconferences were below 350 Kbps, so the Bluetooth link worked perfectly.

Video streaming was a more demanding service tested in our study. RealServer [23,30] with RealPlayer from RealNetworks [26] is one of the most popular solutions for streaming multimedia in the Internet. RealServer by default, uses PNM [23] protocol for transmission, but RSTP/RTP [17,19] stack has been implemented in both server and player for compatibility with other solutions. There is a substantial difference between PNM and RSTP: PNM tries to keep the bandwidth at the lowest possible level, comparable to the recording rate, while RTSP sends data as fast as possible and lets the application buffer them. Streaming video up to 450kbps worked perfectly over the Bluetooth link.

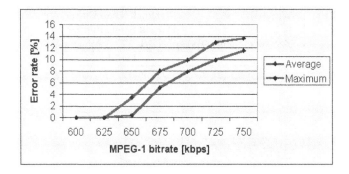

Fig. 6. Error rate with MPEG-1 streaming

To find the limit of error-free multimedia transmission over a Bluetooth link MPEG-1 [14,31] clips have been streamed using the RTSP protocol. The stream ranged from 600 Kbps to 750 Kbps. The observed error rate with MPEG-1 streaming is depicted in Fig. 6. A data rate of up to 625 Kbps was transmitted with any losses.

The streaming MPEG-4 [15,28] over Bluetooth provides very good quality. MPEG-4 offers a variable bit rate of compression, which may be better fitted to the available bandwidth of a Bluetooth link preserving the quality of video in the same time.

5   A Teleconferencing System for Mobile Systems

The presented study has proved that the existing SRW technology could be used for multimedia streaming and teleconferencing. Taking into account modern software architectures for mobile computing we decided to construct [1] a new teleconferencing system which exploits Jini and Jiro technology potential.

The system assumes that there will many clients located in different places using mobile access network devices. Thus, it would not be an easy task to install and update the conference software on each of them. Also the limited resources of handheld devices reduces the number of applications that could be preinstalled. A much better solution is to have a centralised point that would store the software and if needed would send it to the client.

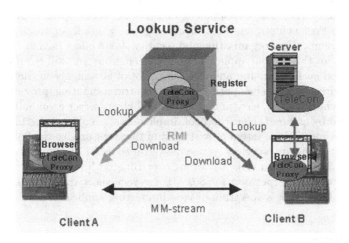

Fig. 7. Jini based teleconferencing system architecture

The architecture of the demonstration system developed by the UMM [1] is presented in Fig. 7. This system exploits Jini and Jiro technology services and JMF (Java Multimedia Framework). JMF supports most of the multimedia stream encoding standards discussed in the previous section.

Proxies of the teleconferencing system implementing the classes for multimedia streaming between users, teleconference opening procedure, multimedia streams capture, and encoding and display functionalities are registered with the Lookup Service. The proxy may be loaded on demand to the user end-device. Next the procedure of user authentication with the system is started. This step is supported by the Jiro Security Service. After successful authentication the user is registered with the conference. All other users are notified that a new member has arrived. The Jiro Event Service supports this activity of the system. Next the user is able to choose the members of the conference he wants to open the multimedia streams with. The negotiation of multimedia streams parameters procedure is performed in the following step. After successful negotiation the multimedia streams are opened and a new user joins the video conference. All events observed during the teleconferencing system activity are registered in a log file organised with Jiro Log Service support.

The implemented architecture fully supports mobility requirements. It has been tested in a WLAN 802.11b environment and with Digianswer/Motorola Bluetooth MK II PCMCIA cards [21,29].

6 Conclusions

Mobile access to the Internet which supports a Web-centric model is at the moment a reality. The fast development of SRW networks opens a great future for Peer-to-Peer computing. This model requires a novel approach to ad-hoc group communication, organisation and security. Jaxta offers the most promising framework for this type of application but this environment still requires further research and evaluation. Jini and Jiro offer a lot of advantages in the context of mobile environments, in comparison to Web-centric computing, providing a scalable deployment model, easy maintenance, and client server communication not constrained by any particular protocol. Implementation of the experimental Jiro based teleconferencing system proved most of these features to the full extent. It also validated the Jiro services as very powerful tools for distributed computing implementations. Multimedia streaming over Bluetooth provides an acceptable QoS and creates competition for 802.11b for very short range communication scenarios. This opens a spectrum of very interesting applications.

References

1. Chlebek J., Jiro Based Multimedia Conference System Design and Implementation, M.Sc. Theses Dept. Of Comp. Sc. At UMM, June 2001.
2. Geish K., Middleware Challenges Ahead, IEEE Computer, June 2001.
3. Leeper D. R., A Long-Term View of Short-Range Wireless, IEEE Computer, June 2001.
4. Michalak M., Multimedia Transmission in Bluetooth-based Networks, Theses Dept. Of Comp. Sc. At UMM, June 2001.
5. Sun Microsystems Inc., Enterprise Java Beans Specification v.1.1 (final), grudzie 1999.
6. Lewis T., UbiNet: The Ubiquitous Internet Will Be Wireless, IEEE Computer, October 1999, pp. 126-128.
7. OMG Inc., Common Object Request Broker (CORBA): Architecture and Specification, Rev. 2.2, 1998.
8. The Internet Society, Service Location Protocol, RFC 2608, 1999.
9. Ericsson, IBM, Intel, Nokia, Toshiba, Specification of the Bluetooth System, v.1.0, 1999.
10. Malik O., Personal Information Bubble - Halla's Latest Mantra, Forbes Magazine, 21 September 1999, available as:
http://www.forbes.com/tool/html/99/sep/0921/feat.htm.
11. The Official Bluetooth SIG Website http://www.bluetooth.com
12. Bluetooth 1.1 Specifications Book, http://www.bluetooth.com/developer /specification/Bluetooth_11_Specifications_Book.pdf
13. Kulwinder Atwal, Ron Akers, Transmission of IP Packets over Bluetooth Networks http://www.ietf.org/internet-drafts/draft-akers-atwal-btooth-01.txt.

14. ISO/IEC 11172: Information technology – Coding of moving pictures and associated audio for digital storage media at up to about 1,5 Mbit/s (MPEG-1).
15. ISO/IEC 14496: Information technology – Coding of audio-visual objects (MPEG-4)
16. RealNetworks.com, http://www.realnetworks.com.
17. H. Schulzrinne, S. Casner, R. Frederick, V. Jacobson: RTP: A Transport Protocol for Real-Time Applications (RFC 1889).
18. ITU-T Recommendation H.323 (11/00) - Packet-Based Multimedia Communications Systems http://www.itu.int/itudoc/itu-t/rec/h/h323.html.
19. H. Schulzrinne, A. Rao, R. Lanphier: Real Time Streaming Protocol (RFC 2326).
20. Recommendation H.263 (02/98) - Video coding for low bit rate communication, http://www.itu.int/itudoc/itu-t/rec/h/h263.html.
21. Bluetooth Products from Digianswer, http://www.digianswer.com/.
22. MBONE Conferencing Applications, http://ww-mice.cs.ucl.ac.uk/multimedia/softwar
23. RealServer 8.01, http://www.realnetworks.com/deliver/index.html.
24. DarwinStreamingServer 2.0, http://www.publicsource.apple.com/projects/streaming/.
25. QuickTime Streaming Server, http://www.apple.com/quicktime/products/qtss.
26. RealPlayer http://www.real.com/player/index.html.
27. QuickTime Player from Apple Computers, http://www.apple.com/quicktime/download/.
28. 3ivx company: MPEG-4-compliant codec http://www.3ivx.com/.
29. Bluetooth Software Suite from Digianswer http://btsws.digianswer.com
30. RealProducer from RealNetworks, http://www.realnetworks.com/products/producer/index.html.
31. MPEG-1 Player for PocketWindows, http://www.mpegtv.com/wince/pockettv/.

Regular Papers

On BAN Logics for Industrial Security Protocols

Nesria Agray[1], Wiebe van der Hoek[1,2], and Erik de Vink[3,4]

[1] Institute of Information and Computing Sciences, Utrecht University,
The Netherlands N.Agray@fss.uu.nl, wiebe@cs.uu.nl
[2] Department of Computer Science, University of Liverpool, United Kingdom
[3] Department of Computer Science, Technische Universiteit Eindhoven,
The Netherlands evink@win.tue.nl
[4] Leiden Institute of Advanced Computer Science, Leiden University, The
Netherlands

Abstract. This paper reports on two case-studies of applying BAN logic
to industrial strength security protocols. These studies demonstrate the
flexibility of the BAN language, as it caters for the addition of appropriate constructs and rules. We argue that, although a semantic foundation of the formalism is lacking, BAN logic provides an intuitive and
powerful technique for security analysis.

1 Introduction

New and upcoming techniques for the internet and also wireless telecommunication require or encourage agents to interchange more and more sensitive data,
like payment instructions in e-commerce, strategic information between commercial partners, or personal information in for instance medical applications. Issues
like authentication of the partners in a protocol, and the confidentiality of information therefore become of increasing importance: cryptographic protocols are
used to distribute keys and authenticate agents and data over hostile networks.
Although many of the protocols used look very intricate and hence waterproof,
many examples are known of sensitive applications that were cracked and then
furnished with new, 'improved' protocols.

The application of logical tools to the analysis of security protocols was pio-
neered by Burrows, Abadi and Needham. In [4] and [9] specific epistemic logics,
collectively referred to as BAN logic, are proposed to deal with authentication
issues. Earlier, standard epistemic logic ([6,12]) has been applied successfully to
reason about communication protocols, cf. the derivation of the alternating bit
protocol in [11] or, more recently, the analysis of TCP [14]). In this setting, contrary to the security set-up of BAN, the implicit assumption is always that the
network is not hostile. The work on epistemic logic has the last decades mainly
focused on theoretical issues like variants of modal logic (cf. also [7] where epistemic notions are mixed with deontic ones), completeness, and derived notions
like Distributed Knowledge and Common Knowledge.

In this paper we discuss the application of the BAN-framework to two of the
most widely used security and authentication protocols. The first is applied in

B. Dunin-Kȩplicz and E. Nawarecki (Eds.): CEEMAS 2001, LNAI 2296, pp. 29–36, 2002.

the Global System for Mobile communication (GSM, see [10]), an integration of
several national cellular networks, which is now world-wide in use to transmit
voice-data on the air, but also to send and receive e-mail, faxes and to get
access to the internet. The second protocol, Secure Electronic Transactions (SET,
see [13]) is an electronic commerce security protocol for doing business over
the internet. It is developed under auspices of Visa and Mastercard, and well
accepted to support credit card payments over the internet.

The aim of our exercise to apply BAN to those two protocols is the following.
First, it goes without saying that such widely used but sensitive protocols have
at least partially to be formally validated. Since the protocols under consideration are apparently not derived from a formal specification, before verifying any
security goals on them one has to first trim down the massive manuals about
the protocols to their bare essentials. Second, we want to demonstrate the flexibility of the BAN-framework by showing how specific issues of the two protocols
can be smoothly accounted for by suitable extensions of the BAN-language and
reasoning rules Here, we give an indication of the needed extensions for each of
the protocols; full proofs are provided in [2]. Finally, the main research question
behind our project is in which direction further fundamental work on BAN, or
any logic for security and authentication, should proceed to sensibly deal with
protocols that are in development or applied on a scale like GSM and SET.

2   BAN Logic

BAN logic is a modal logic with primitives which describe the beliefs of agents
involved in a cryptographic protocol. Using the inference rules of BAN logic the
evolution of the beliefs of agents during a cryptographic protocol can be studied.
Here we present some typical rules that we put to work, on the fly explaining
the language of BAN.

The BAN-formalism is built on three sorts of objects: the agents involved in
a security protocol, the encryption/decryption and signing/verification keys that
the agents possess, and the messages exchanged between agents. The notation
$\{M\}_K$ denotes a message encrypted using a key K. For a symmetric key K we
have $\{\{M\}_K\}_K = M$ for any message M i.e., decrypting with key K a message
M that is encrypted with K reveals the contents M. For a key pair $\langle EK, DK \rangle$ of
a public encryption key EK and a private decryption key DK it holds that
$\{\{M\}_{EK}\}_{DK} = M$ for any message M. Likewise, for a key pair $\langle SK, VK \rangle$
of a private signing key SK and a public verification key VK it holds that
$\{\{H\}_{SK}\}_{VK} = H$ for any hash value H. Hash values are obtained by application of a one-way collision-free hash-function. Proving the hash value $H(m)$
of a message m is a means to demonstrate that m is known, without revealing
it (cf. also [2]).

In BAN, we have a number of operators describing the beliefs of agents,
for which the usual modal properties apply, like P believes $(A \rightarrow B) \rightarrow$
$(P$ believes $A \rightarrow P$ believes $B)$. On top of that we have the operators

sees and possesses (cf. [4,9]). The following rules are an illustration of some of the authentication and encryption rules:

(1) P believes secret$(K, P, Q) \wedge P$ sees $\{X\}_K$
        $\rightarrow P$ believes Q said X

(2) P believes belongs_to $(VK, Q) \wedge P$ sees $\{X\}_{SK}$
        $\rightarrow P$ believes Q said X

(3) P believes fresh$(X) \wedge P$ believes Q said X
        $\rightarrow P$ believes Q believes X

(4) P possesses $DK \wedge P$ sees $\{X\}_{EK} \rightarrow P$ sees X

Intuitively, **(1)** says that if an agent P believes that it shares the symmetric key K with an agent Q, and agent P receives a message X encrypted under K, then agent P believes that agent Q once said message X. This rule addresses symmetric encryption. In a similar way, **(2)** models digital signatures. If an agent P believes that the verification key VK belongs to an agent Q, then P concludes, confronted with a message or hash encrypted with the corresponding signing key SK, that the message or hash originates from the agent Q. Regarding rule **(3)**, if an agent P believes that certain information is new, i.e. constructed during the current protocol run, and P furthermore believes that Q conveyed this information, then P concludes that the agent Q believes himself this information. (Underlying this is the overall assumption in BAN logic of honesty of agents; the participating agents' behavior is consistent with the particular protocol.) According to **(4)**, if an agent P sees an encrypted message and P possesses the decryption key then P can read the message itself.

Analysis of an authentication protocol using BAN-logic is comprised of four steps: (1) first, the initial beliefs of the participating agents are formulated; (2) the protocol security goals are stated; (3) the effect of the protocol's messages is formalized in BAN and (4), the final beliefs are shown to fulfil the goals.

3   Analyzing the GSM Security Protocol

The GSM protocol, Global System for Mobile communication, is a protocol for mobile telephony operating world-wide since the beginning of the 1990s. Abstracting away, in our analysis, from a lot of details we distinguish three parties involved in the protocol: the mobile station MS, which is the subscriber's interface to the network, connected via a radio link, the home location register HLR which is an intelligent database where a subscriber's specific parameters are stored, and the visitor location register VLR, a database that temporarily stores user specific parameters. The VLR's role is to support the HLR by handling most of the user-related queries.

If a mobile station MS wants the GSM service, it must prove its identity to the network. To this end, the mobile station sends a service request via the radio path to the VLR. The VLR then forwards this identity to the HLR, which generates a fresh random number RAND and computes a result RES by applying a one-way and collision free function A_3 to a key K and RAND, i.e. RES $= A_3(K, RAND)$. The identity key K is a shared secret between the HLR and the MS, but not known to VLR. If MS is able to generate the same value RES when provided with RAND, it has proven its identity. The HLR also computes an encryption key K' that will ensure privacy of MS when it further communicates with the VLR. This is done using an algorithm A_8, hence K' $= A_8(K, RAND)$. The HLR then sends the triple $\langle RAND, RES, K' \rangle$ to the VLR. Upon receipt of this triple, the VLR forwards RAND to the MS and waits for an appropriate response from the MS. The mobile station can calculate RES from the key K and the challenge RAND using the algorithm A_3. Then, MS uses RAND together with its key K and the algorithm A_8 to calculate the session key K' and stores it locally.

We next give the crucial rules that we add to BAN. For the modeling we add various auxiliary functions and predicates like ch and comp. Free variables are assumed to be universally quantified.

(4)   VLR believes $[$HLR said $\text{ch}(x, y, z) \rightarrow \text{rand}(x) \wedge \text{res}(y) \wedge \text{skey}(z)]$

(5)   VLR believes $[(\text{MS said } \text{res}(y) \wedge \text{HLR said } \text{ch}(x, y, z) \wedge \text{fresh}(x))$
　　　　$\rightarrow \text{MS possesses } z]$

(6) P believes $(P \text{ possesses } K \wedge Q \text{ possesses } K)$
　　　　$\rightarrow P$ believes $\text{secret}(K, P, Q)$

(7)   MS believes $[(\text{VLR said } \text{rand}(x)) \wedge \text{fresh}(x) \wedge$
　　　　$\text{ikey}(K) \wedge \text{a}_8(A) \wedge K' = \text{comp}(A, x, K) \wedge$
　　　　$\text{secret}(\langle K, A \rangle, \text{MS}, \text{HLR}) \rightarrow \text{VLR possesses } K']$

Rule **(4)** says that the VLR knows the meaning of the three values in the challenge triplet $\text{ch}(x, y, z)$ received from the HLR. Our rule **(5)** expresses that the session key is calculated by the mobile station at the same time the calculation of the res-value takes place. So at the moment that the right fresh res-value is received from the mobile station, the VLR knows that the mobile station is in possession of the right session key. Rule **(6)** is an obvious, but tricky rule. If some agent R possesses the key K as well, it is no longer justified to consider K a secret between P and Q. Finally, concerning rule **(7)**, when the mobile station receives a random challenge, it computes the corresponding response value and session key using the appropriate secret A8-algorithm, the random value and the secret identity key K that it shares with the HLR. It is implicit in the GSM authentication protocol that the mobile station trusts the network on the matter of the random value, i.e. MS assumes that it originates from the HLR. Furthermore, it is assumed that at the moment that the MS receives a random value from the VLR, the MS concludes that the VLR possesses the corresponding session key.

We have omitted rules concerning freshness here. Also, space does not allow us to formulate the initial beliefs of the three partners. Instead, we formulate the authentication question and the question concerning the agreement on the encryption key. The VLR must check whether a mobile station with a given identifier is really registered in the system, and whether the mobile station has the identity it claims. This is done by comparing the res-values received from the mobile station at one side and from the HLR at the other side. If the two values match then the VLR knows that it is indeed talking to the mobile station. The first authentication question is as follows:

(Q1) $\exists x : \texttt{fresh}(x) \wedge \texttt{VLR believes res}(x) \wedge \texttt{MS said res}(x)$

The next question that we discuss concerns the agreement on the session key. At the end of the protocol the VLR must know that it shares the right session key with the mobile station. The mobile station must believe the same statement. This is modeled as follows:

(Q2) $\exists z : \texttt{MS believes } (\texttt{fresh}(z) \wedge \texttt{secret}(z, \texttt{VLR}, \texttt{MS})) \wedge$
        $\texttt{VLR believes } (\texttt{fresh}(z) \wedge \texttt{secret}(z, \texttt{VLR}, \texttt{MS}))$

In our full paper [2], we specify a set of initial beliefs of the three parties involved, translate the effect of the messages into BAN, and prove, amongst others, **(Q1)** and **(Q2)**.

4 Analyzing the SET Protocol

In this section we describe the SET-protocol (see [13]). SET stands for *Secure Electronic Transactions* and is designed for credit card payments over the Internet. By combining both symmetric and public-key cryptographic techniques SET provides several security services at an adequate performance. In particular, SET provides message integrity together with blinding of information, such that (i) no banking information of the customer is revealed to the merchant, and (ii) no purchase information of the customer is disclosed to the bank. For this latter services SET deploys so-called dual signatures.

Let us first explain standard digital signatures. Each agent participating in a run of SET holds a pair of keys $\langle SK, VK \rangle$ consisting of a *signing key* and a *verification key*. The signing key is private, the verification key is public. If Alice wants to sign a message M, she first computes the hash value $\texttt{hash}(M)$ of M, encrypts this value with her signing key SK and attaches this signature $\{\texttt{hash}(M)\}_{SK}$ to the message M, thus yielding $(M, \{\texttt{hash}(M)\}_{SK})$. When Bob receives a signed message (M, S), presumably coming from Alice, he first computes the hash value $\texttt{hash}(M)$ of M, then he retrieves the corresponding verification key VK of Alice, decrypts the signature S with the key VK, and checks whether the resulting value $\{S\}_{VK}$ equals the earlier value $\texttt{hash}(M)$. Note, since $\langle SK, VK \rangle$ is a key pair with private key SK and public key VK, it holds that $\{\{X\}_{SK}\}_{VK} = X$. So, if the two values agree, Bob concludes that Alice signed the message as she is the only agent in possession of the signing key that is needed to produce the signature for the hash value of the message. The BAN rule that we have used to model this is

(8) $P \texttt{ sees } (M, S) \wedge P \texttt{ believes } VK \texttt{ belongs\_to } Q \wedge$
        $\texttt{hash}(M) = \{S\}_{VK} \rightarrow P \texttt{ believes } Q \texttt{ said } M.$

Next we discuss dual signatures. SET makes use of so-called dual signatures to blind some information for one agent while showing the same information to another one, but in the mean time providing the two agents with a reference to the information. Sending each part of the information separately to the intended parties does not work, because the two parts of information are related and this relationship is important for the remainder of the protocol. For example, a purchase request from a card holder C contains both order data and payment data. The payment data is intended for the bank B and must be hidden from the merchant M. Dually, it is no business of the bank to get to know the actual goods that the customer buys. However, at some point in time after the particular purchase request, the merchant M want to capture his money for the purchase from the bank B. For this M and B need to refer to the same procurement.

To see this at work, suppose that an agent P has signing key SK, verification key VK and wants to send some information I to an agent Q. Additionally, Q needs a way to link I to some other information J that will not be revealed to him. To realize this, the agent P sends Q the message

$$(I, \mathtt{hash}(J), \{\mathtt{hash}(\mathtt{hash}(I) \mid \mathtt{hash}(J))\}_{SK}),$$

where the so-called dual hash $\mathtt{hash}(\mathtt{hash}(I) \mid \mathtt{hash}(J))$ is obtained by hashing the juxtaposition of $\mathtt{hash}(I)$ and $\mathtt{hash}(J)$. By encryption of the dual hash with her private signing key, agent P testifies that both the information I and the hash $\mathtt{hash}(J)$ originate from her. The agent Q can verify this by using the corresponding public verification key of P, similar to the case of standard digital signatures as described above. However, Q does not know anything about the information J. Now, if yet some other agent R obtains from P the message

$$(\mathtt{hash}(I), J, \{\mathtt{hash}(\mathtt{hash}(I) \mid \mathtt{hash}(J))\}_{SK}),$$

she knows that the message indeed has been sent by P, but has no clue about the information I. The crucial point is that agents Q and R both are aware that $I\&\mathtt{hash}(J)$ and $\mathtt{hash}(I)\&J$, respectively, are related. Our relevant BAN rule is as follows:

(9) P sees $(I, G, \{H\}_{SK}) \wedge P$ believes   belongs_to $(VK, Q) \wedge$
            $\mathtt{hash}(\mathtt{hash}(I)|G) = H \to P$ believes $(Q$ said $I \wedge \mathtt{dhash}_1(I, G, H))$

Here, $\mathtt{dhash}_1$ is a predicate stating that the hash of I concatenated with G will hash to H. There is also a similar rule for a message $(F, J, \{H\}_{SK})$ for a hash value F, a message J and dual hash H using an auxiliary predicate $\mathtt{dhash}_2$.

Besides user authentication, during a run of SET, the card holder, the merchant and the payment gateway have to agree on a purchase and the corresponding cost. So after the run of the protocol, the three participants must store consistent information about the purchase. For example, the three parties must store the same purchase amount. This is achieved when the three parties agree on the linkage between the order data and the payment instructions. As example, for P, this is modeled in security requirement **(Q3)** as follows:

(Q3) P believes $\big(\mathtt{pay\_instr}(C, \mathtt{PData}) \wedge (\exists \mathtt{OData} : \mathtt{link}_2(\mathtt{OData}, \mathtt{PData}) \wedge$
            M believes $\mathtt{link}_1(\mathtt{OData}, \mathtt{PData}) \wedge$
            C believes $\mathtt{link}_1(\mathtt{OData}, \mathtt{PData}) \wedge \mathtt{link}_2(\mathtt{OData}, \mathtt{PData}))\big)$

The payment gateway P cannot see the order data, but believes in the existence of an order $\mathtt{OData}$ generated by the card holder which is linked to the card holder's payment instructions. Therefore, the well-known Barcan-formula P believes $\exists x : \phi \rightarrow \exists x : P$ believes ϕ is not valid in our framework. Furthermore, P has to trust this link, and has to know that both the merchant and the card holder believe in the same link. Similar rules apply to M and C.

In [2] we present the translation of the protocol in BAN. In order to give the reader a flavor of this, let us consider the third transaction of the protocol, in which the card holder sends its purchase request to the merchant.

(PReq) $C \rightarrow M$:

   (OData, hash(PData), {hash(hash(OData) | hash(PData))}$_{SKC}$),
   {PData, hash(OData), {hash(hash(OData) | hash(PData))}$_{SKC}$}$_K$,
   $\{K\}_{EKP}$,
   sigCert(C, SKC)

That is, card holder C sends to merchant M the following: (1) a message containing the order data and the hash of the payment data as clear text, but dually signed with the signing key of agent C; (2) a message containing the hash value of the order data and the payment data, dually signed with the signing key of C and encrypted with a random session key K; (3) the session key K encrypted by the payment gateway's encryption key EKP, so that only the payment gateway, hence not the merchant, can learn this session key and, consequently, the payment data encrypted with the key K; (4) a public-key certificate sigCert(C, SKC) for the cardholder's signing key which includes the corresponding verification key.

In order to compute the effects of this message on the beliefs of M, one first has to know the beliefs of M prior to performing the transaction **(PReq)**. For example, one belief concerns the possession of the verification key of the root Certification Authority for the public-key certificate for C's signing key. It is clear that the analysis makes such an assumption explicit. Although the SET protocol is rather detailed, in [2] we were able to give a formal proof of **(Q3)** as mentioned, as well as for other authentication goals.

5   Future Research

We see the following lines of research triggered by the experiences reported in this paper. First, the formidable proofs in [2] call for tool-support for the verification of non-trivial security goals. Apart from automated translation, our experiences reveal the need for flexible computer-assistance to incorporate logical extensions and to guide proof construction in the adapted framework.

Second, it is well known that the semantics of BAN logic is under debate (cf. [1,15,16,3]). At present, we cannot claim that our rules are sound or complete. On the one hand, this questions the impact of the derived results (what does it mean that some string has been derived?), but on the other hand, strengthens the call for an adequate model. To our opinion the various proposed semantics for BAN hardly allow for changes in the logic. This raises the question for a model which easily treats extensions as described in this paper. In the protocols considered not only information is exchanged, but also requests. Therefore, one might want to stress the goals of an agent as part of his mental state. However, the framework should not only reflect the state of the agent, but also the *dynamics*: agents learn from the messages they receive, thus calling for a language that deals with knowledge together with epistemic actions like learning and updating. To this aim we try in a current project to exploit the knowledge games semantics of [5] in the setting of authentication logics.

References

1. M. Abadi and M. Tuttle, A Semantics for a Logic of Authentication, in *Proceedings of the ACM Symposium on Principles of Distributed Computing,* p. 201–216, 1991.
2. N. Agray, *The BAN Approach to Formal Verification: Authentication in GSM and SET,* Master Thesis, Utrecht University Number INF/SCR-01-09 and KPN Research, Leidschendam (2001).
3. A. Bleeker and L. Meertens, A Semantics for BAN Logic, *Proc. DIMACS workshop on Design and Formal Verification of Protocols,* 1997,
   http://dimacs.rutgers.edu/Workshops/Security/program2/program.html.
4. M. Burrows, M. Abadi and R. Needham, A Logic of Authentication, *ACM Transactions on Computer Systems,* vol. 8, p. 18–36, 1990.
5. H. van Ditmarsch, *Knowledge Games.* PhD. thesis, Groningen, 2000, available at
   http://tcw2.ppsw.rug.nl/~hans.
6. R. Fagin, J.Y. Halpern, Y. Moses and M.Y. Vardi, *Reasoning About Knowledge,* MIT Press, 1995.
7. M. Fasli, On Commitments, Roles and Obligations. This volume.
8. M. Fitting and R. Mendelsohn, *First order modal logic,* Kluwer, 1998.
9. L. Gong, R. Needham and R. Yahalom, Reasoning about Belief in Cryptographic Protocol Analysis, *Proc. IEEE Symp. on Research in Security and Privacy,* p. 234–248, 1990.
10. H. Gunnar, *GSM Networks: Protocols, Terminology, and Implementations,* Artech House 1999.
11. J.Y. Halpern and L.D. Zuck, A Little Knowledge Goes a Long Way: Simple Knowledge-Based Derivations and Correctness Proofs for a Family of Protocols, *Proc. 6th ACM Symp. on Principles of Distributed Computing,* 1987, p. 268–280.
12. J.-J.Ch. Meyer and W. van der Hoek, *Epistemic Logic for AI and Computer Science,* Cambridge University Press, 1995.
13. The SET Standard Book 2: Programmer's Guide, version 1.0, SETCO 1997, www.setco.org.
14. F. Stulp and R. Verbrugge, A knowledge-based algorithm for the Internet protocol TCP, to appear in the *Bulletin of Economic Research,* 2001. Also at
    http://tcw2.ppsw.rug.nl/prepublications
15. P. Syverson, The Use of Logic in the Analysis of Cryptographic Protocols, in *Proc. IEEE Symp. on Research in Security and Privacy,* 1991.
16. G. Wedel and V. Kessler, Formal Semantics for Authentication Logics, *Proc. ESORICS'96,* p. 219–241, 1996.

A Concept of Agent Language in Agentspace*

Stanislaw Ambroszkiewicz, Tomasz Nowak, Dariusz Mikulowski, and
Leszek Rozwadowski

Institute of Computer Science, Polish Academy of Sciences,
al. Ordona 21, PL-01-237 Warsaw,
and Institute of Informatics, Academy of Podlasie,
al. Sienkiewicza 51, PL-08-110 Siedlce, Poland
{tnowak,sambrosz@ipipan.waw.pl}, www.ipipan.waw.pl/mas/

Abstract. Agentspace is an emerging environment resulting from process automation in the Internet and Web. It is supposed that autonomous software (mobile)
agents provide the automation. The agents realize the goals delegated to them by
their human masters. Interoperability is crucial to assure meaningful interaction,
communication and cooperation between heterogeneous agents and services. In
order to realize the goals, the agents must create, manage and reconfigure complex
workflows. The presentation is focused on language layer of agentspace architecture.

1   Introduction

Cyberspace, the emerging world created by the global information infrastructure and
facilitated by the Internet and the Web, offers new application scenarios as well as new
challenges. One of them is creating new infrastructures to support high-level business-
to-business and business-to-consumer activities on the Web. The second one is so called
"semantic web" [6], i.e. conceptual structuring of the Web in an explicit machine-readable
way.

These two challenges presuppose that all the tasks should be performed automatically
by autonomous software (mobile) agents on behalf of their users. A mobile software
agent is an executing program that can migrate from host to host across a heterogeneous
network under its own control and interact with other agents and services.

Since the software agents are supposed to "live" in the cyberspace, they must be
intelligent, that is, they must efficiently realize the goals delegated to them by their
human masters. To do so they must perceive the world, interact with the world, as well
as with other agents and humans.

Hence, along the development of cyberspace the new world (called agentspace),
inhabited by the new intelligent creatures called software agents, is being created. It
seems that the process automation in the Internet and Web makes the development of
agentspace inevitable, see for example Agentcities initiative [1].

Human users are situated at the border of the agentspace and can influence it only
by their agents by delegating to them complex and time consuming tasks to perform.

---

* The work was done within the framework of KBN project No. 7 T11C 040 20.

B. Dunin-Kęplicz and E. Nawarecki (Eds.): CEEMAS 2001, LNAI 2296, pp. 37–46, 2002.

Since the Internet and Web are open distributed and heterogeneous environments, agents and services can be created by different users according to different architectures. Interoperability is crucial to assure meaningful interaction, communication and cooperation between heterogeneous agents and services. The interoperability is not only restricted to interaction and communication, but it also comprises semantic interoperability. In order to use services established by different users working in heterogeneous domains, agents have to be capable of acquiring knowledge how to use those services and for what purposes. Hence, heterogeneous agents must exchange knowledge and understand each other.

To realize the concept of mobile agents together with agents interactions and service infrastructure, a special middleware called "mobile agent platform" (MAP, for short) is needed. There is a number of platforms available over the Internet, for example IBM Aglets, Concordia, Grasshopper, Mole, Ajanta, and Voyager to mention only some of them. One of them is Pegaz [12] developed in our Institute. These platforms are for creating infrastructures on computer networks so that details of network functioning are hidden from the users as well as from the agents. This makes programming more easy. A programmer need not manually construct agent communication, nor agent transportation. One may ask if agent mobility is essential for agentspace. As we will see in the next sections, besides standard arguments for mobility like disconnected processing, agent mobility provides a means for learning between heterogeneous environments.

Although the MAP technology was designed to provide mobility to the software agents, it seems that the proposals of MASIF / FIPA may be seen as efforts towards building uniform infrastructure analogously to traffic and communication infrastructure consisting of highroads, airports, and telecommunication networks in the real world. Introducing uniform infrastructure does not exclude autonomy and heterogeneity of the environments but it supports their development by the ability to cooperation. Analogously, the agentspace infrastructure should define (as standards) the basic agents / services interactions.

However, the interaction interoperability alone cannot realize our idea of agentspace. We need also semantic interoperability. There must be a common language for expressing tasks by the users, delegating these tasks to agents, and for agent communication with services. The semantic interoperability concerning the meaning of resources on the Web is a subject of current research, see DAML[8] + OIL[11] as the most prominent example.

Our project aims at creating a middleware that provides an absolute minimum necessary for joining applications as services on the one hand and to use them by heterogeneous agents on the other hand. The development of agentspace on the basis of that middleware depends on programmers and users who may find it as a useful and interesting technology.

A work related to our approach is a subject of several ongoing research and implementation projects, see for example LARKS [14], ATLAS [5], CCL [16], and WSDL [15]. The goal of the projects is to achieve a partial interoperability (i.e. semantic interoperability at the level of data), whereas the goal of our middleware is to provide a complete interoperability including interaction, reasoning, and data interoperability. We are trying to realize this goal by constructing layered architecture of the middleware.

The paper is devoted mainly to a presentation of language layer of agentspace architecture. However, for the paper to be self-contained, we describe briefly the basic principles of the agentspace architecture. We try to abstract our language from specific application domain (i.e. agentspace) and show that the language is, in some sense, a universal agent language. Its model and implementation may be specific, however the language itself is generic.

The paper is structured as follows. In Section 2 our approach to interoperability in agentspace is presented. In Section 3 an example explaining the idea of agentspace is presented. In Section 4 language layer of agentspace architecture is presented. Section 5 is devoted to presenting agent architecture.

2 Interoperability in Agentspace

The basic idea of our approach is the construction of open distributed infrastructure that would allow to join applications as services on the one hand and to use them by heterogeneous agents on the other hand. A user, delegating a task to an agent, needs not even to know what and where are services and resources necessary to realize the task. The user expresses the task in our high level common language called Entish. The agent migrates across the agentspace, communicates with services and other agents looking for information, services and resources needed to realize the delegated task.

The architecture of our system consists of three layers: interaction layer, agent/service layer, and language layer. The interaction layer specifies infrastructure that provides basic functionality for agents and services like agent moving from one place to another and communication with agents and services. This layer is to be implemented by a mobile agent platform. In our case it is done by Pegaz2 [12] our own MAP.

The second layer, i.e., agent/service layer specifies some aspects of agent and service architecture that allow them to evaluate formulas (called situations) expressed in the language Entish as well as determining new situations resulting from performing elementary actions. The agents are equipped with mental attitudes: knowledge, goals, intentions and commitments that are represented as Entish formulas. A service is equipped with commitments and intentions.

The language layer consists of Entish, a simple language of first order logic, along with a specification how to "implement" it for open and distributed use. The implementation follows the idea of so called "webizing language" see T. Berners-Lee [6]. The language describes the "world" (i.e. agentspace) to be created on the basis of infrastructure provided by the previous layers. However, this description is purely declarative. Actions are not used in Entish; the formulas describe only the results of performing actions. So that no causal relations can be expressed here. The language is sufficient to express desired situations (tasks) by the users as well as by agents and services, however it can not explicitly express any idea about how to achieve them. This may be done by implementing distributed information service (as an ordinary service), where an agent may get to know how to realize the delegated task, or to get a hint. Usually, as the reply to its query (expressed also in Entish) agent gets a sequence of intermediate situations to follow. We are going to explain it in the next section.

3   Motivations

Perhaps in the near future the development of agentspace reaches the critical mass, i.e. the number of connected applications will be so large that a user, facing hard, complex and time consuming task to perform, first of all will check if this task could be realized in the agentspace. So that she/he will formulate the task in Entish, delegate this task (together with a timeout) to an agent, send the agent to the agentspace and wait for a result. On the other hand if a programmer has implemented an application that performs complex and time consuming routine, and the interface needed to connect it to the agentspace infrastructure is easy to implement, why not to do so?

Suppose that a user faces the following problem. He or she has a file in latex format and wants to transform it onto html format. However, the user has not installed 'LATEXto HTML' converter on his workstation. Since the job is to be performed only once, the user does not want to take all this burden of purchasing the system or looking over Web to download a free copy of it, and then installing it. Supposing that there is a service in agentspace that performs that job, the user formulates the task, describing the job, by using SecretaryService - his interface to the agentspace. The task description is expressed in our language Entish that is supposed to be the common language of the agentspace.

Let us present a rough scenario that may follow from that situation. Suppose, the user delegates the task (along with a timeout) to an agent, and the agent is sent into agentspace. The agent is autonomous and its only goal is to realize the task. The task is expressed in Entish as formula, say f, describing a class of situation that realize the task. Suppose that the agent is equipped with the initial resources described by the Entish formula f^o. First of all, the agent gets in touch with an information service (called InfoService) and sends the following message: *"my intention is f"*. Suppose that the InfoService replies with the following: *"service s^* can realize your intention"*. So that the agent sends again the message *"my intention is f"*, however this time to the service s^*. If the service s^* is ready to do so, it sends back the following message to the agent:
"s^* commits to you to realize f, if f^* is realized".
Let us note that here the formula f refers to the output of service s^*, whereas f^* to the input. Having the commitment, the next intention of the agent is to realize f^*, i.e., the input of s^*. So that agent sends the message *"my intention is f^*"* to any known InfoService. It the agent gets no reply from the InfoServices, it migrates to any randomly chosen remote place and tries again to communicate with new InfoServices. Suppose that finally, the agent got back the following: *"service s^{**} can realize your intention f^*"*. The agent sends to service s^{**} the following message: *"my intention is f^*"*. The service replies with the following: *"s^{**} commits to you to realize f^*, if f^{**} is realized"*. Here again the formula f^* refers to the output of service s^{**}, whereas f^{**} to the input. Now, suppose that f^{**} follows from f^o. So that having these two commitments and knowing that f^{**} follows from f^o, the agent has already arranged the workflow needed to realize the task delegated by the user. If the workflow is executed and performed successfully, the agent notifies the user about that and can finish its activity. However, before the agent does so it is obliged to report its experience (i.e., the operation it has performed in order to realize the delegated task) to an InfoService. In this way the system has ability to learn, so that the next agents having tasks of the same type will be informed how to realize them immediately. If the workflow fails, the agent makes its best to recover it and

tries again unless the timeout is over. In the case the timeout is over, the agent notifies the user about failure and also finishes its activity.

Although our example may be seen as a bit abstract one, it gives an idea how distributed heterogeneous services can be integrated (composed) into a workflow needed for task realization. Another example from e-commerce domain can be given, however the limit of space does not allow to do so.

4   Language Layer: Entish

Our goal is to specify and implement minimum infrastructure necessary to create agentspace. This minimum is a middleware that provides a means for achieving interoperability between heterogeneous agents and services. It is only a means, because interoperability results from submitting to some common rules and standards. We propose a specification of layered architecture of agentspace infrastructure as these common rules. The architecture consists of three layers as it was already mentioned in Section 2. Details of interaction layer implemented by a MAS are presented in [2]. In this paper we focus on language, and agent/service layers.

The language layer consists of a language, called Entish, of first order logic with types where the scopes of quantifiers are limited to finite lists, and specification how to implement it in open distributed environment using space of unique names URI (Universal Resource Identifiers), as suggested by T. Berners-Lee [6]. There is only one deviation from the classic logic; we treat formulas as objects in our language. Of course, this may lead to a paradox, however, it is a convenient way to express agent mental attitudes, like intentions, goals, and commitments in first order language.

Without going into details, Entish consists of types of primitive objects that include: places, agents, resources, services, agent/service mental attributes, and Time. There are also two primitive relations: is_in and leq, and several primitive functions, like $gmt()$. The first relation expresses that something "is in" something else, for example, an agent "is in" a place. The second relation is needed to express timeouts, for example, that a date (object of type Time) is less or equal (leq for short) than the current GMT time. The rest part of Entish consists of standard first order logical operators, for term and formula constructions.

The main purpose of Entish is to provide simple common communication language for users, agents, and services. The communication consists in passing a message, i.e., resource "info" of special type called Info. Intuitively, this resource carries a fact (evaluated formula) expressed in Entish. Using these mental attitudes, a conversation protocol can be constructed in the following way. Agent, say $ag1$, always sends to a service a message containing a formula of the form: $intentions(ag1) => \phi$, where ϕ is an Entish formula. If the service (say ser) agrees to realize agent's intention, it sends back an info containing its commitment that is, (as it was intuitively presented in Section 3) a pair of formulas: $(\psi; \phi)$. Actually, this pair is expressed as one Entish formula:

$$(\psi => form\_in(commitments(ser))) \ \& \ (form\_out(commitments(ser) => \phi)$$

Without going into the notation details, it means that the service ser commits to realize formula ϕ if only the formula ψ becomes true. However, if the service ser is an information service, it sends back an info containing formula of the following form: $form\_out(cos) => intentions(ag1)$, where cos is the pointer (universal address, i.e. a URI [6]) to a service or to a (partial) plan that realizes agent $ag1$'s intention. The conversation protocol is completed by four additional control messages needed for workflow management. Although the protocol is extremely simple, it does work in our applications.

We have presented merely a sketch of the protocol; a detailed presentation must be preceded by formal introduction of Entish notation, however the limit of space does not allow to do so. It seems that the performatives of FIPA ACL, and KQML can be represented in our protocols by using the mental attributes.

Now, we are going to present a formal model of agentspace (presented extensively in [4]) that is based on *event structures* [17]. This formal model will also serve as a formal semantics for our language Entish.

4.1   Formal Model of Agentspace

The main components of the structure created by a MAP (for example: Grasshopper, Mole or Pegaz) are places, services located at the places, and agents that can move from place to place. The agents use services, communicate, and exchange data and resources with other agents. The agents can also collect, store, exchange, and transport the resources. In our formal description the primitives are: **places, agents, resources, services,** and **actions** .

It is important to note that Entish has only places, agents, resources, services, and relation "is_in" as its primitives. So that the language describes relations between these primitives (i.e. something is_in something else), however not using actions.

We can distinguish the following types of primitive actions: **move** to another place, **create agent, pass resource, communicate, finish activity**.

Let us notice that some actions belonging to the core functionality of a MAP are not considered here like agent naming, registration, and actions concerning the security. They are hidden from the user as well as from the agents. In order to have the environment structure as simple as possible we should abstract from those details that are not essential for the agents to realize their goals.

Joint action a (for example a communication action) can be executed if, for all the agents/services needed for an execution: the action a is enabled and selected for execution, i.e., intuitively all the agents/services "can" and "do want" to participate in the execution of this action. If one of the agents/services cannot or doesn't want to participate in the execution, then the attempt to execute action a fails. For this reason we assume that for any joint action a, and any agent i, needed to execute a, there is a local action $fail(a, i)$ of agent i that corresponds to agent i's failure to execute joint action a.

The crucial notion needed to define a representation of agentspace, presented intuitively above, is the notion of "event". Any event corresponds to an action execution, so that it "describes" an occurrence of a local interaction of the agents participating in the execution. The term "local" is of great importance here. Usually, local interaction concerns only few agents so that the event associated with this local interaction describes only the involved agents, services, resources, and places. The events form a structure, that expresses their causal relations.

Having primitive concepts and setting initial conditions for agents, places, and distribution of primitive resources and services, the set E, of all events that can occur in the environment, can be defined. It is important to notice that due to the local interaction, it is easy to extend the set E if new agents, places, resources, and services are added. Hence, the representation is appropriate for open environments. It is also generic in the sense that in order to construct the representation an agent need not know all agents, places, resources, and services in the world. In the course of learning about them the agent can extend the representation or shrink it if it is necessary to forget about some agents, places, etc..

Let A be the set of primitive actions. Let $E_i \subseteq E$ denote the subset of events in which the agent i does participate. Event e is called *joint* if it belongs to at least two different sets E_i. Event structures have been successfully applied in the theory of distributed systems [17] and several temporal logics have adopted them as frames [9].

Now, we present a formal definition of event structure.

A **labeled prime event structure** is a 5-tuple $\mathcal{ES} = (E, A, \rightarrow, \#, l)$, where

1. E is a set of *events* or *action occurrences*,
2. A is a finite set, called a set of *actions*,
3. $\rightarrow$ a subset of $E \times E$ is an irreflexive, acyclic relation, called the *immediate causality relation between the events*, i.e. $e \rightarrow e'$ means that the event e is one of the immediate causes of the event e'. The causality relation satisfies the following condition: $\downarrow e \stackrel{def}{=} \{e' \in E \mid e' \rightarrow^* e\}$ is finite for each $e \in E$, where $\rightarrow^*$ is the reflexive and transitive closure of $\rightarrow$. This means that the past of any event is finite.
4. $\#$ a subset of $E \times E$ is a symmetric, irreflexive relation, called *conflict relation*, such that $\# \circ \rightarrow^*$ is a subset of $\#$ (called *conflict preservation condition*). Two events are in conflict if they cannot occur in the same run. One of the reasons for conflict occurrence is agent choice of action, i.e. which action an agent chooses to execute.
5. $l : E \longrightarrow A$ is a labeling function that indicates for each event which action is executed at that event, i.e., $l(e) = a$ means that event e is an occurrence of action a.

Two events e, e' are in immediate causality relation, i.e. $e \rightarrow e'$ if the same agent participates in them, and the agent has executed the action $l(e')$ immediately after the execution of action $l(e)$.

This formal model presented above serves for three purposes. First of all, it is a formal model of agentspace. It provides also a formal semantics for Entish. This may be seen a bit provocative, since event structures are usually considered as formal semantics for temporal logics, see [9]. As we will see in the next section, agent can evaluate Entish formulas in some way.

Finally, it provides means to represent formally mental attitudes (knowledge, goals, intentions, and commitments) as modalities in a dynamic structure. A modality is represented by a set of runs of the event structure. This allows to specify, and verify agent behavior in terms of these mental attitudes; see [4] for details.

Let us conclude this section with the following important remark. Entish primitives are only places, agents, resources, services, agent/service mental attributes, Time and relations is_in and leq. It seems that these primitives are general enough to capture the essence of agent paradigm. Since Entish does not contain actions, the set of actions A of the model can be arbitrary, i.e., not necessarily corresponding to agentspace and a MAP environment. So that the class of models the Entish describes is broad. Hence, it seems that Entish may be regarded as a universal agent language.

5   Our Agent Architecture

The agent/service layer plays special role in agentspace architecture. It specifies agent and service interfaces to language layer (implemented by Entish) and to interaction layer (implemented by Pegaz2). So that, agent architecture is divided into following three sub layers: mental attitudes (soul), decision mechanism (mind), execution mechanism (body). The "soul" is expressed in Entish and consists of knowledge (a collection of facts), goals, intentions, and social commitments. Agent soul stores all necessary parameters needed to realize the task delegated to agent by its master. This concerns also control parameters of task realization. It is of great importance in our architecture, since we allow a soul to migrate alone without "mind" and "body". This has serious consequences regarding object persistence, security and transactions in our architecture.

The mind controls both the soul and body. It constitutes the proper part of the second layer. It is left open to a programmer how to design and implement his own agent mind. However, to assure interoperability, the programmer must submit to the agent interfaces to soul and to body specified by this layer. Agent body executes actions (directed by the mind) in the interaction layer. Specification of service is a bit different than the agent architecture.

5.1   Design Principles of Agent Mind and Its Functioning

New agent is created if a new task is issued by a user. There is no problem with agent creation. First of all, agent soul is constructed by writing goal, knowledge, and commitment formulas. The agent goal expresses the task. The knowledge is a collection of facts that give the agent initial knowledge about, for example, resources provided by the user for task realization. The commitment expresses that the agent is bound to realize the task for the user. Now, only agent mind and body is needed to complete the agent and send it as an autonomous agent to the agentspace. Agent body is implemented for a specific MAP, so that within the same MAP agent can migrate as a whole, that is, consisting of soul, mind, and body. If MAPs are implemented in Java according to our mind-body interface, then the agent mind and soul together can migrate between these platforms. Otherwise, only agent soul can migrate between platforms provided the platforms implement our soul-mind interface.

So that our agent architecture provides three levels of interoperability that correspond to the layered architecture of agentspace:

- semantic interoperability provided by language layer - agent soul;
- semantic and reasoning interoperability provided by language layer and agent/service layer - agent soul and mind;
- perfect interoperability, i.e., semantic, reasoning, and interaction interoperability provided by all three layers of agentspace architecture - agent soul, mind, and body.

A consequence of layered architecture is that our agent is purely an information agent. Although we allow agent to carry resources, it is not recommended especially if the agent is supposed to migrate (it is autonomous, so it can do so) to unknown platforms. Its capability to perform actions is restricted mainly to migration and communication however, there is a possibility of having more actions implemented as routines in agent body. Its ability to reason is minimal, almost all reasoning job is delegated to information services. It is worth to note that information services are not system services, i.e. they are not a part of basic agentspace infrastructure. Creation of information services as well as creation of agent minds within soul-mind and mind-body interfaces is open and left to users, i.e. to anyone who is willing and is able to implement them. Of course, we provide some pilot implementations of agent minds as well as information services for testing and as examples.

So, the question is what our agent does? The main and only job of the agent is to construct workflow that would perform successfully the task delegated to that agent. This includes: (1) construction of operation (a sequence of sub tasks) of the workflow; (2) arrangement of services needed to perform the sub tasks; (3) control, rearrangement and recovery of the workflow in the case of failure; (4) and finally notification (either positive or negative) of the task realization to be sent to user.

Agent decision mechanism can work according to the following algorithm:

1. compute current situation on the basis of your knowledge; check all your timeouts;
2. check in your history if there is a valid commitment of someone towards you that declares realization of your current intention; if there is one, go to (5);
3. check if there is a routine in your body that can realize your current intention; if there is one, execute it and go to (5);
4. ask an information service how to realize the intention; if you get back a partial plan, go to (5); if all known information services can not help you, migrate randomly to another remote place looking for information services and asking them;
5. if the workflow is completed, execute it; if success, notify the user, otherwise modify your intentions and go to (1);

It seems that our agent architecture can not be classified according to the standard taxonomies, see for example [10,18]. Perhaps it is specific for application domain, that is, for Internet and Cyberspace. Our architecture may be seen as distributed, i.e. information services may be viewed as part of agent architecture where the main part of agent planning and learning is performed. The learning consists on storing and processing agent experience. The difference is that our agent life is short, i.e., it "dies" after performing its task and reporting the way the task was achieved to an information service. On the other hand, it is easy to create a new agent if there is a task to be performed.

6   Conclusion

The limit of space does not allow to present details of our middleware as well as details of Entish and agent architecture. More will be available shortly on English version of our www site. The first version of the specifications of the layers is completed. Prototype of agentspace architecture is already implemented. Now, we are testing our architecture and developing our small agentspace in Pegaz Ring that consists of several research groups, see pegaz.ipipan.waw.pl for details.

References

1. Agentcities - http://www.agentcities.org/
2. S. Ambroszkiewicz and T. Nowak. Agentspace as a Middleware for Service Integration. In Proc. ESAW-2001. To be published by Springer LNAI 2203, December 2001.
3. S. Ambroszkiewicz. Towards Software Agent Interoperability. In Proc. 10th Conf. on Information Modelling and Knowledge Bases, Saariselka, Finland, May 8-11, 2000. Extended version in Kangassalo H., Jaakkola H., (Eds.) Information Modelling and Knowledge Bases XII, IOS Press, Amsterdam, 2001.
4. S. Ambroszkiewicz, W. Penczek, and T. Nowak. Towards Formal Specification and Verification in Cyberspace. Presented at Goddard Workshop on Formal Approaches to Agent-Based Systems, 5 - 7 April 2000, NASA Goddard Space Flight Center, Greenbelt, Maryland, USA. To appear in Springer LNCS.
5. ATLAS - Agent Transaction Language for Advertising Services http://www.cs.cmu.edu/ softagents/atlas/
6. T. Berners-Lee - www.w3.org/DesignIssues/Webize.html -and- /DesignIssues/Logic.html
7. M. E. Bratman. Intentions, Plans, and Practical Reason. Harvard University Press, 1987.
8. DARPA Agent Markup Language (DAML) http://www.daml.org/
9. K. Lodaya, R. Ramanujam, P.S. Thiagarajan, "Temporal logic for communicating sequential agents: I", Int. J. Found. Comp. Sci., vol. 3(2), 1992, pp. 117–159.
10. J.P.Mueller. The Right Agent (Architecture) to Do the Right Thing. In J.P. Mueller, M.P. Singh, and A.S. Rao (Eds.) *Inteligent Agents V, Proc. of ATAL'98,* Springer LNAI 1555, pp. 211-225, 1999.
11. OIL, Ontology Interchange Language, http://www.ontoknowledge.org/oil/
12. Pegaz www.ipipan.waw.pl/mas/
13. A. S. Rao and M. P. Georgeff. Modelling rational agents within a BDI–architecture. In Proc. KR'91, pp. 473-484, Cambridge, Mass., 1991, Morgan Kaufmann.
14. Sycara, K.; Widoff, S.; Klusch, M.; Lu, J.: LARKS: Dynamic Matchmaking Among Heterogeneous Software Agents in Cyberspace. Journal on Autonomous Agents and Multi-Agent Systems, Kluwer Academic, March, 2001.
15. Web Services Description Language (WSDL) 1.0 - http://www-106.ibm.com/developerworks/library/w-wsdl.html?dwzone=web
16. S. Willmott, M. Calisti, B. Faltings, S. Macho-Gonzalez, O. Belakhdar, M. Torrens. "CCL: Expressions of Choice in Agent Communication" The Fourth International Conference on MultiAgent Systems (ICMAS-2000).
17. Winskel, G., An Introduction to Event Structures, LNCS 354, Springer - Verlag, pp. 364–397, 1989.
18. M. Wooldridge. Intelligent Agents. In G. Weiss (Ed.), *Multiagent Systems: A modern approach to Distributed Artificial Intelligence*, The MIT Press. pp. 27-78, 1999.

Agent's Adaptivity – Some Aspects of Theoretical Foundations of a Neural Agent Training Process

Andrzej Bielecki

Institute of Computer Science, Jagiellonian University, Poland
uibielec@cyf-kr.edu.pl

Abstract. In the paper some aspects of theoretical foundations of a neural agent adaptivity is discussed. A method of regularization of a gradient system which models a training process of a layer artificial neural network is considered. The possibilities of applying the result to agent systems are discussed as well.

1 Introduction

Multi-Agent Systems (MASes) schedule their goals according to both the environment state and tasks they should realize. a member of a MAS called *"agent"* is a unit being equipped with the following basic capabilities:

Situatedness - an agent collects information about an environment in which he acts and transforms them in order to obtain predicates for decision making.
Autonomy - an agent controls his own actions.
Flexibility - an agent undertakes decisions by means of responsibility.
Learning ability - an agent has learning abilities allowing him to adapt to the environment.
Goal-orientation - an agent realizes his own goals.
Social abilities - an agent can cooperate with other ones.

The learning ability is strictly connected to other mentioned capabilities and is important for performing effectively the system tasks ([18]). Since artificial neural networks (ANNs) has great adaptive abilities and there are numerous training algorithm for ANNs, MASes are sometimes implemented as neural systems ([6], [9], [20]) especially because ANNs are applied effectively to solution of problems in technical sciences, medicine and economy (see [4], [7], [12], [15], [16], [21]) *i.e.* in these areas in which MASes are widely used. Furthermore, neural algorithms are frequently combined with fuzzy and genetic ones ([9], [15], [19]) which are widespread in MASes as well. Since there emerge problems with neural nets learning process, its mathematical models are created ([13]). Dynamical systems theory is one of the tools for investigating ANNs' learning process ([16], chapter 9). Sometimes, strong theorems concerning dynamical systems can be applied only for systems being sufficiently regular. In this paper a method of regularization of a gradient system modelling a training process of a layer ANN is described. The possibilities of applying the result to MASes are discussed as well.

B. Dunin-Kęplicz and E. Nawarecki (Eds.): CEEMAS 2001, LNAI 2296, pp. 47–53, 2002.

2   Neural Architectures in Agent Systems – Implementations and Possibilities

Neural system can be used in MASes as adaptive ones. They can help to learn an agent profile of a user. In such context ANNs are sometimes used together with fuzzy systems which use if-then rules that store the agent's knowledge. a neural system uses training data to form and tune the rules. An implementation of such system is described in [9]. a function $F : \mathbf{R}^p \to \mathbf{R}^n$ is a model of a fuzzy system and the way of its construction is described - see [9], formulae (1) and (2). An error function is defined in the standard way as a square mapping $E(x) = \frac{1}{2} \cdot (f(x) - F(x))^2$, where f is an approximand. The supervised gradient descent learning low moves and shapes the fuzzy rule patches to give a finner approximation in terms of the error function. There are numerous other descriptions of neural implementation in MASes - the paper [20] can be taken as an example.

On the other hand, developments in the area of synthetic agents have promoted the study of cognitive basis of behaviour (see [3], [11], [17] and references given there). Both the computational models are created and implementations of, for instance, emotional agents are described in literature ([17]). Such approach to modelling of an agent or community of agents is very similar to neojackson models of a human cognitive abilities - compare [11] and [5]. Since there are trials of creating mathematical models of human consciousness considering also consciousness dynamics ([5]) and implementing them using ANNs ([2]), there are possibilities to use ANNs to create agents having some cognitive properties.

Recapitulating, neural networks are used in MASes and studies on agents having cognitive mechanisms, *i.e.* perception, emotions, attention and memory make possible wider use of ANNs in agent systems. One of the key problems in neural implementations is training a network. Therefore, mathematical investigation of the problem widely take places. Since the training process is often modelled by differential equations generating continuous dynamical systems (flows) and a network is trained using an iterative rule being one of the numerical methods for the differential equation, one of the basic question in such context is whether the qualitative properties of flows are preserved under discretization. In this paper we consider this problem with connection to training a nonlinear neuron using the gradient descent method. Conclusion for agent systems is discussed as well.

3   Mathematical Foundations

There are several methods of artificial neural networks learning. Most of them are iterative processes. Let us notice that the descent gradient method which lead to the variation of synapses of the form

$$\boldsymbol{w}^{(p+1)} = \boldsymbol{w}^{(p)} - h \cdot grad\ E(\boldsymbol{w}), \tag{1}$$

where $\boldsymbol{w} = [w_1, ..., w_k]$ is a vector of weights of a neuron, is an iterative process generated by the Euler method for the differential equation

$$\dot{\boldsymbol{w}} = -grad\ E(\boldsymbol{w}). \qquad (2)$$

If we consider a neuron, an output deviation function, called also a criterial function, play a role of the potential E in the gradient equation (2). Most often used square criterial function is, for a single neuron, given by the formula

$$E(\boldsymbol{w}) = \frac{1}{2} \sum_{n=1}^{N} \left[f(\beta^{(n)}) - z^{(n)} \right]^2, \qquad (3)$$

where f is an activation function of a neuron, $\beta^{(n)} := x_1^{(n)} \cdot w_1 + ... + x_k^{(n)} \cdot w_k$ and the vector $\boldsymbol{x}^{(n)} = [x_1^{(n)}, ..., x_k^{(n)}]$ is an input signal. The number $z^{(n)}$ is a desired response of the neuron if a vector $\boldsymbol{x}^{(n)}$ is given to the input and N is a number of input vectors used in the learning process. The finite sequence $((\boldsymbol{x}^{(1)}, z^{(1)}), ..., (\boldsymbol{x}^{(N)}, z^{(N)}))$ is called the learning sequence.

As it has been already mentioned, considering mathematical models of a training process, one of the basic questions is whether the qualitative properties of a contionuous-time system (a flow) are preserved under implementation. Topological conjugacy of a discrete system (cascade) obtained via discretization of the flow and a cascade generated by an applied numerical method is one of theoretical tools for such investigations.

In the applied theorem a differential equation and its Euler method are considered. The time-h-map of the induced solution is compared to the cascade obtained via Euler method.

The result obtained by Bielecki ([Bie1]) is that on a two-dimensional sphere $\mathcal{S}^2$ a gradient dynamical system is, under some natural assumptions, correctly reproduced by the Euler method for a sufficiently small time step. It means that the time-h-map of the induced dynamical system is globally topologically conjugate to the discrete dynamical system obtained via Euler method what can be presented as follows.

Theorem 31 *Let*

$$\phi : \mathcal{S}^2 \times \mathbf{R} \longrightarrow \mathcal{S}^2$$

be a dynamical system having a finite number of singularities, all hyperbolic, and generated by a differential equation

$$\dot{x} = -grad\ E(x), \qquad (4)$$

on the sphere $\mathcal{S}^2$, where $E \in \mathcal{C}^2(\mathcal{S}^2, \mathbf{R})$. Let, furthermore, the dynamical system ϕ has no saddle-saddle connections. Moreover, let us assume that $\phi_h : \mathcal{S}^2 \longrightarrow \mathcal{S}^2$ is a discretization of the system ϕ, i.e. $\phi_h(x) := \phi(x, h)$, whereas a mapping $\psi_h : \mathcal{S}^2 \longrightarrow \mathcal{S}^2$ is generated by the Euler method for the equation (4). Then, for sufficiently small $h > 0$, there exists a homeomorphism $\alpha = \alpha_h : \mathcal{S}^2 \longrightarrow \mathcal{S}^2$ globally conjugating cascades generated by ϕ_h i ψ_h, i.e. the following formula holds

$$\psi_h \circ \alpha = \alpha \circ \phi_h. \qquad (5)$$

The proof of the theorem is presented in [1]. In the paper we concentrate on application of the presented result to analysis of the learning process dynamics of a nonlinear neuron.

4   Dynamics of Learning Process of a Nonlinear Neuron

Let us consider one-layer artificial neural network consisting of nonlinear neurons. Let us assume that the input of each neuron has two component and the learning process is implemented on a computer according to the Euler method. Let us, furthermore, define an activation function of each neuron to be a bounded mapping of a class $C^2(\mathbf{R}, \mathbf{R})$ with the first and second derivatives bounded as well. Most types of activative functions used in practice (for instance bipolar and unipolar functions - see [Oso], page 38, most radial functions - see [Oso], page 168) satisfy the specified assumptions. Since neurons learn independently in a one-layer ANN, we can consider the learning process only for a single neuron. Under such assumptions Theorem 31 implies asymptotical stability of the learning process using the descent gradient method.

Let us consider the sphere S^2, which can be identified, via the homeographic projection, with the compactificated plane $\overline{\mathbf{R}^2}$. The theorem can be used in the analysis of the learning process of a nonlinear neuron having two-componental input provided the potential E in gradient equation (2) can become completed in the north pole of the sphere in such a way that it remains a function of a class $C^2(S^2, \mathbf{R})$ and no additional nonhyperbolic fixed point appears.

The criterial function given by the formula (3) has various limits if an inverse image $\pi^{-1}(\boldsymbol{w})$ of a vector $\boldsymbol{w}$ (where π is the stereographic projection) converges to the north pole i.e. $|\boldsymbol{w}|$ converges to infinity. It follows from the fact that we can converge to infinity in such a way that the scalar product $\boldsymbol{x} \circ \boldsymbol{w}$ remains an arbitrary constant. However it is possible to modify the criterial function in such a way that on a closed ball $B((0,0), r \leq a)$ the potential will not be modified and it will be possible to complete it in the proper way. Furthermore, the radius a can be as large as we need.

Let us remark that the range of number values which can be represented in a computer is bounded. Thus, absolute values of vectors $\boldsymbol{w}$ and $\boldsymbol{x}$ are bounded and, therefore, in modelling numerically artificial neurons we can considered only bounded vectors $\boldsymbol{w}$ and $\boldsymbol{x}$. Therefore, topological conjugacy consideration on a sufficiently large ball is adequate for a learning process analysis.

Let us choice a sufficiently large radius a of a circle on which a training process is modelled. We can modify the potential E using a function defined as follows

$$g(\boldsymbol{w}) := \begin{cases} e^{(r-a)^n} & \text{for } r \geq a, \\ 1 & \text{for } r \in [0, a), \end{cases} \qquad (6)$$

where $r := |\boldsymbol{w}|^2 = w_1^2 + w_2^2$ and a natural number n is selected depending on the potential E and radius a in the way specified below. The function g is of a class $C^2(\mathbf{R}^2, \mathbf{R})$. Define the following mapping

$$E^*(\boldsymbol{w}) := g(\boldsymbol{w}) \cdot E(\boldsymbol{w}), \qquad (7)$$

Solutions of the equation

$$\dot{w} = -grad\ E^*(w) \tag{8}$$

cut the circle $K((0,0),2a)$ transversally "getting" into its interior that is to say the scalar product $-grad\ E^*(w) \circ w$ has for $|w|^2 = 2a$ negative values. Indeed, we have

$$- grad\ E^*(w) \circ w = \tag{9}$$

$$= \sum_{i=1}^{2}\left[E(w) \cdot \frac{\partial g(w)}{\partial w_i} + g(w) \cdot \sum_{n=1}^{N}\left[x_i^{(n)} \cdot \frac{df}{d\beta^{(n)}} \cdot \left(f(\beta^{(n)}) - z^{(n)} \right) \right] \right] \cdot w_i.$$

Because

$$\frac{\partial g(w)}{\partial w_i} := \begin{cases} 2 \cdot w_i \cdot n \cdot (r-a)^{n-1} \cdot e^{(r-a)^n} & \text{for } r > a, \\ 0 & \text{for } r \in [0,a], \end{cases} \tag{10}$$

thus for $r = 2a$, we obtain

$$- grad\ E^*(w) \circ w = -e^{a^n}\sum_{i=1}^{2} \cdot [n \cdot a^{n-1} \cdot w_i^2 \cdot E(w) + \tag{11}$$

$$+ \sum_{n=1}^{N}\left[x_i^{(n)} \cdot \frac{df}{d\beta^{(n)}} \cdot \left(f(\beta^{(n)}) - z^{(n)} \right) \right] \cdot w_i \Big].$$

Since the problem is considered on a closed ball, all variables and functions are bounded. The potential E is nonnegative thus, for a large a, the first term in the sum asymptotically equals a^{n-1} whereas the second one can be negative but is limited. Thus, as a is large, the number n can be choice so large that the value of the first term is greater than absolute value of the second component of the sum.

In order to properly complete the potential in the north pole, let us assume that in a certain neighbourhood of the north pole the potential is of the form $V(w) = -s^2$, where s is the distance from the north pole. This neighbourhood is on the plain $\mathbf{R}^2$ equivalent, via the homeographic projection, to values of $|w|^2$ greater than, for instance, $3a$. Thus, it has maximum in the north pole. Then the dynamical system generated by the differential equation

$$\dot{w} = -grad\ V(w),$$

considered on the mentioned neighbourhood, has in the north pole repelling, hyperbolic fixed point. The completed potential $\tilde{E} \in \mathcal{C}(\mathcal{S}^2, \mathbf{R})$ can be of the form

$$\tilde{E}(w) = \begin{cases} E^*(w) & \text{for } |w|^2 \le 2a, \\ V(w) & \text{for } |w|^2 \ge 3a \end{cases}$$

Since trajectories "get" into the interior of the circle $K((0,0),r = 2a)$, the closed ball $B((0,0),r \le 2a)$ is an invariant set of the system. Therefore, though the potential is modified, the dynamics in the domain interested for us remains unchanged. Thus, if only dynamical system generated by the equation (2) has in the ball $B((0,0), r \leq a)$ a finite number of singularities, all hyperbolic, then the dynamical system generated by the formula (8) satisfies assumptions of Theorem 31.

5 Concluding Remarks

The possibilities of usage of Theorem 31 are limited to systems with only finite number of singularities, all of which have to be hyperbolic. The fact that the set of structural stable systems is open and dense in the set of gradient dynamical systems (see [PM], page 116), and that structural stability implies assumptions of Theorem 31, play an important role in applications. This guarantees that properties specified in assumptions of Theorem 31 are generic.

The conducted analysis concerns a one-layer ANN that consists of double-input neurons. In order for the analysis to be conducted for any multilayer network the Theorem 3.1 should be generalised, so that it encompasses the case of an n-dimensional sphere.

Not only are there numerous neural implementations of agent systems, but also some perspectives of wider usage of ANNs, for instance, in modelling of cognitive properties, as described in Section 2. The presented mathematical tool can be applied to the analysis of the learning process of both neural agent systems and of each system trained through gradient methods. On the basis of the [8] the presented method of regularisation can be, moreover, used for numerical methods of at least 2nd order. The fact that the described method has direct usage in the analysis of the system described in [9], should be clearly emphasised.

Dynamics of gradient systems is very regular. Particularly, it can not be chaotic and there can be no periodic orbits. These properties are preserved under discretization and due to the global topological conjugacy under application of the Euler method. Those facts imply assymptotical stability of the layer neural network learning process modelled by the cascade generated by the Euler method.

References

1. Bielecki, A.: Topological Conjugacy of Cascades Generated by Gradient Flow on a Two-Dimensional Sphere, Annales Polonici Mathematici, vol.73 (2000)
2. Bielecki A.: A Neuronal System for Simulation of Consciousness Dynamics Based on Information Metabolism Theory, Proceedings of the Seventh National Conference on Application of Mathematics in Biology and Medicine, Zawoja, Poland (2001) - accepted.
3. Canamero D.: Modeling Motivations and Emotions as a Basis for Intelligent Behavior, Proceedings of the First International Conference on Autonomus Agents, Marina del Rey, California USA (1997)
4. Hertz J., Krogh A., Palmer R.G.: Introduction to the Theory of Neural Computation, Addison-Welsey Publishing Company, Massachusetts (1991)

5. Kokoszka A., Bielecki A., Holas P.: Mental Organization According to Metabolism of Information and its Mathematical Description, International Journal of Neuroscience, vol 107 (2001)

6. Kisiel-Dorohinicki M., Klapper-Rybicka M.: Evolution of Neural Networks in a Multi-Agent World, Universitatis Iagellonica Acta Scientiarum Litterarumque, vol.10 (2000)

7. Korbicz J., Obuchowicz A., Uciński D.: Sztuczne sieci neuronowe - podstawy i zastosowania, (Artificial Neural Networks - Foundations and Applications), Akademicka Oficyna Wydawnicza PLJ, Warszawa (1994) - in Polish.

8. Li M.: Structural Stability of Morse-Smail Gradient-Like Flows under Discretization, SIAM J. Math. Anal., vol.28. **2** (1997)

9. Mitaim S., Kosko B.: Neural Fuzzy Agent for Profile Learning and Object Maching, Proceedings of the First International Conference on Autonomus Agents, Marina del Rey, California USA (1997)

10. Müller B., Reinhardt J.: Neural Networks, Springer Verlag, New York (1990)

11. Neves M.C., Oliveira E.: A Control Architecture for an Autonomus Mobile Robot, Proceedings of the First International Conference on Autonomus Agents, Marina del Rey, California USA (1997)

12. Osowski S.: Sieci neuronowe w ujęciu algorytmicznym, (An Algorithmical Approach to Neural Networks), Wydawnictwa Naukowo-Techniczne, Warszawa (1996) - in Polish.

13. Owens A.J., Filkin D.L.: Efficient Training of the Back Propagation Network by Solving a System of Stiff Ordinary Differential Equations, Int. Joint Conf. on Neural Networks, vol.II, Washington (1989) New York: IEEE.

14. Palis J., de Melo W.: Geometric Theory of Dynamical Systems, Springer Verlag, New York (1982)

15. Rutkowska D., Piliński M., Rutkowski L.: Sieci neuronowe, algorytmy genetyczne i systemy rozmyte, (Neural Networks, Genetic Algorithms and Fuzzy Systems), PWN, Warszawa-Łódź (1997) - in Polish.

16. Tadeusiewicz R.: Sieci neuronowe, (Neural Networks), Akademicka Oficyna Wydawnicza (1993) - in Polish.

17. Velasquez J.D., Maes P.: Cathexis: a Computational Model of Emotions, Proceedings of the First International Conference on Autonomus Agents, Marina del Rey, California USA (1997)

18. Weiss G., Sen S. (red.): Adaptation and Learning in Multi-Agent Systems, Lecture Notes in Artificial Intelligence (1996)

19. Yao X.: Evolutionary Artificial Neural Networks, International Journal of Neural Systems (1993)

20. Zrehen S., Gaussier P.: A Neural Architecture for Motivated Navigation Behavior in an Animat, Proceedings of the First International Conference on Autonomus Agents, Marina del Rey, California USA (1997)

21. Żurada J., Barski M., Jędruch W.: Sztuczne sieci neuronowe, (Artificial Neural Networks), PWN, Warszawa (1996) - in Polish.

Mobie: Personalized Automated Recharge of Prepaid Mobile Phones

J. Burgett[1], S. Hussain[1], C.M. Jonker[2], A. Razaq[1], and K. Silz

[1] AMS Inc, 51-55 Gresham Street, London EC2V 7JH, JeBu@acm.com
[2] Department of AI, Vrije Universiteit, De Boelelaan 1081a, 1081 HV Amsterdam,
jonker@cs.vu.nl, http://www.cs.vu.nl/~jonker

Abstract. Prepay usage as a percentage of overall mobile phone access has increased sharply over the past several years. However, the recharging process is still largely manual with personalization provided by the user. The MOBIE system described in this paper shows the future service of automatically recharging the prepaid account of a mobile phone in a personalized manner. Special attention is given to the use of industry technology to implement the MOBIE system. The paper addresses some of the difficulties encountered in that process.

1 Introduction

Telecommunication is an interesting domain that offers both opposing and common interests and that is in full development due to the integration of mobile phones, the Wireless Application Protocol (WAP, http://www.wapforum.org), and the Internet. Consumers are interested in accessibility, security, and personal beneficial intent. The telecom industry is interested in improvement of the relationship with its consumers, because this will lead to improvement of market share, and loyalty of good consumers (i.e., customer retention). They are further interested in improved operating efficiencies, and increased revenue.

In this paper the design and implementation of MOBIE an intelligent system to support the telecommunications industry is described. The focus of the MOBIE system lies on the (relatively simple idea of) personalized automated recharge of mobile phones. This choice is motivated by the practical benefits of such an application. Simple reactive variants of automated recharge are already available with some telecom providers. The simple automated recharge that is already provided entails only the automated recharge of the account if the account drops below a certain threshold.

The intelligence provided by MOBIE is new. MOBIE monitors your actual usage patterns and compares that to the expectation that the user has of his usage. In case of a discrepancy, MOBIE enlightens the user. The user can then decide whether his expectation was incorrect, or whether some unapproved usage of the account is in progress.

B. Dunin-Kęplicz and E. Nawarecki (Eds.): CEEMAS 2001, LNAI 2296, pp. 54–61, 2002.

The multi-agent paradigm enables the modeling of opposing and common interests in one system, called MOBIE♣. The interests of each party are modeled in their own agent, thus ensuring that the opposing interests are respected to the full. Cooperation between the agents representing the different parties enables the system to serve the common interests of all parties. The MOBIE multi-agent system consists of personal assistant agents for the consumers and business agents for the mobile telecommunication service providers.

2 Personalized Automated Recharge

On one hand, the user is interested in having an account as low as possible (because s/he will not accrue interest over the money located at the service provider). On the other hand the user wants to call unhindered by an account that is too low. This implies that from a financial point of view it makes sense to recharge his/her mobile account often. However, having to recharge the account is (still) time consuming; having to do this often is inconvenient. The telecom provider can increase consumer comfort by offering personalized automated recharging of the prepaid account by way of a personal assistant agent for each customer. The customer can also use a personal assistant agent offered by another party.

The core functionality of the personal assistant agent required to automate recharging consists of 5 elements. The business agent is designed to match at least the same capabilities. The personal assistant agent has to create and maintain a profile of the customer. The profile contains at least the criteria that tell the agent when to recharge the account and information needed to execute recharging (like the amounts it can use, and payment information). The profile also contains the expected usage pattern for the account. The personal agent has to match the criteria against the actual balance of the prepaid account, and the actual usage pattern against the expected usage pattern. The personal agent has to request the necessary information from the business such as the balance of the prepaid account and the actual usage pattern of the phone for a specified period of time. The personal agent is capable of recharging the prepaid account. The personal agent alerts the user in case of a discrepancy between the actual and expected usage patterns.

The customer initiates the personalized automated recharge by directly selecting the "Recharge" activity. Upon initiation of the recharge process, the Personal Agent retrieves the profile information related to recharging the phone. The Personal Agent replicates the latest account activity from the current service provider to its own Account History Database. The Personal Agent reviews the account activity and determines its actions. If a recharge is needed but the maximum recharge amount was already used up, the personal agent alerts the customer. If a recharge is needed and the maximum recharge amount has not been used up yet, then the personal agent uses

---

♣ MOBIE has been developed by the Intelligent Agent Initiative Team at American Management Systems (AMS).

knowledge rules to determine the appropriate recharge amount (these rules are proprietary information).

If the recharge amount, together with the amount recharged so far this week, exceeds the maximum recharge per week, then the customer is alerted. If a recharge was decided, the personal agent asks the business agent to recharge the account of the phone with the specified amount. If the recharge fails, the customer is alerted. If the recharge is successful, then, in due time, the personal agent notifies the customer about the recharge. The personal agent writes all activities in the agent activity log.

3   Pre-design Decisions

Multi-agent technology supports the development of distributed systems consisting of heterogeneous components that by interacting produce the overall service required [2], [4]. The nature of the domain requires that the MOBIE system consists of heterogeneous components. It should at least consist of a personal agent system, a business agent system, and a number of databases. The databases are needed to store information on the users of the personal agent system and to store information on the consumers but now from the perspective of the business, and there is a billing system database; see Figure 1. The last two of these are already in use by the business, a good reason to keep them as separate entities.

Fig. 1. The Multi-Agent System Functionality

The application should be able to access enterprise systems and enterprise data. Each agent has to be accessible through a number of different access channels: web-based, WAP and voice. Due to inherent restrictions of current WAP implementations (such as slow connection speeds and incompatibilities) and of mobile devices in general (such as small screen and limited input capabilities), a voice-enabled interface has high potential. However, the pilot version of the system only implements web access. The system has to be scaleable, reliable, and easy to maintain. Each agent has to be constructed on the basis of a domain-independent code framework (necessary for rapid and flexible agent development).

Based on an evaluation of the existing industry standards and techniques a decision was made to use some of the Java 2, Enterprise Edition (J2EE; http://www.javasoft.com/products/OV_enterpriseProduct.html) APIs because J2EE is the de-facto industry standard for implementing and scaling Java on the server. The use of J2EE in the development of an intelligent agent framework helps ensure scalability and maintainability. The available agent communication languages were studied (e.g., KQML), but a full ontology was not required for this application. XML (http://www.xml.org) as the industry standard format for data exchange was chosen as the input/output format for MOBIE's agents.

In the design of MOBIE no logic resides on the client side. Running any code on the client side requires the client to have a runtime environment that can execute the code, enough resources to run the code, downloaded and installed the code on the client's machine, and sophisticated security software against malicious attacks. The most popular client-side scripting language for web pages is JavaScript. WAP devices use the Wireless Markup Language (WML) for page description. WMLScript is the client-side scripting language (http://allnetdevices.com/faq/?faqredir=yes). A voice-enabled access channel does not have any scripting at all. An interesting client-side logic alternative to JavaScript that we did not investigate is Macromedia's Flash technology (http://www.macromedia.com/software/flash/). In our system, the MOBIE character on the screen is a Flash animation.

Investigation of commercially available Java agent platforms, namely AgentBuilder (http://www.agentbuilder.com) and Jack (http://agent-software.com.au) revealed a number of disadvantages: no built-in J2EE or XML support, proprietary communication protocol, hardwired reasoning engine, proprietary development environment (AgentBuilder) and high resource consumption. Instead of taking these products and adding missing features, an agent framework has been developed that focuses on scaleable, e-commerce capabilities. The reasoning engine of the framework is OPSJ from PST (http://www.pst.com), a Java rule engine with small memory footprint. VisualAge for Java (http://www.software.ibm.com/ad/vajava/) was used to develop the Java code, because from our experience it is the best available Java IDE.

MOBIE makes use of the following J2EE (http://www.javasoft.com/j2ee) APIs: JavaServer Pages (JSP), Servlets, Enterprise Java Beans (EJB), the Java Naming and Directory Interface, Java Database Connectivity, and the Java Transaction API. Servlets [3] are server-side Java components that can be accessed from HTML pages. Once loaded by the application server, they reside in memory. The application server automatically spawns a new servlet instance in its own thread for every incoming request. A servlet can use the entire Java API and has built-in support for session management (carrying user data while navigating through a web site).

In the design of MOBIE all three tiers of the Enterprise Java Application Model (http://www.javasoft.com/j2ee/images/appmodel.jpg) are used: the client tier („Client-Side Presentation"), the middle tier („Server-Side Presentation" & „Server-Side Business Logic") and the data tier („Enterprise Information System").

4   The Backbone Architecture

In this paper a generic architecture for multi-agent systems is presented that can be accessed over different channels. The architecture is especially suited for multi-agent systems in which there are at least two parties playing a role.

MOBIE has consumers and businesses. The consumer deals with the business indirectly by allowing his/her personal agent system to act on his/her behalf. The consumer can interact with the personal agent through three different access channels: by phone (using ordinary speech), by accessing the web site of the business on the Internet or by using a WAP (device such as a phone or a PDA). The system is designed according to one generic open system's architecture that is presented in Figure 2; it follows the J2EE recommendations by Sun. Each agent is embedded in its own EJB.

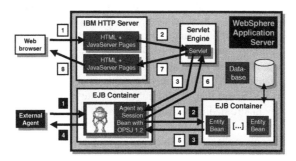

Fig. 2. The MOBIE Backbone Architecture

The upper half shows the control flow of a user – agent interaction. Firstly, the user enters some data into a web page (either an HTML page or a JSP; ①). The servlet extracts the information (②), converts it from Java into XML and sends it to the agent (③). The agent processes the information and then requests data through an entity bean (④). The entity bean is delivered (⑤) and used by the agent. After some more processing, the agent comes up with a result and returns it to the servlet as an XML document (⑥). The servlet examines the results, converts it into a Java object and sends it to the appropriate web page (either an HTML page or a JSP) in the appropriate form (⑦). The user then views the page (⑧).

The lower half shows the agent – agent interaction. The outside agent sends an XML request to the agent (❶). In the same way as before, the agent processes the information and then requests data through an entity bean (❷). The entity bean is delivered (❸) and used by the agent. After some more processing, the agent comes up with a result and returns it to the external agent as an XML document (❹).

In order to formalize and simplify the Java integration with XML, Business Objects (BO) were used. These special Java classes represent the XML data and support XML creation and parsing.

5   Agent Design

Usability engineering tasks included design of the screen look & feel, agent onscreen look, agent onscreen animation, agent onscreen movement, dialog interaction, and agent sound. First the generic agent architecture is introduced, and then the working of the agent is described in the form of a scenario.

5.1   Generic Agent Architecture

The main goal of the agent architecture was to build an industrial strength, domain-independent framework for huge scale e-commerce applications. As a general approach, an EJB like design (the so-called agent container) was chosen. The container offers services to the agent through static methods in the Services class. Each agent has to implement one Java interface. The container services were implemented as static methods since OPSJ rules only have access to objects in their working memory and to static methods (see section 6.1.2). Instead of inserting a service object and referencing it in every rule condition, the agent container uses static methods.

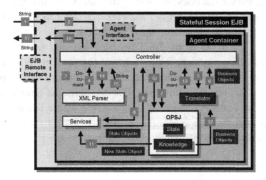

Fig. 3. The Agent Architecture

Figure 3 depicts a more detailed design of the agent (the numbers are referred to in the next section). The agent container is embedded in a stateful session EJB (application specific classes are depicted in white on blue). The EJB classes are just a wrapper around the container; there is little functionality in the EJB. There are two methods in the Agent Interface (and in the EJB remote interface) that trigger the agent reasoning: String reason(String) and Document reason(Document). Both methods expect and return a BO as an XML document – either flattened to a string or as an XML Document Object Model (DOM) tree. In both cases, the EJB just passes the messages on to the agent. Since XML is the data exchange format of the agent, the agent has an XML parser to parse strings into documents and to flatten documents to strings. The business logic resides in the Java rule engine OPSJ. The knowledge (i.e. the rules and Java methods) and the state (i.e. objects in the working memory of the rule engine) are application specific. The agent container uses the application specific Translator class to convert between XML and BOs. The Services class offers functionality through static methods.

As a result of the architecture, there is very little that sets one specific agent apart from another one: a list of rule set classes, an object derived from the Translator class and (implicitly) the BOs used. Each specific agent's remote interface extends (without any changes or additions) the generic agent EJB's remote interface. Similarly, each specific agent implementation class extends the generic agent EJB's implementation class and must implement two methods that return the aforementioned list of rule set classes and the Translator instance.

5.2 A Scenario

The steps in the scenario refer to figure 3. Application specific classes are depicted in white on dark. With regards to Figure 2, this details steps ③ and ⑥ (without the entity bean interaction in steps ④ and ⑤).

The scenario starts with an XML document (stored in a flat string) passed into the agent interface (1). The EJB passes it on to the agent (2) where the controller takes charge. The XML Parser decodes the string into an XML document using the Java class Document (3 and 4). The controller asks the Translator to transform the document into BOs (5 and 6). After the transformation the OPSJ working memory is reset. Then the controller takes each BO from the Translator list and inserts it into the OPSJ working memory. In the next step, it gets a list of the (externally stored) state objects of the agent (8 and 9, see the previous section) and are inserts them into the OPSJ working memory (10). The OPSJ inference process starts. As a result of the reasoning, a BO is stored in the Translator where it is converted into a Document (12). The controller picks it up (13) and the XML parser flattens it to a string (14 and 15). This string is returned to the EJB (16), which then returns it to the EJB client (17).

6 Discussion

Systems can consist of both straightforward and complex tasks. In our opinion, straightforward tasks (e.g., logging activities) should be implemented conventionally (e.g., in plain Java). Complex tasks that require autonomous intelligence (for example, negotiating a better price plan) can be implemented with agents. We found use cases to be an effective way of partitioning system functionality into tasks and assigning them to agents.

The main result of our project is that industry standard methodologies, technologies and tools can be used to build multi-agent systems; software developers can utilize their investments in these areas. Furthermore, in industry, new systems have to co-exist and co-operate with legacy systems. Building the new systems with proven technology in the form of industry standard technology eases the process of the integrating the old with new systems. We demonstrated that for heterogeneous systems requiring autonomous intelligence in a naturally distributed setting, a de-coupled, distributed, XML based architecture like MOBIE eases software development considerably.

However, agent development with industry standard methodologies does have its disadvantages. Those methodologies are based on a different paradigm, which complicates designs. The lack of scalable agent tool integration (e.g., rule engines) makes agent implementation more complex than it should be (e.g., no integrated source code debugger as in Java tools). Also, the concept of (agent) autonomy is absent from object-oriented methodologies.

We imagine that future multi-agent projects will use extended versions of „regular" software system development tools, i.e., an evolutionary improvement - not a revolutionary one. The main difference will be that specific encapsulated roles will be identified, modeled and implemented as intelligent agents. Just as objects brought a higher level of abstraction to software analysis and design, role modeling for agent-based systems will bring a higher level of abstraction than objects [1].

Since the construction of the multi-agent system described here, the world has not stood still. In the mean time the big prepaid mobile phone operators already have some sort of assistance for account recharge. For example, D2 Vodafone in Germany allows a recharge of either 50 DM or 100 DM through an Interactive Voice Response (IVR) service number with direct debit from a bank account. Telecom Italy has an even more advance rang of offerings: IVR, SMS, ATMs, and with an automatic recharge by a fixed amount (through direct debit) if the account falls below a certain threshold. The research presented in this article is therefore of direct applicability.

The chosen domain for the MOBIE project is more in the area of business to consumer (or vice versa) than business to business. However, the results are easily transferable to other applications.

References

1.   Ferber, J., Gutknecht, O., Jonker, C. M., Mueller, J. P., and Treur, J., Organization Models and Behavioural Requirements Specification for Multi-Agent Systems. In: *Proceedings of the Fourth International Conference on Multi-Agent Systems*, ICMAS 2000. IEEE Computer Society Press. In press, 2000. Extended version in: *Proceedings of the ECAI 2000 Workshop on Modelling Artificial Societies and Hybrid Organizations*, 2000.
2.   Giampapa, J., Paolucci, M., and Sycara, K., (2000), Agent interoperation across multi-agent system boundaries. In: *Proceedings of the Agents 2000 workshop on Infrastructure for scalable multi-agent systems.*
3.   Hunter, J., and Crawford, W., (1998), *Java Servlet Programming*, O'Reilly and Associates.
4.   Jennings, N., Sycara, K., and Wooldridge, M., (1998), A roadmap of agent research and development. In: *Autonomous Agents and Multi-agent Systems*, Kluwer Academic Publishers, Boston, pp. 275-306.

A Formal Specification of M-Agent Architecture

Krzysztof Cetnarowicz[1], Pablo Gruer[2], Vincent Hilaire[2], and Abder Koukam[2]

[1] Institute of Computer Science
AGH – University of Mining and Metallurgy
Al. Mickiewicza 30, 30-059 Krakow, Poland
[2] UTBM/Systèmes et Transports
Belfort Technopôle
90000 Belfort, France

Abstract. Complexity of distributed and decentralized systems demands new tools for designing and programming processes. An idea of autonomous agents that arises as an extension of the object and process concepts may be applied to distributed and decentralized systems development. In the paper the authors have undertaken an attempt to describe formally the architecture of multiagent systems using a method of specification based upon the combination of Object-Z, Statecharts and M-agent architecture. The proposed method of multiagent system description may be considered as a starting point to develop a multi-agent system description method covering a gap existing between theoretical analysis and practical realization of multiagent systems.

1 Introduction

Complexity of distributed and decentralized systems demands new tools for designing and programming processes. An idea of autonomous agents that arises as an extension of the object and process concepts may be applied to distributed and decentralized systems development ([4],[5]). The approaches proposed, (BDI architecture, Agent-0, etc.) ([14], [17]), ([15]) make some attempts to a practical model of multiagent system definition, but it seems to the authors that these attempts are not always practically applicable, and particularly they present, among others, the following inconveniences: They take as a base of considerations a low level of abstraction of the problem, and therefore the proposed model of the agent architecture does not cover a wide range of types of agents (or multiagent systems). The formalism proposed is not always convenient in practical applications where the real problem with its characteristic features is to be interpreted in the formal model. The approaches proposed do not take into consideration such problems as testing and debugging of the creating system. It seems that the research work is grouped around two opposite points: - one representing very formal approach that enables to describe some properties of multiagent systems with formal methods, - the other representing a practical approach with tools that enables to develop practical multiagent systems without any control of a number of important properties (such as stability, efficiency, etc.) of the created multiagent systems. In order to provide precise, unambiguous meanings for the concepts and terms introduced previously, we introduce a formal modelling approach. This formal modelling approach is based upon the combination

B. Dunin-Kȩplicz and E. Nawarecki (Eds.): CEEMAS 2001, LNAI 2296, pp. 62–72, 2002.

of Object-Z [6] and Statecharts [9]. In doing so, we can specify many aspects of the MAS that may be verified with theoretical tools and then applied in a practical way. The proposed method of a multiagent system description and modelling may be considered as a starting point to develop a multi-agent system description method covering a gap existing between a theoretical analysis and practical realization of multiagent systems.

The rest of this paper is organized as follows. The M-agent approach and its formal framework are presented in section 2. To illustrate the proposed methodology, a decentralized system of medical help is presented in section 3. Finally, the last section includes a summary and an outline of future research.

2   Formal Framework for M-Agent

2.1   Principle of the M-Agent Architecture

The M-Agent architecture [3]) is based upon the split of MAS in agents and an environment. The environment is what is observed by the agents and represented by a corresponding model. Each agent is related to a subset of the environment which is pertinent to it. The whole reality analyzed from the point of view of the multiagent system may be divided into two parts (fig. 1): *environment* - that may be observed by the agent and represented by a corresponding model, *agent's mind* - an area in which the agent builds and processes a model of the environment.

We can consider that a given agent *a* remains and acts in the environment, and to realize thit for any agent the following notions are defined:

- *models* of the environment, *strategies*, and *goals*.
- operation of the environment observation - *Imagination* and operation of the selected strategy execution *Execute*.

Every agent is characterized by an agent's mind. This mind is composed of strategies, goals and models of the environment. Strategies are what agents can do for modifying their models. Goals are what agents try to satisfy. The main idea of the agent functioning is the following: The agent observes the environment around and builds a *model* of the environment in its mind. For this purpose it uses the *Imagination* operation. The agent forecasts its possibilities using one of the available *strategies*. Applying a given

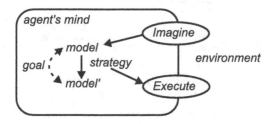

Fig. 1. Principle of the M-agent architecture.

strategy to the *model* of the environment, it obtains the forecasted *model* of the modified environment. Then the agent compares in its mind the *models* (real and forecasted) using the *goal* function that determines the goal of agent functioning. The agent selects the best strategy available according to its goals and realizes it. If the evaluation of the forecasted model is satisfactory, the agent realizes the selected strategy which is represented by the *Execution* operation. The whole decision process is carried out using the models of the environment processing in the agent's mind. In some cases we may observe that beings alter their behaviour as if they were changing their point of view. In this case the agent may be described with a more complex M-agent model called a multiprofile M-agent. Using the multiprofile M-agent architecture we can decompose the agent specification into several *profiles* (fig. 2). The operations of the *strategy execution* is common for all profiles, but the models, strategies, goals and imagination functions are different and characteristic for each profile. Every profile works in the following way:

As a consequence the agent obtains the *optimal strategy* proper for each profile. Then using the common decision function the agent selects the best strategy for the execution.

The final decision to realize the *strategy* is made by the agent with the use of the *Decision* function that takes into consideration the *models* of all the profiles.

The MAS environment is specified by the *Environment* which may take a form of a class. This class is composed of a set of resources, set of agents and topology defining the spatial properties of the environment.

2.2 Formal Framework

We build a framework written with formalism which is a composition of Object-Z and statecharts. The whole composition mechanism is described in [11]. For the sake of clarity this mechanism will only be sketched. In order to compose Object-Z classes and statecharts one can write a class with a schema including a statechart. This statechart specifies the behaviour of the class. Our framework is composed of a set of such classes which specify all meta-model concepts: environment, profile, and agent.

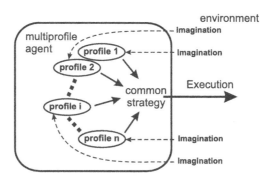

Fig. 2. Principle of the multiprofile M-agent architecture.

The structure of the framework as a class hierarchy allows for inheritance from defined classes in order to define more specific model concepts or to extend existing concepts. Every model concept is given formal semantics by a class of the framework.

The first concept of the model is a profile. The profile is defined by a Model of the environment, a set of actions and a set of goals to be reached. The *behaviour* of sub-schema specifies the behaviour of the profile. This schema is to be refined by including a statechart.

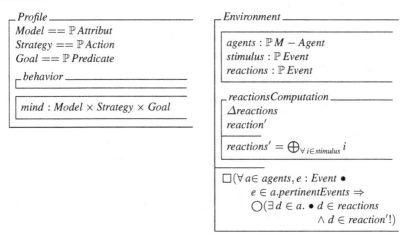

This work deals with situated MAS, that is to say, the MAS in which interactions occur through the environment. Situated MAS environments may have a metric, that is to say a total mapping from the entity which relates it to places. Here we do not assume the existence of such a mapping. The environment groups all agents of the MAS and is the place where all interactions are combined. The MAS environment is specified by the *Environment* class. This class is composed of a set of agents which are the MAS agents. The *stimulus* set groups all events occurring at a moment in time. The *reaction* set is the set of all agent reactions. Reactions are calculated by the reactionsComputation operation. This operation is obviously to be refined to make the combination operator (circled plus) at least more precise.

2.3 M-Agent Specification

In order to specify M-Agents the $M - Agent$ class which specifies a generic agent based upon the M-Agent architecture is added to the agent framework, defined in [12]. A specific M-Agent is then defined as a set of *Event* it reacts to, *pertinentEvents*. The reaction depends on the active agent's mind. The agent's mind defines values of models, strategies and goals. The agent's mind model and strategies are defined on the basis of the agent profiles. Indeed, *agentMind.Model* is a subset of the agent's attributes and *agentMind.Strategy* is a subset of the agent's actions which are an union of profile attributes and profile actions respectively. These profiles define the attributes, actions and stimulus of the M-Agent. The temporal invariant of the class constrains the behavior of the M-Agent so that they react to whatever event belonging to *pertinentEvents*. The reaction consists in applying the best strategy available with respect to the goals of the M-Agent. Intuitively, the best strategy is the strategy which satisfies the maximum number of sub-goals.

$\boxed{\begin{aligned}
&\underline{\ M - Agent\ }\\[4pt]
&\quad attributes : \mathbb{P}\,Attribute\\
&\quad actions : \mathbb{P}\,Action\\
&\quad stimulus : \mathbb{P}\,Event\\
&\quad pertinentEvents : \mathbb{P}\,Event\\
&\quad activeProfiles : \mathbb{P}\,Profile\\
&\quad agentMind : Model \times Strategy \times Goal\\[4pt]
&\quad agentMind = \cup_{\forall\, p \in activeProfiles} p.mind\\
&\quad \forall\, m \in agentMind.Model \bullet m \subseteq attributes\\
&\quad \forall\, s \in agentMind.Strategy \bullet s \subseteq actions\\[8pt]
&\Box(\exists\, e : Event, m : Model, s : Strategy \bullet\\
&\quad (e\ \mathbf{occurs} \wedge e \in pertinentEvents \wedge m = agentMind.Model)\\
&\quad \Rightarrow \bigcirc(agentMind.Model = s(m) \wedge s \in agentMind.Strategy \wedge \forall\, s' : agentMind.Strategy\\
&\quad \bullet s \neq s'\\
&\quad \bullet d : Predicate/s(m) \vdash d,\\
&\qquad d' : Predicate/s'(m) \vdash d'\\
&\quad \Rightarrow (agentMind.Goal \Rightarrow d) \wedge (d \Rightarrow d')))
\end{aligned}}$

3 Example

3.1 The Medical Help System

The objective of the Medical Help System (MHS) consists in selecting the best adapted hospital, capable of providing medical assistance to a patient. The MHS could ideally help to direct, in real time, an ambulance with the victim of some kind of health hazard (accident, stroke, ...) to the appropriate care unit.

The system is to be implemented as a MAS, in which ultimately, active entities will be mobile agents with information about symptoms of the given patient. A hospital is represented by agents (*HospitalAgents*) and constitutes the node of the network, and a patient is represented by *PatientAgent*. Each *PatientAgent* moves in the network and holds negotiations with *HospitalAgent*. The concept of the system structure and the principles of cooperation of each agent is reduced to the following postulates: Hospital (wards) is represented as nodes in the network. The possibilities of a hospital in the given node are represented by a *HospitalAgent*. The patient (sick, injured person) is represented by a *PatientAgent*. It has information about the examination results/treatment and the present symptoms of the given patient. In the system there are nodes authorized to create the *PatientAgent*. These nodes are accessible to general practitioners and emergency services (e.g. firemen, police, etc.) by means of overhead or radio network. In the system there is a unified multiagent platform which enables *PatientAgents* to move around in the network and hold negotiations between them and *HospitalAgents* concerning a possibility of providing help and parameters (conditions) of the service. In the system there are (can be

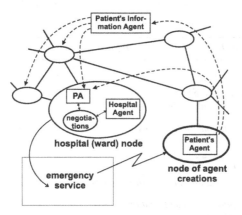

Fig. 3. Scheme of actions of the decentralized multiagent system of providing medical help.

generated) *PatientInformationAgents* which look for information about the given patient in medical centers (outpatient clinics, hospitals) to provide it to *PatientAgent* in order to create the patient's full picture (epicrisis) enlarged by dispersed archival data. In fact, this example has yet been developed in [2]. This paper introduces a retro-engineering approach for this example.

3.2 Profile Specification for the MHS

The specification process begins by identifying the profiles and their interactions. Each agent will encapsulate some profile. Indeed, *Patient* agents will search a hospital, contact an emergency service which will be in relationship with all hospitals services. In this paper, *HospitalSearch* and *AdmissionNegotiation* profiles will be described.

Let us consider now the formal specification of the *HospitalSearch* profile, i.e. Object-Z class *HospitalSearch*. Basic types [*HospitalId, Symptom*] represent hospital identifiers and medical information about the patient respectively.

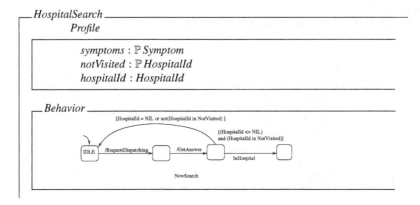

__ INIT _____

     $visited, notVisited = HospitalId$

__ RequestDispatching _____

    $\Xi(HospitalSearch)$
    $description! : \mathbb{P}\ Symptom$

    $description! = symptoms$

__ GetAnswer _____

    $\Delta(HospitalSearch)$
    $identification? : HospitalId \cup \{NIL\}$

    $hospitalId' = identification?$
    $identification? \neq NIL$
     $\Rightarrow notVisited' = notVisited \setminus \{identification?\}$
      $\wedge\ visited' = visited \cup \{identification?\}$
    $identification? = NIL$
     $\Rightarrow notVisited' = notVisited$
      $\wedge\ visited' = visited$

The *HospitalSearch* class includes two operations, *RequestDispatching* and *GetAnswer*. The first operation interacts with the *Dispatching* profile of some *Hospital* agent. In fact, this operation which does not modify the profile states (Ξ notation) outputs *description!*, a list of symptoms. The postfixed notation ! denotes outputs values. As a result of the *GetAnswer* operation, the patient obtains an identifier of the hospital with which negotiations for admission are conducted. This negotiation operation modifies the profile state (Δ notation) and takes as input, ? postfix notation, a hospital identifier. The behaviour defined by *HospitalSearch* is to execute first *RequestDispatching* and then *GetAnswer*. If there are no hospitals available or the one found has already been visited then a new search is started. In the case of a new hospital *InHospital* event is broadcasted.

The admission negotiation profile class is as follows:

__ AdmissionNegotiation _____

    Profile
    $InHospital, NewSearch : Event$

    $hospitalId : HospitalId$
    $symptoms : \mathbb{P}\ Symptom$
    $rights : InsuranceProfile$
    $availableCash : \mathbb{R}^+$
    $admitted : \mathbb{B}$

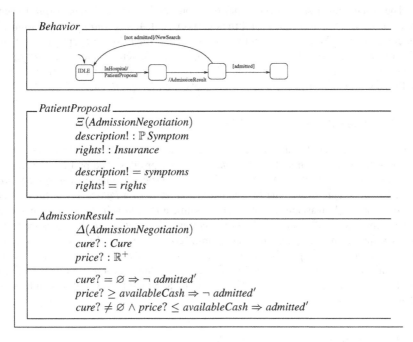

___ Behavior _____

[not admitted]/NewSearch

IDLE   InHospital/   [admitted]
     PatientProposal   /AdmissionResult

___ PatientProposal _____

$\Xi(AdmissionNegotiation)$
$description! : \mathbb{P}\, Symptom$
$rights! : Insurance$
_____
$description! = symptoms$
$rights! = rights$

___ AdmissionResult _____

$\Delta(AdmissionNegotiation)$
$cure? : Cure$
$price? : \mathbb{R}^+$
_____
$cure? = \varnothing \Rightarrow \neg\, admitted'$
$price? \geq availableCash \Rightarrow \neg\, admitted'$
$cure? \neq \varnothing \wedge price? \leq availableCash \Rightarrow admitted'$

___ Patient _____

$M - Agent$

Profile
$= \{HospitalSearch, AdmissionNegotiation\}$
$pertinentEvents = \{InHospital, NewSearch\}$
mind
    $= \{hospitalSearch, AdmissionNegotiation\}$
$hospitalSearch.Model == (visited, notVisited)$
$hospitalSearch.Strategy == getAnswer$
$hospitalSearch.Goal == InHospital$ **occurs**
$AdmissionNegotiation.Model == admitted$
$AdmissionNegotiation.Strategy$
    $== AdmissionResult$
$AdmissionNegotiation.Goal == admitted$

___ INIT _____

$agentMind = hospitalSearch$

_____

$InHospital$ **occurs**
    $\Rightarrow \bigcirc(mind = AdmissionNegotiation)$
$NewSearch$ **occurs**
    $\Rightarrow \bigcirc(mind = hospitalSearch)$

The behaviour of *AdmissionNegotiation* consists in waiting for *InHospital* event, then executing *PatientProposal* and then carrying out *AdmissionResult* operations. If not admitted then *NewSearch* event is broadcasted. *PatientProposal* operation outputs a list of symptoms and details on the insurance of the patient. *AdmissionResult* operation decides if treatment is compatible with patient symptoms and available cash. Both profiles communicate by the intermediate of events *InHospital* and *NewSearch*.

3.3   Agent Specification for the MHS

The *Patient* class specifies a specific M-Agent of the MAS for Medical Help. This agent proposes *HospitalSearch* and *AdmissionNegotiation* profiles. The pertinent events for this agent are *InHospital* and *NewSearch*. The mental states available are *hospitalSearch* and *admissionNegotiation*. The first active mental state of a *Patient* is *hospitalSearch*. The two temporal invariants specify that each time a *Patient* is in hospital (resp. begins a search for a hospital) *admissionNegotiation* (resp. *hospitalSearch*) becomes the active mental state. The model for *hospitalSearch* mind consists in *visited* and *notVisited* hospitals. Each time a new hospital is visited its identifier is added to *visited*. The *goal* is to enter a hospital which happens when *InHospital* occurs. The model for *admissionNegotiation* mind is Boolean *admitted*. The goal here is to be admitted to hospital, which happens when *admitted* is true.

4   Conclusion

The language used by the specification framework can describe reactive and functional aspects. It is structured as a class hierarchy so one can get inheritance from these classes to produce its own specification. As an example, we have specified the M-Agent specific agent architecture by adding a new class to the framework. Several MAS have already been specified with this framework without using a specific agent architecture [10,12]. These MAS have been applied to the radio-mobile network field and foot-and-mouth disease simulation.

The specification language allows prototyping of specification [12]. Prototyping is not the only means of analysis, indeed, in another work [7], we have introduced a formal verification approach. Moreover, the specification structure enables incremental and modular validation and verification through its decomposition. Eventually, such a specification can be refined to an implementation with multi-agent development platform like MadKit [8] which is based upon an organizational model.

Formal theories are numerous in the MAS area but they are not all related to concrete computational models. Temporal modal logic, for example, have been widely used [19]. Despite an important contribution of this work to a solid underlying foundation for MAS, no methodological guidelines are provided concerning the specification process and how an implementation can be derived. Another type of approach consists in using traditional software engineering or knowledge based formalisms [16]. Among these approaches a few [16,1] provide the specifier with constructs for MAS decomposition. However, there are no proposed methodologies for these approaches. In [13] there is a survey of MAS methodologies. MaSE is more detailed in terms of guidance for system designer but necessitates several differents models. Gaia is based upon a logical formalism which is difficult to refine down to an implementation.

The presented approach of coupling the M-agent architecture with Object-Z and State-chart formalism gives a homogenous system for the description of the multiagent systems. Taking as a starting-point a properly defined description of the problem we may developed a base for the Agent Oriented Analysis, Design and even Programming and use the specified model of a given problem to go toward formal verification or practical realization.

References

1. F.M.T. Brazier, B. Dunin Kęplicz, N. Jennings, and J. Treur. Desire: Modelling multi-agent systems in a compositional formal framework. *International Journal of Cooperative Information Systems*, 6:67–94, 1997.
2. K. Cetnarowicz and E. Cetnarowicz. Multi-agent decentralised system of medical help. In *Management and Control of Production and Logistics. IFIP, IFAC, IEEE Conference*, Grenoble, France, 2000. ENSIEG, LAG Grenoble, France 2000.
3. K. Cetnarowicz and E. Nawarecki. Système d'exploitation decentralisé realisé à l'aide de systèmes multi-agents. In *Troisième Journées Francophone sur l'Intelligence Artificielle Distribuée et les Systèmes Multiagents*, pages 311–322, St Baldoph, Savoie, Francja, 1995.
4. Y. Demazeau and J.-P. Müller. Decentralized artificial intelligence. In Y. Demazeau and J. P. Müller, editors, *Decentralized A.I.*, pages 3–14. North-Holland ISBN 0-444-88705-9, 1990.
5. Y. Demazeau and J. P. Müller. From reactive to intentional agents. In Y. Demazeau and J. P. Müller, editors, *Decentralized A.I. 2*, pages 3–10. North-Holland, 1991.
6. Roger Duke, Gordos Rose, and Graeme Smith. Object-z: Specification language advocated for the description of standards. Tech. rep. no. 94-95, Software Verification Research Centre, Dept. of Computer Science, the University of Queensland, Quinsland, Australia, 1994.
7. Pablo Gruer, Vincent Hilaire, and Abder Koukam. an Approach to the Verification of Multi-Agent Systems. In *International Conference on Multi Agent Systems*. IEEE Computer Society Press, 2000.
8. Olivier Gutknecht and Jacques Ferber. The madkit agent platform architecture. In *1st Workshop on Infrastructure for Scalable Multi-Agent Systems*, june 2000.
9. David Harel. Statecharts: A visual formalism for complex systems. *Science of Computer Programming*, 8(3):231–274, June 1987.
10. V. Hilaire, T. Lissajoux, and A. Koukam. Towards an executable specification of Multi-Agent Systems. In Kluwer Academic Publisher, editor, *International Conference on Enterprise Information Systems'99*, 1999.
11. Vincent Hilaire. *Vers une approche de spécification, de prototypage et de vérification de Systèmes Multi-Agents*. PhD thesis, UTBM, 2000.
12. Vincent Hilaire, Abder Koukam, Pablo Gruer, and Jean-Pierre Müller. Formal specification and prototyping of multi-agent systems. In *Engineering Societies in the Agents' World*, number 1972 in Lecture Notes in Artificial Intelligence. Springer Verlag, 2000.
13. Carlos Iglesias, Mercedes Garrijo, and José Gonzalez. A survey of agent-oriented methodologies. In Jörg Müller, Munindar P. Singh, and Anand S. Rao, editors, *Proceedings of the 5th International Workshop on Intelligent Agents V : Agent Theories, Architectures, and Languages (ATAL-98)*, volume 1555 of *LNAI*, pages 317–330, Berlin, July 04–07 1999. Springer.
14. D. Kinny, M. Georgeff, and A. Rao. A methodology and modelling technique for systems of bdi agents. In Van Velde and Perram [18], pages 56–71.

15. Crowley J. L. and Demazeau Y. Principles and techniques for sensor data fusion. In *Signal Processing*, volume 32, pages 5–27, Elsevier Science Publishers B. V., 1993.
16. Michael Luck and Mark d'Inverno. A formal framework for agency and autonomy. In AAAI Press/MIT Press, editor, *Proceedings of the First International Conference on Multi-Agent Systems*, pages 254–260, 1995.
17. A. Rao. Agentspeak(l): Bdi agents speak out in a logical computable language. In Van Velde and Perram [18], pages 42–55.
18. W. Van Velde and J. W. Perram, editors. *7th European Workshop on Modelling Autonomous Agents in Multi-Agent World, MAAMAW'96*. Number 1038 in Lecture Notes in Artificial Intelligence. Springer-Verlag ISBN 3-540-60852-4, Berlin, 1996.
19. Michael Wooldridge and Nicholas R. Jennings. Intelligent agents: Theory and practice. Available by FTP, 1994. Submitted to The Knowledge Engineering Review, 1995.

Multi-agent System for Flexible Manufacturing Systems Management*

Krzysztof Cetnarowicz and Jarosław Koźlak

Institute of Computer Science
AGH - University of Mining and Metallurgy
Al. Mickiewicza 30, 30-059 Krakow, Poland
cetnar@agh.edu.pl

Abstract. The paper focuses on the application of a multi-agent system for a management process. The presented system is working on the structure of graph, where nodes represent decision modules and edges – technological processes. Kinds of agents working in such environment are presented and an overview of the interaction protocols which can be used in such a system is given.

1 Introduction

The development of production systems introduces new tasks, such as optimal production systems designing, efficient and safe production systems structure management or management of optimal functioning of a production process. On the other hand, proper management of a production system structure is very important for the enterprise rentability and common problem. The contemporary production system becomes more and more complex and must be flexible for modifications. It makes a management process very difficult, inefficient and expensive.

It seems that these tasks should be supported in their realization by computer systems, or even totally managed by them. It may be realized when management systems are provided with models of a production process realized as decentralized systems. Attempts at realizing such systems improving the process of production systems functioning can be found in [7].

An optimal movement of processed objects in the production system depends on a proper structure of the production system layout and real time routing, which can make use of the current production system structure in an optimal way. A proper choice of the production system layout structure has a basic influence on the effectiveness of activity. Consequently, it seems that multi-agent systems can be used as a model for a more complex computer management by means of effective object (parts) routing, but the evolution of the production system layout must be steered dynamically, thus adapting its structure to the current needs.

---

* This work is supported by KBN Project 7 T11C 040 20

B. Dunin-Kęplicz and E. Nawarecki (Eds.): CEEMAS 2001, LNAI 2296, pp. 73–82, 2002.

2 Principles of Functioning of Decentralized System Managing Computer Network

We may determine two goals of the computer management system for the production process [1,5,10,14] (fig. 1):

– management in real time to obtain the optimal functioning of the production process,
– management of the production process structure (layout) to be adapted to the production realization.

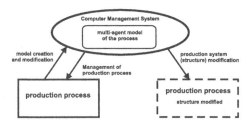

Fig. 1. Schema of a computer system (with multiagent model) for production process management

To develop a multi-agent managing system for the production process we have to take a particular point of view to consider the production process as a graph environment for the agents population. In general, the production system may be represented as a network with boxes representing technological operations such as: milling machine, lathers, drills, grinder, etc. with a common operation: transport of parts fig. 2. The parts enter the system, are treated and leave the system at the output.

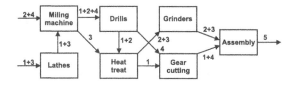

Fig. 2. Schema of the production system layout consisting of milling machine, lathers, drills, heat treat, grinders, gear cutting and assembly as an output with circulating parts 1, 2, 3, 4.

So the environment of that production system could be considered as a directed graph created in the following way (fig. 3):

– The production system is composed of a technological operation and edges representing the operation, that follows.
– The transport of parts between operations is considered as a technological operation.

- A node is placed between every technological operation.
- The whole production system layout may be mapped to a graph called a precedence diagram.
- The edges represent technological operations, the nodes - decision nodes linking following operations and enables to take decision to switch the way of a part and select a proper path in the system.
- The part is treated in the system following a properly chosen path in the graph.

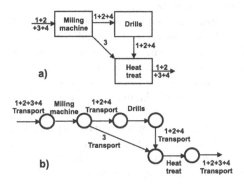

Fig. 3. Schema of the production system layout - a, corresponding precedence diagram - b.

The optimal treatment of a given part may be considered from two points of view:

- point of view of the part: use the cheapest or the quickest way of operation execution with a given quality standard,
- point of view of the system: prepare the best adaptation of the system to perform demanded operations (be competitive) or use the cheapest way of the system modification to adapt it to the treated parts needs (demand).

The optimal management may be expressed in two ways:

- Production management system functioning is based on the essential principle that defines conditions of a sending treated parts between the nodes following the optimal path (that is created in real time) of the part treatment.
- The production system layout must be dynamically adapted to the treatment needs in an optimal way.

These two points are dependent between them and must be considered as an integrity during the management process.

The main principle of the multiagent management system functioning is that the management process bases on the marked oriented decisions methods. To make a possible application of the marked oriented management, it is necessary that every part pay for the technological operation executed on it. It means that a part pays for transfer through every edge between the nodes. Therefore a part is considered as a special agent (Part

Agent - PA). Its task is to go by the graph from the source node to the destination node in given conditions and follow a path corresponding to the demanded technological operations [2].

The conditions (the quickest, the cheapest treatment, etc.) are known to a given agent PA and are a basis for realizing a routing process of choosing dynamically the proper path.

The payment may be done

– directly:
  • For the purpose, each node (exactly - output port on an edge) has an account opened. Appropriate sums may be paid into the account by the treated part,
  • Each processed part which is to be treated in the system has its account and transfers an appropriate payment for sending to an account of a sending port for the treatment by the corresponding edge.
  • Agents authorized to use the founds accumulated on accounts may perform all operations on the accounts with the intermediary of network operations.
– indirectly:
  • In a simplified case, a sending port obtains a generalized payment in a form of some number of (stipulated) points. The number of points collected makes evidence on activity of a given port, and what follows - a given operation (treatment) corresponding to the edge in a graph.
  • The points collected may then be changed into cash and transferred from the funds, (e.g. centrally fixed), planned to be spent on production system functioning or development.
  • The points collected may then be used as a basis to take decisions concerning the optimal functioning and development of production system.

The payments make a basis for market oriented decisions related to modifications (extension, decrease) of certain parts of a production system. Decisions are undertaken and then realized by the multi-agent system managing the production system.

3   Multi-agent System Managing the Production System

The production system is dynamically mapped into the model (of the form of graph). The model is managed by the multiagent system. The multi-agent system consists of two main parts: a population of different kinds of agents and the environment in which the agents work. The environment is determined by the model of the production system, and may be considered as a particular graph (Fig. 3). The model is created and dynamically updated to take into consideration the circulation of the treated parts in the system. There are the following types of agents in the system:

– **Input Part Agent (IPA)** that provides the interface between the external reality and production system and creates the Part Agent.
– **Path Agent (PthA)** that provides the proper path selection for the treated part.
– **Path Messenger Agent (PMA)** that collects and transfers information around the graph about available operations (treatments) in the system.

- **Port Agent (PoA)** that makes possible for agents to leave a given node to reach the neighboring one by the selected edge, and to be treated by an operation represented by the edge.
- **Part Agent (PA)** that represents a given treated part in the system, and provides a transfer of a given part from the beginning to the end following the proper path (i. e. sequence of operations) in the system.
- **Linker Agent (LA)** that collects necessary information around the graph (or its part) to enable detection of a problem of traffic in the graph (such as overloaded operations, waiting lines for operations etc.).
- **Investor Agent (IA)** that enables to undertake decisions with investment in the graph (extension or reduction of connections, new operations etc.) to modify the production system layout.
- **Investor Proxy Agent (IPxA)** that participates in negotiations concerning investments in the graph.

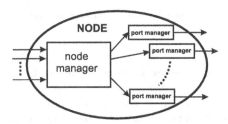

Fig. 4. Schema of the graph node where the agent undertake an action to establish new itinerary continuation

The real time optimal system management consists of a properly composed path for the treated part navigation in the production system graph. Using its own required sequence of operations Part Agent goes across the graph from the beginning node to the ending node. At every node it enters the *nodemanager* where cooperating with PthA, PMA, LA agents it obtains information about the possibilities of the path continuation. Accordingly to its need (cheapest, quickest) it selects the best continuation of the itinerary and goes to the appropriate port where it pays (cooperation with PoA agent) for entering the following edge in the graph (which means that the corresponding operation will be executed on the part)

The decisions concerning investments in the production process layout (which results in the layout modifications) are settled as a result of negotiations among Investors and Investor Proxy agents (IA, IPxA). We can consider that the edge linking node A with the node E is overloaded (it means that the technological operations - drills between A and E has insufficient efficiency rate). A scenario of the action undertaken by agents to establish a new connection (or to raise operation rate) may consists of the following steps (fig. 5):

- Port at the node A linking it with the node B is overloaded and the agent AoP corresponding to the port creates the LA agent that is sent to the node B.

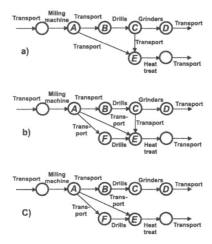

Fig. 5. Schema of the graph where the agent undertake action to establish new edges (operations, treatments)

- At the node B the AL agent verifies the traffic linking the node B with the node C.
- If the traffic from the node B to the node C going via the node B is too heavy, the agent Linker goes back to the node A with a proposition to create a direct link between the nodes A and C, or looks for the next overloaded node (for example node E). This proposition is paid to the Investor agent at the node A.
- Investor agent at the node A builds a financial project of the enterprise, and sends the Investor-Proxy agent to the node E to negotiate its participation in the project.
- If the negotiations are completed successfully the agent Investor-Proxy realizes the connection (direct or complex) placing order for the appropriate service with the appropriate company.

4   Interactions in the Multi-agent System for the Production System Management

An interaction protocol is a set of rules of interaction that describes what action each agent can take at each time. In this chapter typical interaction protocols used in the multi-agent systems are presented, then a presentation is given how these protocols can be applied to the interactions in the system for the production process management, which was presented in the previous chapter.

4.1   The Interactions Protocols Used in the Multi-agent Systems

Contract net. Its idea is based on the mechanism of contracting, used in business [13]. There are two roles of the agents in the protocol: manager – agent, which orders the realization of the task. and contractors – the agents – potential executors of the task.

Voting. In some situations the agents can hold a vote on certain decisions. The result of the voting is obligatory for all agents participating in the voting. In [12] some protocols of voting are presented: plurality protocol, binary protocol and Bord's protocol.

Auctions. The exchange of goods between the agents may be realized by auction. The agents participating in the auction can perform one of the followings roles: auctioneer or participant of the auction. There are many different protocols of auctions which are associated with particular strategies of the agents. On the basis of an overview from [11] we can enumerate: English (first-price open cry) auction, Vickrey auction (second-price sealed-bid), all-pay auction.

Market interactions. The interactions based on the market approach have several advantages, such as well analyzed (in economic science) theory and a low cost of communication. There are two kinds of agents in the system: producers and consumers. Producers transform the goods using technologies they have and the consumers put demands for the goods needed and their decisions are undertaken on the basis of their utility function [16,4]. The market approach was used for creation of systems strictly connected with the management of the graph or network:

- the system for analysis of the distributed multi-commodity flow problem [15],
- finding the optimal localization of the mirrors of services in the Internet [8],
- system of routing of the packages in the Internet based on market mechanisms [6].

4.2   The Types of the Interactions in the Multi-agent System for the Management of the Production Process

Introduction. This sub-chapter will analyze what interactions protocols can be chosen for particular tasks of the production management system. We concentrate on the following problems:

- choosing the Port by PA agent, which enables the best quality of the connection (using the criterion based on the cost and/or the performance of the treatment),
- gaining information about the state of the graph,
- adding or removing the links to/from the graph by Investor and Investor Proxy.

Choosing the Port by Part Agent. The process of choosing the Port by the Part Agent may be realized using the following interactions protocols:

- Contract Net – PA agent informs all Ports on the Node that it wants to get a defined treatment (which means that it is looking for a particular node in the graph). The Ports inform what price it has to pay for the available treatment, and what are other properties of the treatment (time elapsed, quality etc.) The PA agent chooses the best from its point of view of treatment – it means the corresponding Port.
- voting – The PA agents vote which treatment is the best and the corresponding edge gets a privilege to be selected for such treatment.

- auction – If the production system is heavily loaded (overloaded), the PA agents can take part in the auctions of treatment offered by the Ports (i.e. edges).
  The opposite situation is also possible – the agent PA demands to buy the treatment offered by one of the Ports at a given node. There are more than one available ports offering similar kinds of treatment and the Ports participate in the auction offering lower and lower prices and better treatment. The PA agent chooses the lowest price, the best treatment. This algorithm may be used if the production system is currently not loaded.
- market – The complex negotiation of the cost of the treatment between PA agents considered as consumers and Ports playing a role of producers can be implemented using a market model.

Collecting the information about the current state of the network. Linker Agent can gain the information about the state of the network using the following interaction protocols:

- Contract Net – LA announces that it is ready to buy information about the state of the network. The group of the nodes (Node Managers) can send their proposals concerning the quality and the costs of the possessed information.
- Market – LA and Port Agents participate in the exchange of the information about the structure of the network. The prices of the information are set by the market methods.

The modification of the structure of the production process structure (graph) - adding or removing the operations (edges). The modification of the structure of the network by adding or removing the edges representing technological operations can be performed using the following interaction protocols:

- Auction – Agents Investors take part in the auction of adding a new edge to the graph or selling the one by the Investor who actually owns it. It is also possible to increase or reduce the efficiency, productivity or quality of a given operation (edge).
- Market – The Investors can buy or sell technological operations (edges).

5   Simulation of the Multi-agent System for the Production System Layout (Graph Management)

The multi-agent system proposed for the production system layout management has been modelled and verified by simulation (fig. 6).

It has a limited function – provides only the migration of the Part Agents using the Contract Net Protocol. Other tasks, such as collecting information about the structure of the network and changing the structure of the network (adding/removing nodes) are not realized.

The following interaction among the agents has been realized:

- Part Agent when arriving at a given node tries to reach the destination node by the edge with demanded operation at the lowest costs.
- At the node a number of options of transfer continuation at different prices are proposed to the Part Agent.

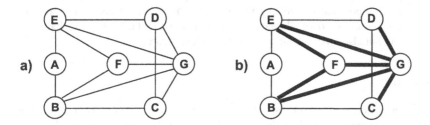

Fig. 6. Schema of the examined production system layout - graph corresponding to the system: a - at the beginning of simulation, b - at the end of simulation after the improvement of the system layout (extension of operations - corresponding edges)

- Part Agent accepts the solution, taking into consideration the price of the following operation versus its own resources and the quality of the treatment versus the time it can waste for all the operations from the beginning to the end of the part treatment.
- Part Agent pays the Port Agent for the treatment. With the resources saved the Port Agents (and Node Manager) undertake modification of the production system layout (graph).

The simulation of the system was performed on the computer network composed of 6 nodes with edges representing technological operations.

Technology needs and pricing policy favour the following edges of the graph: (B,F), (B,G), (C,G), (D,G), (E,F), (E,G), (F,G). The initial state of the network with the same productivity rate of all edges (technological operations) is shown in fig. 6a. After a number of operations execution and transfers of parts in the system the nodes using collected funds modify the parameters of the network. The result of the system investment is presented in fig. 6b. After the improvement (changes of the efficiency of operations corresponding to the edges) realized by the system the overloaded operations (edges)were reinforced (thick lines in the fig. 6b).

6   Conclusion

The proposed system of a automatic management of production system enables both optimal real-time management of the production system functioning, and optimal, self-acting adaptation of the network structure to users' needs, also in real-time [3]. Both aspects of optimal management, considered together may bring very interesting results. The application of the above mentioned system will lower costs of production system exploitation. In the future it will enable the realization of optimal management of production systems layout for large, extensive production systems. It may be applied also to the realization of the disassembly process [9]. The proposed system enables flexible production systems management (of graph structure) with the use of economic criteria of optimization. The system takes advantage of possibilities given by the decentralized, multi-agent system, that enables making local decisions, taking into account local, and if necessary and possible - a global point of view. The presented system may be easily extended to uniform, optimal management of network, including not only hardware management but also other resources, e. g. network software.

References

1. K. Cetnarowicz, E. Nawarecki, and M. Żabinska. M-agent architecture and its application to the agent oriented technology. In *Proc. of the DAIMAS'97. International workshop: Distributed Artificial Intelligence and Multi-Agent Systems*. St. Petersburg, Russia, 1997.
2. K. Cetnarowicz, M. Żabińska, and E. Cetnarowicz. A decentralized multi-agent system for computer network reconfiguration. In J. Stefan, editor, *Proc. of the 21st International Workshop: Advances Simulation of Systems - ASSIS'99*. MARQ, Ostrava, Czech Republic, 1999.
3. Krzysztof Cetnarowicz and Jarosław Kozlak. Multi-agent system for decentralized computer network management. In *Proceedings of the Second Conference on Management and Control of Production and Logistics (MCPL'2000)*, Grenoble, July 2000.
4. John Q. Cheng and Michael P. Wellman. The WALRAS algorithm: A convergent distributed implementation of general equilibrium outcomes. *Computational Economics.*, 1997.
5. N. Gaither. *Production and Operations Management*. The Dryden Press, New York, 1994.
6. M.A. Gibney and N.R. Jennings. Dynamic resource allocation by market based routing in telecommunications networks. In Garijo F.J. Albayrac S., editor, *Intelligent Agents for Telecommunications Applications (IATA'98)*. Springer Verlag, 1998.
7. G. Dobrowolski K. Cetnarowicz, E. Nawarecki. Multi-agent mrp class system for production and disassembling. In *Management and Control of Production and Logistics. IFIP, IFAC, IEEE Conference*, Grenoble, France, 2000. ENSIEG, LAG Grenoble, France 2000.
8. Tracy Mullen and Michael P. Wellman. A simple computational market for network information services. In *ICMAS*. 1995.
9. Ales Pavliska and Vilem Srovnal. Robot disassembly proces using multi–agent system. In Barbara Dunin-Kęplicz and Edward Nawarecki, editors, *Proceedings of the Second International Workshop of Central and Eastern Europe on Multi-Agent Systems CEEMAS'01 (in this volume)*. Springer Verlag.
10. J. F. Proud. *Master Scheduling*. John Wiley & Sons Inc., New York, 1994.
11. Tuomas W. Sandholm. *Negotiation among self-interested computationally limited agents*. PhD thesis of University of Massachusetts Amherst, 1996.
12. Tuomas W. Sandholm. Distributed rational decision making. In Gerhard Weiss, editor, *Multiagent Systems. A Modern Approach to Distributed Artificial Intelligenc*, volume II, chapter 7, pages 201–258. The MIT Press, 1999.
13. Reid G. Smith. The contract net protocol: High-level communication and control in a distributed problem solver. *IEEE Transactions on Computers.*, C-29(12):1104–1113, 1980.
14. W. J. Stevenson. *Production/Operations Management*. Richard D. Irwin Inc., Homewood IL 60430, 1990.
15. Michael P. Wellman. A market-oriented programming environment and its application to distributed multicommodity flow problem. *Journal of Artificial Intelligence Research*, pages 1–23, 1993.
16. Michael P. Wellman. Market-oriented programming: some early lessons. In S. Clearwater, editor, *Market-Based Control: A Paradigm for Distributed Resource Allocation*. World Scientific, 1996.

Motivational Attitudes of Agents: On Desires, Obligations, and Norms

Frank Dignum[1], David Kinny[2], and Liz Sonenberg[2]

[1] Institute of Information and Computing Science, Utrecht University
3508 TB Utrecht, The Netherlands
dignum@cs.uu.nl
[2] Department of Information Systems, The University of Melbourne
Victoria 3010, Australia
{dnk,LizS}@staff.dis.unimelb.edu.au

1 Introduction

Many papers about agents mention BDI as a reference logical model for agents, but this model does not offer a thorough formal account of the connections between the different modalities of Beliefs, Desires and Intentions. Of course, work such as that of Rao and Georgeff [14] and of Cohen and Levesque [5] has pointed to some specific constraints, but does not offer a complete logical theory that explains all possible connections between, e.g., goals and intentions. Another point of concern often voiced is the long-standing gap between the BDI logical model and practical agent implementations. Judged by its applicability, it might seem that the BDI model is becoming less important, due to the looseness of its connection to practical systems, and because of its failure to guide research into implementation directions in any obviously useful way.

One reaction to such criticisms might be to ignore the formalism and focus on refining implementations, however this would risk losing intuitions that could guide further development of the agent paradigm, and extensions of BDI agents with concepts like emotions, power relations, obligations, etc. would be *ad hoc*, lacking an adequate theoretical basis. There would be no way of determining how these extensions might relate with the basic components of BDI agents if the link between BDI logic and the implementation is not clear. The implementation will not impose any inherent restrictions or guidelines on these relations. The BDI logic might give some insights, but if there is no relation between the logic and the implementation, these insights are of dubious value.

Our long-term goal is to extend the BDI model with social concepts such as norms and obligations. Elsewhere we and others have argued that such concepts are an important tool to "glue" autonomous agents together in a multi-agent system [8,2,4,6]. However, little has been said about the way norms and obligations influence the decision processes of agents. In this paper we do two things towards this goal. After presenting a motivating example, we revisit the relationships between goals, desires and intentions in the BDI model with a view to understanding the kinds of situations in which both goals and desires should be represented (Section 2). We then look at ways in which norms and obligations might be added to this model and make some general comments about such

B. Dunin-Kęplicz and E. Nawarecki (Eds.): CEEMAS 2001, LNAI 2296, pp. 83–92, 2002.

formalisations (Sections 3 and 4). In particular, we propose that for goal generation, interactions between desires, obligations and norms can resolved by preference orderings, and discuss how an agent might form intentions given certain desires, goals, norms and obligations.

2 Sources of Motivation

Consider the following situation. I want my software agent to buy me a certain book as cheaply as possible. It has found the book listed at Amazon for $40, and on offer at an eBay auction, and it has also sent a request to the book broker El Cheapo, with a commitment to buy if El Cheapo can negotiate a price under $30 dollars. At eBay the price is still going up, and it has decided to bid $35 there, but knows there is no guarantee of that being the winning bid. The search at El Cheapo has been going on for some time without any positive result. Then I inform the agent that I need the book by next Monday, and it immediately places an order at Amazon to ensure that I have it in time. At that moment the results come in from Ebay: it transpires that its bid of $35 at eBay has won the auction after all; a moment later, before my agent can cancel the El Cheapo request, El Cheapo's agent reports back that it has found the book at a discounter not far from my home and negotiated a price of $28. My agent now has incurred three obligations. It should pay $40 to Amazon, it should pay $35 to eBay and it has committed to order the book for $28 through El Cheapo. But I don't need three copies, and a quick check of my budget reveals that I can't afford to spend more than $50 anyway, so the agent now must somehow decide which of the three suppliers to pay.

Cancelling the Amazon order will probably require paying a $10 cancellation fee, but there's a chance that they may waive the fee. Not paying at eBay will result in damage to my reputation, but no fee. Not placing the order through El Cheapo may result in some hassle but no monetary cost, and any loss of reputation will be confined to El Cheapo and not seen by others. In terms of these outcomes, fulfilling the obligation to Amazon seems the preferred solution for the agent. However, it also has some norms and desires involved in the decision. The norms in this case are that all commitments should be fulfilled whenever possible, but if they conflict that public commitments should take priority, because loss of public reputation is most socially harmful. So, the agent's norms will dictate that fulfilling the obligation to eBay has the highest priority. Obviously, however, the agent's (and my) desire is to pay as little as possible for the book, which can be achieved by ordering through El Cheapo, even if a fine must also be paid to Amazon. So, according to its desires the agent prefers to order through El Cheapo, according to the consequences of not fulfilling obligations it prefers to pay Amazon, but according to its norms it prefers to pay eBay. How should it decide what goals for payment to adopt?

We will discuss some rules for making such a decision in section 4, however this example reveals that an agent will often need to balance its own interests (desires) against the interests of other agents (obligations) or society (norms), and also need to balance potentially conflicting obligations towards different parties. In more general cases it may even need, as a member of different communities, to balance conflicting norms.

In the BDI approach, the behaviour of an individual agent is shaped by the agent's state of knowledge of the world (its *beliefs*), the states of the world it seeks to bring about (sometimes termed *desires*, sometimes *goals*), and the execution of stored *plans* that have been designed to bring about certain world states in pre-specified circumstances. The plans selected by the agent for execution are referred to as its *intentions*, of which at any time there may be many. Our focus here will be on exploring how an agent's goals should arise from the various sources of motivation to which it may be subject.

From the literature [13,14] it is clear that desires are a very abstract concept with few general logical properties, and that they are only loosely coupled with beliefs and intentions. Taking desires to be identical to goals, as has often been done in the past, makes them more tangible and practically usable. We suggest, however, that the main reason to consider desires as a separate interesting concept arises when they are not the sole source of motivation, i.e., when obligations or norms are also present, and goals must be determined by balancing desires against such external sources of motivation.

Norms, as manifest in human societies and organizations, assist in standardising the behaviour of individuals. Commitment to membership of a society means that an agent will tend to follow its norms, i.e., an agent will weigh up goals suggested by other sources against those suggested by societal norms. Similar considerations apply to obligations, which are associated with specific enforcement strategies that involve punishment of violators. Obligations are explicit mechanisms for influencing the behaviour of agents and providing some stability and reliability in their interactions while allowing some flexibility. They provide a level of "freedom of choice" with known explicit consequences.

The main difference between norms and obligations as we use them is that norms are more abstract and are inherent to the society of which the agent is a member. Obligations are (usually) a consequence of a direct action of the agent itself and entered by choice (e.g. the obligation to pay when something is ordered). The distinctions that we make in this paper are thus relatively crude; we are however including at least these two concepts as representatives of a whole spectrum of external motivational influence.

3   B-DOING Agents

As discussed above, an agent typically has intrinsic desires that it tries to satisfy by achieving some concrete goals, but these desires must be balanced with the norms of the society in which the agent operates and with the obligations it may have to other members of the society. Norms can be seen as the desires of the society, and obligations as a mechanism to balance the desires of individual agents. So, an agent which functions in a multi-agent system should not only take into account its own desires, but also the desires of other individual agents and the desires of the agent society as a whole. Desires, norms and obligations are three motivational sources for the goals of the agent[1]. The influence of these sources might differ for different agents and also for different situations.

Although norms and obligations are important concepts to include in the theory of agents that operate in a multi-agent system, their inclusion also has the indirect effect of highlighting the differences between goals and desires. Here, we model the effect of motivational influences by a two stage process. First, a goal maintenance process is

---

[1] For agents built around these notions: beliefs, desires, obligations, intentions, norms and goals, we affectionately adopt the term *B-DOING agents*.

responsible for determining which of the goals that might arise from an agent's obligations, desires and norms are sufficiently realistic, valuable and urgent, given its beliefs, to warrant adoption as goals.

In the second stage, an intention maintenance process is responsible for determining which of an agent's feasible goals it should commit to by forming new intentions, and how its existing intentions might need to be modified, due to changed beliefs and goals. Commitment to goals means that current goals also influence the choice of new goals. If commitment to goals is high then the chance that an agent will change its goals based on new desires, obligations and norms is small.

An aspect of the goal maintenance process not captured in the figure are the direct relationships between desires, obligations and norms, which are depicted as independent influences. However, there are many possible relationships between these concepts. For instance, it might be a norm in a society to fulfill one's obligations.

B-DOING Logic

Having argued that the concepts of belief, desire, goal, intention, norm and obligation are important to model agents in a multi-agent system, in this section we will offer some ideas as to how these concepts should be defined in a logical framework. A sketch of a possible formal logical description has been given in previous work [6], but the resulting logic is very complicated. Here we will just give pointers to the formalization of goals, beliefs and intentions, which have been discussed elsewhere already, and discuss a possible formalization of norms, obligations and desires. Note that this is only one possible way to do so, and for the argument of this paper it does not really matter which logical theory is used as long as the requirements that we define for the concepts are met.

Goals, beliefs and intentions. The formalisation of these concepts is quite conventional. A belief ϕ of an agent i is represented as $B_i(\phi)$. For the beliefs of agents we will use a KD45 axiomatization relative to each agent. This induces a standard relation in the Kripke semantics which we will not further expand upon.

A goal ϕ of an agent i is represented as $G_i(\phi)$. Although goals have been defined in the literature in terms of other primitives (see e.g. [5,13]) we will define them as a primitive notion here and indicate some relations with desires, norms and obligations later on. We assume a (minimal) KD axiomatization to ensure the consistency of the goals. The semantics of $G_i(\phi)$ is defined in the standard way in the Kripke model.

Finally, the intentions of an agent are represented in a manner similar to its goals. $I_i(\phi)$ stands for the intention of an agent i to achieve ϕ. Just like goals, intentions have a KD axiomatization and a straightforward semantic representation.

Desires. A desire ϕ of an agent i is represented in the logic as $D_i(\phi)$. As desires are almost completely opaque and the K-axiom does not hold, their semantics cannot easily be represented by a Kripke semantics where desires are represented by a relation between possible worlds. We will avoid the problems with opaqueness by defining desires to be an explicit (infinite) set of formulas, denoted by $DES_i(s)$, that are desired by each agent i in each state s. This set of formulas should comply with the following constraint:

$$\forall \phi, \psi, s, i : \phi \in DES_i(s) \land \Box(\phi \to \psi) \text{ then } \psi \in DES_i(s)$$

which states that the set of desires is closed under implication by necessity. Although the K-axion does not hold for desires in general, making the set of desires closed under implication by necessity at least avoids the problem of distinguishing desires that only differ syntactically but are logically equivalent. E.g. if $\phi \wedge \psi \in DES_i(s)$ then also $\psi \wedge \phi \in DES_i(s)$. The semantics of $D_i(\phi)$ is now given as follows:

$$M, s \models D_i(\phi) \text{ iff } \phi \in DES_i(s)$$

Related to the set of desires there is a preference ordering on the set of possible worlds indicating their relative desirability. This preference ordering is relative to the present state of the agent, i.e. it might change depending on the state of the agent.

If all desires were consistent it would be possible to determine a situation in which all of them would be fulfilled. This situation could then be adopted as a goal, or if not realizable from the current situation, one as close to it as possible could be chosen. As desires do not have to be consistent this "ideal" situation may not exist, and so the preference ordering may not necessarily have a top element.

Norms and obligations. The formal semantics of obligations (and norms) is based on Prohairetic Deontic Logic (PDL) [17]. PDL is a logic of dyadic obligation defined axiomatically in terms of a monadic modal preference logic. Only dyadic obligation is defined, i.e., all obligations are conditional, $O(p|q)$, however unconditional obligation can be represented using a tautology for the condition, $O(p) = O(p|q \vee \neg q)$. PDL allows the representation of *contrary-to-duty* obligations (obligations that hold in in sub-ideal circumstances) without contradiction, yet true deontic conflicts (conflicting obligations) imply inconsistency.

We extend PDL to allow for *multiple* modalities to denote norms and obligations from different "sources". Norms for different societies are distinguished, as are obligations to different individuals or within different organisational contexts. We take the view that obligations from the same source must be consistent, but it is allowable for obligations from two *different* sources to conflict. For example, one can't simultaneously have two obligations to Bill: one to achieve p and the other to achieve $\neg p$. However, one can have an obligation to Bill to achieve p and an obligation to Chris to achieve $\neg p$:

- $N^z(p|q)$ – it is a norm of the society or organisation z that p should be true when q is true.
- $O_{ab}^z(p|q)$ – when q is true, individual a is obliged to b that p should be true. z is the society or organisation that is responsible for enforcing the penalty.

The semantics of each modality is based on a preference ordering over worlds, unique to the modality, and an equivalence relation, POS, common to all modalities, that is used to interpret "possibility".

The preference ordering of norms is based on the social benefit of situations, while the preference ordering of obligations is based on the punishments for their violation. For each society x, each state w has a social worth $SW(w, x)$ which defines the preference ordering for the operator N^x. In the same way, for each state w there is a value of that world for an individual a, with respect to its relation to individual b and society x:

$PW(w, a, b, x)$. This value can be seen as the cost of the punishment in case a does not fulfil its obligation towards b and defines the preference ordering for the operator O^x_{ab}.

We now follow [17] for describing a preference semantics of the conditional norms and obligations. Refer to [17] for an extensive explanation of the choice of operators.

Start with three sets of monadic modal operators $\overset{\leftrightarrow}{\Box}$, $\Box^N_x$, and $\Box^O_{a,b,x}$. The formula $\overset{\leftrightarrow}{\Box}p$ can be read as "p is true in all possible worlds" defined in terms of the access condition, POS, which is required to satisfy the minimal constraints below. The formula $\Box^N_x p$ can be read as "p is true in all worlds that are preferred according to the norms of society x". The formula $\Box^O_{a,b,x}p$ can be read as "p is true in all worlds that are preferred according to the obligations of a towards b with respect of society x". As usual $\Diamond p \equiv \neg\Box\neg p$.

$$M, w \models \overset{\leftrightarrow}{\Box}p \text{ iff } \forall w' \in W \text{ if } POS(w, w') \text{ then } M, w' \models p$$
$$M, w \models \Box^N_x p \text{ iff } \forall w' \in W \text{ if } SW(w, x) \leq SW(w', x) \text{ then } M, w' \models p$$
$$M, w \models \Box^O_{a,b,x}p \text{ iff } \forall w' \in W \text{ if } PW(w', a, b, x) \leq PW(w, a, b, x) \text{ then } M, w' \models p$$

The $\Box^N_x$ and $\Box^O_{a,b,x}$ are S4 modalities, while the $\overset{\leftrightarrow}{\Box}$ is an S5 modality. Assume that if $SW(w, x) \leq SW(w', x)$ or $PW(w', a, b, x) \leq PW(w, a, b, x)$ then also $POS(w, w')$.

From the monadic operators $\Box^N_x$ and $\Box^O_{a,b,x}$, define binary "betterness" relations for the norms and obligations: $p \succ^N_x q$ states that "p is preferred according to the norms of society x to q". More precisely, it holds in a world w if for all possible worlds w_1 where $p \wedge \neg q$, and w_2 where $\neg p \wedge q$, w_2 is not preferred to w_1. Introduce $\succ^O_{a,b,x}$ similarly.

$$p \succ^N_x q \equiv \overset{\leftrightarrow}{\Box}((p \wedge \neg q) \rightarrow \Box^N_x \neg(q \wedge \neg p))$$
$$p \succ^O_{a,b,x} q \equiv \overset{\leftrightarrow}{\Box}((p \wedge \neg q) \rightarrow \Box^O_{a,b,x}\neg(q \wedge \neg p))$$

Also from the monadic operators, define $Id^N_x(p|q)$ and $Id^O_{a,b,x}(p|q)$. [We use the non standard notation Id rather than I to avoid later confusion with intentions.] These state that of all the worlds that are possible from the current world, (i) in all the maximally preferred (ideal) worlds where q holds, p also holds, and (ii) in all infinite chains of increasingly preferred worlds, p eventually holds:

$$Id^N_x(p|q) \equiv \overset{\leftrightarrow}{\Box}(q \rightarrow \Diamond^N_x(q \wedge \Box^N_x(q \rightarrow p)))$$
$$Id^O_{a,b,x}(p|q) \equiv \overset{\leftrightarrow}{\Box}(q \rightarrow \Diamond^O_{a,b,x}(q \wedge \Box^O_{a,b,x}(q \rightarrow p)))$$

Finally, define a *norm*, $N^x(p|q)$, or *obligation*, $O^x_{ab}(p|q)$, to be that not only is $p \wedge q$ preferred to $\neg p \wedge q$ but also the preferred (or ideal) q-worlds all satisfy p.

$$N^x(p|q) \equiv ((p \wedge q) \succ^N_x (\neg p \wedge q)) \wedge Id^N_x(p|q)$$
$$O^x_{ab}(p|q) \equiv ((p \wedge q) \succ^O_{a,b,x} (\neg p \wedge q)) \wedge Id^O_{a,b,x}(p|q)$$

4   Decision Making and Priorities

In the previous section we have shown that the motivational inputs for goal generation all induce a preference ordering on the possible worlds and thus on the possible goals.

In general we can distinguish two situations in which the agent has to make a decision about which new goals to choose. The first situation is characterised by the fact that the agent has either achieved or dropped its former goals, and can, in principle, choose new goals freely among all possible alternatives. The second situation arises when an agent is trying to achieve some goals, but either a new opportunity or obligation arises (through some event in the world) or its goals become less "interesting". For example, the goal to work in order to earn money can become uninteresting if one wins a million dollars in a lottery. In this second situation the agent first decides upon the best alternative goal, which is then compared with its current goals. If the agent has a strong commitment to its current goals the alternative has to be really much better to cause a current goal to be dropped. In the framework of this paper we will not distinguish the two cases, but undoubtedly this will be important in an implementation of a B-DOING agent.

We have not discussed the role of commitment in the previous sections, because we did not want to introduce it as a separate modality in the logic. Rather, we take commitment (in this context) to be an aspect of an agent's decision processes, measured by the resistance to change of its current attitudes; one which can determine how often the agent will reconsider its goals and intentions and how big a change between the actual situation (considering both mental as well as physical parameters) and the planned situation will be needed to cause a change, as in [12]. Due to space limits, we will not further expand upon this concept here, but assume it as a design characteristic of an agent.

Combining Preferences

In this section we will expand on the combination of the different preference orderings induced by the obligations, norms and desires of the agent. As said before, these preference orderings have to be combined into one ordering on possible goals. In order to achieve this it would be nice to have a general, intuitive mechanism. Unfortunately, social choice theory [1,7] points out that it is not possible to find such an aggregation mechanism if it has to possess a number of intuitive properties. These properties are:

- *Collective rationality.* The aggregate preference ordering is a function of the separate preference orderings.
- *Pareto principle.* I.e. the ordering of the goals agrees with uncontested strict preferences.
- *Independence of irrelevant alternatives.* Other formulas do not influence the final ordering.
- *Nondictatorship.* There is no preference ordering that solely determines the ordering on the goals.
- *Conflict resolution.* If two formulas are comparable in one of the preference orderings they also are comparable in the resulting ordering of goals.

The above properties seem to be all very intuitive. However, by a well known theorem due to Arrow [1] the above constraints are not simultaneously satisfiable.

Although the integration of preferences is not perfectly possible in the general case, we will sketch a number of general rules that might be used as heuristics in the case of combining the three preference orderings related to the different mental attitudes in a domain independent way. In principle we have three sources: desires, obligations and norms. We assume that a choice for a goal has to be made between mutual exclusive situations. Each source will have zero, one or more preferred alternatives. Obligations and norms might have no preferred alternative if there are no obligations or norms applicable to any of the alternatives.

From the above discussion we can easily formulate the first rule:

Rule 1: An agent should adopt one of its most preferred desires as its next goal whenever there are no norms or obligations applicable to any of the alternatives, or when they are applicable, they prefer the same alternative.

The more interesting case occurs when the desires and norms and/or obligations prefer different alternatives. In the general case there is very little to say about how the decision should be made, but if we limit ourselves to two possible alternatives then the following very simple (default) rule can be used:

Rule 2: An agent should adopt as its next goal an alternative that is preferred by at least two of the three sources.

Although this is a very simple numerical heuristic one can also argue in favor of it for the specific cases. Of course when an alternative is preferred from all three viewpoints it is clear that it should be chosen. If an alternative is most desirable and also most preferred with respect to the obligations of an agent, but not with respect to the norms, then one might argue that the conflict between the norms and the obligations be resolved in favour of the obligations. For it seems that the agent has committed to some obligations that cannot be fulfilled in a normative way. Because they are still in line with its own desires it should choose for that alternative again.

If an alternative is most desirable and also most preferred with respect to the norms, but not with respect to the agent's obligations, then one might argue that the desires of the agent are in line with that of the whole society. It will not fulfil the obligations in the preferred way. However, this (only) affects mainly the beneficiary of the obligation. Apparently the agent values the norms of the society higher at this moment, because they are in line with its own desires. This argument would lead the agent to pay eBay in the example of section 2!

If an alternative is most preferred with respect to both obligations and norms, but not the most desirable, then the agent should comply to the preferences of the society. Just following its own desires in this case would incur sanctions from the other agents and might thus hamper achieving its own goals in the future.

If an agent has a choice from three or more alternatives, as was the case in our example, we can still use the above rule if one of the alternatives is the preferred one according to at least two of the three sources. The rule does not work, however, if all sources prefer a different alternative (as was the case in our example). In that case one could either design the agent in a simple way such that it would order the alternatives in a fixed order and, for instance, always choose an alternative preferred by its obligations first, one preferred by its norms second and one preferred by its own desires third. Using these rules means that an agent does not have to do any sophisticated reasoning, but also that it will not distinguish between the consequences of different situations.

A more complex approach is to let the agent decide based on reasoning about the consequences of choosing each alternative. Returning to the example, if we represent the agent's obligations by $O^{law}_{a\ Am}(paid(40))$, $O^{com}_{a\ eBay}(paid(35))$ and $O^{law}_{a\ ElC}(paid(28))$, and the norms which apply by $N^{law}(G(\phi)|O^{law}_{a\ Am}(\phi))$, $N^{com}(G(\phi)|O^{com}_{a\ eBay}(\phi)))$ and $N^{com}(G(\phi)|O^{com}_{a\ ElC}(\phi)))$, such a decision process may occur as:

$$O^{law}_{a\ Am}(paid(40)) \wedge O^{com}_{a\ eBay}(paid(35)) \wedge O^{law}_{a\ ElC}(paid(28)) \wedge$$
$$D_a(paid(minimum)) \wedge N^{com}(G(\phi)|O^{com}_{a\ b}(\phi))) \wedge$$
$$\neg paid(Am, 40) \wedge \neg paid(eBay, 35) \wedge paid(ElC, 28) \ \rightarrow$$
$$DO(Am, PayFine) \wedge BadReputation(eBay) \wedge paid(minimum)$$

Note that this is a simplified presentation, because we did not include all the consequences of not fulfilling the norms of fulfilling obligations (this would require some more notation about achieving goals which we do not want to add at this place). However, in the same vein as the rule above the agent could reason about the consequence of each choice and determine the most preferable situation. In fact my agent was able to reason in a more sophisticated way about possible outcomes: it first successfully negotiated that the Amazon fine be waived, then offered to pay eBay, only to discover that the goods in question had been misdescribed and hence the bid could be cancelled, so it finally ordered via El Cheapo and so fulfilled all its norms, obligations and desires.

Although the above arguments can be undercut by counterexamples in each case, it seems that the rules could function well as a heuristic. However, we should emphasise that every solution inherently depends on domain specific properties, such as the fact that we combine three preference orderings and the nature of these preferences.

5   Conclusions

Our long-term goal is to extend the BDI model with social concepts such as norms and obligations. Towards this aim, in this paper we have attempted to do two things: (i) by critically reviewing the relationships between the basic modalities in the BDI model, we have elicited an account of situations in which both goals and desires should be represented; (ii) further, we have argued that to represent complex external influences on an individual agent's behaviour, norms and obligations have a role to play, and to capture the interaction between these, and the internal motivations for goals, explicitly representing desires, as well as goals, becomes important. In support of this analysis we have proposed a way in which norms and obligations might be added to the BDI model, while making the point that the particular logic referred to is just one way of accomplishing this. The main point in this logic is the fact that desires, obligations and norms can all be based on preference orderings, which can be used to direct the choice of future actions.

Clearly a great deal of further work is required before the framework presented here can be regarded as comprehensive. We see the contribution being in the conceptual analysis, supported by the example formalism, rather than resting on the details of the formalism itself.

Acknowledgements. We thank the anonymous reviewers for their very useful comments. This work was supported by a grant from the Australian Research Council.

References

1. K.J. Arrow. *Social Choice and Individual Values*. Yale University Press, 1963.
2. C. Castelfranchi, F. Dignum, C. Jonker and J. Treur. Deliberate Normative Agents: Principles and Architectures, In *Proceedings of ATAL-99*, Orlando, 1999, pp. 206–220.
3. L. Cavedon, L. Padgham, A. Rao and E. Sonenberg. Revisiting rationality for agents with intentions, In *Bridging the Gap*, pp. 131-138, World Scientific, 1995.
4. L. Cavedon and L. Sonenberg. On social commitments, roles and preferred goals, In *Proceedings of ICMAS'98*, Paris, July 1998, (ed) Y Demazeau, pp 80–87.
5. P. Cohen and H. Levesque. Intention is choice with commitment. *Artificial Intelligence*, vol.42, pages 213–261, 1990.
6. F. Dignum, D. Morley, L. Sonenberg and L. Cavedon. Towards socially sophisticated BDI agents In Proceedings of the Fourth International Conference on MultiAgent Systems July, Boston, USA, pp 111-118
7. J. Doyle and M. Wellman. Impediments to Universal Preference-Based Default Theories, *Artifical Intelligence*, Vol.49, Nr.1-3, pages 97-128, 1991.
8. M. Fasli. On Commitments, Roles and Obligations, *in this volume*.
9. L. Hogg and N. Jennings. Variable Socialability in Agent-based decision making, In N. Jennings and Y. Lesperance (eds.) *Proceedings of ATAL-99*, Orlando, 1999, pages 276- 290.
10. N. Jennings. Commitments and Conventions: The foundation of coordination in Multi-Agent systems. *Knowledge Engineering Review*, vol. 8(3), pages 223-250, 1993.
11. N. Jennings and J. Campos. Towards a Social Level Characterisation of Socially Responsible Agents. *IEEE Proc. on Software Engineering*, vol.144, 1, pp.11-25, 1997.
12. D. Kinny and M. Georgeff. Commitment and Effectiveness of Situated Agents. In *Proceedings of IJCAI'91*, Sydney, 1991, pages 82–88.
13. B. van Linder. Modal Logics for Rational Agents, PhD thesis, 1996, University of Utrecht.
14. A.S. Rao and M.P. Georgeff. Modeling rational agents within a BDI architecture. In: R. Fikes et.al. (eds.), *Proceedings of the 2nd CKRR*, Morgan Kaufman, pp. 473-484, 1991.
15. A.S. Rao and M.P. Georgeff. BDI Agents: From Theory to Practice. *Proceedings of ICMAS 95*, San Francisco, 1995.
16. Y. Shoham and M. Tennenholtz. On social laws for artificial agent societies: off-line design. *Artificial Intelligence* 73(1995)231-252.
17. L. van der Torre and Y.-H. Tan. Contrary-To-Duty Reasoning with Preference-based Dyadic Obligations. Submitted to *Annals of Mathematics and AI*.
18. M. Wooldridge. *Reasoning about Rational Agents*, MIT Press, 2000

On Commitments, Roles, and Obligations

Maria Fasli*

Department of Computer Science, University of Essex
Wivenhoe Park, Colchester CO4 3SQ, UK
mfasli@essex.ac.uk

Abstract. This paper presents a formalisation of obligations, social commitments and roles for BDI agents. We present a formal analysis of general obligations and *relativised-to-one* obligations from a bearer to a single counterparty and we examine obligations and *relativised-to-one* obligations in the context of strong realism for BDI agents. We also discuss how *relativised-to-one* obligations arise as a result of social commitments and the adoption of roles. In our framework, if an agent adopts a role, then this role is associated with one or more social commitments. Social commitments give rise to relativised obligations and consequently, roles, social commitments and relativised obligations are interwoven.

1 Introduction

Agent-based systems have become increasingly popular as a means of conceptualising and implementing a wide range of applications. One of the accepted ways of viewing agents is as intentional systems that have certain mental attitudes which comprise their cognitive state and shape their decision making. Bratman [2] argued that intentions play a prominent role in an agent's decision making and based on his work researchers in AI have developed logical formalisms in order to reflect this. The most well known such formalism is the BDI [17], [18] in which agents are characterised as having beliefs, desires, and intentions.

As agents are required to work in increasingly complex environments and interact and coordinate with other agents, we need some means of regulating their behaviour in order to avoid disruption and to ensure smooth performance, fairness and stability. In this direction, norms and obligations can be adopted to facilitate the means for basic social interaction. The case for adopting obligations and their importance and relevance in multi-agent systems was discussed by Krogh in [15]. In this paper we investigate how obligations, roles and commitments can be incorporated into the BDI framework. We identify two broad categories of obligations: general and relativised. The former express normative states that ought to be the case for all agents, whereas the latter express obligations which explicitly involve a bearer and one or more counterparty agents. We concentrate on relativised-to-one obligations where the counterparty is a single agent and we present axioms for general obligations and relativised obligations for BDI agents based on strong realism [18]. Relativised obligations seem

---

* The author would like to thank the anonymous reviewers for their helpful comments.

to result from social commitments of an agent towards another agent and the adoption of roles. A definition of social commitments is presented which involves among other things the adoption of a relativised-to-one obligation. Commitment strategies regarding social commitments and a generic condition for successful de-commitment from relativised obligations are also provided. In our framework the adoption of a role by an agent implies the adoption of social commitments. Since social commitments are interwoven with relativised obligations our approach provides a natural way of connecting roles with relativised obligations.

The paper is organised as follows. In the following section the logical framework is presented. Next we discuss the deontic concepts of obligation and relativised obligation. Then we present a formal analysis of these concepts and we discuss relativised-to-one obligations in the context of strong realism. The following section discusses social commitments and how they give rise to relativised obligations. Moreover, commitment strategies for social commitments and a generic condition that allows de-commitment from relativised obligations are also presented. We then present an analysis of social commitments resulting from the adoption of roles. Finally, the paper discusses related work, and ends with a summary of the main results and a pointer to future work.

2   The Logical Framework

The logical framework is based on the BDI paradigm which we extend into a many-sorted first order modal logic. Due to space limitations we will only describe the basic ideas and the extensions made to the original framework briefly; the reader is referred to [17], [18] for the details of the BDI paradigm.

The logical language $\mathcal{L}$ includes, apart from the usual connectives and quantifiers, three modal operators B, D, and I for expressing beliefs, desires and intentions respectively. There are three sorts: *Agents* , *Groups* of agents, and *Other* which indicates all the other objects/individuals in the universe of discourse. In addition the framework uses a branching temporal component based on CTL logic [10], in which the belief-, intention-, and desire-accessible worlds are themselves branching time structures. The operator *inevitable* is said to be true of a path formula γ at a particular point in a time-tree if γ is true of all paths emanating from that point. O-formulas are wffs that contain no positive occurrences of *inevitable* outside the scope of the modal operators B, D and I. The temporal operators *optional*, $\bigcirc$ (next), $\diamond$ (eventually), $\square$ (always), U (until) are also included. Furthermore the operators: $succeeds(e)$, $fails(e)$, $does(e)$, $succeeded(e)$, $failed(e)$ and $done(e)$, express the past and present success or failure of an event e, [17].

Semantics is given in terms of possible worlds relativised to time points. A model for $\mathcal{L}$ is a tuple $M = < W, E, T, \prec, U, \mathcal{B}, \mathcal{D}, \mathcal{I}, \pi >$ where W is a set of worlds, E is a set of primitive event types, T is a set of time points, $\prec$ is a binary relation on time points, U is the universe of discourse which is a tuple itself $U = < U_{Agents}, U_{Groups}, U_{Other} >$, $\mathcal{B}$ is the belief accessibility relation, $\mathcal{B} : U_{Agents} \rightarrow \wp(W \times T \times W)$, and $\mathcal{D}$ and $\mathcal{I}$ similarly for desires and intentions.

Finally π interprets the atomic formulas of the language. Satisfaction of formulas is given in terms of a model M, a world w, a time point t and a mapping v of variables into elements of U. For instance, the semantics for belief is as follows:

$M_{v,w_t} \models B(i,\phi)$ iff $\forall\ w_t'$ such that $\mathcal{B}_i(w_t, w_t')$ we have $M_{v,w_t'} \models \phi$

By imposing restrictions on the respective accessibility relations for the modalities we adopt the KD45 system for belief, and the K and D systems for desires and intentions. We illustrate the axioms of belief:

K. $B(i,\phi) \wedge B(i,\phi \Rightarrow \psi) \Rightarrow B(i,\psi)$ (Distribution Axiom)

D. $B(i,\phi) \Rightarrow \neg B(i,\neg\phi)$ (Consistency axiom, $\mathcal{B}_i$: Serial)

S4. $B(i,\phi) \Rightarrow B(i, B(i,\phi))$ (Positive Introspection axiom, $\mathcal{B}_i$: Transitive)

S5. $\neg B(i,\phi) \Rightarrow B(i,\neg B(i,\phi))$ (Negative Introspection axiom, $\mathcal{B}_i$: Euclidean)

Nec. if $\vdash \phi$ then $\vdash B(i,\phi)$ (Necessitation Rule)

The K axiom and the Necessitation rule are inherent of the possible worlds approach and they hold regardless of any restrictions that we may impose on the accessibility relations. Hence, agents are logically omniscient [11] with respect to their attitudes. Furthermore, we adopt the strong realism axioms:

$I(i,\phi) \Rightarrow D(i,\phi)$

$D(i,\phi) \Rightarrow B(i,\phi)$

These correspond to the following semantic conditions respectively:

$\forall i \in U_{Agents}, \forall w_t, w_t'$ if $\mathcal{D}_i(w_t, w_t')$ then $\exists w_t''$ s.t. $\mathcal{I}_i(w_t, w_t'')$ and $w_t'' \sqsubseteq w_t'$

$\forall i \in U_{Agents}, \forall w_t, w_t'$ if $\mathcal{B}_i(w_t, w_t')$ then $\exists w_t''$ s.t. $\mathcal{D}_i(w_t, w_t'')$ and $w_t'' \sqsubseteq w_t'$

Hence, for all desire-accessible worlds w_t' from w_t, there is an intention-accessible world w_t'' from w_t which is also a sub-world of w_t'; similarly for the second condition. A world w_t' is a sub-world of w_t ($w_t' \sqsubseteq w_t$) if the tree structure of w_t' is a subtree of w_t, and w_t' has the same truth assignment and accessibility relations as w_t. By imposing the sub-world restriction between worlds the application of the above axioms is restricted to O-formulas. The BDI system with the axioms of strong realism will be called S-BDI. Strategies for the maintenance of intentions as in [17] can be adopted here as well.

We extend the language to include two additional modal operators $EB(g,\phi)$ and $MB(g,\phi)$ for "Everybody in a group of agents g believes ϕ" and "ϕ is a mutual belief among the agents in group g" respectively. Following [11]:

$EB(g,\phi) \equiv_{def} \forall i \in g \Rightarrow B(i,\phi)$

Intuitively everybody in a group of agents believes ϕ if and only if every agent i in this group believes ϕ. Then a proposition ϕ is mutually believed among a group of agents if everyone believes it, and everyone believes that everyone believes it, and everyone believes that everyone believes that everyone believes it..., and so on. If EB^k expresses the k-th level of nesting of belief of the agents in group g, then the group has mutual belief of ϕ as follows:

$M_{v,w_t} \models MB(g,\phi)$ iff $M_{v,w_t} \models EB^k(i,\phi)$ for $k = 1, 2, \dots$.

This property requires the notion of reachability [11]. Using this property and the notion of reachability the following axiom and rule can also be adopted:

$MB(g,\phi) \Leftrightarrow EB(g, \phi \wedge MB(g,\phi))$

From $\phi \Rightarrow EB(g, \psi \wedge \phi)$ infer $\phi \Rightarrow MB(g,\psi)$ (Induction Rule)

3   Obligations

Deontology is in principle the study of norms and associated concepts such as obligations and permissions for human agents [1], [12]. In the same sense it seems reasonable to employ obligations to express what ought to be the case for artificial agents. Obligations seem to be external to agents, they are usually imposed by another agent or perhaps a larger body, such as a group, an organisation or society. We distinguish between two broad categories of obligations: general and relativised. General obligations express what ought to be the case for all agents and they are impersonal, that is no explicit reference is being made to a particular agent. They express normative sentences for all agents and can be seen as rules that provide the minimal means of social interaction.

Furthermore, individual agents may hold obligations towards another specific individual or a group of agents. We distinguish between relativised-to-one obligations which are obligations of one agent towards another, and relativised-to-many obligations of an agent towards a group. Relativised-to-one obligations can be the result of social commitments. Castelfranchi [3] argues that if an agent is socially committed to another agent to bring about a state of affairs, then the former has an obligation towards the latter. Thus if agent i commits to deliver a piece of work to agent j, this social commitment implies, among other things, the creation of a relativised-to-one obligation of i towards j. Although related, we believe that social commitments and relativised obligations are different in the following sense: if an agent commits to another agent to bring about a certain state, then this involves not only a relativised obligation on behalf of the bearer towards the counterparty, but an intention (a personal commitment) of the bearer to bring about that state of affairs. On the other hand a relativised obligation may not necessarily mean that the bearer is personally committed to bring about the state of affairs. Thus, if i is obliged to deliver a piece of work to j, this does not necessarily mean that i has committed itself by adopting an individual intention to do so. If however, i makes a promise that it is going to deliver it, then i is declaring that it has made a personal commitment, an intention to do so. Another way that relativised-to-one obligations arise is via the adoption of roles. If i adopts the role of the supervisor towards j and j adopts the role of the student, then this creates certain social commitments for the two agents. By adopting these roles, j socially commits itself to submitting draft chapters of the thesis and i to providing feedback on j's chapters. Since, social commitments are intimately related with the adoption of obligations, the adoption of roles through social commitments creates relativised obligations.

Relativised-to-many obligations will be addressed in future research.

3.1   Formal Analysis

In standard propositional deontic logic (SDL), an obligation operator O prefixes propositions $\phi, \psi, \ldots$ to create formulas of the form $O(\phi)$. Such a formula is read "It ought to be the case that ϕ". In formula $O(\phi)$ there is no explicit reference to the individual agent for whom ϕ ought to be the case. Therefore the standard obligation operator cannot capture relativised-to-one obligations. We extend the language to include two modal operators $O(\phi)$ and $O(i, j, \phi)$. $O(\phi)$ is read as "It ought to be the case that ϕ", and $O(i, j, \phi)$ as "Agent i is obligated to j to bring about ϕ". The model for the language needs to be extended as well. Thus $M = < W, E, T, \prec, U, \mathcal{B}, \mathcal{D}, \mathcal{I}, \pi, \mathcal{O}, \mathcal{O}^* >$ where $\mathcal{O}$ is the accessibility relation for general obligations and $\mathcal{O}^* = \{\mathcal{O}_{ij} | \forall i, j \in U_{Agents} \wedge i \neq j\}$ is the accessibility relation for relativised obligations between pairs of agents. $\mathcal{O}$ is considered to yield the deontically ideal worlds [6] relative to a world w at time point t:

$M_{v,w_t} \models O(\phi)$ iff for all w'_t such that $\mathcal{O}(w_t, w'_t)$ we have $M_{v,w'_t} \models \phi$

$M_{v,w_t} \models O(i, j, \phi)$ iff for all w'_t such that $\mathcal{O}_{ij}(w_t, w'_t)$ we have $M_{v,w'_t} \models \phi$

The D system is adopted for general obligations. This ensures that there may not be deontic conflicts, that is not both ϕ and $\neg\phi$ ought to be the case:

$O(\phi) \Rightarrow \neg O(\neg\phi)$

A permission operator is defined as the dual of the general obligation operator:

$P(\phi) \equiv_{def} \neg O(\neg\phi)$

The principle of veracity $O(\phi) \Rightarrow \phi$ is rejected since what ought to be the case may not be the case after all. We do not impose any restrictions on the accessibility relation for relativised obligations $\mathcal{O}_{ij}$. In particular we do not impose seriality; in other words deontic conflicts are allowed for relativised obligations. Hence, the K system is adopted for the relativised obligations operator.

3.2 Further Properties

It seems reasonable to suggest that if ϕ is a general obligation then each agent believes that this is the case (special constant g_0 denotes the set of all agents):

$\forall(i \in g_0) \Rightarrow (O(\phi) \Rightarrow B(i, O(\phi)))$ \hfill (i)

In other words, if ϕ ought to be the case, then each agent i believes that it ought to be the case. This axiom requires the following semantic condition:

$\forall i \in U_{Agents}, \forall w_t, w'_t, w''_t$ if $\mathcal{B}_i(w_t, w'_t)$ and $\mathcal{O}(w'_t, w''_t)$ then $\mathcal{O}(w_t, w''_t)$

Since general obligations ought to be believed by all agents we also derive the following from (i) by the axiom defining EB and the induction rule for MB:

$O(\phi) \Rightarrow MB(g_0, O(\phi))$

This means that normative statements are mutually believed (ideally) by all agents. For instance driving to the left is mutually believed by all agents in UK. It also seems reasonable to suggest that if such an ought-to relation between an agent (counterparty) and another agent (bearer) is in place, both of them should be aware of it, or in other words, they should believe that this is the case:

$O(i, j, \phi) \Rightarrow B(i, O(i, j, \phi))$

$O(i, j, \phi) \Rightarrow B(j, O(i, j, \phi))$

Moreover we can accept the stronger axiom that such a relativised-to-one obligation is mutual belief between the bearer and the counterparty:

$O(i, j, \phi) \Rightarrow MB(\{i, j\}, O(i, j, \phi))$

Another plausible principle is that if i is obligated to j to bring about ϕ, then at least j should desire that state of affairs. Although there seem to be counter-arguments (parents may have relativised obligations regarding their children's education, which the children may not desire) we can accept this property here since in the current analysis relativised-obligations are the result of roles and social commitments. We assume that the counterparty agent will take the necessary steps to free the bearer from the obligation (although this is not present in the current formalism), if it doesn't desire ϕ to be brought about:

$O(i, j, \phi) \Rightarrow D(j, \phi)$

This in turn requires the following semantic restriction:

$\forall i, j \in U_{Agents}, \forall w_t, w_t'$ if $\mathcal{D}_j(w_t, w_t')$ then $\exists w_t''$ s.t. $\mathcal{O}_{ij}(w_t, w_t'')$ and $w_t'' \sqsubseteq w_t'$

The application of the axiom is restricted to O-formulas and accordingly it should be understood as stating that if agent i is obligated to j to bring about $optional(\psi)$, then j also desires $optional(\psi)$. In S-BDI the axiom $D(j, \phi) \Rightarrow B(j, \phi)$ in combination with the axiom that connects relativised-to-one obligations and the counterparty's desire entails $O(i, j, \phi) \Rightarrow B(j, \phi)$. Again this formula states that if i is obligated to j to bring about $optional(\psi)$, then the counterparty agent j believes $optional(\psi)$. The following are also theorems:

$O(\phi) \Rightarrow \neg D(i, \neg O(\phi))$
$O(\phi) \Rightarrow \neg I(i, \neg O(\phi))$

Counterparty Agent   *Bearer Agent*
$O(i, j, \phi) \Rightarrow \neg I(j, \neg\phi)$ $O(i, j, \phi) \Rightarrow \neg I(i, \neg O(i, j, \phi))$
$O(i, j, \phi) \Rightarrow \neg I(j, \neg O(i, j, \phi))$ $O(i, j, \phi) \Rightarrow \neg D(i, \neg O(i, j, \phi))$
$O(i, j, \phi) \Rightarrow \neg D(j, \neg O(i, j, \phi))$

4   Social Commitments

One way in which relativised-to-one obligations seem to arise is as a result of social commitments. The term commitment intuitively means "promise" [14]. Following Castelfranchi [3] the basic idea behind our formal analysis is that social commitments involve the creation of obligations as well as individual commitments (intentions) on behalf of the bearer. We will explicate this idea via an example: Agent i agrees to rent a house from j and commits itself to paying a monthly rent. Since i has made a commitment to j, this seems to have created an obligation now towards j to pay the monthly rent. i's commitment expressed its intention to do so. Moreover, its obligation and intention have now become a mutual belief among i and j. In other words, social commitments give rise to relativised obligations and personal intentions. Formally:

$SCom(i, j, \phi) \Leftrightarrow O(i, j, \phi) \wedge I(i, \phi) \wedge MB(\{i, j\}, (O(i, j, \phi) \wedge I(i, \phi)))$

Intuitively there should be conditions under which an agent should be allowed to drop its social commitments as discussed in [14] and [9]. In what follows we describe two different commitment strategies for social commitments: *blind* and *reliable*. These are very closely related to the social commitment strategies of Dunin-Kęplicz and Verbrugge [9]. We define an agent to have a *blind* social commitment strategy if it maintains its commitment until it actually believes that it has been achieved:

$SCom(i, j, inevitable \diamond \phi) \Rightarrow inevitable(SCom(i, j, inevitable \diamond \phi)U\ B(i, \phi))$

Clearly such a strategy towards social commitments is very strong. If this requirement is relaxed then we can define a *reliable* strategy. An agent following a *reliable* strategy will keep its commitment towards another agent as long as it believes that it is still an option:

$SCom(i, j, inevitable\diamond\phi) \Rightarrow inevitable(SCom(i, j, inevitable\diamond\phi)U$

$(B(i, \phi) \vee \neg B(i, optional\diamond\phi)))$

After agent i has managed to bring about the desired state of affairs for agent j, or it has come to its attention that the state of affairs is not an option any more, it needs to take some further action in order to ensure that the counterparty agent is aware of the situation. The agent successfully de-commits itself from a relativised obligation in the following way:

$succeeded(decommit(i, j, inevitable\diamond\phi)) \Rightarrow$

$(\neg O(i, j, inevitable\diamond\phi) \wedge done(communicate(i, j, B(i, \phi))))$

$\vee(\neg O(i, j, inevitable\diamond\phi) \wedge done(communicate(i, j, \neg B(i, optional\diamond\phi)))$

$\wedge done(communicate(i, j, \neg O(i, j, inevitable\diamond\phi))))$

According to the above formula an agent can successfully de-commit itself from a previously adopted relativised obligation towards another agent j if: i) The agent has come to believe that it has achieved its commitment and in this case it drops its obligation towards j and lets it know that the state of affairs has been achieved, or ii) The agent has come to believe that the state of affairs that is committed to is not an option anymore, and in this case it successfully de-commits itself by dropping the relative obligation and by letting the other agent know that the state of affairs is not achievable and finally that it no longer holds the relativised obligation to bring about that state of affairs. We use *communicate* in a generic way to indicate that the agent needs to communicate with the other agent involved in order to de-commit successfully.

5   Roles

We follow and adopt the approach of Cavedon and Sonenberg [5] regarding the formalisation of roles into our framework. However, they are more interested in the adoption of goals as a result of roles and the degree of influence of roles, whereas we are more interested in obligations that result from the adoption of roles. We begin by introducing three additional sorts *Reln*, *RelType* and *Role*. *Reln* constants represent relationship instances. E.g. if *Ray* is in a supervisor-student relationship with two different students then these relationships will be represented by different *Reln* constant symbols. *RelType* constants represent a collection or type of relationship. E.g. all student-supervisor relationships will be of the same type. *RelType* objects allow us to abstract and associate properties with a collection of such relationships. *Role* constants represent "role types", e.g. the same constant symbols are used to represent the supervisor roles and the student roles in each supervisor-student relationship.

Roles are related to relationship types via a predicate $RoleOf(a, R)$ which describes that a is one of the roles in relationship of type R. As in [5] although a relationship can have multiple roles, we assume that each role is associated with only a single type of relationship for simplicity:

$\forall a, R_1, R_2, RoleOf(a, R_1) \wedge RoleOf(a, R_2) \Rightarrow (R_1 = R_2)$

A three place predicate $In(i, a, r)$ which asserts that agent i is in role a of relationship r is introduced. Moreover only one agent can fill a role in a given relationship at any given time:

$\forall i, j, a, r \ \ In(i, a, r) \wedge In(j, a, r) \Rightarrow (i = j)$

We require that roles of a relationship type are filled when any role of that type is filled (Note: given a relationship r, $\widehat{r}$ denotes its corresponding type.):

$\forall r, \forall i, a \ \ \ In(i, a, r) \Rightarrow \forall b(RoleOf(b, \widehat{r}) \Rightarrow \exists j \ In(j, b, r))$

In order to express that a role a involves the adoption of a social commitment ϕ we introduce a new modality $RoleSCom(a, \phi)$. No particular restrictions are imposed on the accessibility relation for this modality. $RoleSCom$ is used in order to define the general social commitments associated with a particular role. This then provides a way of associating relativised-obligations to roles. Intuitively if role a involves the social commitment ϕ and agent i has the role a in relationship r, then there exists another agent j (different to i) that has the role b in relationship r towards whom agent i has the social commitment ϕ:

$RoleSCom(a, \phi) \wedge In(i, a, r) \Rightarrow \exists j, b \ In(j, b, r) \wedge SCom(i, j, \phi) \wedge \neg(i = j)$

This approach of associating roles to social commitments which in turn give rise to relativised obligations provides a way of explaining how relativised obligations arise in a unified way. The commitment strategies for social commitments and the generic condition for de-commitment from relativised obligations can be used in the context of roles as well. However, we haven't touched the issue of dropping roles here. For the time being we assume that once an agent adopts a role it adheres to it forever. The agent can only drop social commitments and de-commit from relativised obligations.

6   Related Work

Obligations and their relevance to Multi-agents systems were discussed in [15]. Krogh distinguishes between general and special obligations. A special obligations operator $_iO$ expresses the fact that an agent i has an obligation, without reference to a counterparty agent. An operator O_i expresses what is ideal from i's perspective and a praxiological operator $_iEA$ is read as "i sees to it that A", where A indicates an action. Finally, special obligations with a bearer and a counterparty agent are defined as $_iO_j(_iEA) \equiv_{def} {_iO}(_iEA) \wedge O_j(_iEA)$. Our approach is simpler than Krogh's since we only adopt two modal operators. Furthermore, in this paper we have accepted that obligations are external to agents, they are either imposed by another agent or by a larger body. The omission of the $_iO$ operator under this assumption does not seem to reduce expressiveness. The O_i operator can be regarded here as replaced by the D operator which expresses the states the agent would like to be, i.e. the agent's ideal states.

Another recent approach involving obligations and BDI agents is [16] . The authors offer an alternative to the BDI logic, in which the primitive modalities are beliefs, desires and obligations, whereas intention is not a primitive modality but an obligation of an agent towards itself. Beliefs and desires are individual modalities but obligations are defined as social modalities. An operator $OBL(x, y, \phi)$ similar to our $O(i, j, \phi)$, expresses that an agent x has an obligation towards agent y to bring about ϕ. The definition of an intention as an obligation of an agent towards itself seems unintuitive. Intentions express the individual agent's commitments to itself to bring about certain states of affairs. Obligations on the other hand express what ought to be the case and in this sense they are weaker. Such a definition of intentions results in unnecessarily depriving intentions of their strong character of personal commitment. BDO logic is only able to capture agents as the ones described by the strong realism constraints, whereas our approach could easily be extended to the other notions of realism.

A different treatment of obligations and norms within the context of the BDI paradigm is presented in [8]. In this approach which is based on Prohairetic Deontic Logic, obligations and norms are conditional, and preferences can be expressed over them.

Roles were discussed by Castelfranchi and Falcone [4] but their analysis is delegation and plan-based. Dignum *et.al.* formalised intentions, commitments and obligations in a modal framework, albeit from a different perspective [7]. Dunin-Kęplicz and Verbrugge [9] also formalised social commitments and conditions under which an agent can drop its social commitments, but the notion of a relativised obligation is not part of their formalism. Although much of the work in deontic logic and norms has been carried out in an implicit single-agent framework, a lot of work in AI [13],[19] ,[20] extends to the multi-agent case.

7   Conclusions

The paper presented an extension of the classical BDI formalism which accommodates the concepts of obligation, social commitment and role. We distinguished between general obligations that apply to all agents, and relativised obligations from a bearer to a counterparty single agent. We investigated how social commitments give rise to relativised obligations and individual intentions and we argued that the adoption of roles entails social commitments. Thus, in the proposed framework relativised obligations are treated in a unified way in the context of social commitments and roles.

There are a number of possible avenues for future development. Firstly, since agents may adopt social commitments or roles towards different agents, nothing prevents an agent ending up with conflicting relativised obligations. In this case a conflict resolution mechanism needs to be in place. This aspect is not present in the current formalism. Secondly, conditions for punishment for breaking one's obligations are yet to be formalised. Another issue that hasn't been touched is conditions under which an agent can abandon a role. Finally, farther goals include the formalisation of relativised-to-many obligations and their relation to commitments and roles, as well as a delegation-based analysis of roles as in [4].

References

1. L. Åqvist, Deontic Logic. In *Handbook of Philosophical Logic Vol.II* (D. Gabbay and F. Guenthner eds). Reidel Publishing Company, pp.605-714, 1983.
2. M.E.Bratman, *Intentions, Plans, and Practical Reason.* Harvard Univ. Press, 1987.
3. C. Castelfranchi, Commitments: From Individual Intentions to Groups and Organisations. In *Proceedings of the First International Conference on Multi-Agent Systems* (ICMAS-95). AAAI Press, pp. 41-48, 1995.
4. C. Castelfranchi and R.Falcone, From Task Delegation to Role Delegation. In *Proceedings of the AI*IA 97: Advances in Artificial Intelligence Congress.* LNAI: 1321, pp.278-289, 1997.
5. L. Cavedon and L.Sonenberg, On Social Commitments, Roles and Preferred Goals. In *Proceedings of the Third International Conference on Multi-Agent Systems* (ICMAS-98). IEEE Computer Society, pp. 80-87, 1998.
6. B.F.Chellas, *Modal Logic.* Cambridge University Press, 1980.
7. F. Dignum, J.-J.Ch.Meyer, R.J.Wieringa, R.Kuiper, A Modal Approach to Intentions, Commitments and Obligations: Intention plus Commitment yields Obligation. In *Deontic Logic, Agency and Normative Systems*, Springer Workshops in Computing (M.A Brown and J.Carmo eds), pp. 80-97, 1996.
8. F. Dignum, D. Kinny and L.Sonenberg, Motivational Attitudes of Agents: On Desires, Obligations and Norms. In *Proceedings of the Second International Workshop of Central and Eastern Europe on Multi-Agent Systems* (in this volume), 2001.
9. B. Dunin-Kȩplicz and R. Verbrugge, Collective Motivational Attitudes in Cooperative Problem Solving. In *Proceedings of the First International Workshop of Central and Eastern Europe on Multi-Agent Systems*, pp. 22-41, 1999.
10. E.A. Emmerson and J. Srinivasan, Branching Time Temporal Logic. In *Linear Time, Branching Time and Partial Order in Logics and Models for Concurrency* (J.W.de Bakker, W.P. de Roever and G.Rozenberg eds), pp.123-172, 1989.
11. Fagin *et.al, Reasoning about Knowledge.* The MIT Press, 1995.
12. R.Hilpinen (ed.), *Deontic Logic: Introductory and Systematic Readings.* Reidel Publishing Company, 1971.
13. H.Herrestad and C.Krogh, Deontic Logic Relativised to Bearers and Counterparties. In *Anniversary Anthology in Computers and Law* (J.Bing and O. Torvund eds), pp. 453-522, 1995.
14. N.R.Jennings, Commitments and Conventions: The Foundation of Coordination in Multi-Agent Systems. *Knowledge Engineering Review*, Vol.8:3, pp. 223-250, 1993.
15. C. Krogh, Obligations in Multi-Agent Systems. In *Proceedings of the Fifth Scandinavian Conference on Artificial Intelligence.* ISO Press, 1995.
16. G.Ma and C.Shi, Modelling Social Agents in BDO Logic. In *Proceedings of the Fourth International Conference on Multi-Agent Systems* (ICMAS-00). IEEE Computer Society, pp. 411-412, 2000.
17. A. Rao and M. Georgeff, Modeling Rational Agents within a BDI Architecture. In *Proceedings of the Second International Conference on Principles of Knowledge Representation and Reasoning.* Morgan Kaufmann Publishers, pp. 473-484, 1991.
18. A.Rao and M.Georgeff, Decision Procedures for BDI Logics. *Journal of Logic and Computation*, 8(3), pp. 293-343, 1998.
19. M.P. Singh, An Ontology for Commitments in Multiagent Systems: Towards a Unification of Normative Concepts. *AI and Law*, Vol:7, pp. 97-113, 1999.
20. L.van der Torre and Y.-H. Tan, Rights, Duties and Commitments between Agents. In *Proceedings of the International Joint Conference on Artificial Intelligence* (IJCAI-99). Morgan Kaufmann Publishers, pp.1239-1244, 1999.

Automata-Based Multi-agent Model as a Tool for Constructing Real-Time Intelligent Control Systems

Mariusz Flasiński

Institute of Computer Science, Jagiellonian University
Nawojki 11, 30-072 Cracow, Poland
flasinski@softlab.ii.uj.edu.pl

Abstract. The multi-agent model for constructing process control intelligent systems is discussed in the paper. Agents of the model are based on three paradigms: pattern recognition, formal (string and graph) automata and rules. The efficient syntactic pattern recognition schemes are used for analysing string and graph structures that represent a structured knowledge. For string-like structures DPLL(k) quasi-context sensitive languages are applied. Graph structures are analysed with ETPL(k) graph parsers in a polynomial time. Grammatical inference algorithms can be used for both kinds of structures. It allows one to embed self-learning schemes in agents of the model.

1 Introduction

An intelligent control of complex real-time systems is one of the most challenging problems in the area of Artificial Intelligence. The difficulty in satisfactory solving the problem is caused by its two fundamental requirements: a cognitive overload met in such systems and hard timing constraints. The use of a fully-decentralized system architecture seems to be the most efficient approach to fulfill these two requirements.

A model presented in the paper is a result of the research[1] led within a project started in the middle of 1990s at the Deutsches Elektronen Synchrotron, Hamburg, Germany and concerning a distributed real-time control expert system ZEX (ZEUS Expert System) for a ZEUS detector at a HERA elementary particle accelerator [1,8]. Although, specific methods and algorithms developed for constructing ZEX have been published in mentioned papers, the aspect of its distributed architecture at succeeding phases of the system life cycle and conclusions drawn from an implementation of these phases have not been published yet. They are presented and discussed in this paper.

The complexity of a problem has resulted not only from the complexity of the system to be controlled, but also from its multi-aspect nature. The intelligent system had to operate in the following four aspects of the ZEUS detector functioning:

---

[1] This work was supported by the European Commission under grant ESPRIT 20288-13 *Intelligent Control of Complex and Safety Critical Systems with the Help of Artificial Intelligence- and Pattern Recognition- Based Software Technologies* within the *European Strategic Programme for Research in Information Technology.*

- an equipment[2] and hardware[3] monitoring and control (including a safety-critical control),
- software (data processing) system control[4],
- an equipment work operating (setting up, shutdown, setting operating modes for hundreds of system components), and
- monitoring and analysis of a quality of an equipment performance.

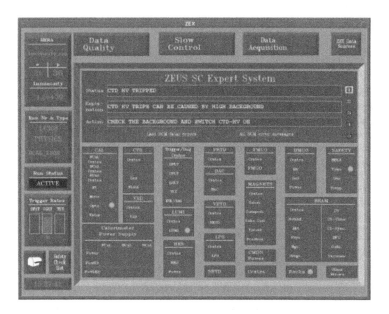

Fig. 1. One of 250 ZEX displays corresponding to an equipment and hardware monitoring and control at the system layer.

One can easily notice that these aspects are not the specific ones only for this particular type of machinery, but they are typical for any industrial-like equipment. For all these aspects ZEX Expert System had to perform four generic tasks with respect to the equipment under control, namely:
- monitoring and identifying the equipment behaviour,
- analysing and diagnosing the equipment behaviour,
- predicting consequences of the equipment behaviour, and

---

[2] The ZEUS detector consists of more than 20 various subdetectors. Its dimensions are 12 m × 10 m × 19 m and its total weight is 3600 tons. It is located about 20 m deep under ground at the 6.3 km long HERA accelerator ring tunnel.

[3] The detector hardware consists of more than 300 network computer nodes and transputer networks of totally 620 transputers.

[4] The software is a fully decentralized distributed system receiving 10 GBytes/s data flow at the front of the detector from more than 250 000 readout channels.

- controlling, i.e. taking proper actions.
Since these four generic tasks are performed simultaneously:
- at various layers of the equipment functioning, i.e. the system layer, the subsystems (subdetectors) layers, the components layers,
- with respect to hundreds of elementary components of the equipment, and
- for four aspects defined above (see Fig. 1),
only fully-decentralized, distributed expert system consisting of autonomous components acting in a parallel way, can meet hard real-time constraints mentioned above. The architecture model of such a system is discussed in the paper.

In the next section we characterize three types of agents defined in our model. The multi-agent architecture of the model proposed is discussed in Section 3, whereas concluding remarks are contained in the final section.

2   Agents

First two types of lowest (component)-layer agents are cognitive agents with reactive features. They can perform some diagnostic tasks, communicate in the environment and they possess *learning capability*. The first group of agents, called *Component State Characteristics Agents, CSCAg* and shown in Fig. 2, are able to perceive data from the sensors of a detector environment. After CSCAg preprocesses data and builds an aggregated feature vector for some phenomenon it identifies a state of a system component with respect to this phenomenon. The identification is made with the help of pattern recognition methods working on the internal knowledge base of the form of a feature space. In case the agent is unable to make a decision concerning the category of a state, it uses its learning module based on clustering methods to modify the feature space.

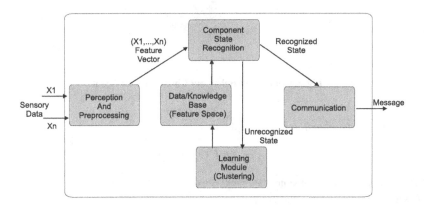

Fig. 2. Component State Characteristics Agent

The agents of the second type, called *Component Behaviour Characteristics Agents, CBCAg* and shown in Fig. 3, reason over a *symbolic representation*. An analysis of system components behaviour in time series is their basic task. A CBCAg receives a series of states from a CSCAg. Then, its Perception and Symbolic Preprocessing module constructs a symbolic representation of transitions between pairs of states. This symbolic representation of the form of a trend string is treated as a sentence of a certain formal language and it is put to a parser, which recognizes the component behaviour with respect to some group of process parameters [8]. For a control of parser transitions rewriting rules (productions) of a formal grammar are used. They are stored in a local knowledge base of the agent. If there is no sequence of rules deriving some trend string, then it is sent to a learning module, which uses a grammatical inference algorithm to modify a set of grammar rules in order to be able to identify such a trend pattern of a component behaviour. The automaton interpreting the rewriting rules presented in [8] is a special case of a *programmed automaton* defined in [6]. This *syntactic pattern recognition* approach prevails over computationally inefficient symbolic (logicist) AI [11], since the automaton (parser) is of $O(n^2)$ time complexity. Let us formalize a notion of a programmed automaton.

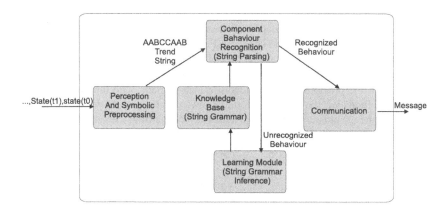

Fig. 3. Component Behaviour Characteristics Agent

A *programmed automaton* is a six-tuple

$$A = (Q, I, O, M, \delta, q_0)$$

where Q is a finite set of states,
I is a finite set of input structures,
O is a finite set of output structures,
M is a finite set of working memory objects,
$\delta : Q \times I \times \Pi \longrightarrow Q \times A \times O$ is the transition function, in which
$\Pi : A_I \cup A_M \longrightarrow \{TRUE, FALSE\}$ is the predicate of the transition permission,
A_I, A_M are sets of attributes of the input structure I and memory objects M (respectively),

$A : A_O \cup A_M \longrightarrow V$ is a set of attributing functions, A_O is the set of attributes of the output structure O, and V is the set of admissible values,
$q_0 \in Q$ is the initial state.

The single step of the programmed automaton step δ is performed in the following way. Being in some state $q \in Q$ and reading some input structure $i \in I$ (e.g. a part of a trend symbolic string) the automaton intends to make a transition. Earlier, however, it has to check whether conditions defined for such a transition by the predicate Π, being analogous to the *IF condition* in rule-based systems, are fulfilled. If so, it changes a state, generates some output (e.g. generates some command forcing external control actions), and ascribes values to parameters of output A_O (e.g. values of parameters of the command) and to parameters of working memory objects A_M (e.g. some flags, mode variables).

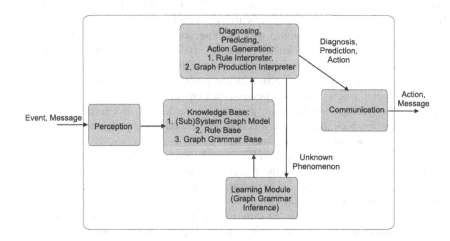

Fig. 4. (Sub)System Agent

At the highest layers social *Subsystem* and *System Agents, SSAg, SAg* are situated (see Fig. 4). SSAgs are basic agents responsible for a proper functioning of the system under control. They keep a model of their part of the system in one of four aspects discussed in Introduction as an attributed graph. The nodes of graphs represent subsystem components and edges relations among them. SSAgs perceive behaviour characteristics of components from CBCAgs and store them as attributes of graph nodes. Such an attributed graph is treated as an input structure for the automaton of the class defined above. In fact it is implemented as an efficient ($O(n^2)$, n is a number of graph nodes) graph grammar parser [5,7]. So, it differs from the string automaton used by CBCAg in processing graph structures, not string structures. An analysis of the attributed graph is used for diagnosing the subsystem functioning and predicting future events in case of some problems. For learning unknown graph configurations a learning module using a graph grammar inference algorithm [4] is used. It modifies a set of graph grammar rules (productions) in order to be able to identify an unknown phenomenon relating to an unknown graph configuration. For the purpose of an action generation, a local rule base implemented with the *RTworks, Talarian* expert system shell is used. At the level of *System Agents, SAgs,* the nodes of attributed graphs in local knowledge bases represent subsystems instead of system components. There are four SAgs corresponding to four aspects of the system monitoring and control introduced in Introduction.

3   Multi-agent Model

A subsystem layer consisting of interacting Subsystem Agents SSAgs is the basic one in functioning of multi-agent model. Each SSAg monitors its subsystem performance in one of four aspects. For such permanent monitoring, *critical sensory data* are analyzed by cooperating pairs of CSCAg-CBCAg. As long as the subsystem works in a proper way, SSAg does not interact with other agents in the environment. However, if something unusual happens, then SSAg tries to give a diagnosis, a prediction, and to make a decision concerning an action. As we have mentioned in a previous section, a diagnosis and a prediction is generated by the programmed automaton via transforming the attributed graph of the subsystem with a proper transition δ (corresponding to a proper rule (production of a graph grammar). In order to perform the transition, it has, however, to check its permission conditions defined in the predicate Π. There are following scenarios of interacting with other agents depending on the availability of variables (attributes) contained in conditions of the predicate Π.

1. All the variables of Π concern the aspect of the subsystem that SSAg is responsible for. If SSAg needs some additional information, it can request its CSCAgs and CBCAgs, which can monitor auxiliary (non-critical) sensory data.

2. Some variable of Π concerns the same aspect of functioning of *another subsystem*. If the variable describes a general state of another subsystem, then our SSAg requests System Agent SAg covering this aspect to deliver required information that it keeps in its attributed graph of the system. If the variable describes a detailed parameter relating to one of components of another subsystem, then our SSAg requests a proper Subsystem Agent to deliver required information, as it is shown in Fig. 5.

3. Some variable of Π concerns *another aspect* of system functioning. For example, no data for processing in a software system of our subsystem can be a result of either deliberate shutting down of an equipment of our subsystem by an operator (the equipment work operating aspect) or a failure of hardware delivering data (the hardware monitoring and control aspect). The scenario is similar as in point 2, but an interaction is among various aspect groups of agents.

Of course, in such a real-time and safety-critical environment an efficient communication among agents should be one of the most important issues of our model. Fortunately, the ZEX message passing is implemented with the interprocess communication (IPC) facilities of *RTworks* expert system shell from *Talarian* that allows one to send and receive messages in an asynchronous manner across a heterogeneous (multiple server) network. Groups of agents can be implemented with the so-called datagroups in *RTworks IPC*. The shell not only enables sending simple messages, but also high-priority

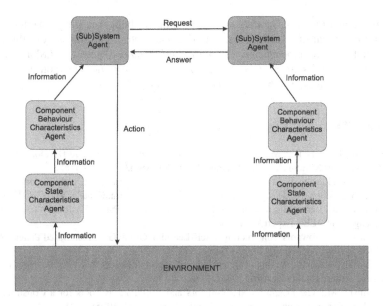

Fig. 5. One of possible scenarios of (sub)system agents cooperation.

ones like warnings and alerts and even the sophisticated messages creating/destroying rules in knowledge bases.

4 Conclusions

Although multi-agent systems are used in an increasingly wide variety of applications [11], their application for a process control is not so frequent, and a few such systems for electricity transportation management [3], monitoring and diagnosing faults in nuclear power plants [13], spacecraft control [10] are known from the literature. As we have mentioned in Introduction, it results from a neccessity of meeting real-time constraints that can be fulfilled with difficulty, because for implementing symbolic reasoning of agents the logicist, computationally inefficient, approach is mainly used [11].

Fortunately, recently, some multi-agent models for real-time applications have been proposed. In the Cardon approach [2], an effective self-adaptation of a multi-agent system is obtained with specialized dynamic agents belonging to a very flexible layered system architecture. State dynamics of agents of one layer is implemented with augmented transition networks (ATN). Dynamic adaptability of the agents' behaviour with ATNs is also used by Guessoum and Dojat [9]. Another interesting approach introduced by Lesser et al. has been presented in [12] for controlling *soft* real-time systems.

Summing up, the approach presented in this paper focuses strongly on fulfilling *hard* real-time constraints, if compared with other models known from the literature. The advantage of the approach presented in the paper is that it uses *efficient syntactic pattern recognition-based model* for implementing symbolic reasoning and inference for the purpose of real-time intelligent monitoring and control. The efficiency of this model results not only from the *efficiency of reasoning/inference schemes* [5,7,8] applied, but also from using the same *syntactic pattern recognition paradigm* at various architecture layers, which makes the whole model consistent and coherent.

References

1. Behrens, U., Flasiński, M., Hagge, L., Jurek, J., Ohrenberg, K.: Recent Developments of the ZEUS Expert System ZEX, IEEE Trans. Nucl. Sci. **NS-43** (1996), 65–68.
2. Cardon, A., Lesage, F.: Toward Adaptive Information Systems, Proc. 11th Workshop Knowledge Acquisition, Modeling and Management, Banff, Alberta, Canada, April 18–23, 1998.
3. Correra, J.M. Laresgoiti, I., Jennings, N.R.: Using Archon, Part 2: Electricity Transportation Management, IEEE Expert **11** (1996), 71–79.
4. Flasiński, M.: Towards Constructing a Self-Learning Graph Grammar-Based Pattern Recognition System, Archives of Control Sciences **37** (1992), 223–248.
5. Flasiński, M.: On the Parsing of Deterministic Graph Languages for Syntactic Pattern Recognition, Pattern Recognition **26** (1993), 1–16.
6. Flasiński, M.: The Programmed Grammars and Automata as Tools for a Construction of Analytic Expert Systems, Archives of Control Sciences **40** (1995), 5–35.
7. Flasiński, M.: Power Properties of NLC Graph Grammars with a Polynomial Membership Problem, Theoretical Computer Science **201** (1998), 189–231.
8. Flasiński, M., Jurek, J.: Dynamically Programmed Automata for Quasi Context Sensitive Languages as a Tool for Inference Support in Pattern Recognition-Based Real-Time Control Expert Systems, Pattern Recognition **32** (1999), 671–690.
9. Guessoum, Z., Dojat, M.: A Real-Time Agent Model in an Asynchronous-Object Environment, Proc. 7th European Workshop Modelling Autonomous Agents in a Multi-Agent World, Eindhoven, The Netherlands, January 22–25, 1996.
10. Ingrand, F.F., Georgeff, M.P., Rao, A.S.: An Architecture for Real-Time Reasoning and System Control, IEEE Expert **7** (1992).
11. Jennings, N.R., Sycara, K., Wooldridge, M.: A Roadmap of Agent Research and Development, Autonomous Agents and Mutli-Agent Systems **1** (1998), 7–38.
12. Vincent, R., Horling, B., Lesser, V., Wagner, T.: Implementing Soft Real-Time Agent Control, Proc. 5th Intern. Conf. Autonomous Agents, Montreal, Canada, June 2001, 355–362.
13. Wang, H., Wang, C.: Intelligent Agents for the Nuclear Industry, IEEE Computer **30** (1997), 28–34.

Rascal – A Resource Manager for Multi Agent Systems in Smart Spaces*

Krzysztof Gajos

MIT AI Lab, Cambridge, MA, USA,
kgajos@ai.mit.edu,
http://www.ai.mit.edu/people/kgajos

Abstract. Multi Agent Systems (MAS) are often used as a software substrate in creating smart spaces. Many of the solutions already developed within the MAS community are applicable in the domain of smart spaces. Others, however, need to be modified or re-developed. In particular, it has to be noted that many agents acting in a physical space domain are restricted in number and capability by the scarce physical hardware available. Those limitations need to be taken into account when coordinating agent activities in a MAS in a smart space.

In this paper we present Rascal, a high-level resource management system for the Intelligent Room Project, that addresses physical resource scarcities. Rascal performs the *service mapping* and *arbitration* functions for the system. Rascal is an implemented tool and has been partially deployed for day-to-day use.

1   Introduction

Building smart spaces requires distributing computation across a number of computers. The software components of a smart space need to cooperate robustly and the system must be able to cope with components being added and removed dynamically. For that reason a number of research groups have adopted an approach in which a multi-agent system (MAS) is the software substrate connecting all of the computational components of a smart space [9,5,8].

Agents in smart spaces have to deal with many of the same issues as agents in other MAS. At the same time, physical spaces are a domain with their own features and constraints that affect how the agents deal with certain situations.

Agents in a smart space are heavily resource-bounded because they are embedded in a physical world where all physical resources are scarce. This makes the coordination of multiple agent in a smart space all the more difficult because these physical constraints have to be taken into account. For that reason, an explicit resource management system is required in a smart space.

In this paper we present Rascal, a resource manager for the Metaglue agent platform. Metaglue [5] is a MAS developed at the MIT AI Lab for the Intelligent Room project. Rascal provides service mapping and resource access arbitration mechanisms

---

* The work presented here was supported in part by the Advanced Research Project Agency of the Department of Defense under contract number F30602–92–C0204, monitored through Rome Laboratory, and in part by the MIT Project Oxygen Alliance.

for Metaglue agents. Rascal has been implemented and partially deployed for every-day use. Some of its advanced features are still being tested and optimized for speed.

1.1 Definitions

What Is a Resource Manager for a Smart Space? We believe a resource manager should be capable of performing two fundamental tasks: *resource mapping* and *arbitration*.

Resource mapping (i.e. match-making) is the process of deciding what resources can be used to satisfy a specific request.

Arbitration is ensuring that, at a minimum, resources are not being used beyond their capacities. Ideally, arbitration ensures optimal, or nearly optimal, use of scarce resources via appropriate allocation of resources to requests.

This paper is concerned with the management of high-level resources. As opposed to OS level management (memory, files, etc.) and load-balancing computationally intensive agents over multiple machines, these high-level resources include physical devices and large software components, for example, projectors, multiplexors, wires, displays, modems, user attention, software programs, screen real estate, sound input and output devices, CD players, drapes, and lamps.

For clarity, we define some potentially ambiguous terms that are used throughout the remainder of this paper:

Metaglue. Metaglue [5,10,11] is the MAS forming the software base for all work at the Intelligent Room Project. Unlike most MAS, Metaglue provides infrastructure for close-coupling of agents (that is, it facilitates direct method calls) in addition to a message passing mechanism in order to enable faster communication among agents. Metaglue is intended for use in environments where most agents are physically close and thus good network connectivity can be assumed. Metaglue makes it easy to coordinate the startup and running of agents on any number of machines with different operating systems.

Metaglue agents are collected into "societies" which are distinct name-spaces for multiple users and spaces. A new communication and discovery model is currently being developed for inter-society communication.

Agent. Agents are distinct object instances capable of providing services and making requests of the resource manager. This means agents themselves are considered to be a type of resource because they provide services (see below).

Device. A physical or logical device is something akin to a projector, screen, or user-attention; devices are often, but not necessarily, represented by agents. Devices provide services and therefore are resources.

Service. Services are provided by agents and devices; a single agent or device can provide more than one service and any kind of service can be provided by a number of agents or devices. For example, the ShortTextOutput service can be provided by the on-wall display, scrolling LED sign or a text-to-speech program. An A/V receiver is a provider of a number of services, such as an amplifier, an audio multiplexor and a radio receiver.

Resource. A resource is a provider of a service. Both agents and physical devices are resources. For example, a physical LED sign is a resource (providing the LED sign hardware service) obtained and used by the LEDSignText Agent, which is in turn a resource (providing TextOuput service and LEDSign service) that can be obtained and used by any other agent needing those services.

2 Summary of Design Requirements

This section summarizes the essential requirements for designing a high-level resource management system for a smart space. Space permits only a brief overview; potential design issues are discussed in more detail in [7]. In particular, the needs for on-demand agent startup and "smart re-allocations" are motivated more extensively in [7].

2.1 Closed System Assumption

We assume that Rascal will work in a closed system, i.e. one where all agents can be assumed to be trusted (but where agents can appear or leave dynamically). We can make this assumption without reducing the scalability of the system by dividing agents into *societies* . An agent society is a collection of agents that act on behalf of a single entity, such as a physical space, a person, a group of people, an institution, an information store, etc. Rascal's job is to coordinate use of resources within a society.

In cases where agents from one society need to access resources owned by a different society, a resource manager of one society can make requests of the resource manager from the other one. The resource manager from the society that owns the resource is the sole owner of the resource and can decide to take it back at any moment if necessary. The negotiation for resources among a number of societies is a somewhat different problem from managing resources within a society. For one thing, this is now an open system and access control mechanisms need to be put in place to ensure that all requesters act within their authority.

Extending our resource management system to a world with multiple societies requires having an access control system in place (see [7] for discussion) and is not covered here because this work is still in a preliminary phase.

A most common kind of situation where one society needs to make resource request of another is one in which agents acting on behalf of the user need resources to communicate information to the user. Agents acting on behalf of the user belong to one society and those controlling the space, belong to another (as in Figure 1). User's society usually will not contain physical devices and thus if, for example, an email alert agent acting on my behalf needs to tell me that a new mail has arrived for me, it will need resources (such as speech output or a display) from my office to pass the message on to me. In such situation, the email alert agent will still make a resource request of the resource manager in my society. My resource manager, seeing that it has no good resources on its own, will make a request of the resource manager of my office's society. My office will then decide whether to fulfill the request and if so, how.

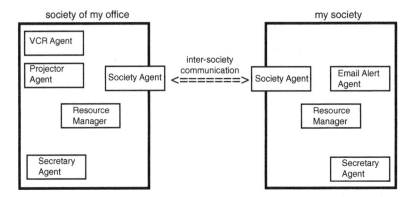

Fig. 1. Our view of the world: a society is viewed as a closed system. All agents within a society are trusted yet self-interested. A world composed of many societies is, on the other hand, viewed as an open system where, to an extent, every society can be viewed as a single agent providing a number of capabilities.

2.2 Self-Interested Agents

Although we assume that all agents are trusted, we also assume that they are self-interested. All agents admitted to a society are assumed to be truthful in that they do not misrepresent their needs and capabilities. They are, however, concerned solely with performing the task or tasks they were built for. For example, an agent that controls the flow of a presentation is only concerned with ensuring that slides are visible on an appropriate display; it has no knowledge of how its actions affect the abilities of other agents to perform their tasks. The assumpiton that agents have no knowledge of their peers allows a more modular design of the system.

2.3 Tightly Tied to External Physical Resources

A special characteristic of a MAS based in a smart space, as noted before, is that it is very tightly coupled to the physical resources within that space. At the simplest level, the number of physical displays in the space is a limiting factor that determines how many visual activities (such as web browsing, sketching, watching movies, writing email) can be performed simultaneously. At a deeper level, the layout of physical connections among devices also limits their use. For example, the output of a VCR may be connected to only one projector and a TV, while computers can be dynamically connected – via a multiplexor – to any of the available displays in the space. A resource management system, such as Rascal, is necessary to keep track of available resources and arbitrate among conflicting requests for those resources.

2.4 Reasoning about Absent Agents

In smart spaces components can be added or removed at any moment. More often than not, however, components that are available one day, are also available the next.

We believe that our system should not only be able to cope with dynamic changes of configuration, but also that the stability and predictability of the physical environment should be used to the system's advantage. One consequence of a predictable enviroment is the plausibility of reasoning about agents even before they have been started. In other words, in smart spaces, agents can be started when needed using the resources that at a given moment can be spared. For example, when one of the users within a space needs to make a slide presentation, an appropriate agent will be started on an available computer that has the appropriate presentation software, available screen space, and can be connected to an on-wall display device (such as a projector). If another presentation is started at the same time, another available computer and display device will be chosen. On-demand agent startup allows the system to adapt to the current set of available resources and prevents the system designer from having to predict all possible configurations that might be required in a space (such as the unusual case where two presentations need to run simultaneously).

2.5   Need for Smart Re-allocations

In our system, it happens frequently that a new request can only be satisfied by taking a resource away from a previously satisfied request. But that previous request does not have to be left resource-less – there is often an alternative resource that can be used to fill it. Suppose, for example, that I request to watch the news in an office equipped with an on-wall projector and a TV set (see Figure 2). The projector is assigned to the job because it produces the largest image and has the best resolution. Then, while watching the news, I decide to also access my email agent. This agent must use the projector because it is the only display that can be used by a computer. Therefore, the projector is taken away from the news agent; ideally, instead of stopping the news agent, Rascal moves it to the TV set.

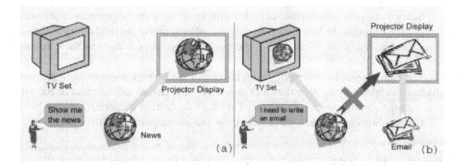

Fig. 2. Sample interaction. (a) user requests to see the news – on-wall projected display is allocated as the best resource for the task. (b) user accesses email; the only possible display for email is the on-wall projector previously allocated to the news agent. Instead of being stopped, the news agent is moved to a TV set.

3 Building Rascal

3.1 Centralized vs. Distributed

Conceptually, Rascal is a centralized system. This decision was not made lightly, but we believe the advantages of a centralized system outweigh its drawbacks (such as, e.g., being a single point of failure).

Rascal was built as a separate centralized system primarily because it had to reason about absent agents. If we instead chose a distributed solution involving direct negotiation, all agents would have to be "alive" to be considered as candidates for a request. Also, a resource manager in an smart interactive, space has to be efficient. Rascal must make its decisions within a couple of seconds or less. A lot of inter-agent communication would make this goal nearly impossible.

Despite centralization, Rascal is actually not a single point of failure in the system. This is because two features of Metaglue make any agent nearly "invincible:" automatic restarting of agents ([11]) and persistent storage ([5]). If any agent dies, it will be restarted the next time any other agent tries to make a call to it. The dead agent will be restarted on any available computer, so even if the original computer hosting the agent fails, the agent will be restarted somewhere else. The persistent storage mechanism allows agents to save changes to their state whenever such changes occur. Consequently, if the agent dies and gets restarted, it can retrieve its state from before the failure and continue as if nothing had happened.

3.2 Structure

Rascal performs two major functions: *service mapping* and *arbitration* among requests for services (as defined in Section 1.1) and it is composed of three major parts: the knowledge base, the constraint satisfaction engine, and the framework for interacting with other Metaglue agents.

Service mapping is performed entirely by the knowledge-based component of Rascal. Arbitration begins in the knowledge-based part (where relative cost and utility of various resources are determined) but most of the work on arbitration is done by the constraint satisfaction engine.

The components for interacting with the rest of the Metaglue agents facilitate communication with service providers and requesters, and enable enforcement of Rascal's decision (i.e., taking previously allocated services away from requesters).

In the following sections, we present these major components of the system.

Representation and the Knowledge Base. Upon startup, information about all available resources is loaded into Rascal's knowledge base (if more resources become available later on, they can be added dynamically). It is important to reiterate here that Rascal relies on all resources having descriptions of their needs and capabilities separate from the actual code. Those external descriptions contain a list of services that the resource can provide. Agents who provide services may in addition specify what other resources they will need in order to provide that service. For example, the MessengerAgent that provides a message delivery service will need one or more resources capable of providing text output service. Agents may also specify their startup needs, i.e. a list of requests that need to be fulfilled for the agent to exist. For example, an agent providing speech recognition service will need a computer, with appropriate speech recognition software installed, in order to be able to start and configure itself properly.

When Rascal considers candidates for a request, it not only makes sure that those candidate services are adequate and available – it also makes sure that the needs of those candidates can be satisfied, and so on recursively. The final selection of candidates for requests is performed by the constraint satisfaction engine. Therefore, the knowledge-based part evaluates all possible candidates for all possible requests. This request chaining proves to be extremely valuable: when the email alert agent, for example, requests a text output service, several different agents may be considered, including the LED sign and the speech output agents. The email alert agent may have its own preference as to what kind of rendition of the text output service it prefers. However, if the communication link with the actual LED sign is broken, the needs of the agent controlling the LED sign will not be satisfied and so it will not be assigned to the request.

Rascal's knowledge base is implemented in a rule-based system (JESS [6]) written in Java. The role of this component of the system is to find all plausible candidates for all requests. In addition, for each request-candidate pair, a measure of utility has to be calculated (see the next section).

In terms of representation, services provided by agents are described by the names of the Java interfaces that can be used to access them. For services provided by entities other than agents, similar hierarchical names are used (e.g. hardware.Computer for a computer). In addition, attribute-value pairs are used to describe services in more detail and to refine requests.

Cost-Benefit Analysis. When resources are scarce, part of the arbitration process is deciding which requests are more important. This could be done with self-assigned priorities or economic models may be involved (e.g. [3]). In Rascal, self-assigned need levels are used in conjunction with the concept of utility of a service to the requester and its cost to others. This is a very simple and arbitrary scheme. It could easily be replaced by a different system should there be a need for that. This simple model is sufficient for the current implementation of Rascal, because of our assumption that all agents within a society can be trusted.

The basic assumption of this schema is that, given a request, each candidate resource has some utility to the requester. This utility depends on how badly the requester needs a particular request r fulfilled and on how well the resource s matches the request (Equation 1). A variety of monotonically increasing functions can be used as f_u.

$$utility(r, s) = f_u(need(r), match(r, s)) \qquad (1)$$

The same method is used to calculate the utility of the already allocated resources. When a resource is taken from its current user, the system as a whole incurs cost equal to the utility of that resource to that user. Also, when a resource s_i, currently allocated to fulfill request r, is replaced with a different resource s_j, a cost is incurred. This cost is a sum of a fixed "change penalty" and the difference in utilities between the new allocation and the old one (if this difference is negative, it is set to zero) as shown in Equation 2.

$$cost(r, s_i, s_j) = changePenalty(r) + max\{0, utility(r, s_i) - utility(r, s_j)\} \quad (2)$$

The arbiter has to make sure that whenever it awards a resource to a new request, the cost of doing so should never exceed the utility of the awarded resources to the new requester.

Rascal provides a number of methods for calculating utilities and evaluating matches between requests and resources. Each resource or request description can also be accompanied by its own custom tools for performing those calculations.

Finding the Right Solution – The Constraint Satisfaction Engine. When the knowledge-based subsystem selects and rates all candidates for requests, a constraint satisfaction engine (CSE) is invoked to find an optimal or nearly optimal configuration that fulfills the new request without breaking any of the previous assignments.

Rascal uses a Java-based CSE (JSolver [4]) in order to enable close coupling with its other components. In order to find the right solution, a number of constraints and heuristics are involved:

- respecting limits – there are limits on how many requests can share a service.
- only some requests need to be satisfied – CSE needs to find services only for some of the requests that it knows about: the newly made request, the needs of the services assigned to satisfy this new request and all the previously satisfied requests.
- preference to local solutions – As explained in Section 2.5, it is sometimes necessary to change the assignment to a previously satisfied request. However, it is necessary to minimize such changes to the absolute minimum. Rascal's CSE has been set up in such a way that changes to old requests are only made as a last resort and have to be limited in scope. That is, it should not be possible for a new request to cause changes to a large number of other assignments. For that reason, Rascal's CSE uses following heuristics:
  - the first service considered for any previously satisfied request is the service previously allocated to the request;
  - if a different service has to be assigned, the cost of service substitution is calculated and added to the overall cost of the current new request – if the cost exceeds a preset limit, CSE backtracks;
  - the CSE is run several times, each time with a different limit to the overall cost: the first time CSE runs, the limit is set to zero in hope that a solution can be found that does not disturb any of the previously assigned requests. If this fails, the CSE is run again with a higher limit. The process is repeated until a solution is found or until the CSE is ran with a limit equal to the need of this request. In Rascal, the cost of satisfying a request cannot exceed the need to have it satisfied.

Rascal-Metaglue Connection. There are two major components to the Rascal-Metaglue connection mechanism: the `RascalAgent` and the `ManagedAgent`. The former makes Rascal's methods available to the rest of the Metaglue agents. The latter is a simple implementation of a Metaglue agent that all other "managed" agents inherit from. That is, all agents that want to make their services available through Rascal, or that wish to make requests through it.

4   Related Work

The Facilitator Agent in Open Agent Architecture (OAA) [8] performs *task* not *resource* management. Implicit in the OAA design is the assumption that each agent has sole control over all of the resources it might need.

Applications in Hive [9] agent platform are created by explicitly connecting various components together. Thus resource conflicts are diminished because connections among agents are long-lived and pre-designed, contrary to the on-demand configurations created within Rascal-enhanced Metaglue.

Jini [2] is a framework with a number of discovery and description tools but no arbitration capabilities. The arbitration component is supposed to be provided by the user.

Intentional Naming System (INS) [1] provides an extensive naming mechanism and a mechanism for choosing the best available service but it does not provide explicit arbitration mechanisms or tools for smart re-allocations.

5   Contributions

Multi-Agent Systems constitute a very powerful programming paradigm. Applying MAS to new domains often poses a number of challenges. This paper shows how the MAS approach can be applied in the domain of smart spaces, where agent coordination is constrained by the availability of physical resources. Rascal—an implememnted and tested tool for managing such resources—is presented.

Acknowledgments. Luke Weisman did most of the fundamental work on the Rascal-Metaglue interface. He has also done a lot of research on other approaches to resource management in Metaglue-based MAS. Dr. Howard Shrobe has provided invaluable advice throughout the duration of the project. Finally, the author would like to thank Mark Foltz for his thorough and insightful comments on this paper.

References

1. W. Adjie-Winoto, E. Schwartz, H. Balakrishnan, and J. Lilley. The design and implementation of an intentional naming system. In *17th ACM Symposium on Operating Systems Principles (SOSP)*, Kiawah Island, SC, December 1999.
2. Ken Arnold, Bryan O'Sullivan, Robert W. Scheifler, Jim Waldo, and Ann Wollrath. *The Jini Specification*. Addison-Wesley, Reading, MA, 1999.

3. Jonathan Bredin, David Kotz, Daniela Rus Rajiv T. Maheswaran, Çagri Imer, and Tamer Basar. A market-based model for resource allocation in agent systems. In Franco Zambonelli, editor, *Coordination of Internet Agents*. Springer-Verlag, 2000.

4. Hon Wai Chun. Constraint programming in Java with JSolver. In *First International Conference and Exhibition on The Practical Application of Constraint Technologies and Logic Programming*, London, April 1999.

5. Michael Coen, Brenton Phillips, Nimrod Warshawsky, Luke Weisman, Stephen Peters, and Peter Finin. Meeting the computational needs of intelligent environments: The Metaglue system. In *Proceedings of MANSE'99*, Dublin, Ireland, 1999.

6. Ernest J. Friedman-Hill. Jess, the Java Expert System Shell. Technical Report SAND98-8206, Sandia National Laboratories, 1997.

7. Krzysztof Gajos, Luke Weisman, and Howard Shrobe. Design principles for resource management systems for intelligent spaces. In *Proceedings of The Second International Workshop on Self-Adaptive Software*, Budapest, Hungary, 2001. To appear.

8. David L. Martin, Adam J. Cheyer, and Douglas B. Moran. The Open Agent Architecture: A framework for building distributed software systems. *Applied Artificial Intelligence*, 13(1-2):91–128, January-March 1999.

9. Nelson Minar, Matthew Gray, Oliver Roup, Raffi Krikorian, and Pattie Maes. Hive: Distributed agents for networking things. In *Proceedings of ASA/MA'99, the First International Symposium on Agent Systems and Applications and Third International Symposium on Mobile Agents*, August 1999.

10. Brenton Phillips. Metaglue: A programming language for multi agent systems. Master's thesis, Massachusetts Institute of Technology, Cambridge, MA, 1999.

11. Nimrod Warshawsky. Extending the Metaglue multi agent system. Master's thesis, Massachusetts Institute of Technology, Cambridge, MA, 1999.

Software Development Kit for Multi-agent Systems Design and Implementation[1]

Vladimir Gorodetski, Oleg Karsayev, Igor Kotenko, and Alexey Khabalov

St. Petersburg Institute for Informatics and Automation
{gor, ok, ivkote, khab}@mail.iias.spb.su

Abstract. The paper presents the developed technology and software tool for design and implementation of knowledge-based multi-agent systems. The software tool comprises two components that are *"Generic Agent"* and *"Multi-agent System Development Kit"* (MAS DK). The former comprises reusable Visual C++ and Java classes and generic data and knowledge base structures, whereas the latter comprises several developer-friendly editors aimed at formal specification of the applied multi-agent system (MAS) under development and installation of the resulting application in particular computer network environment. The developed technology and MAS DK were used in the design and implementation of the MAS prototype for computer network assurance and intrusion detection and distributed attack simulator. Several other applications are currently under development.

1 Introduction

At present development of software tools for design and implementation of multi-agent systems (MAS) is the task of great concern. Till now a good deal of such software tools has been developed. Between them, the most known ones are such as AgentBuilder [1], MadKit [9], Bee-gent [2], FIPA-OS [10], JADE [3], Zeus [4], etc.

However, unless the great deal of such tools they do not meet wholly the present-day requirements. The latter can be divided in two groups ([11]). *The first group* corresponds to the *properties of the technology* supported by a software tool. They are ability to support for the entire circle of MAS design, development and deployment, friendly interfaces for all categories of users, visual programming style, concurrency of the development, automated documenting, etc. *The second group* of requirements concerns to the *properties of the target MAS*. These requirements are such as support for the ontology development, support for the development of the basic MAS components (agent mental components and inference mechanisms, agent behavior scenarios, communication component, etc.) and support for modifiability of MAS on the whole.

These requirements form the focus of the Multi-agent System Development Kit (MAS DK) that is being developed by authors. Below its first version and application examples are described. Section 2 outlines ideas implemented in MAS DK. Section 3 describes the basic phases of the supported technology. Section 4 describes generic

---

[1] This research is being supported by grants 01-01-00109, 01-01-108 of Russian Foundation of Basic Research and European Office of Aerospace R&D (Projects #1994 P)

B. Dunin-Kęplicz and E. Nawarecki (Eds.): CEEMAS 2001, LNAI 2296, pp. 121–130, 2002.

architecture of agents generated by MAS DK. Section 5 outlines capabilities of MAS DK in communication component development. Section 6 presents several applied MAS prototypes, which have already been developed or in progress of development now on the basis of MAS DK. The concluding remarks outline the future research.

2 Peculiarities of the Developed MAS Technology

In general, the life cycle of knowledge-based MAS, like any other information system consists of a number of standard phases. They are development of a business model and the requirements, analysis, design development and deployment, testing, maintenance, and evolutionary modification. The quality of any information technology (IT) is assessed over such properties as time spent for a system design, development and deployment and quality of the resulting system.

Despite the visible diversity of MAS applications, and variants of their implementations, one can notice a high percentage of common functionalities that are practically independent conceptually from application to application. It is reasonable to implement these "commons" within a software tool as generic classes and data structures, and reuse them as "ready software components" in various applications. Such "ready components" could decrease substantially the total MAS development time.

This view is the first idea of MAS DK. Its practical realization supposes to carry out a formidable work to find such "commons" over many applications. Within the developed MAS DK this principle is realized in the form of so-called "*Generic Agent*", which comprises a hierarchy of standard software classes and generic data structures. *Generic Agent* is a nucleus that is "bootstrapped" by the developer via specialization of the software classes and data structures and via cloning software agent instances composing MAS. These procedures are supported by a user-friendly editors of MAS DK, which is the second component supporting the MAS technology.

The second idea of the technology aims at providing for modifiability of an application during its life cycle. Sometimes it is necessary to modify an agent's knowledge base, to add a new template of message, to install a new agent, etc. MAS DK provides these capabilities due to formal specification of the target MAS in terms of so called "*System Kernel*". The latter contains the complete information about the developed MAS. It is stored and if necessary is capable to re-generate MAS software code in a semi-automatic mode. If MAS has to be modified, it is necessary to modify *System Kernel* and to re-generate the respective software code.

3 Summary of MAS Technology

The MAS technology comprises two main phases. At the first one the application is specified in terms of a MAS DK specification language resulting in so called "*System Kernel*". At the next phase *System Kernel* is used for MAS deployment. At this phase the software of MAS is generated and software agents are situated in computers of the network according to the MAS specification in *System Kernel*.

3.1 "Generic Agent" and "System Kernel"

Generic Agent typifies classes of agents to be specified in *System Kernel* and is used further for cloning of the software agent instances. *Generic Agent* consists of three components: (1) Invariant scheme of agents' databases, (2) Library of invariant Visual C++ and Java classes implementing the basic mechanisms of data processing and (3) Library of reusable Visual C++ and Java classes supporting message exchange. The latter include implementation of KQML language, message content specification language based on XML, message templates, parsers needed to interpret message content.

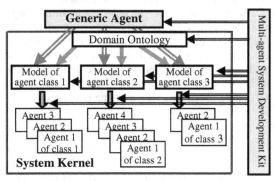

Fig. 1. High level structure of MAS technology

Generic Agent data structures are used to represent the data- and knowledge bases of agent classes (Fig.1). Data-and knowledge bases of an agent class are specified in context of the domain ontology intending to provide their integrity and agents' mutual understanding via using common terminology and its shared interpretation. Also, ontology defines functionalities of the particular agent classes. The above specification form *System Kernel*. Apart from specification of agent classes generated from *Generic agent, System Kernel* contains also information about the numbers of instances of each agent class and the names of hosts of the local network, in which they have to be situated.

3.2 Multi-agent System Development Kit

MAS DK consists of several specialized editors as follows:
1. *Ontology editor* used to specify domain ontology concepts and their attributes.
2. *Editor of agent classes.* It defines the list of the agent classes to be generated according to the model of the target MAS. Every such agent class inherits the methods and data structures of *Generic agent.* In the developed case study of a Computer Network Assurance System (CNAS) the examples of agent classes are "*Access control agent*" (*ACA*), "*Intrusion detection agent*" (*IDA*), etc. At the posterior development steps each class of agents can be represented in MAS by several instances situated in different computers.
3. *Agent class ontology editor.* It aims to allocate the subset of the domain ontology concepts, which the particular agent deals with, and to generate agent class database according to the above allocation. If necessary, this editor supports definition and specification of new concepts of the agent class. The agent class database structure is generated on the basis of the entire set of its concepts.
4. *Editor of agents' behavior scenarios.* It specifies the scenarios of input message processing and rules of knowledge base determining the scenario to be executed.

5. *Editor of message templates.* This editor aims at specification of the set of the templates of output messages of each agent class.

6. *Agents' cloning manager.* This function aims at generation of the instances of each agent class according to the MAS model. For example, in CNAS the cloning procedure performs generation of four copies of each of seven agent classes and values of their parameters, e.g. agent's identifier, the name of host to situate, etc.

The second step of technology is installation of the software agents in the target computers of the network. This procedure is carried out in the semi-automatic mode. The only information that can be defined by the developer is to point out the name of hosts (*IP*-addresses), in which each agent must be situated as it is specified in *System Kernel.* Special software generates the parameters of the message templates to tune addressee(s) for each message, and copies the data associated with the agent to a folder in the host computer. Several simple operations follow up the last ones.

4   Agent Architecture

MAS agents have the same architecture (Fig.2). Differences are reflected in the content of particular agents' data and knowledge bases. Let us outline agents' architecture.

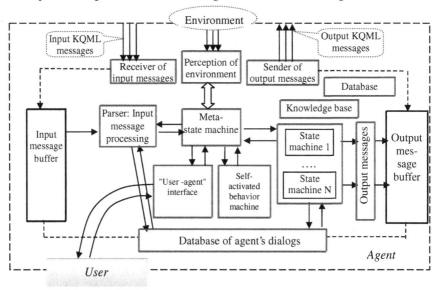

Fig. 2. Agent architecture

Each agent's neighborhood comprises other agents, with which it communicates, environment which is perceived, and, possibly, modified by agents, and user interacting with agents through his interface. *Receiver of input* and *Sender of output messages* perform the respective functions. Messages received are recorded in *Input message buffer.* The order of its processing is managed by *Input message processor.* In addition, this component performs syntax analysis and KQML messages interpretation and extracts the message contents. The component *Database of agent's dialogs* stores for each input message its attributes like identifiers, type of message and its source. If a message supposes to be replied it is mapped the respective output message when it is sent. *Meta-state machine* manages the semantic processing of input messages directing it for processing by the respective *State machines*. An additional functionality of this component is allocation of management of the parallel performance of agent's processes. The basic computations of agent corresponding its role in MAS are executed by *State machine 1,..., State machine N*. Each of them is implemented as automata realizing a scenario of processing of some kind of input messages.

The selection of scenario and therefore the output result depend on the input message content and inner state of the *State Machine*. In turn, inner state of this Machine depends on pre-history of its performance; in particular, this prehistory is reflected in the state of agent's *Knowledge base и Database*. One more state machine called "*Self-activated behavior machine*" is changing its inner state depending on the state of the data and knowledge bases. In some combinations of these states it can activate functionality independently on input messages or state of the environment.

It should be noted that the described architecture is not BDI one because its capabilities are restricted still by representation and dealing with agent's local knowledge. The architecture does not represent explicitly such mental abilities of agent as belief and obligations (commitments). Fortunately, to expand the MAS DK in order to provide it with the above capabilities is rather technical problem than principal one and is planned for the future research and development.

5   Communication Environment

Each agent class is provided with a set of particular message templates according to its functionalities. These templates are formed through specialization of the of *Generic agent* component called *generic message template*. The developer carries out the specialization procedure with *Editor of message templates*, which, in turn, is a component of MAS DK. The message templates are specified in KQML language and specialization corresponds to the assignment to each template the respective performatives. At current phase of MAS DK development only standard KQML performatives are used. Communication component of each agent includes also data regarding potential addressees of messages of given template. The last data are assigned at the phase of agent class instances cloning. Message content is specified in XML. The XML content of each message is formed on-line according to the chosen scenario depending on the input message and agent's internal state. The package KQML+XML is configured by the procedure called in fig.2 as "Output message".

6   Applications

Below several prototypes of applied MAS are described in brief. The first of them that is Computer Network Assurance System has already been implemented on the basis of MAS DK. Two more applied MAS are now in progress of implementation.

6.1 Multi-agent Computer Network Assurance System

A peculiarity of this MAS is that it is responsible for detection of a user's suspicious activity or distributed attacks against the whole computer network. Multi-agent CNAS is the system, which agents are distributed over the defended network hosts and interact both within the host and within the network. The host-based part of CNAS architecture comprises the following basic components (Fig.3):

Agent-demon AD-E is responsible for the input traffic preprocessing. It monitors traffic and extracts sequences of so-called "events" that are semantically meaningful from intrusion detection viewpoint. These events are sorted, stored in *AD-E* database and forwarded to the posterior processing to one or several agents. *Agent-demons for identification and authentication (AIA)* and *for access control (ACA)* perform their conventional functionalities, record the results into their data bases and send messages to the *Intrusion detection agent* (IDA) if a suspicious behavior or attempt of an attack has been detected. *Agent-demons AD-P1* and *AD-P2* are responsible for extraction of the predefined ("interesting", "meaningful") patterns of "events" and for making decisions (both preliminary and final) regarding to the user's behavior. In the implemented case study *AD-P1* agent is responsible for extracting patterns associated with the attacks like *port scanning* (on application level), *finger search* and *buffer overflow*. The agent *AD-P2* is intended to extract patterns corresponding to the *denial of service* attack, *syn-flood* attack and *port scanning* (on transport level). *IDA* are responsible for

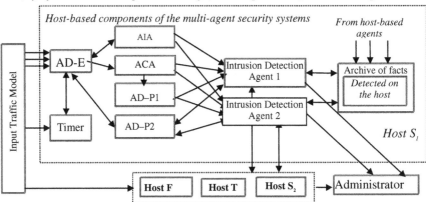

Fig. 3. Architecture of host-based part of multi-agent CNAS

high-level input data processing. *IDA*s make rule-based decisions on the basis of input facts contained in the received messages. They can receive messages about detected suspicious behavior from agent-demons of the same host as well as from security agents of other hosts. The distinction between *IDA*s is that they deal with different situations. *IDA1* processes situations like *combined spoofing attacks*, whereas *IDA2* performs high level data processing in order to detect distributed multi-phase attacks.

The results of testing of the CNAS prototype exhibited the capability of the system to detect multi-phases distributed attacks performed from different source computers (*IP*-addresses) and through several entry points of the computer network. More detailed description of this system prototype can be found in [8].

6.2 MAS for Simulation of Distributed Attacks against Computer Network

The competition between computer security systems and malefactors is such that the latter have an advantage, which is growing if they implement distributed attacks targeted against the whole computer network. This is a cogent argument for the study of distributed attacks. The intentions, objects and strategies of attacks must be the prime subjects of this study. Software tool for simulation of distributed attacks could be very valuable mean for this study. Also, attack simulation tool if used together with security scanners could play an important role in the validation of security policies.

In the developed simulator, distributed attack is specified as a sequence of coordinated actions of the distributed malefactors acting as a team of agents. While performing a distributed attack, malefactors interact in order to coordinate their activity. These messages are specified in KQML+XML languages. Let us outline the basic components of the of distributed attack model implemented by means of MAS DK.

1. Scenario of distributed attack. A distributed attack is specified as a sequence of phases resulting from cooperative activity of malefactors. The latter perform an attack according to a shared *scenario* represented in high-layer terms. At every scenario phase the malefactor intends to achieve a particular sub-goal. Every phase of the scenario is detailed in terms of sub-goals of the lower layer. At the lowest one the attack is represented as a sequence of commands. Every scenario phase can be successful or ineffective. In the last case malefactors have to modify the scenario on-line, i.e. attack scenario is formed dynamically depending on the results of its previous phases.

2. Basic intentions. Malefactor's activity is specified on the basis of the intention-centric approach. This means that basic domain notions correspond to the malefactor intentions and all other ones are structured accordingly. The following *classes of high-layer malefactor's intentions* are used in the developed simulator:

a) R^1–*Reconnaissance* aiming to get information about the network. The followings are the particular cases of such intention: *IH–Identification* of the operating *Hosts*; *IS–Identification* of the host *Services, IO–Identification* of the host *Operating* system, *CI–Collection* of other *Information; RE*–shared *Resource Enumeration, UE–Users* and groups *Enumeration, ABE–Applications* and *Banners Enumeration.*

b) *I–Implantation* and threat realization. The followings are its lower layer representatives*: GAR–Getting Access to Resources* of the host*; EP–Escalating Privilege* with regard to the host resources, *GAD–Gaining Additional Data* needed for threat realization*, TR–Threat Realization, CT–Covering Tracks* to avoid detection of malefactors' presence, *CBD–Creating Back Doors* in order to use them for intrusion. **TR** can be detailed at the lower layer in terms of *CD*–Confidentiality destruction, for example, through getting access to file reading, *ID – Integrity Destruction* realizing through attacks against integrity of the host resources, *DOS –* Violation of resource availability achieved, for example, through *Denial of Service attack.*

3. Attack goal. It is specified by triple *<Network (host) address, Intention, Attack object>.* The attack intention determines the class of scenarios that leads to the result.

---

[1] The same denotations are used below in formal grammars specifying a distributed attack.

Attack object is an optional variable. It is absent in attacks like **R**. E.g., if the intention corresponds to the attacks like **CD** or **ID** then the object is specified as follows:

[**Account**,] [**Process** {*Process name* >/< *Process mask* >},] [**File** {<*file name* >/< *file mask* >},] [**Data in transit** {< *file (data) name* >/< *file (data) mask* >}],

where **Account** –object account, **Process**–running process(es), **File**–file(s) that is the attack target(s), **Data in transit**– transmitting data, []–optional variable, {}–element that can be repeated, and symbol "/" is interpreted as "*OR*". The attack objects are either the whole network (host) resources ("*All*"), or at least anyone of them ("*Anyone*").

Attack formal model is represented as knowledge base, which is shared by all agents and structured according to the developed domain ontology, which comprises a hierarchy of notions specifying malefactors' activities. The developed ontology includes detailed description of the "*Network attack*" domain in which the notions of the bottom layer ("*terminals*") can be specified in terms of audit data and *network packets*.

Mathematical model of distributed attacks is specified in terms of the set of *formal grammars* interconnected through "*substitution*" operation. The symbol sequences generated by *each* of grammars correspond to the sequences of time ordered malefactor's intentions and/or actions. All formal grammars are specified in the standard form:

$$G=<V_N, V_T, S, P, A >,$$

where **G**–is the grammar identifier, V_N is the set of non-terminals, V_T is the set of its terminals, $S \in V_N$ is the axiom, **P** is the set of production, and **A** is the set of attributes and algorithms of their computations. Analysis of the syntactical structures of distributed attack scenarios and also structures of particular cases of attack justified that all they can be generated by context free right-recursive grammars, in which productions are represented as $X \rightarrow aY$, where $X, Y \in V_N, a \in V_T$.

Attribute component of a grammar serves for several purposes. The basic one is to specify randomized choice of a production at an inference step. Also the attribute component used to check admissibility of using a production at the current inference step. These conditions depend on attack goal, configuration of attacked network and its resources and on the results of the previous actions of the malefactor.

Example. Let us consider a simple example of the family of grammars interconnected with "substitution" operation that specifies a subset of scenarios for the particular case of intention **R** ("*Reconnaissance*") that is **IH** ("*Identification* of Hosts*"). The attack goal is specified as follows: <*51.111.125.60, IH, ∅*>.

Formal grammar G("Network attack")=G(NA)

$V_N=\{A, A1\}$, $V_T=\{R,I\}$, $S=\{A\}$, $P=\{A \rightarrow A1 (p1), A1 \rightarrow I (p2), A1 \rightarrow R (p3), A1 \rightarrow R A1 (p4), A1 \rightarrow I A1 (p5)\}$, where *p1–p5* are the probabilities assigned to the productions.

Formal grammar G("Reconnaissance")=G(R)

$V_N=\{R, R1\}$, $V_T=\{IH, CI, IS, IO, RE, UE, AB\}$, $S=\{R\}$, $P=\{R \rightarrow R1 (p1), R1 \rightarrow IH (p2), R1 \rightarrow IH R1 (p3), R \rightarrow CI (p4), R \rightarrow CI R1 (p5), R \rightarrow IS (p6), R \rightarrow IS R1 (p7), ...\}$.
Note, terminal symbol **R** of the upper grammar **G(NA)** plays here the role of *axiom*.

Formal grammar *G(Identification of Hosts")=G(IH)*

$V_N=\{IH, IH1\}$, $V_T=\{DC, SPI\}$, $S=\{IH\}$, $P=\{IH \rightarrow IH1 (p1), IH1 \rightarrow DC (p2), IH1 \rightarrow DC IH1 (p3), IH1 \rightarrow SPI (p4), IH1 \rightarrow SPI IH1 (p5)\}$.

In the same way all the grammars are specified. The probabilities assigned to the productions determine the choice if a multiple choice is possible. They provide also the necessary infinite diversity of the instances of attack generated by the model.

An attack can be successful or ineffective. The result depends on the malefactor's "skill", information about network, which he possesses, and security policy implemented in the attacked network. An attack is developing as interactive process, in which the network is reacting on the malefactor's actions. Computer network plays the role of environment for attacker and therefore the environment model must be a part of the attack simulation tool. *The main attributes* of the host model include such of them as *IP*-address, its *mask*, type and version of *OS*, users' identifiers, their domain names, *passwords*, users' *security identifiers* (*SID*), domain parameters, active ports of the hosts (services used, busy *TCP* and *UDP* ports, etc.), running applications, security indices, shared resources, trusted hosts and some other attributes.

Success or ineffectiveness of an attack action is computed in accordance with the probabilistic model of the network reactions. The malefactor's strategy depends on the results of his intermediate actions. This is the reason for using of on-line generation of the attack development depending on the attacked network reaction. The proposed context-free grammar syntax provides the model with this capability.

6.3   Other Applications under Development

Two other applications are currently in progress. The first is MAS for knowledge discovery from databases (KDD) and the second is MAS for Operation planning.

KDD is interactive and iterative technology in which the user plays an active role. The KDD MAS aims to assist to a user in mining large scale distributed data to develop knowledge base of a decision making system. As a case study we consider a data fusion system. The task peculiarities are diversity of data to be mined (format, precision, measurement scale, etc.), data distribution, etc. These entail peculiarities of this MAS architecture. The model of KDD for data fusion was described in [7].

Multi-agent System for Operation Planning is now in progress. In general case operation planning task is formulated in terms of *bounded resource* allocation under *temporal* and *real-time* constraints. Every operation consists of a number of partially ordered sub-operations and every of such sub-operation can be performed in several ways and by different entities. Conceptually, the problem can be specified as the task of allocation of a partially ordered and real time constrained contracts over eventual contractors that, in turn, are capable to perform particular contracts. The operation planning system architecture includes *meta-agent* that is responsible for high level management of planning realized on the basis of auction-based protocol and *agent-contractors*, performing particular types of sub-operations. More information about conceptual model of this prototype can be found in [5] and [6]. At the current phase of research, as a case study the task of ship servicing in a large SeaPort is considered.

7   Conclusion

The paper presents the developed software tool called Multi-agent System Development Kit that aims at supporting for the basic phases of MAS technology, i.e. design, implementation and deployment. This technology is implemented on the basis of Visual C++ 6.0, JAVA1.3 и XML programming languages.

MAS DK software tool was validated through the development of the multi-agent CNAS and Agent-based simulator of distributed attacks. Those made it possible not only to validate the software tool itself, but also to explore the advantages of using multi-agent technology implemented for new application area, i.e. computer network security area [8]. Several applied MAS are now in progress of implementation.

The future research is intended to expand MAS DK in the following aspects:

1. To expand the capabilities of the MAS specification language in order to make it possible to specify agents' mental states like belief and commitments, and mechanisms to deal with them.
2. To improve computational efficiency of the resulting MAS through using generation of executable code instead of interpretation of high-level software code.
3. To enrich the visual components of the technology, in particular, for analysis of system specification represented by *System Kernel*.

References

1. AgentBuilder: An Integrated Toolkit for Constructing Intelligent Software Agents. Reticular Systems, Inc. Revision 1.3 (1999) http://www.agentbuilder.com.
2. Bee-gent Multi-Agent Framework. Toshiba Corporation Systems and Software Research Laboratories (2000) http://www2.toshiba.co.jp/beegent/index.htm.
3. F.Bellifemine, A.Poggi, G.Rimassa: JADE – A FIPA-compliant agent framework. In: Proceedings of PAAM'99, London UK (1999) http://sharon.cselt.it/projects/jade.
4. J.Collis, D.Ndumu: The Zeus Agent Bilding Toolkit. ZEUS Technical Manual. Intelligent Systems Research Group, BT Labs. Release 1.0 (1999) http://193.113.209.147/projects/agents/index.htm.
5. V.Gorodetski and A.Lebedev: Multi-agent Technology for Planning, Scheduling and Resource Allocation. In: Proceedings of the Third International Conference on Multi-agent systems. IEEE Computer Society (1998) 429-430.
6. V.Gorodetski, A.Lebedev: Multi-agent Model for Real Time Resource Allocation. In: International Journal "Computacion y Sistemas", Vol. 3, No.1, Mexico-City (1999) 17-24.
7. V.Gorodetski, V. Skormin, L.Popyack, O.Karsaev: Distributed Learning in a Data Fusion System. In: Proceedings of the Conference of the World Computer Congress (WCC-2000) "Intelligent Information Processing" (IIP2000), Beijing (2000) 147-154.
8. V.Gorodetski O.Karsaev, I.Kotenko, L.Popyack, and V.Skormin: Agent–based model of Network Security System: A Case Study. Lecture Notes in Computer Science, vol. 2052 (Eds. V.Gorodetski, V.Skormin, L.Popyack), Springer Verlag (2001) 39-50.
9. http://www.madkit.org.
10. S.J.Poslad, S.J.Buckle, and R.Hadingham: The FIPA-OS agent platform: Open Source for Open Standards. In: Proceedings of PAAM 2000, Manchester, UK (2000) http://fipa-os.sourceforge.net/.
11. A.Sloman: What's an AI Toolkit For? In: Proceedings of the AAAI-98 Workshop on Software Tools for Developing Agents. Madison, Wisconsin (1998).

Formal Semantics for Behavioural Substitutability of Agent Components: Application to Interaction Protocols

Nabil Hameurlain

LIUPPA Laboratory, Avenue de l'Université, BP 1155, 64013 Pau France.
nabil.hameurlain@univ-pau.fr

Abstract. This paper presents formal semantics for behavioural substitutability of agent components, and argues that the traditional approaches used in software multi-agent systems are not rigorous and have some limitations. We propose various substitutability relations based upon the preorder relations which are considered in the study of concurrent systems. Examples of interaction protocols such as the Contract-Net-Protocol are given to illustrate our approach.

1 Motivation

One of the challenging and emerging problems of agent-based computing is to apply the basis principles of Software Engineering to the development of open multi-agent systems [1]. Up to now, most of existing software agent applications are developed in an ad hoc fashion. The elements of software (components), the relation between the components (connectors) and the composition of components and connectors are developed following a limited and not rigorous specification of the components. Our main contribution is to propose formal semantics for behavioural composition and substitutability of agent components in open multi-agent systems context. The new semantics take into account property preservation and some validation and verification aspects. We argue that integrating methods and validation and verification techniques into the requirement of behavioural substitutability of agent components is necessary for developing software agent systems.

Component based approach [13] is one of the well-known approaches used to develop software agents. In this approach, an agent is made of a collection of components, which are able to interact with the environment (other agents), and can easily be upgraded by changing components or integrate new ones. Components are then used for incremental design and reuse. Several software platforms based on agent components approach have been developed. Recently, [19] proposes SoftComponent Description (SCD) language providing a formal expression language to describe components. It enables the designer to model an agent's behaviour by defining component classes and then composing component instances. The type of software component is characterised by the way in which its behaviour is described: *Petri net* components, *Primitive* components (describe the 'behaviour' in Java), *Generic connector* compo-

plicz and E. Nawarecki (Eds.): CEEMAS 2001, LNAI 2296, pp. 131–140, 2002.
© Springer-Verlag Berlin Heidelberg 2002

B. Dunin-Kę

nents (Synchronizer and Selector components), and *compound* component, which are constructed by composition of other components. SCD compiler translates compositional model to Java source program, and Petri net components are described by BRIC (Block-like Representation for interacting Component) component [5] using coloured Petri nets [11]. Petri net components and their interactions are validated, analysed and simulated in order to check safety and liveness properties of cooperating agents using conversation protocols such as the Contract Net Protocol [16]. Nevertheless the composition and the semantics of components in SCD has been addressed only intuitively but not formally.

This paper aims to provide a formal framework for behavioural composition and substitutability of Petri net components. We develop the software engineering's proposal presented in [9], and propose some behavioural *substitutability* relations based on behavioural subtyping relations suited for modelling the behaviour extension in agent components systems. Our approach is related to the behavioural subtyping according to the Wegner and Zdonik's *substitutability* principle [18]. We also investigate the characterisation of these behavioural subtyping relations to their degree of change by property preservation.

The paper is organised as follows: the second chapter presents the basic definitions of Petri nets components and their semantics together with the notions based on action observation. In the third chapter we propose results about two behavioural substitutability relations and their property preservation. These relations are based upon Request Substitutability preorder [12], and proved to be quite easy to use in practice. The Contract Net Protocol is considered as an example to illustrate our approach.

2   Agent Petri Net Components and Their Semantics

Our definition of Petri net components is related to BRIC formalism [5], which enables to model a system as a collection of agent components. Each component is described both by its interface and by its basic components, and the behaviour of a basic component is formalised using coloured Petri nets. For the simplicity, and in order to make our approach more general, we will describe the behaviour of Petri net components by classical Labelled Petri nets instead of Coloured Petri nets since from theoretical point of view, any coloured Petri nets may be translated to classical Labelled Petri nets [11][1].

Backgrounds on Labelled Petri nets. Formally, a marked Petri net $N = (P, T, W, M_N)$ consists of a finite set P of places, a finite set T of transitions where $P \cap T = \varnothing$, a weighting function $W : P \times T \cup T \times P \to \mathbf{N}$, and $M_N : P \longrightarrow \mathbf{N}$ is an initial marking. We denote as $LN = (P, T, W, M_N, l)$ the (marked, labelled) Petri net (see [17] for further information) in which the events represent actions, which can be observable. It consists of a marked Petri net $N = (P, T, W, M_N)$ with a labelling function $l : T \longrightarrow A \cup \{\lambda\}$, where A is the set of services, that is the alphabet of observable actions, and $\{\lambda\}$ denotes the special unobservable action, which plays the usual role of an internal

---

[1] This result is valid if and only if the coloured Petri nets does not contain inhibitor arcs.

action, whose execution is under the control of the net alone. A sequence of actions w $\in$ A* $\cup$ {λ} is enabled under the marking M and its occurrence yields a marking M', noted M(w >> M', iff either M = M' and w = λ or there exists some sequence $\sigma \in$ T* such that l(σ) = w and M(σ > M'. (The first condition accounts for the fact that λ is the label image of the empty sequence of transitions).

Agent Petri net component. An agent Petri net component [5] is a labelled Petri net (P, T, W, M$_N$, l) together with two labelling functions *la* and *lr* such that *l* = *la* $\cup$ *lr* and :

> *la* : T $\longrightarrow$ SA $\cup$ {λ}, where SA is the set of Accepted Services,
> *lr* : T $\longrightarrow$ SR $\cup$ {λ}, where SR is the set of Requested Services.

This distinction allows to focusing either upon the server side of an agent or its client side. One hand it makes some services available to other agents and is capable of rendering these services. On the other hand it can request services from other agent components and needs these requests to be fulfilled. Each offered service is associated to one or several transitions, which may be requested by other agent components, and the service is available when one of these transitions is enabled. These transitions are referred to as *accept-transitions*. To request a service, a component includes one related transition for issuing the request (referred to as a *request-transition*). The interface of an agent is the union of the set of *accepted services* (that is the mapping of the accept-transitions) and the set of *requested services* (that is the mapping of request-transitions).

A Petri net component may be a server agent (and/ or resp. client agent) if and only if it accepts at least one service, that is SA $\neq \emptyset$ (resp. it requests at least one service, that is SR $\neq \emptyset$).

Composition of Petri net components. A Client agent C and a Server agent S are *composable* if SR$_c$ $\cap$ SA$_s$ $\neq \emptyset$; then they may be *composed* into a third Petri net component denoted by CS. When composing a Client Agent with a Server Agent, each accept-transition of this latter is provided with an *entry-place* for receiving the requests/replies. Then, the Client Agent is connected with the Server through this communication place by an arc from each request-transition towards the suitable entry-place and an arc from the suitable entry-place towards each accept-transition. In the following, we will assume that Petri net components which are composed are composable, without recalling the hypothesis SR$_c$ $\cap$ SA$_s$ $\neq \emptyset$.

Example. Figure 1 shows the compound *ACP* obtained from the composition of the two Petri net components AC and AP, describing different steps of Von Martial's agents conversation model [19]. The component *AC* is a basic Petri net component of agent *coordinator*; the component *AP* is a component of Agent *planner*. Each of these two components can send a message to another one (transition *send* may occur) and receive a message from each other (transition *receive* may occur).

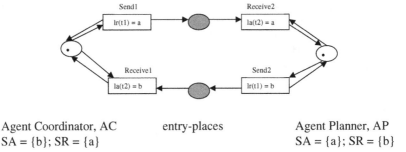

Agent Coordinator, AC   entry-places   Agent Planner, AP
SA = {b}; SR = {a}   SA = {a}; SR = {b}

Fig. 1. Agent Coordinator/Planner, *ACP, SA = SR = {a, b}*.

Semantics of Petri net components. Among the numerous semantics, which may be used to study the behaviour of Petri net components, we consider *Trace* semantics. Indeed, Trace semantics are the coarsest one; they are the less demanding and it is meaningless to compare nets whose languages are not comparable. However Trace semantics is related to the safe properties and it is often regarded as too weak for many applications because it is not able to express deadlock behaviour. Failure semantics have to be considered which are sensitive to liveness properties (deaddlock-free and Liveness).

Definition 2.1 (Trace and Language)
Let $N = (P, T, W, M_N, l)$ be a Petri net component.
$Tr(N) = \{\sigma \in T^*; M_N(\sigma >\}$ is the trace of N, i.e. the set of enabled transition sequences of N. The label image of the trace of N is its language $L(N) = l(Tr(N)) = \{w \in A^*; \exists \sigma \in Tr(N), l(\sigma) = w\}$.

Definition 2.2 (Failure)
The failure of the net N, noted by $F(N) = \{(\sigma, S); \sigma \in T^*, S \subseteq T$, and there exists some marking M such that $M_N(\sigma > M$, and $\forall t \in S$, <u>not</u> $(M(t >)\}$, are the pairs (σ, S) where σ is a sequence of transitions processed by a net, and S is a set of transitions that the net may refuse to perform after undergoing σ and reaching a stable marking[2].
The label image of the failure of N is $F(N) = F(N, l) = \{(w, X); w \in A^* \cup \{\lambda\}, X \subseteq A$, and there exists some marking M such that $M_N(\sigma > M, l(\sigma) = w$, M stable, and $\forall a \in X$, <u>not</u> $(M(a>>)\}$.

In this paper, we will consider only trace and failure semantics based upon the *la* labelling and the Accepted Services, without referring to the Requested Services. We adopt a top-down approach where the compound CS obtained from the composition of agent components C and S is considered as a refinement of C; this approach gives a greater place to Clients than to Servers. Similar results to the ones provided in this paper hold for the Client side of Petri net components, but the semantics must be based upon labelling *lr* instead of *la* [9]. In fact, adapting our requirements to a bot-

---

[2] A marking is *stable* if no unobservable action λ is enabled.

tom-up approach, is just achieved by focusing on the client side of the component nets instead of their server side.

For instance, let us consider the Petri net component Agent Coordinator/Planner, ACP, presented in figure 2. {send1.receive2.send2.receive1} is a word of the component's trace, (send1, receive1) is a pair of the component's failure, and then (a, b) is a pair of the component's failure image, that is (a, b) $\in$ F(ACP, 1). In the agent Petri net component Coordinator AC (resp. Planner, AP), presented in figure 1, we have (b*, a) $\in$ F(AC, la) and (a*, b) $\in$ F(AP, la).

3   Behavioural Substitutability for Petri Net Components

Our main interest is in capturing *substitutability* that is the ability to replace a component with another component without losing behaviours. From a software engineering point of view, a behavioural *substitutability* relation is a *subtyping* relation, that is a preorder relation (reflexive and transitive relation). Reflexivity allows that each component is substitutable by itself, and transitivity allows that if a component S_2 extends the capabilities of a component S_1 and a component S_3 extends the capabilities of S_2, then S_3 extends the capabilities of S_1. Our proposal is to base substitutability relations on the preorder which have been introduced to compare the behaviour of concurrent systems, such as the language, and failure (see [14] for a comparative study of these relations). Indeed, these relations are defined on a formal basis, without regard for the peculiarities of a given language, so that they are suitable for the study of the behavioural properties of any concurrent system. In the rest of this paper, we are interested in components having deterministic behaviour, since for non-deterministic behaviour checking a preorder become semi-decidable.

Operations on the Petri net components. To define our subtyping relations we need two basic operations on the nets, encapsulation and abstraction:

- *Encapsulation* of an action a from the component N removes all transitions labelled with a from N. Thus the *encapsulation operator* τ on $I \subseteq A$ removes some transitions from a Labelled net. Formally, given a Labelled Petri net N = (P, T, W, M_N, l), for each $I \subseteq A$, $\tau_I(N) = N' = (P, T', W', M_N, l')$ such that T'={t $\in$ T, l(t) $\notin$ I},W '= W $\cap$ ((P $\times$ T') $\cup$ (T' $\times$ P)), and l' = l $\cap$ (T'$\times$ A).

- *Abstraction* of an action a renames all a transitions into λ transitions; abstraction introduces new non-stable states, from which the refusal sets are not taken into account for the failure semantics. The *abstraction operator* λ labels as not observable and internal actions, some transitions of a Labelled net. Formally, given a Labelled Petri net N = (P, T, W, M_N, l), for each $I \subseteq A$, $\lambda_I(N) = N' = (P, T, W, M_N, l')$ such that l'(t) = l(t) = s, if t $\in$ T and s $\in$ A \ I, l'(t) = λ else.

Subtyping relations. For the definitions of our subtyping relations, we use *extension* [4], which is the most popular one as a choice for subtyping relation in Object-Oriented formalisms. It allows extension of functionality, that is the subtype may have new services in addition to the ones of the supertype. Extension has been used by

Nierstrasz in order to define the Request Substitutability (RS) preorder for active objects [12]. This relation requires that the sequences of service that a net can accept to process constitute a regular language, since when the behaviour is non-deterministic, reflexivity is lost (a component is not substitutable for itself). In our context we will use the RS preorder according to the Wegner and Zdonik's substitutability principle [18]. Then, there are basically two possibilities to treat the new services: we restrict them (encapsulation), and we hide them (abstraction). First, we start to define RS preorder on the la labelling and the accepted services, then using the encapsulation operator, we define the strong subtyping relation, and finally using the abstraction operator, we define the weak subtyping relation. Weak subtyping relation is less restrictive than strong subtyping relation.

Definition 3.1 (*Request Substitutability (RS) preorder*)

Let N_1 and N_2 be two components such that $SA_1 \subseteq SA_2$.

N_2 is less or equal to N_1 w.r.t *Request Substitutability (RS) preorder* denoted $N_2 \leq_{RS} N_1$ iff $la_1(L(N_1)) \subseteq la_2(L(N_2))$ and $\forall\ (w, X') \in F(N_2, la_2)$, $w \in la_1(L(N_1))$, there exists $(w, X) \in F(N_1, la_1)$ such that $X' \subseteq X$.

If N_2 is less or equal to N_1 w.r.t *Request Substitutability*, then the language of N_2 must include the language of N_1, and if the language of N_1 is performed by N_2, then its possible failures must be a subset of the corresponding failures of N_1.

Definition 3.2 (*Strong Subtyping*)

Let N_1 and N_2 be two Petri net Components such that $SA_1 \subseteq SA_2$.

N_2 is less or equal to N_1 w.r.t *Strong Substitutability*, denoted $N_2 \leq_{SS} N_1$, iff there exists a set $I \subseteq SA_2 \setminus SA_1$ such that $\tau_I(N_2) \leq_{RS} N_1$.

If N_2 is less or equal to N_1 w.r.t *Strong Substitutability*, then the component N_1 can be substituted by a component N_2 and the agent component interacting with N_1 will not be able to notice the difference since the new services added in the component N_2 are encapsulated, through the encapsulation operator τ_I.

Example: The Contract Net Protocol. As an example, let us take the *Contract-Net-Protocol (CNP)* [16]. For the simplicity we will consider only the manager part of the protocol. In figure 2, we show the (Manager's) component of the CNP protocol, and in figure 3, we show the (Manager's) component of the *FIPA-Iterated-CNP* [6], which is obtained from the CNP component by adding a basic component (represented in a dashed box)[3]. Initially the manager may accept one or more begin-of-contracts (action *BeginContract* may occur), then he announces the call for proposal (action *Cfp*) for the contract, and waits for biding from the contractors. When the bids are received, he evaluates and select the most interesting (transition *reject* or *accept* may occur). If there is one interesting bidder, the manager informs the successful bidder (action *award*). In the *FIPA-Iterated-CNP*, ICNP (figure 3), if there are no bids once the deadline occurs (simulated by the occurrence of the transition timeOut), that is the manager does not receive any bids from the contractors, it reformulates a new offer

---

[3] When the label of a transition is not empty ($\{\lambda\}$), it is written inside its box.

and re-announces the task: the manager makes a request to the basic component (action *Beginrepropose*); this latest component makes a new definition of the call for proposal (transition *repropose*), and actives the basic component CNP (action *Begincontract).* It is easy to prove that ICNP $\leq_{SS}$ CNP holds, since with I = {*Beginrepropose*}, we have $\tau_I(ICNP) \leq_{RS}$ CNP.

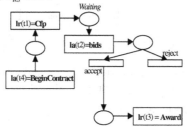

SA = {BeginContract, bids}, SR={Cfp, Award}.

Fig. 2. The Manager's Contract-Net Protocol component, CNP.

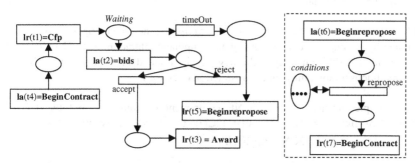

SA = {BeginContract, bids, Beginrepropose},
SR = {Cfp, Award, Beginrepropose, BeginContract}.

Fig. 3. The Manager's FIPA-Iterated-Contract-Net Protocol component, ICNP.

Now, let us take another implementation of the Manager's FIPA-Iterated contract net Protocol component, I2CNP (shown in figure 4). It is obtained by adding a basic component to the CNP component, which is different from the one added in figure 3. In this case, the basic component makes a new definition of the call for proposal, once it requests to (action *repropose*) and gets (action *Nproposal*) from another component of the system. It easy to prove that I2CNP $\leq_{SS}$ CNP, but neither ICNP $\leq_{SS}$ I2CNP nor I2CNP $\leq_{SS}$ ICNP holds, that is ICNP and I2CNP are not related by strong substitutability relation. This is captured by the second type of Substitutability, called *Weak Substitutability*, which is less restrictive than *Strong Substitutability*.

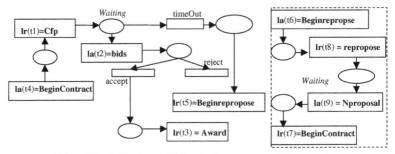

$$SA = \{BeginContract, bids, Beginrepropose, Nproposal\},$$
$$SR = \{Cfp, Award, Beginrepropose, BeginContract, repropose\}.$$

Fig. 4. The Manager's FIPA-Iterated-Contract-Net Protocol component, I2CNP.

Definition 3.3 *(Weak Subtyping)*

Let N_1 and N_2 be two Petri net components that $SA_1 \subseteq SA_2$.
N_2 is less or equal to N_1 w.r.t *Weak Substitutability*, denoted $N_2 \leq_{WS} N_1$, iff there exists a set $I \subseteq SA_2 \setminus SA_1$ such that $\lambda_1(N_2) \leq_{RS} N_1$.

If N_2 is less or equal to N_1 w.r.t *Weak Substitutability,* then the component N_1 can be substituted by a component N_2 and the agent component interacting with N_1 will not be able to notice the difference since the new services added in the component N_2 are considered unobservable, through the abstraction operator λ_1.

As an example, let us take the ICNP component of figure 3, and the I2CNP component of figure 4; we prove that I2CNP $\leq_{WS}$ ICNP holds; in fact with I = {Nproposal}, we have $\lambda_1(I2CNP) \leq_{RS}$ ICNP.

Now, we have two subtyping relations for extension of functionality in Petri net components: weak and strong subtyping relations. Strong subtyping relation is stronger than weak subtyping relation.

Property 3.1 (hierarchy of subtyping relations)

The subtyping relations form a hierarchy: $\leq_{SS} \Rightarrow \leq_{WS}$.

Property preservation. Petri net components allow to analyse the behaviour of MAS in an incremental way, since the behaviour of a compound may be deduced from the behaviour of its components [7]. Then, we show that the strong and weak behavioural substitutability relations are compositional for the components composition operation. This property is necessary to ensure the compatibility of the substitutability relations with the incremental design of MAS; we investigate the substitutability principle by property preservation for these two substitutability relations and prove that they are suited for modelling extension in MAS; they can be characterised by property preservation in the following way: weak subtyping is the right relation if we would like to preserve safety property (language) and deadlock-free property, and strong subtyping is useful to preserve both safety and liveness property (deadlock-free and liveness). All these results are available in [8].

4   Related Works

From validation and specification of MAS point of view, [3] proposes a model formalising the joint intention model by generic and refined components. It enables to design a system by the composition of several layers. The language description is based on temporal logic, which allows to validate the properties of the system and to specify both the static and dynamic aspects; unfortunately, the reuse of generic components is not well defined. Recently [15] proposes CPDL language (Communication Protocol Description Language) based on the combination of components called micro-protocols, which represent pieces of an interaction. CPDL is based on finite state automata including extra characteristics such as tokens, time, and loop predicate. The combination of micro-protocols is done with some logic formulae encompassing a sequence of micro-protocols. The authors address the reuse of components in the context of the contract net protocol by refinement. Their approach is related to our Strong subtyping relation by adding formulae. Nevertheless this requires that no formula be non-deterministic and that two formulae cannot be fired at the same time. In addition the preservation of property is not addressed, and no semantics are associated to the refinement.

5   Conclusion

This paper proposes formal semantics for the definition of behavioural substitutability relations for agent components in the area of open MAS. It consists of requirements that any substitutability relation ought to satisfy, and it is based upon the preorder relations commonly considered in the study of concurrent systems. It is in accordance with the principle of substitutability and extends Liskov's approach [10]. We have proposed two relations which are suitable as behavioural substitutability relations for Petri net components: weak subtyping relation is the right relation if we would like to preserve safety properties, and strong subtyping relation is useful to preserve both safety and liveness properties. The results can be applied in an incremental design with inheritance by checking what kind of subtype a sub-component is, and then deduce what properties of the super-component are preserved.

It is clear that the approach presented in this paper could be fruitfully applied to other formalisms supporting agent components, where the behaviour of a compound may be deduced from the behaviour of its components. The next intended problem is to apply our approach to compositional multi-agent Languages such Agent UML (Unified Modelling Language) [2]. Our intention is to apply the semantics presented in this paper to activity diagrams and state charts together with the concept of components.

References

1. AgentLink News, Issue 3, july 1999.
2. B. Bauer, J. Odell. Extending UML for the Specification of Interaction Protocols, ICMAS 2000, IEEE Computer Society Press, 2000.
3. F. M.T.Brazier, C. M. Jonker, J. Treur. Formalisation of a Cooperation Model Based on Joint Intentions. ATAL'96, LNCS/LNAI 1193, pp141-155.
4. E. Brinksma, g. Scollo, and Ch. Steenbergen. LOTOS specifications, their implementations and their tests. In Protocol Specification, Testing and Verification VI, pages 349-358, Elsiever, 1987.
5. J.Ferber. Les systèmes multi-agents : vers une intelligence collective, InterEditions Paris, 1995.
6. FIPA. Specification Part 2: Agent Communication Language, November 1997.
7. N. Hameurlain. Composition et Substitution d'agents: sémantique et préservation de propriétés; in proceedings of JFIADSMA'01, pp 135-147, Hermès Science publications, 2001.
8. N. Hameurlain. Behavioural Subtyping and Property Preservation for Active Objects; Fifth IFIP International Conference on Formal Methods for Open Object-Based Distributed Systems, FMOODS'02, Chapman and Hall, March 2002 (to appear).
9. N. Hameurlain, C. Sibertin-Blanc. Behavioural Types in CoOperative Objects; Second International Workshop on Semantics of Objects As Processes, SOAP'99. BRICS NS-99-2, Hüttel et al. (eds.), pp 29-38, 1999.
10. B. H. Liskov, J. M. Wing. A Behavioral Notion of Subtyping; in ACM Trans. on Programming Languages and Systems, Vol 16, n° 6, Nov. 1994.
11. T. Murata. Petri Nets: Properties, Analysis and Applications; Proc. of the IEEE, vol. 77, N° 4, pp. 541-580.
12. O. Nierstrasz. Regular Types for Active Objects; in ACM Sigplan Notices, 28 (10); Proceedings of OOPSLA'93, pp. 1-15, 1993.
13. O. Nierstrasz, T. D. Meijler. Requirements for a Composition Language, ECOOP'94 Workshop on Models and Languages for Coordination of Parallelism and Distribution, LNCS 924, Springer-Verlag, 1994.
14. L. Pomello, G. Rozenberg, C. Simone. A Survey of Equivalence Notions for Net Based System. Advances in Petri Nets 1992; G. Rozenberg Ed., LNCS 609, Springer-Verlag 1992.
15. J-L. Koning, M-P. Huget. A Semi-formal Specification Language Dedicated to interaction Protocols. 10th European-Japanese Conference on Information Modelling and Knowledge Bases, IOS Press, May 2000.
16. G. R. Smith. The Contract Net Protocol: High-Level Communication and Control in Distributed Problem Solver. IEEE Transaction on Computers, Vol. C-29, N° 12, 1980, pp 1104-1113.
17. W. Vogler. Modular Construction and Partial Order Semantics of Petri Nets. LNCS 625, Springer-Verlag, 1992.
18. P. Wegner, S. Zdonik. Inheritance as an Incremental Modification Mechanism, or What Is and Isn't Like; in Proc. ECOOP 88, LNCS 322, Springer-Verlag, pp. 55-77, 1988.
19. M-J. Yoo. Une Approche Componentielle pour la Modélisation d'Agents Coopératifs et leur Validation, Ph. D Thesis, University of Paris 6, 2000.

A Modelling Environment for Mind and Matter Aspects of Intentional Behaviour

Catholijn M. Jonker, Jan Treur, and Wouter C.A. Wijngaards

Department of Artificial Intelligence, Vrije Universiteit Amsterdam,
De Boelelaan 1081a, 1081 HV Amsterdam, The Netherlands
{jonker,treur,wouterw}@cs.vu.nl
http://www.cs.vu.nl/~{jonker,treur,wouterw}

Abstract. In this paper the internal dynamics of mental states, in particular states based on beliefs, desires and intentions, is formalised using a temporal language. A software environment is presented that can be used to specify, simulate and analyse temporal dependencies between mental states in relation to traces of them. If also relevant data on internal physical states over time are available, these can be analysed with respect to their relation to mental states.

1 Introduction

Dynamics has become an important focus within Cognitive Science in recent years; e.g., [12]. As one of the aspects, the dynamics of the interaction with the external world, and its implications for the representational content and dynamics of mental states have received attention; e.g., [2], [5]. Another important aspect is the internal dynamics of mental states, as can be found, for example in the dynamics of intentional notions (such as beliefs, desires and intentions) and their interaction with each other and with the external world. An example of a pattern for such internal dynamics is: if a desire and an additional reason (in the form of a belief about the world) to do some action are both present, then the intention to do the action is generated.

In this paper the internal dynamics of mental states, based on beliefs, desires and intentions (which also may include dynamics of the interaction of mental states with the external world) is addressed. A modelling environment is presented that can be used to specify, simulate and analyse models for these dynamics taking into account mental aspects (mind), physical aspects (matter), or both. A basic notion underlying the modelling is the notion of functional role or profile of a mental state, cf. [3].

A question is how such functional roles can be modelled in a precise and formal manner that stays close to the original idea. In this paper functional roles of belief, desire and intention states are modelled in a *temporal language* in such a manner that causal relationships are formalised by temporal dependencies they entail. Since dynamics is a phenomenon occurring over real time, the real numbers are used as time frame; no approximation by a sequence of fixed discrete time steps is needed. The temporal language can be used on the one hand for the *specification* of temporal relationships between mental states involving beliefs, desires and intentions (and between mental states and the external world). Such a temporal specification can be used to express a theory for these dynamics. On the other hand the language is the basis of a *software environment* that has been implemented and which can be used for the simulation and analysis of the internal dynamics.

B. Dunin-Kęplicz and E. Nawarecki (Eds.): CEEMAS 2001, LNAI 2296, pp. 141–150, 2002.

Simulation takes place within this software environment by generating consequences over time from the specified set of temporal relationships, according to the paradigm of executable temporal logic [1]. To predict the internal dynamics, the software takes the temporal relationships, some initial values, and a pattern of environment dynamics to produce implied traces of internal belief desire and intention states. *Analysis* of given traces (in comparison to certain temporal relationships) is supported by the software environment as well. For example, these given traces can have the form of successively attributed intentional states over time. The automated support displays any discrepancies between such data and a background theory of the dynamics expressed by (assumed) temporal relationships. Another use of the software environment is the analysis of the relationship between mental and physical internal states. If observations (e.g., by advanced scanning techniques) can be made of the physical states assumed to be related to mental states, these empirical physical traces can be used as input, after which the software environment generates the related mental traces and checks the temporal relationships.

In Section 2 the intentional notions on which the paper focuses are introduced; for each type of intentional notion its functional role with respect to the other notions is discussed informally. In Section 3 the formalisation for the dynamics is presented. An example is discussed in Section 4. Subsequently in Section 5 the software environment, and some results are presented. Section 6 addresses the use of the environment when relevant physical internal state data over time are available, while Section 7 concludes with a discussion.

2   The Intentional Notions Addressed

The intentional notions from the BDI model (belief, desire and intention), are addressed in a static manner in e.g. [13], [11]; in our approach they are used in temporal perspective, see Figure 1. For an approach exploiting such a temporal perspective to attribute intentional notions on the basis of observed behaviour, see [10].

Beliefs are based on observation of the outside world in the present or in the past. Beliefs are modified in response to changes perceived in the external world. A belief denoted by the property $\beta(x, pos)$ means that the agent thinks that the property x holds. The property $\beta(x, neg)$ means that the agent thinks that the property x does not hold. Beliefs can be incorrect (a *false belief*), e.g. due to some faulty sensory input.

It is possible to have both the belief that something holds and the belief that it does not hold, at the same time. Although such a state of affairs may have deplorable consequences for the agent, it is expressible.

Desires are states of the world or changes to the world that are desired. Desires are formed based on the agent's history. Desires are created and stay in existence for a while. The property $\delta(x)$ denotes a desire for x. The desire can be for a situation or an action. The desires the agent has at one time can conflict with each other.

From the set of desires that exist in a given situation some can be chosen to be pursued by creating an *intention* for them. For example, when a desire exists and an additional reason ρ (i.e. a particular co-occurrence of beliefs) also holds then an intention to fulfil the desire is created. This intention lasts until the desire or the additional reason for it disappears. *Additional reasons* perform at least two functions. Firstly, they inhibit the selection of conflicting intentions. Secondly, they cause the selection of particular intentions when those intentions are appropriate. The first and second uses can overlap. For example, if an animal obtains food, it could intend to eat it, or store it for later use. The intention to store the food for later, could need the reason that winter is approaching, selecting the intention when appropriate. The intention to store the food is used under the condition (additional reason) that it is not hungry, preventing a conflict with the intention to eat the food, which it only does when hungry.

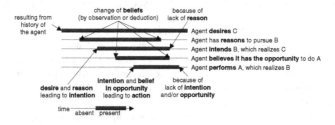

Fig. 1. BDI notions over time

The intentions are states or changes in the world that are intended to be accomplished. An intention is denoted $\iota(x)$. The intentions of an agent at a particular time do not conflict with each other. When the intention exists and it is believed that an *opportunity* o presents itself, the *action* is performed. The action is undertaken until the intention or the belief in the opportunity for it disappears. An action atom θ of the form $\alpha(x)$ refers to process x in the external world. Actions can have the intended effect, but can also fail or produce unexpected results.

3 Dynamical Formalisation

In BDI-logics such as [13], [11], internal processes are considered instantaneous. However, a more sincere formalisation is obtained if also internal processes take time. In this paper real time is used (represented by real numbers); time is not measured in computational steps. Real time temporal relationships are defined that take into account the delay between cause and effect, together with the durations of those cause and effect situations. The delay and durations may be measured. In this setting, the BDI-notions can be defined by the functional role they play. In the following the term *agent* is used to refer to the subject and *system* is used to refer to both the agent and the external world together. Intervals of real numbers are denoted like: [x, y) meaning $\{p \in \mathbb{R} \mid p \geq x \land p < y\}$. Thus, '[' or ']' stands for a closed end of the interval, and '(' or ')' stands for an open end of the interval.

Definition (state properties)

The states of the system are characterised by *state properties*. The state properties are formalised using (logical) formulae over a specific ontology. For an ontology Ont, the set of *atoms* AT(Ont) contains the atomic properties expressed in terms of the ontology. The set of *state properties* SPROP(Ont) contains all the propositional formulas built out of the atoms using standard propositional connectives. More specifically, the following ontologies are used. Firstly, *world state properties* express properties of a particular situation in the material world, using ontology EWOnt. Secondly, the internal physical state properties of the agent are expressed using IntOntP. The combined physical ontology is OntP $=_{def}$ EWOnt ∪ IntOntP. Thirdly, the ontology for internal mental state properties is denoted by IntOntM. The ontology for all state properties is denoted by AllOnt $=_{def}$ EWOnt ∪ IntOntP ∪ IntOntM.

Definition (states)

a) A *physical state* P of the system is an assignment of truth values {true, false} to the set of physical state atoms AT(OntP) of the system. The set of all possible physical states is denoted PS.

b) A (partial) *mental state* M of the system is an assignment of truth values {true, false, unknown} to the set of internal mental state atoms, AT(IntOntM). The set of all possible mental states is denoted by MS. Three valued states are used to avoid commitment to closed world assumptions or explicit specification of negative conclusions.

c) At each time-point the system is in one state. This state is from the set States $=_{def}$ PS x MS.

d) The standard satisfaction relation ⊨ between states and state properties is used: s ⊨ φ means that property φ holds in state s.

Definition (traces)

The system when viewed over a period of time, will produce several states consecutively. The function T returning the state for each time point is called a trace, T: ℝ → States. The notation state(T, t, m), where T is a trace, t ∈ ℝ and m ∈ {physical, mental}, means the physical or mental state at time t in trace T. The notation state(T, t) is by definition T(t). Thus using the last notation both physical and mental terms can be used interchangeably, under the assumption that PS ∩ MS = ∅. The set of all possibly occurring traces is denoted W.

The behaviour of the agent and environment is defined by a set of traces. Temporal relationships between the state properties over time specify such a set of traces: they express certain constraints on the relative timing of the occurrence of state properties. These constraints on the timing reflect a causal relationship between the arguments.

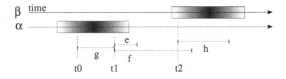

Fig. 2. The time relationships between variables

Definition (the '⇢' relation and the '•—' relation)

Let α , β ∈ SPROP(AllOnt). The state property α *follows* state property β, denoted by α $\rightarrowtail_{e, f, g, h}$ β, with time delay interval [e, f] and duration parameters g and h if ∀T ∈ W ∀t1:

[∀t ∈ [t1 - g, t1) : state(T, t) ⊨ α ⇒ ∃d ∈ [e, f] ∀t ∈ [t1 + d, t1 + d + h) : state(T, t) ⊨ β]

Conversely, the state property β *originates from* state property α, denoted by $\alpha \bullet\!\!-\!\!\!-_{e,f,g,h} \beta$, with time delay in [e, f] and duration parameters g and h if $\forall T \in W \; \forall t2$:

$[\forall t \in [t2, t2 + h) : state(T, t) \models \beta \Rightarrow \exists d \in [e, f] \; \forall t \in [t2 - d - g, t2 - d) \; state(T, t) \models \alpha]$

If both $\alpha \rightarrow\!\!\!\rightarrow_{e,f,g,h} \beta$, and $\alpha \bullet\!\!-\!\!\!-_{e,f,g,h} \beta$ hold, this is denoted by: $\alpha \bullet\!\!\rightarrow\!\!\!\rightarrow_{e,f,g,h} \beta$.

The relationships between the variables α, β, e, f, g, h, t0, t1 and t2 are depicted in Figure 2.

Definition (continuous)

Let $\varphi, \psi \in$ SPROP(AllOnt). The relationship $\varphi \bullet\!\!\rightarrow\!\!\!\rightarrow_{e,f,g,h} \psi$ is continuous if:
$\forall T \in W \; \forall t0 \; \forall t1 > t0$: if $(\forall t \in [t0, t1) : state(T, t) \models \varphi)$ then

$\quad (\forall t2, t3 \in [t0+g+e, t1+f+h]: state(T, t2) \models \psi \wedge state(T, t3) \models \psi)$
$\quad \Rightarrow (\forall t4 \in (t2, t3): state(T, t4) \models \psi)$.

Loosely phrased, continuous means that when φ holds for a continued length of time, then ψ will also hold for a continued length of time, without gaps.

Lemma

a) If T is a given trace, $\varphi, \psi \in$ SPROP(AllOnt), $\varphi \rightarrow\!\!\!\rightarrow_{e,f,g,h} \psi$ and $(\forall t \in [t0, t0+g) : state(T, t) \models \varphi)$ then a *guaranteed result* exists:
$\quad (\forall t \in [t0+g+f, t0+g+e+h) : state(T, t) \models \psi)$.
b) If T is a given trace, $\varphi, \psi \in$ SPROP(AllOnt), $\varphi \bullet\!\!-\!\!\!-_{e,f,g,h} \psi$ and $(\forall t \in [t0, t0+h) : state(T, t) \models \psi)$ then a *guaranteed precondition* exists:
$\quad (\forall t \in [t0-e-g, t0-f) : state(T, t) \models \varphi)$.

Proposition

If $\varphi \bullet\!\!\rightarrow\!\!\!\rightarrow_{e,f,g,h} \psi$ and $e + h \geq f$, then $\varphi \bullet\!\!\rightarrow\!\!\!\rightarrow_{e,f,g,h} \psi$ is continuous.

An interval of ψ of [t0+g+f, t1+e+h) can be seen to hold continuously when given an interval of φ of [t0, t1), using the lemma of guaranteed result, to assure there are no gaps in between. In order for the result to keep holding, when the antecedent keeps holding, the parameters of $\bullet\!\!\rightarrow\!\!\!\rightarrow$ should have certain values. If $e + h \geq f$ then for each application of the definition of the relation we can be sure that the period [t1 + f, t1 + e + h] holds. To see how this can be, consider that a range of resulting intervals is possible, with at the earliest [t1 + e, t1 + e + h] and at the last [t1 + f, t1 + f + h]. With $e + h \geq f$ holding, the two intervals will overlap, this overlap is exactly the interval [t1 + f, t1 + e + h]. Thus if $e + h \geq f$ and the φ holds in a long interval [t3, t4], where $t4 - t3 \geq g$ then ψ will hold in the interval [t3 + f + g, t4 + e + h].

Definition (internal belief representation)

Let $\varphi \in$ SPROP(OntP) be a physical state property.
a) The internal mental state property $\beta \in$ SPROP(IntOntM) is called an *internal belief representation* for φ with time delay e and duration parameters f, g if: $\varphi \bullet\!\!\rightarrow\!\!\!\rightarrow_{e,f,g,h} \beta$.

b) Two belief representations β_1 and β_2 are *exclusive* if
$\quad \forall T \in W: \neg \exists t: state(T, t) \models \beta_1 \wedge \beta_2$.

In a) of this definition the $\twoheadrightarrow$ part is necessary, as the occurrence of external state φ should lead to the creation of the belief β. The $\bullet\!\!-$ part must also hold, since a belief β must have an explanation of having being created, in this case φ. This consideration also holds for intentions and desires in an analogical fashion.

When the world situation suddenly changes, the beliefs may follow suit. The belief β_1 and the belief β_2 of two opposite world properties should not hold at the same time; they should be exclusive. As the external world state fluctuates, the beliefs should change accordingly, but never should there be both a belief for a world property and a belief for the opposite world property at the same time. If two belief representations for opposite world properties are exclusive, this inconsistency is avoided, and the belief representations are called *non-conflicting*.

Definition (internal intention representation)

Let $\alpha \in$ SPROP(OntP) be a physical state property, $\beta \in$ SPROP(IntOntM) a belief representation for α and $\theta \in$ SPROP(IntOntM) an action atom. The internal mental state property $\gamma \in$ SPROP(IntOntM) is called an *internal intention representation* for action θ and opportunity α with delay e, f and duration parameters g, h if $\gamma \wedge \beta \bullet\!\!\twoheadrightarrow_{e,f,g,h} \theta$.

Definition (internal desire representation)

Let $\rho \in$ SPROP(OntP) be a physical state property, β a belief representation for ρ and γ an intention representation. The internal mental state property $\delta \in$ SPROP(IntOntM) is an *internal desire representation* for intention γ and additional reason ρ with delay e, f and duration parameters g, h if $\delta \wedge \beta \bullet\!\!\twoheadrightarrow_{e,f,g,h} \gamma$.

4   An Example Formalisation

In order to demonstrate the formalisation and automated support put forward in this paper, a simple example description is presented. In this example, the test subject is a common laboratory mouse, that is presented with cheese. Mostly, the mouse will try to eat the cheese, but a transparent screen can block access to the cheese. First, an intentional perspective on the mouse is constructed. Then, assuming a mouse-brain-scanning-technique, it is analysed how specific brain area activity can be correlated to the intentional notions.

The formalised physical external world description of this experiment has two properties; screen_present and cheese_present. The internal physical state has the property hungry. The intentional description of the mouse makes use of the following beliefs on the relevant parts of the world for this experiment: β(hungry, pos), β(hungry, neg), β(screen_present, pos), β(screen_present, neg), β(cheese_present, pos) and β(cheese_present, neg). These beliefs are all based on perceptions by the mouse.

The beliefs should persist continuously if the perceptions stay the same. So if φ holds in the interval [t0, t2) then the belief will hold in a continuous resultant interval. The timing parameters of the belief observations indeed guarantee that a continuous belief representation is obtained.

When the world situation changes, the beliefs change. The g and h of the belief generation relations are chosen equal, so that the belief representations become double-seamless: the belief in a world property starts to be there exactly at the same time the belief in the opposite property stops to be there. By fixing the delays, as done in the double-seamless settings, the belief representations are non-conflicting.

Furthermore, the intentional description includes desires. If the mouse is hungry, it desires to eat, δ(eat_food). When sufficient additional reason, ρ_1, is present – the belief that there is cheese – the mouse will intend to eat the cheese, ι(eat_cheese). When the mouse believes that the opportunity, o_1, presents itself, the screen not being present, the mouse will eat the cheese, the action denoted by α(eat_cheese).

The temporal relationships for the intentional description of the mouse are given below. All e, f, g and h values for the temporal relationships are given in sequence, after the $\bullet\!\!\rightarrow\!\!\!\rightarrow$ symbol, in a certain time unit (e.g., 0.1 second). In this example only the positive and negative beliefs need to be present, in general however, the predicates of the properties could contain numbers to describe the world in more detail.

·· **Sensing** ··

hungry $\bullet\!\!\rightarrow\!\!\!\rightarrow_{1,\,5,\,10,\,10}$ β(hungry, pos) $\wedge$ $\neg\beta$(hungry, neg).

$\neg$hungry $\bullet\!\!\rightarrow\!\!\!\rightarrow_{1,\,5,\,10,\,10}$ β(hungry, neg) $\wedge$ $\neg\beta$(hungry, pos).

cheese_present $\bullet\!\!\rightarrow\!\!\!\rightarrow_{1,\,5,\,10,\,10}$ β(cheese_present, pos) $\wedge$ $\neg\beta$(cheese_present, neg).

$\neg$cheese_present $\bullet\!\!\rightarrow\!\!\!\rightarrow_{1,\,5,\,10,\,10}$ β(cheese_present, neg) $\wedge$ $\neg\beta$(cheese_present, pos).

screen_present $\bullet\!\!\rightarrow\!\!\!\rightarrow_{1,\,5,\,10,\,10}$ β(screen_present, pos) $\wedge$ $\neg\beta$(screen_present, neg).

$\neg$screen_present $\bullet\!\!\rightarrow\!\!\!\rightarrow_{1,\,5,\,10,\,10}$ β(screen_present, neg) $\wedge$ $\neg\beta$(screen_present, pos).

·· **Internal Processes** ··

β(hungry, pos) $\bullet\!\!\rightarrow\!\!\!\rightarrow_{1,\,5,\,10,\,10}$ δ(eat_food).

δ(eat_food) $\wedge$ ρ_1 $\bullet\!\!\rightarrow\!\!\!\rightarrow_{1,\,5,\,10,\,10}$ ι(eat_cheese).

ι(eat_cheese) $\wedge$ o_1 $\bullet\!\!\rightarrow\!\!\!\rightarrow_{1,\,5,\,10,\,10}$ α(eat_cheese).

ρ_1 = β(cheese_present, pos).
o_1 = β(screen_present, neg).

·· **World Processes** ··

α(eat_cheese) $\wedge$ cheese_present $\bullet\!\!\rightarrow\!\!\!\rightarrow_{1,\,5,\,10,\,10}$ $\neg$hungry.

In order to derive the converse of the previous temporal relationships, a temporal variant of Clark's completion is used [7].

$\neg\beta$(hungry, pos) $\bullet\!\!\rightarrow\!\!\!\rightarrow_{1,\,5,\,10,\,10}$ $\neg\delta$(eat_food).

$\neg(\delta$(eat_food) $\wedge$ ρ_1) $\bullet\!\!\rightarrow\!\!\!\rightarrow_{1,\,5,\,10,\,10}$ $\neg\iota$(eat_cheese).

$\neg(\iota$(eat_cheese) $\wedge$ o_1) $\bullet\!\!\rightarrow\!\!\!\rightarrow_{1,\,5,\,10,\,10}$ $\neg\alpha$(eat_cheese).

$\neg(\alpha$(eat_cheese) $\wedge$ cheese_present) $\bullet\!\!\rightarrow\!\!\!\rightarrow_{1,\,5,\,10,\,10}$ hungry.

Also, at the start of derivation the intentional notions will be false, in particular the mouse initially does not believe anything. The starting value of each property is given for $e + \lambda(f\text{-}e) + g$ time units.

5 Implementation of the Software Environment

A software environment has been made which implements the temporal formalisation of the internal dynamic behaviour of the agent. Following the paradigm of executable temporal logic, cf. [1], a 2700 line simulation program was written in C++ to automatically generate the consequences of the temporal relationships. The program is a special purpose tool to derive the results reasoning forwards in time, as in executable temporal logic.

The graph in Figure 3 shows the reaction of the mouse to changes in the environment. Time is on the horizontal axis. The world state properties and the intentional notions are listed on the vertical axis. The parameter λ is fixed at 0.25. A dark box on top of the line indicates the notion is true, and a lighter box below the line indicates that the notion is false.

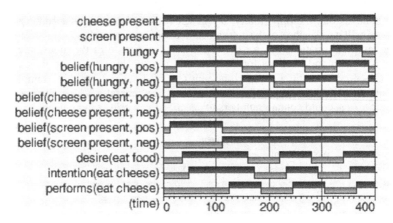

Fig. 3. Simulation results: initially cheese and screen are present; later the screen is removed

As can be seen, the mouse is not hungry at the very start, but quickly becomes hungry. It desires to eat the cheese, and intends to do so, but the screen blocks the opportunity to do so. When the screen is removed, the mouse eats. After a while it stops eating, as it is not hungry anymore. Subsequently it enters a cycle where it becomes hungry, eats, and becomes hungry again. Intention revision is handled here by the leads-to operator and its duration parameters. After the consequent duration has passed, the intention is no longer required to hold. For example see Figure 3, where the intention to eat cheese ceases to hold, shortly after the desire to eat stops to hold.

Another program, of about 4000 lines in C++, has been constructed that takes an existing trace of behaviour as input and creates an interpretation of what happens in this trace and a check whether all temporal relationships hold. The program is configured (amongst others) by giving a set of intentional temporal relationships, see Section 4 for example relationships. The program marks any deficiencies in the trace compared with what should be there due to the temporal relationships. If a relationship does not hold completely, this is marked by the program. The program produces yellow marks for unexpected events. At these moments, the event is not produced by any temporal relationship; the event cannot be explained. The red marks indicate that an event has not happened, that should have happened. In addition to checking whether the rules hold, the checker produces an informal reading of the trace. The reading is automatically generated, using a simple substitution, from the information in the intentional trace.

6 Mind and Matter: Relating Physical and Mental States

In the formalisation, each internal state has a mental state and a physical state portion. The physical state is described by a set of (real number) value assignments to continuous variables. The automated support also supports the assignment of internal physical properties to intentional notions; also material data can be used as input. For the assignment of physical properties to intentions, each intentional property has one physical property associated. The values true and false of the intentional notion are assigned to particular ranges of values of the material in the data.

For the example, it is assumed that a scanner provides signal intensities for different brain areas, for modern scanning usage see [4]. Some of these may correlate with the intentions as described above. An assumed example assignment of intentional notions to the signal intensities of specific brain areas is given in Table 1.

The simulation program, having derived an intentional trace, can output a physical trace based on it. The physical trace consists of the possible ranges of values for all physical state variables in each time-interval.

The checker can read back a physical trace as generated by the simulator, but it can also read back a trace where for time-points a value for each physical state variable is given. It will then interpret this physical trace, comparing the given (range of) value(s) to the true and false ranges as given per intentional notion. It will then check whether all the given temporal relationships hold correctly.

Table 1. Related physical and mental state properties.

Intentional notion in SPROP(IntOntM)	Physical condition in SPROP(IntOntP)
β(hungry, pos)	intensity of area_01 $\geq$ 1.0
β(hungry, neg)	intensity of area_02 < 1.0
β(cheese_present, pos)	intensity of area_03 $\geq$ 1.0
β(cheese_present, neg)	intensity of area_04 < 1.0
β(screen_present, pos)	intensity of area_05 $\geq$ 1.0
β(screen_present, neg)	intensity of area_06 < 1.0
δ(eat_food)	intensity of area_07 $\geq$ 1.0
ι(eat_cheese)	intensity of area_08 $\geq$ 1.0
α(eat_cheese)	intensity of area_09 $\geq$ 1.0

Using the interpretation and checking of relationships the program can assist in the verification of hypothetical assignments of physical properties to intentional notions, and the verification of hypothetical intentional temporal relationships.

7 Discussion

This paper addresses formalisation of the internal dynamics of mental states involving beliefs, desires and intentions. In available literature on formalisation of intentional behaviour, such as [13], [11], the internal dynamics of intentional mental states are ignored. The formalisation of the internal dynamics of mental states introduced in this paper is based on a real time temporal language. Within this (quite expressive) temporal language a specific format is defined which can be used to specify temporal relationships that describe (constraints on) the dynamics of mental states (and their interaction with the external world). Specifications in this specific format have the advantage that they can be used to perform simulation, based on the paradigm of executable temporal logic, [1]. The approach subsumes discrete simulation, for example as performed in Dynamical Systems Theory [12] as a special case (with $e=f=1$ and $g=h=0$).

A software environment has been implemented including three programs. The first simulates the consequences of a set of temporal relationships of mental states over time. The second program interprets a given trace of intentional states over time (in terms of beliefs, desires and intentions), and makes an analysis whether the temporal relationships hold, and, if not, points at the discrepancies. A third program takes into account physical states and their (possible) relation to beliefs, desires and intentions. Physical traces, for example obtained by advanced scanning techniques [4, pp. 59-105], can be input and analysed with respect to possible interpretations in terms of mental properties such as beliefs, desires and intentions.

An example has been presented and explained: the internal dynamics of intentional eating behaviour of a mouse that in an experimental setting has to deal with a screen and cheese. The formalisation and supporting software environment is useful for simulation of the internal dynamics of mental states. In addition, they are useful for checking the attribution of intentions, (e.g., [8]) and predicting behaviour based on an attribution of intentions. Another use is if advanced scanning techniques provide empirical data. These data can be related to mental states and checked on correctness with respect to the required dynamics. The checking program can easily be used to check various assignments, and, for example, the number of bad marks per assignment. In this manner an assignment of materials to intentional notions can be selected from a set of hypothetically possible assignments.

In further research the attribution of intentional notions to explain the behaviour of some of the simpler biological organisms is addressed. Some first results have shown that the nutrient import behaviour, and the dynamics and control of the internal metabolism of the bacterium *E. Coli* can be explained using these notions.

References

1. Barringer, H., M. Fisher, D. Gabbay, R. Owens, & M. Reynolds (1996). *The Imperative Future: Principles of Executable Temporal Logic*, Research Studies Press Ltd. and John Wiley & Sons.
2. Bickhard, M.H. (1993). Representational Content in Humans and Machines. *Journal of Experimental and Theoretical Artificial Intelligence*, 5, pp. 285-333.
3. Bickle, J. (1998). *Psychoneural Reduction: The New Wave*. MIT Press, Cambridge, Massachusetts.
4. Chen, L. & Zhuo, Y., eds. (2001). *Proceedings of the Third International Conference on Cognitive Science (ICCS'2001)*. Press of University of Science and Technology of China.
5. Christensen, W.D. & C.A. Hooker (2000). *Representation and the Meaning of Life*. In: [5].
6. Clapin, H., Staines, P. & Slezak, P. (2000). *Proc. of the Int. Conference on Representation in Mind: New Theories of Mental Representation*, 27-29th June 2000, University of Sydney. To be published by Elsevier.
7. Clark, K.L. (1978). Negation as Failure. *Logic and Data Bases*. Gallaire, H. & Minker, J. (eds), Plenum Press, New York, pp. 293-322.
8. Dennett, D.C. (1987). *The Intentional Stance*. MIT Press. Cambridge Massachusetts.
9. Hodges, W. (1993). *Model Theory*. Cambridge University Press.
10. Jonker, C.M., Treur, J. & de Vries, W. (2001). "Temporal Requirements for Anticipatory Reasoning about Intentional Dynamics in Social Contexts", in: Y. Demazeau and F.J. Garijo (eds.), *Proceedings of MAAMAW'2001 (Modelling Autonomous Agents in a Multi-Agent World)*, to appear in LNCS.
11. Linder, B. van, Hoek, W. van der & Meyer, J.-J. Ch. (1996). How to motivate your agents: on making promises that you can keep. In: Wooldridge, M.J., Müller, J. & Tambe, M. (eds.), *Intelligent Agents II. Proc. ATAL'95* (pp. 17-32). Lecture Notes in AI, vol. 1037, Springer Verlag.
12. Port, R.F. & Gelder, T. van (eds.) (1995). *Mind as Motion: Explorations in the Dynamics of Cognition*. MIT Press, Cambridge, Massachusetts.

Temporal Languages for Simulation and Analysis of the Dynamics within an Organisation

Catholijn M. Jonker, Jan Treur, and Wouter C.A. Wijngaards

Department of Artificial Intelligence, Vrije Universiteit Amsterdam,
De Boelelaan 1081a, 1081 HV Amsterdam, The Netherlands
{jonker,treur,wouterw}@cs.vu.nl
http://www.cs.vu.nl/~{jonker,treur,wouterw}

Abstract. In this paper a modelling approach to the dynamics within a multi-agent organisation is presented. A declarative, executable temporal modelling language for organisation dynamics is proposed as a basis for simulation. Moreover, to be able to specify and analyse dynamic properties, another temporal language is put forward, which is much more expressive than the executable language for simulations. Supporting tools have been implemented that consist of a software environment for simulation of multi-agent organisation models and a software environment for analysis of dynamic properties against traces organisation dynamics.

1   Introduction

Multi-agent systems often have complex dynamics, both in human society and in the non-human case. Organisational structure is used as a means to handle these complex dynamics. It provides a structuring of the processes in such a manner that an agent involved can function in a more appropriate manner. For example, at least partly the behavioural alternatives for the other agents are known. Put differently, the flow of dynamics within a given organisational structure is much more predictable than in an entirely unstructured situation. This assumes that the organisational structure itself is relatively stable, i.e., the structure may change, but the frequency and scale of change are assumed low compared to the more standard flow of dynamics through the structure. Both types of dynamics, dynamics within an organisational structure, and dynamics of an organisational structure are quite relevant to the area of organisation modelling. In this paper, for reasons of focussing the former type of dynamics is addressed, leaving the latter type out of consideration.

Modelling of dynamics within an organisation has at least two different aspects of use. First, models for the dynamics can be specified to be used as a basis for simulation, also called *executable models*. These types of models can be used to perform (pseudo-)experiments. Second, modelling dynamics can take the form of specification of *dynamic properties* of the organisation. These properties can play the role of requirements, and can be used, for example, in evaluation of sample behaviours of (real or simulated) organisations. These two different uses of models of dynamics impose different requirements on the languages in which these models are to be expressed.

A language for executable organisation models should be formal, and as simple as possible, to avoid computational complexity. Expressivity can be limited. Software tools to support such a language serve as *simulation environment*. A language to

B. Dunin-Kęplicz and E. Nawarecki (Eds.): CEEMAS 2001, LNAI 2296, pp. 151–160, 2002.
© Springer-Verlag Berlin Heidelberg 2002

specify and analyse dynamic properties of the flow within an organisation, on the other hand, should be sufficiently advanced to express various dynamic properties that can be identified. Expressivity should not be too limited; executability, however, is not required for such a language. What is important, though, is that properties specified in such a language can be checked for a given sample behaviour (e.g., a simulation run) without much work, preferably in an automated manner. Moreover, it is useful if a language to specify properties provides possibilities for further analysis of logical relationships between properties, and to generate theories about organisation dynamics. For these reasons also a language to specify properties of the dynamics within an organisation should be formal, and at least partly supported by software tools (*analysis environment*).

In this paper, for the Agent-Group-Role (AGR) organisation modelling approach (formerly called the meta-model Aalaadin) introduced in [4], two different temporal specification languages are put forward and illustrated for an example organisation. In Section 2 the static and dynamic view of the AGR modelling approach is briefly introduced. In Section 3 it is shown how the two languages (one aiming at simulation, the other one aiming at analysis) to model dynamics within such a model can be defined. In Section 4 the analysis and simulation software environment is discussed.

2   The Agent/Group/Role Organisation Modelling Approach

To obtain a useful specification of an organisation model not only the static, structural aspects, but also the dynamics within the organisation have to be taken into account. Thus, according to our view, an organisation model consists of a specification of the static *organisation structure* (Section 2.1), and a specification of the *organisation dynamics* (Section 2.2).

2.1   Static View

To model an organisation, the Agent/Group/Role (AGR) approach, adopted from [4] is used. The *organisational structure* is the specification of a specific multi-agent organisation based on a definition of groups, roles and their relationships within the organisation. A central notion is the *group structure*. It identifies the roles and (intragroup) interaction between roles within a group. The group structure is defined by the set of roles, interaction schemes and an (intragroup) transfer or communication model within the group. In addition, (intergoup) role relations between roles of different groups specify the connectivity of groups within an organisation.

Within this paper examples are taken from a case study that has been performed in the context of the Rabobank, one of the largest banks in the Netherlands, see [3]. The case study addressed design and analysis of a multi-agent approach for a bank service provision problem using a Call Centre. However, in the reference mentioned no organisation modelling approach such as AGR was incorporated. From an organisation modelling perspective, an organisation model can be defined using the following two groups: Client Service (sometimes also called Open Group) and Distribution. The roles within the groups are as follows:

Client Service:	Group Manager, Customer Relator, Client
Distribution:	Group Manager, Distributor, Participants

Within the Client Service group the service requests of clients are identified in an interaction between Client Relator and Client (this takes place within the Call Centre). Within a Distribution group, an identified service request is allocated in mutual interaction between Distributor and Participants. Actually this process takes place in two steps, making use of different instantiations of the Distribution group: once in a first line Distribution groups (relating a Call Centre agent to local bank work manager agents) and once in second line Distribution groups (work manager and employees within a local bank). The agents with role Participant in the first line Distribution group have the role of Distributor in a second line Distribution group. Also an agent with role Customer Relator in the Client Service group has a role of Distributor in the first line Distribution group.

2.2 Dynamic View

To be able to simulate or analyse dynamics within an organisation, in addition to the static organisation structure specification discussed above, as part of an organisation model also a specification of the dynamics within the organisation is needed. To this end, partly based on the types of requirements identified in [6], in the specification of an organisation model six different types of specifications of *dynamic properties* are distinguished: single role behaviour properties, intragroup interaction properties, intragroup transfer properties, intergroup interaction properties, global group properties, global organisation properties. These properties serve as constraints on the dynamics of the respective roles and interactions. To be able to specify ongoing interaction between two roles for which multiple appearances exist, the notion of *role instance* is used. This notion abstracts from the agent realising the role as actor, but enables to distinguish between appearances of roles.

The AGR modelling approach itself does not make commitments nor provides support for the use of any particular language to specify the dynamic view within the organisation model. In Section 3 below two temporal languages are introduced to specify the different types of dynamic properties. These languages and the supporting software environments can be used as an extension to the AGR modelling approach.

3   Specification of Dynamics within an Organisation Model

First the temporal trace language TTL to specify and analyse dynamic properties is introduced (Section 3.1). Next, the executable temporal language to specify simulation models is introduced (Section 3.2).

3.1 The Temporal Trace Language to Specify Dynamic Properties

To specify properties on the dynamics within the organisation, the temporal trace language used in [11], [8], is adopted. This is a language in the family of languages to which also situation calculus [14], event calculus [13], and fluent calculus [9] belong.

An *ontology* is a specification (in order-sorted logic) of a vocabulary, i.e., a signature. A state for ontology Ont is an assignment of truth-values {true, false} to the set of ground atoms At(Ont). The *set of all possible states* for ontology Ont is denoted by STATES(Ont). The standard satisfaction relation ⊨ between states and state properties is used: S ⊨ p means that state property p holds in state S.

To describe behaviour, explicit reference is made to time in a formal manner. A fixed *time frame* T is assumed which is linearly ordered. Depending on the application, it may be dense (e.g., the real numbers), or discrete (e.g., the set of integers or natural numbers or a finite initial segment of the natural numbers), or any other form, as long as it has a linear ordering. For example, for human organisations discrete time may be suitable, but for our planned future work on modelling the organisation in the living cell, a dense time frame will be more appropriate. A *trace* $\mathcal{M}$ over an ontology Ont and time frame T is a mapping $\mathcal{M} : T \to$ STATES(Ont), i.e., a sequence of states $\mathcal{M}_t$ (t ∈ T) in STATES(Ont). The set of all traces over ontology Ont is denoted by TRACES(Ont) , i.e., TRACES(Ont) = STATES(Ont)^T.

States of a trace can be related to state properties via the formally defined satisfaction relation ⊨ between states and formulae. Comparable to the approach in situation calculus, the sorted predicate logic *temporal trace language* TTL is built on atoms referring to traces, time and state properties, such as state($\mathcal{M}$, t, output(R)) ⊨ p. This expression denotes that state property p is true at the output of role R in the state of trace $\mathcal{M}$ at time point t. Here ⊨ is a predicate symbol in the language (in infix notation), comparable to the Holds-predicate in situation calculus. Temporal formulae are built using the usual logical connectives and quantification (for example, over traces, time and state properties). The set TFOR(Ont) is the set of all *temporal formulae* that only make use of ontology Ont. We allow additional language elements as abbreviations of formulae of the temporal trace language. Ontologies can be specific for a role. In Section 4, for simplicity explicit reference to the specific ontologies per role are omitted; the ontology elements used can be read from the property specifications themselves. As an example, a dynamic property for the dynamics within the organisation as a whole is shown.

GR1 All requests answered
The first global property specifies that at any point in time, if a client communicates a request to the receptionist, then at some later time point the receptionist will communicate either an acceptance or a rejection of the request to this client.

∀ T : TRACES ∀ tid : TaskId, ∀ t1, tf : T ∀ C: CLIENT:open_group ∀ R: RECEPTIONIST: open_group
[state(T , t1, output(C)) ⊨ comm_from_to(requested(tid, tf), C, R) ⇒
    ∃ t2 : T [t2 ≥ t1 & [state(T , t2, input(C)) ⊨ comm_from_to(rejected(tid), R, C) ∨
                          state(T , t2, input(C)) ⊨ comm_from_to(accepted(tid), R, C)]]

Note that this property is relevant, but is not of a format that can be executed easily within a simulation. Although it generates properties of future states out of current states, it entails nontrivial complexity since, due to the disjunction in the consequent, two possibilities would have to be considered. To avoid this, the executable sub-language introduced in the next section is more restrictive.

IaRI1 Client-Receptionist Intragroup Interaction
As an example of a more local property, within the Client Service group (or open group) instance the following intragroup role interaction property is shown. It specifies that within this group proper co-operation takes place: if a client communicates a request, then some time later, either the request will be rejected or accepted.

∀ T : TRACES, ∀ tid : TaskId ∀ t1, tf : T ∀ C: CLIENT: open_group,
∀ R: RECEPTIONIST: open_group

[state(T , t1, output(C)) ⊨ comm_from_to(requested(tid, tf), C, R)
⇒ ∃ t2 : T [t2 ≥ t1 &   [state(T , t2, output(R)) ⊨ comm_from_to(rejected(tid), R, C)
∨ state(T , t2, output(R)) ⊨ comm_from_to(accepted(tid), R, C)]]]

The temporal trace language used in our approach is much more expressive than standard temporal logics in a number of respects. In the first place, it has *order-sorted predicate logic* expressivity, whereas most standard temporal logics are propositional. Secondly, the explicit reference to *time points and time durations* offers the possibility of modelling the dynamics of real-time phenomena, such as sensory and neural activity patterns in relation to mental properties (cf. [16]). Especially when the language is applied to the internal organisation of (biological or chemical) processes within a biological organisation, as is planned for the near future, this is an important feature. Third, in our approach states are *three-valued*; the standard temporal logics are based on two-valued states, which implies that for a given trace a form of closed world assumption is imposed. This means that, for example, in Concurrent MetateM (cf., [7]), if the executable temporal logic specification leaves some atom unspecified, during construction of a trace the semantics will force it to be false. To avoid this, an atom has to be split into a positive and a negative variant.

Fourth, the possibility to quantify over traces allows for specification of *more complex types of dynamics*. As within most temporal logics, reactiveness and pro-activeness properties be specified. In addition, in our language also properties expressing different types of adaptive behaviour can be expressed. For example a property such as 'exercise improves skill', which is a relative property in the sense that it involves the comparison of two alternatives for the history. This type of property can be expressed in our language, whereas in standard forms of temporal logic different alternative histories cannot be compared. Fifth, in our language it is possible to define *local languages for parts* of an organisation. For example, the distinction between internal, external and interface languages is crucial, and is supported by the language, which also entails the possibility to quantify over organisation parts; this allows for specification of organisation modification over time. Sixth, since state properties are used as first class citizens in the temporal trace language, it is possible to explicitly refer to them, and to quantify over them, enabling the specification of what are sometimes called *second-order properties*, which are used in part of the philosophical literature (e.g., [12]) to expres functional roles related to state properties.

In the current paper only part of the features of the language as discussed above are exploited. Due to simplicity of the chosen example, for this focus the job could also be done by a less expressive language. However, then the approach is less generic and will not be extendable to more complex dynamics, such as, for example, relative adaptive organisational behaviours. The language used is meant to support a more *generic* perspective and anticipates on these types of more complex behaviours which are in the focus of our further research.

3.2 The Executable Temporal Language to Specify Simulation Models

To obtain an executable language, in comparison with the temporal trace language discussed above strong constraints are imposed on what can be expressed. These constraints define a temporal language within the paradigm of executable temporal logic; cf. [1]. Roughly spoken, in this executable language it can only be expressed that if a certain state property holds for a certain time interval, then after some delay another state property should hold for a certain time interval. This specific temporal relationship •–» (*leads to*) is definable within the temporal trace language TTL. This definition is expressed in two parts, the forward in time part and the backward in time part. Time intervals are denoted by [x, y) (from and including x, to but not including y) and [x, y] (the same, but includes the y value).

Definition(The •–» relationship)

Let α and β be state properties, and let P1 and P2 refer to parts of the organisation model (e.g., input or output of particular roles). Then β *follows* α, denoted by P1:α –»$_{e, f, g, h}$ P2:β, with time delay interval [e, f] and duration parameters g and h if

$\forall T \in$ TRACES $\forall t1$:   [$\forall t \in$ [t1 - g, t1) : state(T, t, P1) $\models \alpha \Rightarrow$

$\exists \lambda \in$ [e, f] $\forall t \in$ [t1 + λ, t1 + λ + h) : state(T, t, P2) $\models \beta$]

Conversely, the state property β *originates from* state property α, denoted by P1:α •—$_{e, f, g, h}$ P2:β, with time delay in [e, f] and duration parameters g and h if

$\forall T \in$ TRACES $\forall t2$:   [$\forall t \in$ [t2, t2 + h) : state(T, t, P2) $\models \beta \Rightarrow$

$\exists \lambda \in$ [e, f] $\forall t \in$ [t2 - λ - g, t2 - λ) state(T, t, P1) $\models \alpha$]

If both P1:α –»$_{e,f,g,h}$ P2:β, and P1:α •—$_{e,f,g,h}$ P2:β hold, this is called a *leads to* relation and denoted by P1:α •–»$_{e,f,g,h}$ P2:β. Sometimes also conjunctions or negations on one of the sides (or both) of the arrow are used.

The definition of the relationships as given above, can be applied to situations where the sources hold for longer than the minimum interval length g. The additional duration that the source holds, is also added to the duration that the result will hold, provided that the condition e + h ≥ f holds. This is because under the given constraint the definition can be applied at each subinterval of α, resulting in many overlapping intervals of β. The end result is that the additional duration also extends the duration that the resulting notion β holds.

To use the language for simulation of organisations only role behaviour, intergroup role interaction and transfer properties are specified in the executable language. The other types of properties emerge during the simulation process. An example property in the executable language is:

IrRI2 Distributor-Receptionist Intergroup Role Interaction

This expresses that any information regarding the request of a client that the distributor instance of the distribution group instance cc receives is forwarded to the client by the receptionist role instance of the client server group instance (also called open group). In the example, for reasons of presentation we assume that only one client exists. For more clients an additional condition is needed.

∀ tid : TASKID, ∀ R : RECEPTIONIST:open_group:OPEN_GROUP,
∀ C : CLIENT:open_group:OPEN_GROUP, ∀ info : TASKINFORMATION
∀ D : DISTRIBUTOR:cc:DISTRIBUTION, ∀ P : PARTICIPANT:cc:DISTRIBUTION,
INTERGROUP_ROLE_RELATION(R, D) ⇒
        [input(D):comm_from_to(info(tid)), P, D) •–»$_{5,5,10,10}$ output(R):comm_from_to(info(tid), R, C)]

Role behaviour properties specify the behaviour of a role within a group. For each role within a group, and for all groups, the role behaviour must be specified. Given that for the Call Centre application three types of groups have been identified with three roles each, nine role behaviours must be specified. The behaviour of one role can take more than one property to specify. For brevity, a few of the kernel role behaviours specified here:

E1 Accepting jobs

If a Participant of a local bank group instance is asked to perform some task, and he has time to do so, then he communicates to his Distributor of the local bank group instance that he accepts the task.

$\forall$ tid : TASKID, $\forall$ tf : COMPLETIONTIME, $\forall$ f : FIFOSLOTS, $\forall$ GI : DISTRIBUTION,
$\forall$ D : DISTRIBUTOR:GI:DISTRIBUTION, $\forall$ P : PARTICIPANT:GI:DISTRIBUTION

[GI $\neq$ cc] $\Rightarrow$ [input(P):comm_from_to(requested(tid, tf), D, P) & internal(P):fifo_empty(f) $\bullet\!\!\twoheadrightarrow_{0,0,10,10}$
output(P):comm_from_to(accepted(tid), P, D)]

E2 Rejecting jobs

If a Participant of a local bank group is asked to perform some task, and he has no time to do so, then he communicates to his Distributor of the local bank group that he rejects the task.

$\forall$ tid : TASKID, $\forall$ tf : COMPLETIONTIME, $\forall$ GI : DISTRIBUTION,
$\forall$ D : DISTRIBUTOR:GI:DISTRIBUTION, $\forall$ P : PARTICIPANT:GI:DISTRIBUTION

[GI $\neq$ cc] $\Rightarrow$ [input(P):comm_from_to(requested(tid, tf), D, P) & not(internal(P):fifo_empty(fifo2))
$\bullet\!\!\twoheadrightarrow_{0,0,10,10}$ output(P):comm_from_to(rejected(tid), P, D)]

4 Analysis Environment

The analysis environment includes three different tools:
1. a tool that, given a set of traces, checks any dynamic property of the organisation.
2. a tool that, given a trace and an executable specification checks any property expressed in terms of $\bullet\!\!\twoheadrightarrow$ against the trace and interprets which rules of the executable specification are satisfied in the trace and which are falsified by the trace.
3. a tool that, given an executable specification, proves or disproves any property expressed in terms of $\bullet\!\!\twoheadrightarrow$.

All three these tools assume a finite time frame. Simulation software has been created that allows the generation of traces using properties in the executable language.

To *check* whether a given behavioural property is fulfilled in a given trace or set of traces, a software environment based on some Prolog programmes (of about 500 lines) has been developed. The temporal formulae are represented by nested term structures based on the logical connectives. For more information see [10].

Another program, of about 4000 lines in C++, has been constructed that takes an existing trace of behaviour as input and creates an *interpretation* of what happens in this trace and a *check* whether all temporal relationships in a set of properties hold in that trace. The program marks any deficiencies in the trace compared with what should be there due to the temporal relationships. If a relationship does not hold completely, this is marked by the program. The program produces yellow marks for unexpected events. At these moments, the event is not produced by any temporal relationship; the event cannot be explained. The red marks indicate that an event has not happened, that should have happened.

In addition to checking whether the rules hold, the checker produces an informal reading of the trace. The reading is automatically generated, using a simple substitution, from the information in the given trace. For example, the properties GR1, GR2, IaRI1 and a number of other properties (not shown in this paper) have been checked and shown to be valid.

The complexity of checking properties is limited. Let the number of properties be #p, the length of the properties be |m|, the number of atoms be #a and the number of value changes per atom in the trace be #v. The length of properties is measured by the total number of atoms and connectives in the antecedent and the consequent. A first inspection of the complexity of checking is that it is polynomial in #a, #p, #v and |m|. The complexity of simulation is comparable.

A third software tool (about 300 lines of code in Prolog) addresses the *proving* of dynamic properties (expressed in terms of $\bullet\!\!-\!\!\twoheadrightarrow$) of an organisation from an (executable) specification of the organisation dynamics without involving specific traces. This dedicated prover exploits the executable nature of the specification and the past/current implies future nature of the property to keep complexity limited. For example, given the executable specification of the Call Centre organisation model, an instantiated form of global level property GR1 (see Section 4.1) can be proven.

Using this prover, dynamic properties of the organisation can be checked that hold for all traces of the organisation, without generating them all by subsequent simulation. The efficiency of finding such a proof strongly depends on the complexity of the specifications of the role behaviour dynamics for the different roles.

5   Discussion

In this paper specification and uses of models of the dynamics within a multi-agent organisation are addressed. A declarative temporal language is proposed as a basis for simulation. This language belongs to the class of executable temporal languages; cf. [1]. Models can be specified in a declarative manner based on a temporal 'leads to' relation; within the simulation environment these models can be executed. Moreover, to specify dynamic properties another language is put forward: a temporal trace language that belongs to the family of languages to which also situation calculus [14], event calculus [13], and fluent calculus [9] belong. The executable language for simulations is definable within this much more expressive language. Supporting tools have been implemented that consist of:

- A software environment for simulation of a multi-agent organisation model
- A software environment for analysis of dynamic properties against traces for such a model

A simple example organisation model illustrates the use of both languages and of the software environments.

In [4] no commitment to a specific dynamic modelling approach is made. In contrast, the modelling approach put forward here, makes a commitment to particular temporal languages, and provides detailed support of the dynamic modelling aspect, both for (automated) simulation and evaluation. Within [6] also a temporal trace language to specify dynamic properties is used. However, in that paper no automated support of specification, simulation and evaluation is included, which is the main subject of the current paper. A difference with [10] is that in the current paper at a conceptual level an executable declarative temporal language and an associated simulation environment are introduced, whereas simulation within [10] is based on an implementation environment such as Swarm, without conceptual specification language. Another difference is that in [10] a diagnostic method to analyse organisational dynamics is addressed, which is not the subject of the current paper.

In comparison to the environment SDML [15], our work differs in that a specific organisation modelling approach, AGR is taken as a basis, whereas SDML does not make such a commitment, nor provides specific support for such a more specific modelling approach enabled by this commitment. Moreover, in contrast to SDML (which is restricted to simulation), in our case in addition a specification language for dynamic properties is provided, and tools to check properties. As the multi-agent system design method DESIRE [2] is similar to SDML in perspective and scope, the approach proposed in the current paper has the same differences to DESIRE as it has to SDML.

In comparison to the executable temporal logic language Concurrent MetateM [7], this language is based on discrete time whereas our approach is able to use continuous time. Moreover, our temporal language is more expressive. The possibility to compare and quantify over traces allows for specification of more complex behaviours. Properties expressing different types of adaptive behaviour can be expressed. Consider, for example properties such as 'exercise improves skill', and 'the better the experiences, the higher the trust' (trust monotonicity) which are relative in the sense that they involve the comparison of two alternatives for the history. This type of property can be expressed in our language, whereas in Concurrent MetateM and standard forms of temporal logic different alternative histories cannot be compared. The same difference applies to situation calculus, event calculus, or fluent calculus.

In future research, the diagnostic method introduced in [10] will be integrated within the organisational modelling environment described above. Moreover, support will be developed for the identification and checking of logical relationships between dynamic properties specified at different levels within the organisation.

References

1. Barringer, H., Fisher, M., Gabbay, D., Owens, R. & Reynolds, M. (1996). The Imperative Future: Principles of Executable Temporal Logic, Research Studies Press Ltd. and John Wiley & Sons.
2. Brazier, F.M.T., Jonker, C.M. & Treur, J., Principles of Compositional Multi-agent System Development. In: J. Cuena (ed.), *Proceedings of the 15th IFIP World Computer Congress, WCC'98, Conference on Information Technology and Knowledge Systems, IT&KNOWS'98*, 1998, pp. 347-360. To be published by IOS Press, 2002.
3. Brazier, F. M. T., Jonker, C. M., Jüngen, F. J. & Treur, J. (1999). Distributed Scheduling to Support a Call Centre: a Co-operative Multi-Agent Approach. In: Applied Artificial Intelligence Journal, vol. 13, pp. 65-90. H. S. Nwana and D. T. Ndumu (eds.), Special Issue on Multi-Agent Systems.
4. Ferber, J. & Gutknecht, O. (1998). A meta-model for the analysis and design of organisations in multi-agent systems. In: Proc. of the Third International Conference on Multi-Agent Systems (ICMAS '98) Proceedings. IEEE Computer Society, 1998

160   C.M. Jonker, J. Treur, and W.C.A. Wijngaards

5. Ferber, J. & Gutknecht, O. (1999). Operational Semantics of a role-based agent architecture. Proceedings of the 6th Int. Workshop on Agent Theories, Architectures and Languages. Lecture Notes in AI, Springer-Verlag.
6. Ferber, J., Gutknecht, O., Jonker, C.M., Mueller, J.P. & Treur, J. (2000). Organisation Models and Behavioural Requirements Specification for Multi-Agent Systems (extended abstract). In: Proc. of the Fourth International Conference on Multi-Agent Systems, ICMAS 2000. IEEE Computer Society Press, 2000. Extended version in: Proc. of MAAMAW'01.
7. Fisher, M., A survey of Concurrent METATEM — the language and its applications. In: D.M. Gabbay & H.J. Ohlbach (eds.), Temporal Logic — Proceedings of the First International Conference, Lecture Notes in AI, vol. 827, pp. 480–505.
8. Herlea, D.E., Jonker, C.M., Treur, J. & Wijngaards, N.J.E. (1999). Specification of Behavioural Requirements within Compositional Multi-Agent System Design. In: F.J. Garijo & M. Boman (eds.), Multi-Agent System Engineering, Proc. of the 9th European Workshop on Modelling Autonomous Agents in a Multi-Agent World, MAAMAW'99. Lecture Notes in AI, vol. 1647, Springer Verlag, 1999, pp. 8-27.
9. Hölldobler, S. & Thielscher, M. (1990). A new deductive approach to planning. *New Generation Computing*, 8:225-244, 1990.
10. Jonker, C.M., Letia, I.A. & Treur, J. (2001). Diagnosis of the Dynamics within an Organisation by Trace Checking of Behavioural Requirements. In: Wooldridge, M., Ciancarini, P., and Weiss, G. (eds.), *Proc. of the 2nd International Workshop on Agent-Oriented Software Engineering, AOSE'01*. Lecture Notes in Computer Science, Springer Verlag, to appear.
11. Jonker, C.M., & Treur, J. (1998). Compositional Verification of Multi-Agent Systems: a Formal Analysis of Pro-activeness and Reactiveness. In: W.P. de Roever, H. Langmaack, A. Pnueli (eds.), Proceedings of the International Workshop on Compositionality, COMPOS'97. Lecture Notes in Computer Science, vol. 1536, Springer Verlag, 1998, pp. 350-380. Extended version in: *International Journal of Cooperative Information Systems*. In press, 2002.
12. Kim, J. (1998). *Mind in a Physical world: an Essay on the Mind-Body Problem and Mental Causation*. MIT Press, Cambridge, Mass, 1998.
13. Kowalski, R. & Sergot, M. (1986). A logic-based calculus of events. *New Generation Computing*, 4:67-95, 1986.
14. McCarthy, J. & P. Hayes, P. (1969). Some philosophical problems from the standpoint of artificial intelligence. *Machine Intelligence*, 4:463--502, 1969.
15. Moss, S., Gaylard, H., Wallis, S. & Edmonds, B. (1998), SDML: A Multi-Agent Language for Organizational Modelling, *Computational and Mathematical Organization Theory* **4**, (1), 43-70.
16. Port, R.F. & Gelder, T. van (eds.). (1995) *Mind as Motion: Explorations in the Dynamics of Cognition*. MIT Press, Cambridge, Mass, 1995.

Syntactic Pattern Recognition-Based Agents for Real-Time Expert Systems

Janusz Jurek

Institute of Computer Science, Jagiellonian University
Nawojki 11, 30-072 Cracow, Poland
jwj@ii.uj.edu.pl

Abstract. Syntactic pattern recognition-based analyzers (parsers) have been proposed [4,7] as efficient tools for analysis of complex trend functions (patterns) which describe a behaviour of an industrial equipment. In this paper we present the application of the parsers in a real-time diagnostic and control expert system. The expert system has been designed as a sophisticated multi-agent system, where the parsers have been embedded in the agents of pattern recognition-type. The architecture of the agents and their role in the system is discussed in the paper.

1 Introduction

In the paper we describe the results of research[1] into defining efficient tools for constructing real-time diagnostic and control expert systems. The research started in 1993 for the purpose of diagnosing a behaviour of a big detector in a high energy physics experiment [1,2]. One of the main goals has been to define an efficient method of the on-line analysis of patterns representing trend functions related to the performance of a very complex industrial-like equipment. The problem has been difficult since the patterns have been highly complicated, and they have had to be analysed on-line (diagnostic results have had to be given in real-time). As it has been described in [4,7], the problem can be solved via application of syntactic pattern recognition methods: the trend functions can be treated in an analogous way, as it is made while applying syntactic pattern recognition for ECG or EEG analysis [5]. The research into the problem has resulted in defining of a new class of string grammars, DPLL(k) grammars [4]. DPLL(k) grammars, which are characterised by a big descriptive power (the grammars are stronger than context-free grammars [8]), have been proved to be a suitable tool to describe the trend functions. On the other hand, it has appeared that it is possible to define an efficient, $O(n)$, parser for DPLL(k) grammars [7]. A construction of the parser of linear computational complexity has been an important achievement because computational time is a crucial

---

[1] This work was supported by the European Commission within European Strategic Programme for Research in Information Technology, ESPRIT, (CRIT2 project *Intelligent Control of Complex and Safety Critical Systems with the Help of Artificial Intelligence- and Pattern Recognition- Based Software Technologies*).

B. Dunin-Kęplicz and E. Nawarecki (Eds.): CEEMAS 2001, LNAI 2296, pp. 161–168, 2002.
© Springer-Verlag Berlin Heidelberg 2002

factor if we consider applications in real-time systems. Finally, a grammatical inference algorithm (i.e. an algorithm of automatic construction of a grammar from the sample of a pattern language [5]) for DPLL(k) grammars has been developed [10], and in this way we have solved a problem of *syntactic pattern learning* in case of this class of grammars.

After establishing the pattern recognition "theoretical background", new research, both software engineering and artificial intelligence related, has been started. The research has been aimed at developing a model of using the pattern recognition formalisms in the real application mentioned above, i.e. the expert system (the ZEUS Expert System, ZEX) responsible for on-line monitoring, diagnosing, and controlling of a high energy physics detector. The pattern recognition formalisms have been chosen as a base for setting up one of the main software modules of the expert system. In order to fulfil the hard real-time constraints required by the system, it has been necessary to design a proper architecture of the system that would guarantee high efficiency. The intensive methodological studies and practical experiments have resulted in the development of sophisticated multi-agent architecture of the system, where the DPLL(k) parsers have been embedded in the agents of syntactic pattern recognition-type.

In the paper we discuss the structure of the agents and their role in the system. In the next section we present the application requirements which a DPLL(k) parser-based agent has had to fulfil and the outline of the multi-agent architecture of ZEX syntactic pattern recognition subsystem. The structure of the agents is characterised in the third section. Concluding remarks are presented in the final section.

2   The Application of DPLL(k) Parser-Based Agents

A DPLL(k) parser has been developed in order to be used as a diagnostic tool in the ZEUS Expert System, called ZEX, which has been designed at the Deutsches Elektronen-Synchrotron, Hamburg, Germany [1,2] with the help of the real-time expert system building shell *RTworks* from *Talarian*. The system monitors and makes diagnoses of various aspects of a work of the ZEUS detector[2], including monitoring detector electronics, data acquisition computers, data flow processes. ZEX is also able to react when it detects errors, and perform suitable actions to eliminate them (e.g. it alerts the shift crew and gives them instructions about what should be done).

The DPLL(k) parser has been designed to support diagnosing of the ZEUS detector Data Acquisition System (the DAQ system), which is a typical hard real-time complex distributed system. The DAQ system data flows exceed 10 GBytes/s at the front of the detector (collisions in the detector take place every 96 ns). Input rate to the data acquisition system is 10.4 MHz, information is

---

[2] The ZEUS detector consists of more than 20 various subdetectors. Its dimensions are 12 m × 10 m × 19 m and its total weight is 3600 tons. It is located about 20 m deep under ground at the 6.3 km long accelerator tunnel. It is operated by a collaboration of about 450 scientists coming from more than 50 institutions in 11 countries.

read from more than 250 000 readout channels. The system consists of about 300 network computer nodes (VAX-VMS, SGI-UNIX, DEC-UNIX, MVME147-OS9, etc.) and transputer subnetworks. The aim of constructing the syntactic pattern recognition-based subsystem of ZEX has been to monitor critical characteristics of the components of the DAQ system: processing times, available memory space, data throughput, interface memory buffers, and give a diagnosis in case of problems.

The multi-agent architecture of ZEX is the result of research into design of such a software model that can fulfil the hard real-time constraints described above. The architecture guarantees high efficiency of the system, what has been practically proven [1,2], and makes the system flexible and easily maintainable. Let us mention that process diagnostic and control is a natural application for agents, since process controllers are themselves autonomous reactive systems. This is the reason why a number of agent-based process control applications have been already implemented around the world [6].

According to the developed model, DPLL(k) parsers have been embedded in the agents of syntactic pattern recognition-type. The syntactic pattern recognition subsystem of ZEX consists of several DPLL(k) parser-based agents. Each agent is responsible for diagnosing a behaviour of one particular component of the DAQ system. The agents are of *reactive* type [3,6]: they should be able to respond timely to changes in their environment (i.e. DAQ system) and to acquire knowledge about the environment.

The agents receive symbolic data representing *critical* characteristics of a component behaviour and they make a diagnosis in case of problems (an erroneous behaviour). The symbolic data is delivered to the DPLL(k) agents by the monitoring agents. Each monitoring agent collects numerical multi-dimensional characteristics of a component behaviour (processing times, load of interface memory buffers, and data flow parameters) taken from several sources (the transputer network, hardware components, an SGI computer farm). As a result of the processing of the data, the monitoring agent produces symbolic representation of the current component state and sends it to the DPLL(k) agent.

After detecting an error or identifying an abnormal behaviour, a DPLL(k) agent sends a message to another agent of ZEX (of different type) which is responsible for reasoning over *all* accumulated information about the DAQ system behaviour including information on its all components. The message contains a symbolic information of the identified behaviour. The decision about whether to eliminate the submitted error and how to do it lies with the ZEX agent that receives the message.

We do not show and discuss very sophisticated architecture of the rest of the ZEUS Expert System [2] in this section, because this is beyond the scope of the paper. Let us only notice that ZEX contains many types of agents implemented with the use of many different techniques (C++, *RTworks* expert system shell). The community of agents is hierarchically organised. A multi-layered blackboard system is the main tool for coordination and communication between agents.

3 DPLL(k) Parser-Based Agents

3.1 Definitions

Let us introduce a few basic definitions [4] needed to discuss the functioning of a DPLL(k) parser-based agent.

Definition 1.   A *dynamically programmed context-free grammar* is a quintuple

$$G = (V, \Sigma, O, P, S)$$

where V is a finite, nonempty alphabet; $\Sigma \subset V$ is a finite, nonempty set of terminal symbols (with N we denote a set of nonterminal symbols $N = V \setminus \Sigma$); O is a set of operations on a tape : *add, read, move*; $S \in N$ is the starting symbol; P is a finite set of productions of the form :

$$p_i = (\mu_i, L_i, R_i, A_i, DCL_i)$$

in which $\mu_i : \bigcup DCL_k \longrightarrow \{TRUE, FALSE\}$ is the predicate of applicability of the production p_i; $L_i \in N$ and $R_i \in V^*$ are left- and right-hand sides of p_i respectively; a pair (L_i, R_i) will be called a core of p_i (we assume that for each two various productions p_i, p_j from P, the core of p_i is different from the core of p_j, i.e. either $L_i \neq L_j$ or $R_i \neq R_j$); A_i is the sequence of actions of a type *add, move* $\in O$ performed over $\bigcup DCL_k$; DCL_i is a derivation control tape for p_i. $\square$

A derivation for dynamically programmed grammars is defined in the following way. Apart from testing whether L_i occurs in a sentential form derived, we check the predicate of applicability of a production p_i. The predicate is defined with use of $read(x)$ operation which is responsible for reading a current position of a head of a derivation control tape of a production x. If it is true, then we replace L_i with R_i, and then we perform the sequence of actions over derivation control tapes: $add(x, y)$ action is responsible for adding an index of a production y to a derivation control tape of a production x; $move(x)$ action is responsible for moving a head of a derivation control tape of a production x.

Definition 2.   Let $G = (V, \Sigma, O, P, S)$ be a dynamically programmed context-free grammar. The grammar G is called a *Dynamically Programmed LL(k) grammar*, DPLL(k) grammar, if the following two conditions are fulfilled.

1. Let $w \in \Sigma^*$, $A \in N = V \setminus \Sigma$, $x, y, \alpha, \beta, \gamma \in V^*$. Then, for every two left-hand side derivations in G:

   $$S \xrightarrow{\;*\;} wA\alpha \longrightarrow w\beta\alpha \xrightarrow[\text{core}]{\;*\;} wx$$
   $$S \xrightarrow{\;*\;} wA\alpha \longrightarrow w\gamma\alpha \xrightarrow[\text{core}]{\;*\;} wy$$

   such, that: $First_k(x) = First_k(y)$, the following condition holds: $\beta = \gamma$.

2. For a grammar G there exists a certain number ξ such, that for any left-hand side derivation $S \xrightarrow{\;*\;} wA\alpha \xrightarrow{\;\pi\;} w\beta\alpha$ (where $w \in \Sigma^*$, $A \in N$, $\alpha, \beta \in V^*$) fulfilling a condition : $|\pi| \geq \xi$, the first symbol of $\beta\alpha$ is the terminal one.

(The following notations have been used: $\xrightarrow{G}$ denotes a single derivation step in G; $\xrightarrow[G]{*}$ denotes the transitive and reflexive closure of $\xrightarrow{G}$; $\xrightarrow[G]{\pi}$ denotes such a derivation in G, which consists in application of succeeding productions from π, where π is a string of indices of productions; $\xrightarrow{G_{core}}$ denotes such a single derivation step in G that consists in an application of only a production core as a rewriting rule; $\xrightarrow[G_{core}]{*}$ denotes the transitive and reflexive closure of $\xrightarrow{G_{core}}$; $First_k(x)$ is a simple extension of a $First_k(x)$ notation used for $LL(k)$ grammars.) □

The algorithm of the parser for DPLL(k) grammars (DPLL(k) parser) has been described in [7]. We will not present it in the paper, but let us notice that the algorithm exactly reflects the way how the derivation in the grammar is performed. The algorithm uses top-down approach during the derivation. FIFO (first-in, first-out) queues are used to simulate all DCL tapes. Before application of a production the algorithm checks its predicate of applicability. After application of a production (i.e. after application of the re-writing rule) the algorithm performs *actions* on the queues, adding or removing elements, and in this way it *dynamically programs* future steps of the derivation.

3.2 Structure of the DPLL(k) Agents

All DPLL(k) parser-based agents have been generated from one template. The template has been designed according to the object-oriented methodology and implemented in C++ language. Fig. 1 shows the general structure of a DPLL(k) parser-based agent.

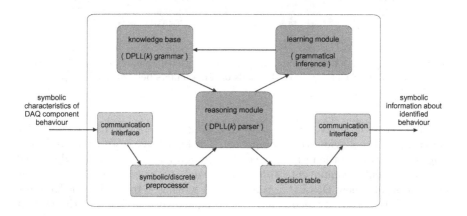

Fig. 1. A general scheme of a DPLL(k) parser-based agent

The agent contains communication interfaces, a symbolic/discrete prepro-cessor, a DPLL(k) parser-based reasoning module, a knowledge base containing a definition of a DPLL(k) grammar, a learning module based on grammatical inference, and a decision table.

The agent has two *communication interfaces*: the first one for receiving data from agents that monitor DAQ components, and the second one for sending messages to the "higher-level" agent responsible for reasoning over information about all components of the DAQ system.

The main task of *the symbolic/discrete preprocessor* is to filter symbolic information in order to eliminate mistakenly detected states of a DAQ component (the monitoring agents can make mistakes because of the simplicity of the algorithm of symbolic representation generation or by inexactitude of monitoring devices). The filtering is time-based: it takes into account previously detected states. The detailed description of the symbolic preprocessor is included in [9].

The preprocessor delivers symbolic information to *the reasoning module* which is based on a DPLL(k) parser. The history of changes of the information can be treated as a pattern representing a trend function related to the performance of a DAQ component. The role of the module is to recognise such a time-series trend, and identify *the behaviour* of the component. Fig. 2 shows an example of time-series trends which are displayed and analysed by ZEX.

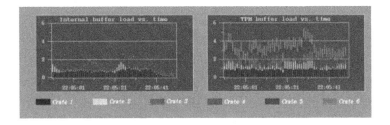

Fig. 2. A fragment of an example display in the ZEUS Expert System. Two charts graphically illustrate changing of the loads of some buffers belonging to components of the DAQ system.

In order to recognise a pattern, the reasoning module has to have a knowledge about possible behaviours of a component. The knowledge is stored in *the knowledge base module* in the form of the definition of a DPLL(k) grammar dedicated to one particular component. *The learning module* is responsible for automatic generation of a new DPLL(k) grammar and writing it to the knowledge base, when a new pattern (which cannot be recognised on the basis of the current grammar) has been detected by the reasoning module.

The last element of the agent is *the decision table*. The table is a simple structure assigning actions (messages to be sent) to the output of the reasoning module.

3.3   Scenarios of the DPLL(k) Agent Functioning

There are two scenarios of the DPLL(k) agent functioning: *reasoning* and *learning*. Usually, the first scenario, *reasoning*, takes place. The reasoning module (a DPLL(k) parser) interprets symbolic information in similar way, as it is done in a rule-based artificial intelligence system. The validation of the predicate of DPLL(k) grammar production is analogous to the testing of "IF" part of a rule, while dynamical programming of the DCL tapes is analogous to the executing of the "THEN" part. However, it is worth to point out that the reasoning made by a DPLL(k) parser, as distinct from rule-based system, is done in a very good, $O(n)$, time [7].

As it has been mentioned in the introduction, DPLL(k) grammars and languages have been defined as the result of research into languages that both have a big descriptive power and could be recognised efficiently. In case of DPLL(k) grammars these two contradictory requirements (i.e. the bigger descriptive power of a grammar the bigger computational complexity of a corresponding parser is expected) are fulfilled. DPLL(k) grammars generate quasi-context sensitive languages (they are stronger than context-free languages) and the parser for the languages performs syntax analysis in the linear time. Both preliminary experimental tests and then the real application of the DPLL(k) parser-based agent have proved that DPLL(k) languages are strong enough to describe very complicated time-series trends representing DAQ component behaviour, and that the reasoning module based on a DPLL(k) parser, which recognises the trends, meets all time constraints.

The second scenario, *learning*, happens rarely, and only if an input pattern cannot be interpreted by the reasoning module. Such situations means that the current DPLL(k) grammar should be replaced by a broaden one which generates the missing pattern. Learning is done via grammatical inference. The reasoning module delivers the pattern sample to the learning module, and on the basis of the sample a new DPLL(k) grammar is created (according to the inference algorithm described in [10]). Finally, the learning module updates the knowledge base with a new grammar.

4   Concluding Remarks

In the paper we have discussed the application of syntactic pattern recognition-based agents in the real-time multi-agent expert system, which has been designed at the Deutsches Elektronen-Synchrotron, Hamburg, Germany, for monitoring, and diagnosing of various aspects of the work of a high-energy physics detector.

The syntactic pattern recognition-based reactive agents have been used in the expert system as a tool for monitoring and diagnosing data flow processes of the detector. The kernel of the agents is a DPLL(k) parser, responsible for on-line analysis of complicated time-series trends related to the performance of the components of the data acquisition system (the trends are treated in an analogous way, as it is made while applying syntactic pattern recognition for ECG or EEG analysis). Although good computational and discriminative properties of the DPLL(k) parser have been proven theoretically, only the real application of the DPLL(k) parser-based agents has demonstrated practically high efficiency and big diagnosing power during their everyday operating.

The agents described in the paper are characterised not only by its good computational and diagnosing properties, but by its *learning capabilities* as well. The grammatical inference algorithm designed as an important element of the agent allows to accumulate knowledge about the environment and flexible react to the changes in the environment.

The agents can be used in such real-time systems where processes are being analysed and controlled. The process diagnostic and control is a natural application for agents, since process controllers are themselves autonomous reactive systems.

Acknowledgement. The author wishes to thank Prof. Mariusz Flasiński for his contribution to the concept of syntactic pattern recognition-based agents, valuable discussions and comments on the paper.

References

1. Behrens, U., Flasiński, M., Hagge, L., Jurek, J., Ohrenberg, K.: Status of the ZEUS expert system (ZEX), Proc. Conf. on Computing in High Energy Physics, Rio de Janeiro, Brasil, September 18–22,(1995), 888–891
2. Behrens, U., Flasiński, M., Hagge, L., Jurek, J., Ohrenberg, K.: Recent developments of the ZEUS expert system ZEX, IEEE Trans. Nucl. Sci. **NS-43** (1996), 65–68
3. Chaib-draa, B., Moulin, B., Mandiau, R., Millot, P.: Trends in distributed artificial intelligence, Artif. Intell. Rev., **6**, (1992), 35–66
4. Flasiński, M., Jurek, J.: Dynamically Programmed Automata for Quasi Context Sensitive Languages as a Tool for Inference Support in Pattern Recognition-Based Real-Time Control Expert Systems. Pattern Recognition, Vol. 32 (1999) no. **4**, 671–690
5. Fu, K.S.: Syntactic Pattern Recognition and Applications, Prentice Hall, Englewood Cliffs (1982)
6. Jennings, N.R., Sycara, K., Wooldridge, M.: A Roadmap of Agent Research and Development, Journal of Autonomous Agents and Multi-Agent Systems, **1** (1998), 7–38
7. Jurek, J.: On the Linear Computational Complexity of the Parser for Quasi Context Sensitive Languages, Pattern Recognition Letters, no. **21** (2000), 179–187
8. Jurek, J.: On the Pattern Generation Power of Parsable DPLL(k) Languages, Proc. First National Conf. On Computer Recognition Systems, KOSYR'99, Trzebieszowice, Poland, 24-27 May 1999, 367–373
9. Jurek, J.: Syntax-Directed Translation Scheme as a Tool for Building Symbolic/Discrete Preprocessors for Real-Time Expert Systems, Universitas Iagellonica Acta Scientiarum Litterarumque: Schedae Informatica, **6** (1995), 175–186
10. Smaglowski, J.: Grammatical inference for DPLL(k) grammars, Ph.D. Thesis, Academy of Mining and Metallurgy in Cracow, (2000).

Learning User Preferences in Multi-agent System

Adorjan Kiss and Joël Quinqueton

LIRMM, Multiagent Team, 161 rue Ada, F-34392 Montpellier Cedex, France
{kiss,jq}@lirmm.fr,
http://www.lirmm.fr/ kiss

Abstract. We present in this paper some attempts to design a Machine Learning method to predict preference knowledge in a multi-agents context. This approach is applied to a corporate knowledge management system.

1 Introduction

In this paper we will present some attempts to design a Machine Learning method to predict preference knowledge in a multi-agents context. Here we define preference knowledge as knowledge about a preference between elements of a set.

For instance, the documents found by a search engine on the web are ordered according to a preference function computed from the user request. Thus, they can be considered as ordered according to a preference relation.

The framework that gave birth to this work is a joint research project, CoMMA[1], dedicated to corporate memory management in an intranet. The main objective of the project is to implement and test a Corporate Memory management framework integrating several emerging technologies in order to optimize its maintenance and ease the search inside it and the use of its content by the members of the organization.

The main challenge is to create a coherent system that relies upon several promising new technologies which are in the middle of their struggle to become standards:

- Multi-agent architecture: it is well suited to the heterogeneity of the Corporate Memory; its flexibility eases the system maintenance and keeps the rhythm with the dynamics and evolution of the Corporate Memory; cooperating and adaptive agents assure a better working together with the user in his pursuit to more effectively achieve his goals. The FIPA standard, supported by the CoMMA project, offers the specifications for interoperable intelligent multi-agent systems.

---

[1] This work was supported by the CoMMA (Corporate Memory Management through Agents) project [5] funded by the European Commission under Grant IST-1999-12217, which started beginning of February 2000.

B. Dunin-Kęplicz and E. Nawarecki (Eds.): CEEMAS 2001, LNAI 2296, pp. 169–178, 2002.

- XML: is a standard recommended by the World Wide Web Consortium intended to offer a human and machine understandable description language: a good choice if it is important to ensure an easy maintenance, and seamless flow through various information processing systems that evolve in time.
- RDF/RDFS another W3C recommendation, that creates a semantic level on the top of XML formal description. RDF annotations allow having an integrated, global view of the Corporate Memory keeping untouched (in terms of storage, maintenance) the heterogeneous and distributed nature of the actual info sources. RDF also allows us to create a common ontology to represent the enterprise model. The ontological commitment, a fundamental choice in our approach to design the Corporate Memory, is motivated by our belief that the community of corporate stakeholders is sharing some common global views of the world that needs to be unified and formalized (RDFS) to form the basis of the entire information system.
- Machine Learning Techniques make the system adaptive to the user, and comes even more naturally due to the previous choices, as presented in the following section.

2   The Role of Preference in Knowledge Management

The purpose of this section is to discuss how our work (preference learning) fits into the Knowledge Management system.

2.1   Getting the User Profile

One of the advantages of an enterprise that should be exploited by such a corporate information management system is that the users (i.e. the employees) can be known (their domains of interest/competence, their current activities/tasks). This can be especially useful in some cases where users are likely to be overwhelmed by the quantity of information to process and navigate themselves through (new employees during accommodation, technology monitoring scientists) who would appreciate personalized, automated help in their process of information retrieval.

2.2   Using Semantic Annotations

On the other hand, we have "human and machine understandable" semantic information upon the corporate knowledge offered by the RDF formalization, based upon an "enterprise ontology" (RDF schema).

The combination of these two sources of information can provide a rich ground to infer knowledge about the users probable/possible preferences. This combination is made possible due to the fact that we use the same RDF standard for formalizing the user profile; the same base ontology for the enterprise and user models.

It can be imagined that the information combined from these sources will form sets of attributes that will be used as input for a Machine Learning (ML) mechanism.

In order to set up such a ML mechanism, there are two main tasks to carry out:

1. Getting and formalizing the information to be decomposed as attributes to feed the ML mechanism.
2. Defining the ML methodology to process this info

2.3   Collecting the Information to Create a Set of Most Meaningful Attributes

We will need to answer the following question: *Why does a user prefer a document?*

In our attempt to give an example of some possible answers, we are gradually going deeper and deeper into details in case of complex answers: *The document is interesting.*

- Because it has been stated so:
    - By the user himself (the user has already seen the document, and "told" the system, that he is interested in)
    - By someone else (someone, maybe "close" to the user, wanted to share a favorable opinion about a document)
- Because it concerns a topic close to the users *interest fields*:
    - by the relation with the user:
        * Personal interest fields
        * Professional interest fields (known by his role in the enterprise)
    - by the way they are obtained:
        * Declared interest fields (the user has stated his interest in documents concerning a topic)
        * Implied interest fields (the user is included in a community of interest which is close to a topic, like in [13])

The second question, that introduces the notion of temporality into the preference: Why does a user prefer a document at a given moment?

In other words, to make the difference from the first question: *Why does a user prefer a document at a given moment, and does not prefer it at another moment?*

The document is interesting only if seen the first time (or the first few times)

- It is interesting during a certain period:
- When the user performs a certain activity
- Etc.

These answers are just some samples, one can think of many other possible reasons. Though, it is a very important to find the right questions and answers, that include the majority of possible situations. Indeed, getting the right questions and answers and translating them into quantifiable attributes, and making sure that the highest number of possible situations are observed is a key to the success of such a learning mechanism, that may even outclass in importance the chosen learning technique.

Nevertheless, we will present our approach in the Comma project to choose some typical answers and attributes, but we will focus more on the second issue: the preference learning methodology.

3   The Design of the CoMMA System

The design of CoMMA, presented in this section, can be viewed as our attempt to implement a corporate knowledge management framework.

3.1   The Agent Architecture

The chosen MAS consists of a society of coarse-grained agents, that fulfill in general multiple roles, and are organized in a small number of functional sub-societies. The MAS architecture was designed in order to optimize task-division, flexibility and robustness of the system, and network layout (extensibility, scalability, traffic optimization).

For the implementation of the prototype system, the Jade agent platform was chosen, which is an Open Source Project developed by project partners, University of Parma and CSELT. Jade is an agent platform implemented in Java, which is Fipa compliant, thus having the advantage of a wide opening towards Internet and the Web, interoperability with other MAS-s, and future systems.

In the current status of implementation, the CoMMA system will help the user in three main tasks:

- insertion and RDF annotation of documents,
- search of existing documents, and
- autonomous document delivery in a push fashion to provide the user with information about new documents that the system predicts interesting for him.

The agent categories present in the system can be classified into four main areas:

1. Document and annotation management.
2. Ontology (Enterprise and User Models) management.
3. User management.
4. Agent interconnection and matchmaking.

The agents from the document dedicated sub-society are concerned with the exploitation of the documents and annotations composing the corporate memory, they will search and retrieve the references matching the query of the user with the help of the ontological agents.

The agents from the ontology dedicated sub-society are concerned with the management of the ontological aspects of the information retrieval activity especially the queries about the hierarchy of concepts and the different views.

The agents from user dedicated sub-society are concerned with the interface, the monitoring, the assistance and the adaptation to the user. Finally the agents from the interconnection dedicated sub-society are in charge of the matchmaking of the other agents based upon their respective needs.

We have already experimented such an architecture in Network Supervision [6], with Machine Learning abilities [9]. More recently, an interaction-based strategy has been experimented [12].

3.2   The Learning Agent

The first context to assess preference learning was chosen to be the document retrieval scenario, via semantic annotations. The search engine used for document retrieval in the CoMMA system is an inference engine called CORESE [4] developed by INRIA, one of the partners of the project. CORESE uses Conceptual Graphs and combines the advantages of using the RDF language for expressing and exchanging metadata, and the query and inference mechanisms available in CG formalism. In order to produce inferences, CORESE exploits the common aspects between CG and RDF: it defined a mapping from annotation statements (RDF triples) to Conceptual Graphs and vice-versa.

One of the shortcomings of such a query retrieval engine is that there is no standard method to sort the information returned, such as keyword frequency in keyword-based search engines. The returned data set must be post-processed, filtered and sorted to present the user with the relevant information. Here comes the aid offered by our ML mechanism.

In the CoMMA system, information that feeds the ML comes from several sources: The document sub-society (the annotations accompanying a query response), the user sub-society (user monitoring and explicit user feedback), and ontology sub-society (to help getting the meaning of the results). Therefore, the learning behavior was awarded to the User Profile Manager agent, which belongs to the connection dedicated sub-society, and performs notably a role of middleman between agents. This decision was justified also by network traffic optimization reasons, especially because in reaction to a user action (query), several interactions can be triggered between agents of different roles.

For example, during a query retrieval, the main interactions are as described in the following figure.

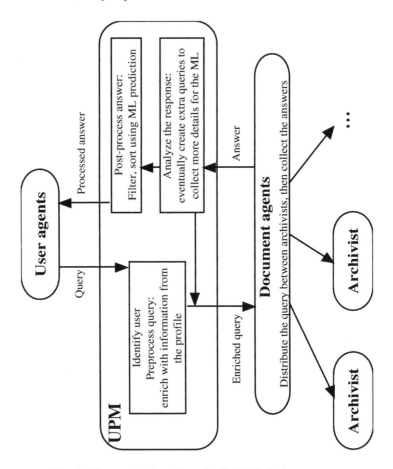

Fig. 1. The main interactions in CoMMA during a query

3.3 The Learning Cycle

The goal of the ML component is to produce a set of rules that will be used to produce predictions about user preferences. It can be supposed that the system starts with a set of predefined rules, that will be gradually improved during the process of adaptation to users. Otherwise, the system would start with an empty knowledge base, and will undergo a training period, to accumulate sufficient knowledge to allow its deployment.

In our approach, user adaptability comes from both implicit observation of the user (user monitoring subsystem), and explicit user feedback.

Within the ML subsystem, we use a "predict-or-learn" type protocol, that is, when the input is coming from query answers, the system tries to use its knowledge to predict, otherwise, when the input comes from the user in the form of negative feedback, the system tries to update its rules set.

3.4   A Sample Set of Attributes

A sample set of attributes is used to create instances from the answers we gave as examples to the question of preference. We tried to make it diverse and for most of them restricted the scope as much as possible for the sake of simplicity of our prototype. We also tried to stick close to the concepts defined in the prototype ontology, that we used as a basis for our first enterprise model.

The first set of attributes relates the document to knowledge recorded in the user profile. Concepts defined in the ontology which are used for this purpose are *Topic*, *Concerns*, *Interestedby*, *CommunitiesofInterest*, etc .

We have also used a number of attributes automatically generated by *user monitoring*. In our example we have imagined a simple user monitoring scenario, that supposes tracking each consultation of a document by the user, and building a navigation history (or consultation trace). These attributes refer to statistics about document and document category visits.

Finally we have a set of attributes containing specific information about the particular document being analysed (ratings for the document of the user in question, public ratings of other users eventually close to the user).

The issue regarding the correctness of the choice of these concepts, how to make them more generic or how they can be adapted to a specific enterprise, we are addressing in the next stage of our project: there we will intend to create a generic process for attribute collection, instead of analyzing how these attributes are fit for their purpose.

4   The Use of Preference Knowledge

As mentioned in the introduction we define preference knowledge as knowledge about a preference between elements of a set. Such knowledge can be stated in various forms: a numerical value assigned for each item, a total ordering relation, a partial ordering relation or even a preordering of the set.

Logical models have been proposed to deal with such knowledge, some dealing directly with the comparison abilities [10].

It is generally admitted that a preference stands for an order that maybe partial, even a preorder, but that it is often convenient to represent it by a linear extension (which is a total order) or a numeric value compatible with the known orderings.

Then, in terms of Machine Learning, different strategies may be used, depending on the form of the preference knowledge.

4.1   Numeric Labelling

A numeric labeling, i.e. a mapping of our set of examples into a set of real numbers, is a convenient way to summarize a preference relation. Some Machine Learning methods are available to learn numerical variables [7,3,2].

Generally, the methods for learning to predict a numerical variable v measure the quality of a predictive rule R by the standard deviation $Q(R, v) = \sigma^2(v|R)$ of the value of the variable among the set of objects verifying the concept R to be tested.

The lower $Q(R, v)$ is, the better R is to predict v, because the mean value of v can be used with less error. With such criteria, any learning method will lead to grouping several neighbour values around their mean. Then, the learnt rules will not be very different from rules learnt from examples roughly rated with a finite set of values.

4.2   The Order Relation

By definition, a binary relation, which we note $\lhd$, is an order if it has the following properties:

- reflexive $x \lhd x$,
- transitive: if $x \lhd y$ and $y \lhd z$, then $x \lhd z$,
- antisymmetric: if $x \lhd y$ and $y \lhd x$, then $x = y$.

Then, we can imagine to learn the binary relation by learning each of its elements, that is, learn on each couple of objects (a, b) such that $a \lhd b$. Then, let us summarize the suitable properties of such a learning set for this approach to work correctly.

First, if (a, b) with $a \lhd b$ is an example, then (b, a) is a counter-example. Then, what happens to (a, a)? We can see that they would be both examples and counter-examples, then it is better to consider the strict order relation, and eliminate diagonal elements.

With these hypotheses, the description of an example is made of 2 parts: the attributes which are modified between a and b, and those which keep the same value. We can notice here that these attributes are the same as those involved in the sorting tree of our examples.

Finally, our method appears to be "half lazy", in comparison with lazy learning methods, like kNN or LWR [1]. Our learned knowledge is partly explicit, but in the classification step, we need to compare a new instance with several elements of the learning set (maybe in a dichotomic way) to put it in the right place.

4.3   Statistical Evaluation Criteria

Usually in Machine Learning, particularly for building of decision trees, the learned classification rules are evaluated by their similarity to the desired classification.

We can use the same principle here, and we have two possible families of criteria. If we can compute a rank for each element, the similarity is computed by measuring the rank correlation to the expected ranking. Otherwise, each pair must be given: then we use a pairwise comparison between the expected order and the learnt order.

Several measures of similatity between 2 different orderings of the same data have been proposed. In each case, one has to deal with tied elements.

The Spearman rank order correlation. The Spearman rank order correlation r_s is a correlational measure that is used when both variables are ordinal. The traditional formula for calculating the Spearman rank-order correlation is

$$Corr(r, r') = 1 - \frac{6 \sum_{i=1}^{i=n} (r_i - r'_i)^2}{n(n^2 - 1)}$$

where r and r' are the ranks to compare of paired ranks. When there are tied cases they should be assigned the mean of their ranks. The mean of the ranks from $p+1$ to $p+n$ is $\frac{1}{n}(\frac{(n+p)(n+p+1)}{2} - \frac{p(p+1)}{2})$, which become after simplification $\frac{n+2p+1}{2}$.

The Kendall pairwise τ criterion. When we have to compare each pair of data, they can be classified as either tied (T), concordant (P), or discordant (Q).

The best measure for this case is Kendall's τ_b which takes into account a correction for tied pairs. Its formula is

$$\tau_b = \frac{P - Q}{\sqrt{(P + Q + T_x)(P + Q + T_y)}}$$

where T_x is the number of pairs tied on X but not Y, and T_y is the number of pairs tied on Y but not X.

4.4   Verifying the Consistency of the Method

In the case we perform a pairwise learning of the order relation, we can notice that a fundamental property, the transitivity, can be guaranteed by the learning process itself, as we show below for a version space method [8].

We can check that, if, for 3 examples the transitivity holds, then it is not necessary to add the 3rd pair as example to learn the relation :

- let $(a, b) = (a_1 \dots a_n, b_1 \dots b_n)$ and $(b, c) = (b_1 \dots b_n, c_1 \dots c_n)$. Then, S is of the form $L \wedge R$, with the left part L as a generalisation of both a and b, and the right part R of both b and c. Then, as L is a generalisation of a and R of c, S is a generalisation of (a, c).
- with the same conventions, G has a disjunctive form whose elements reject all the examples, then, if we represent any of its elements as $L \wedge R$. If (b,a) and (c,b) are rejected, it means that L rejects b or R rejects a, and L rejects c or R rejects b. But G must also be a generalisation of S.

Of course, this is only a scheme of the proof, and is, strictly speaking, only available for version-space-like learning. In a more general case, like decision tree learning, we can only make the hypothesis that it is true. We concluded that we could learn directly a sorting rule (in a greedy way, like decision trees) and evaluate the obtained rule with the τ criteria defined in section 4.3.

5 Conclusion

The Machine Learning and user adaptability component is a very important aspect in the CoMMA project. In this paper we presented the advances that we have made in this domain, especially focussing on the learning of preference data for document retrieval. The main choice we focus on does not only present the usefulness of Machine Learning, but also tries to overcome some of the gaps and limitations of semantic based information retrieval systems. The first implementation of our algorithm has given the expected quick results during the intermediate trials during the project, and allowed experimental validation through feedback from the users. The next stage of our research is focusing on the "generic lerning problem", that instead of being built upon a predefined set of attributes, will try to offer a formal procedure to collect the attributes from "observable concepts" present in the ontology.

References

1. D. Aha. Tolerating noisy, irrelevant, and novel attributes in instance-based learning algorithms. *International Journal of Man Machine Studies*, 36(2):267–216, 1992.
2. L. Breiman. Bagging predictors. *Machine Learning*, 24:123, 1996.
3. L. Breiman. Stacked regression. *Machine Learning*, 24:49, 1996.
4. Olivier Corby, Rose Dieng, and C. Hébert. A Conceptual Graph Model for W3C Resource Description Framework. In *the 8th International Conference on Conceptual Structures (ICCS'00)*, number LNCS 1867 in Lecture Notes in Artificial Intelligence, Darmstadt, Germany, 2000. Springer Verlag, Springer Verlag.
5. CoMMA Consortium. Corporate Memory Management through Agents. In *E-Work and E-Business conference, Madrid*, October 2000.
6. Babak Esfandiari, Gilles Deflandres, and Joël Quinqueton. An interface agent for network supervision. In *Intelligent Agents for Telecommunication Applications*, Budapest, Hungary, 1996. ECAI'96 Workshop IATA, IOS Press.
7. O. Gascuel. A conceptual regression method. In Katharina Morik, editor, *EWSL-89, 4th European Working Session on Learning*, pages 81–90, Montpellier, France, Décembre 1989. Jean Sallantin and Joel Quinqueton, CRIM, Pitman, Morgan Kaufman.
8. Tom M. Mitchell. *Machine Learning*. Mac Graw Hill, 1997.
9. Joël Quinqueton, Babak Esfandiari, and Richard Nock. Chronicle learning and agent oriented techniques for network management and supervision. In Dominique Gaïti, editor, *Intelligent Networks and Intelligence in Networks*. Chapman & Hall, September 1997.
10. P-Y. Schobbens. A comparative logic for preferences. In Pierre-Yves Schobbens, editor, *Working Notes of 3rd ModelAge Workshop: Formal Models of Agents*, Sesimbra, Portugal, January 1996.
11. P.-Y. Schobbens and J.-F. Raskin. The logic of "initially" and "next": Complete axiomatization and complexity. *Information Processing Letters*, 69(5):221–225, March 1999.
12. Nicolas Sabouret and Jean Paul Sansonnet. Learning collective behavior from local interactions. In this book, 2001.
13. Michal Pechoucek, Vladimir Marik, and Jaroslav Barta. Cplant: An acquaintance model based coalition formation multi-agent system. In this book, 2001.

Towards Requirements Analysis for Autonomous Agent Behaviour

Sorabain Wolfheart de Lioncourt[1] and Michael Luck[2]

[1] Department of Computer Science,
University of Warwick,
Coventry, CV4 7AL, UK
bane@dcs.warwick.ac.uk

[2] Dept of Electronics and Computer Science
University of Southampton
Southampton SO17 1BJ, UK
mml@ecs.soton.ac.uk

Abstract. The importance of methodologies for the construction of agent-based systems has recently begun to be recognised, and an increase in efforts directed at addressing this concern is currently being seen. Yet the focus of the majority of such work is on the *design* aspects of methodology or on the *higher-level* aspects of analysis. Of no less importance, however, are the behavioural requirements and specification of autonomous agents, which in some sense precede these phases of the development process. In this paper, we provide a detailed analysis of these requirements, and offer a preliminary view on how to focus design on meeting these requirements.

1   Introduction

An intelligent autonomous agent is expected to act for extended periods without human intervention. Although the agent is free to set its own goals and decide how best to achieve them we, as designers or developers, will have particular roles in mind for the agent, and will expect it to act accordingly. This paper details how we might specify behavioural constraints on an autonomous agent, and how to motivate the agent to direct its behaviour accordingly, while still retaining the benefits of autonomy.

At any moment an agent may have several feasible actions that it can perform, and it needs to select the appropriate action according to the external stimuli and its internal needs. Mechanisms for deciding which action is most appropriate are normally termed *action selection mechanisms* [10,5,2,8]. For some types of behaviour the external stimuli are enough to determine the appropriate action, as in obstacle avoidance [4]. For other types of behaviour both external and internal stimuli need to be taken into account, such as dealing with the short-term need for food [12]. In some cases we wish the agent's behaviour to exhibit goal-directedness. For example, if an agent finds itself in a situation where there is no food in the local area then the appropriate behaviour is to move to a new area. Where an appropriate behaviour requires a significant amount of directed action over time we need the concept of an intention [3,9] as a special kind of internal drive, otherwise the agent will have to constantly notice that it needs to move to a new

B. Dunin-Kęplicz and E. Nawarecki (Eds.): CEEMAS 2001, LNAI 2296, pp. 179–186, 2002.

area, and may dither as the external simulti and internal needs change [7,11]. We refer to a mechanism for generating, assessing, and dropping goals and intentions as a *goal management mechanism*.

In this paper we examine these issues in more detail, using the example of a multi-agent solution to a highly simplified emergency services coordination problem. The problem facing the designer is to motivate autonomous ambulance agents to pick up and deliver patients to hospital in such a way as to minimize some performance measure.

In the next section, we look at the different types of behavioural requirement we might impose on an autonomous agent.

2   Behavioural Requirements

If we choose to field an autonomous agent in a particular domain then it must be the case that the environment is too complex or time-consuming for us to develop a control system using conventional software engineering methods. Instead of prescribing the appropriate action to take under all possible circumstances we delegate the responsibility for choosing the appropriate actions to the agent itself. An autonomous agent architecture that is capable of directing its own behaviour towards maintaining a set of requirements in a complex environment would greatly reduce the development time and costs of such systems.

In this section we look at the requirements we may place on agent behaviour, and introduce a performance measure that allows us to measure how effective an agent is at meeting the requirements over time. The kinds of behavioural requirement are similar to those described in [1].

We argue that without an adequate specification of the behavioural requirements, or without any general measure of how well an agent meets these requirements, any agent development process will remain ad-hoc and impossible to generalize.

2.1   Avoidance and Maintenance Requirements

The first type of constraint on agent behaviour we consider is where the agent is required to avoid or maintain particular states of affairs over some timeframe (up to and including the lifetime of the agent). Such requirements include maintaining homeostasis in a simulated biological entity [6], or avoiding situations that puts the agent in danger. In our example, an autonomous ambulance agent must avoid running out of fuel at any point over its lifetime. Maintenance and avoidance requirements are equivalent – a requirement to avoid some set of states (such as any state where the fuel level is zero) is the same as a requirement to maintain the complement of those states (any state where the fuel is greater than zero).

2.2   Periodic Requirements

A periodic requirement is one where we wish the agent to perform a set task periodically over some timeframe. Such requirements may include information gathering, performing diagnostics, or general maintenance. For an autonomous ambulance agent, a periodic requirement will be to check and service the ambulance to reduce the chance of a breakdown.

2.3 One-Off Tasks

The previous two types of requirement both relate to matters that persist over time. As well as such requirements, an agent may be acting as a part of a system where it will be delegated one-off tasks to perform. Such tasks may include those that should be completed as soon as possible, or before a given deadline. A new one-off task is created every time an emergency call is received by the system, with the goal of ferrying the patient to a hospital.

2.4 Types of Violation

Clearly we would ideally prefer that an agent never violates any of its requirements, but in general this may not be possible. Circumstances may arise where the agent cannot possibly maintain all of its requirements, but is faced with a choice between which requirements to fulfil, and which to let slip. Before examining how to specify preferences between violations, we examine the different types of violation that can occur.

Flexible Violation. A flexible violation is one that can be rectified by an appropriate choice of actions. For example, an ambulance agent can put off its regular maintenance checks and servicing during times of crisis, and perform them later instead.

Trap Violation. A trap violation is one which can never be rectified, once violated it remains violated for all time. For example, a patient may urgently require an organ transplant, and a suitable organ becomes available at another hospital. The ferrying of the organ to the patient is highly time-critical, and after a certain deadline has passed the organ is rendered useless. Allowing this deadline to pass cannot be rectified by any future action (another organ may become available, but this would form a seperate one-off task to ferry it).

Lethal Violation. A lethal violation is similar to a trap violation in that it will remain violated for all time. But more than this, a lethal violation means that the agent becomes incapable of any action from the time of violation onwards. For an ambulance, allowing itself to run out of fuel is a lethal violation as it will be unable to continue on its current assignments, or undertake any new ones (in this simulation we do not allow the recovery of such ambulances).

We would normally expect an agent to prefer flexible violations over trap and lethal violations; and to prefer trap violations to lethal violations. We would not expect an ambulance to prefer carrying a non-urgent patient to ferrying a vital organ; nor would we normally wish an ambulance to run itself out of fuel in an attempt to ferry a vital organ.

3 Specifying Preferences between Violations

When the agent is faced with no way of satisfying all of its requirements it needs a way to choose which requirement violations are most preferrable. In general we cannot simply specify a strict preference ordering between requirements such that higher requirements are never violated in preference to lower ones, as there are many different levels of violation and we may be faced between choosing between sets of violations (suffering the violation of more than one requirement). It may be preferrable to suffer a short duration flexible violation of a particularly important requirement in favour of trap violations of several lower level requirements.

The solution proposed by the authors is to provide the agent with a method of deriving a quantitative measure of the *badness* of a violation (violation cost). The choice between requirement violations is then a matter of choosing the course of action that leads to the minimum expected badness.

3.1 Violation Cost

In general we will be dealing with agents with an indeterminate life-span. In order to measure their performance meaningfully over any period of time, we will derive a measure of *instantaneous* violation cost for each requirement that is not being satisified at that moment in time. The agent's performance over any interval can then be calculated by a summation of the instantaneous violation costs accrued over that interval. The alternative to the accruement of instantaneous costs is to impose the overall cost of a violation either after it has been rectified, or once a course of action that will lead to this overall cost has been committed to. However, this kind of solution will penalize an agent if the period its performance is being measured does not cover the complete violation. For example, if a patient has not been recovered by the end of a performance measurement period, then an agent that only accrues costs after rectification of a violation will not have been penalized for leaving the patient unrecovered. However, an ambulance that performed *better* and collected the patient before the end of a performance measurement period would have accrued the cost of recovering that patient, and would have fared worse in the measurement period, despite actually doing better. A similar problem occurs if the cost is accrued when a violation is committed to, where an agent that puts off committing to anything is measured as performing better, although in practice is performing worse. The only way to avoid such problems is to take on a continuous instantaneous measure of violation cost, which is the approach taken in this paper.

Definition 1. *For an agent with n requirements $r_1, r_2, \ldots, r_n$, and associated cost functions $c_1, c_2, \ldots, c_n$, the instantaneous violation cost of being in a state s is given by*

$$\mathcal{V}(s) = \sum_{i=0}^{n} c_i(s)$$

If the environment's state changes over time with the function, $s(t)$, then we can calculate the overall violation cost over a given interval by the formula given in Definition 2. This measure can be used to compare different agent architectures, or action choices under the same conditions.

Definition 2. *The overall violation cost of an agent whose state at time, t, is given by* $s(t)$ *over the interval* $[t_1, t_2]$ *is given by*

$$C(s) = \int_{t_1}^{t_2} \mathcal{V}(s(t)) \, dt$$

Clearly we can exploit this simple relationship both ways, being able to derive an overall violation cost function from instantaneous cost functions, or reversing the process and being able to recover an instantaneous cost function from an overall cost function (by simply taking the instantaneous cost to be the derivative of the overall cost function).

3.2   Violation Cost Functions

The formulae given in the previous definitions are designed to be as general as possible, where the instantaneous violation cost can depend on any combination of environmental state variables. In practice, the violation cost functions with be considerably simpler than this generality allows, often depending on only a single measurable variable.

Example instantaneous violation cost functions for the simple ambulance agent are shown in Figure 1.

The cost function for a violation of the fuel maintenance requirement is simple: if the agent runs out of fuel then it incurs an immediate cost of 100 (this number has been chosen arbitrarily). Note that this is the instantaneous cost, so it will incur a cost of 100 at every instant beyond the time it ran out of fuel as well, which will penalize an agent that ran out of fuel early on more than one that ran out late it its lifetime.

The periodic requirement to service the ambulance can be violated flexibly, and the service deadline at time $t1$ is soft (that is, there is still reason to get the ambulance serviced after the ideal date has passed). Here the instantaneous violation cost increases steadily, as it becomes increasingly likely that the ambulance will breakdown in proportion to the time that has passed since the last service. The cost function is always increasing, and is bounded above at 100, which is the same level as the instantaneous cost of running out of fuel. This is because if the ambulance actually breaks down then it is effectively the same as if it ran out of fuel (for demonstration purposes, this scenario does not allow the recovery of ambulances that have either broken down, or run out of fuel). Note again that the upper bound on the instantaneous violation cost does not indicate a bounded cost for a violation – the instantaneous violation cost is effectively the derivative of the overall cost function, and in the limit the overall cost function is still increasing with a slope of 100.

Finally, the cost functions relating to one-off tasks to recover patients are of a similar form to the servicing requirement cost function, except that in this case the ideal solution would be if the patient were instantly recovered and placed in hospital. This is unlikely to ever be the case, so an ambulance agent will always expect to incur some cost in recovering a patient. Here the instantaneous cost function is again increasing, this is to ensure that no single patient is ever left waiting for an unreasonable amount of time. If the instantaneous cost function was at a fixed level then ambulances would be striving to minimise the mean waiting time for patients, but would favour patients that are easier to

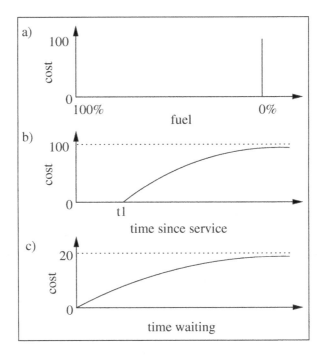

Fig. 1. Cost functions for violations of the ambulance requirements. a) cost of violating fuel maintenance requirement. b) cost of not receiving regular servicing. c) cost of patient not being delivered to hospital.

pick up (i.e. are near the hospital and ambulance stations) over those that are far away. This kind of behaviour could lead to patients being left indefinitely, although the mean waiting time was still minimized. Rather than just wanting to minimise the mean waiting time, we also want to ensure that the maximum waiting time is also kept low. Here we have chosen to bound the maximum instantaneous cost at 20. This number was chosen quite arbitrarily for this example, but represents our desire for ambulance agents to not risk running out of fuel or breaking down in their desire to recover patients. In order to decide to risk running out of fuel an ambulance would have to reason that it will recover 5 patients in doing so, which would otherwise never be recovered. This is unlikely to be the case, even if there is only one ambulance, since the agent deciding this course of action can choose to refuel and service itself and then collect those patients safely.

4   Choosing Appropriate Requirements

We make two assumptions about each requirement of an agent, namely that:

1. there exists at least one possible situation where the requirement is violated; and

2. at least one of the situations in which the requirement is violated could either have been predicted and avoided, or is a flexible violation that is detectable and can be rectified by an appropriate choice of agent actions.

Both of these assumptions serve to protect the agent from worrying about situations that it can do nothing about. The first assumption means that it must be possible for each requirement to be violated. For example, it would be pointless to give an ambulance agent the requirement *avoid being in two places at once*, since the ambulance can never find itself in such a situation.

The second assumption states that an agent must be able to predict and avoid at least some lethal and trap violations for each requirement (ideally, but not necessarily all). This will depend on the perceptual and physical capabilities of an agent. For example, a vampire with the requirement *avoid having a wooden stake driven into the heart* needs to be able to perceive a would-be vampire slayer with stake in hand, and then be able to run away very fast in the other direction. A vampire without the senses to detect the danger, or the ability to avoid it once it has been detected can do nothing to avoid the requirement being violated.

In the case of a flexible violation the agent need not necessarily be able to predict and avoid the violation before it arises, but should be able to rectify at least some of the possible situations in which a flexible violation has occurred (not necessarily all). This will again depend on the physical capabilities of an agent, it would be reasonable to expect a vampire to be able to rectify a violation of the requirement *avoid sunlight* should it be unfortunate enough to find itself in such a situation, but giving a tree the same requirement would be pointless since the the average tree is powerless to rectify such situations.

If either assumption is not met then the behaviour of the agent with such a requirement will be identical to an agent without the requirement. If requirement serves no purpose in directing the agent, it should be removed.

5   Conclusion

The analysis of requirements for autonmous agents considered above provides a first pass towards the first stage in the software development process. The method provided in this paper gives both a general way for agents to calculate the utility of their actions, and an effective performance measure that is independent of an agent's capabilities.

The violation costs assigned to requirements play a dominant role in prescribing how an autonomous agent should behave. In order for this framework to be successful there needs to be a clear methodology for selecting appropriate values to match the behaviour that the designer has in mind. This is a general problem with many motivational systems [12,2], where the appropriate parameters for specific agents are often found by trial-and-error rather than by a formal analysis.

References

1. C. Balkenius. The roots of motivation. In J.-A Meyer, H. L. Roitblat, and S. W. Wilson, editors, *From Animals to Animats II*, Cambridge, MA, 1993. MIT Press.

2. Bruce Mitchell Blumberg. *Old Tricks, New Dogs: Ethology and Interactive Creatures*. PhD thesis, Massachusetts Institute of Technology, 1997.
3. M. E. Bratman. *Intentions, Plans and Practical Reason*. Harvard University Press, Cambridge, MA, 1987.
4. R. Brooks. A robust layered control system for a mobile robot. *IEEE Journal of Robotics and Automation*, 2:14–23, 1986.
5. Pattie Maes. How to do the right thing. *Connection Science Journal*, 1(3), 1989.
6. D. McFarland and T. Bösser. *Intelligent Behaviour in Animals and Robots*. MIT Press, Cambridge, MA, 1993.
7. M. Minsky. *The Society of Mind*. Heineman, 1987.
8. Paolo Pirjanian. *Multiple Objective Action Selection & Behaviour Fusion Using Voting*. PhD thesis, Department of Medical Informatics and Image Analysis, Aalborg University, 1998.
9. Anand S. Rao and Michael P. Georgeff. Modeling rational agents within a BDI-architecture. Technical Report 14, Australian Artificial Intelligence Institute, February 1991.
10. J. K. Rosenblatt and D. Payton. A fine-grained alternative to the subsumption architecture for mobile robot control. In *Proc IEEE/INNS Int'l Joint Conf on Neural Networks*, page 65ff, 1989.
11. M. K. Sahota. Action selection for robots in dynamic environments through inter-behaviour bidding. In D. Cliff, P. Husbands, J.-A.Meyer, and S.W. Wilson, editors, *From Animals to Animats III*, pages 138–142, Cambridge, MA, 1994. MIT Press.
12. Toby Tyrrell. *Computational Mechanisms for Action Selection*. PhD thesis, University of Edinburgh, 1993.

Messages, Clocks, and Gravitation*

Antoni Mazurkiewicz and Dobiesław Wróblewski

Institute of Computer Science of PAS
Ordona 21, 01-237 **Warsaw**
{amaz,wrobldob}@ipipan.waw.pl

Abstract. The message system considered in the paper consists of a finite set of places, each of them capable to store a fixed number of messages. Places can be joined by links and then they are called neighbours. Messages are created and moved from neighbour to neighbour until reaching their destinations, and then disappear. The aim of this paper is to define a rule of message moving, which ensures responsiveness of the system, i.e. a rule that guarantees any message appearing in the system to eventually reach its destination. Such a rule, based on so-called "potential function" of messages, is found and its adequacy is proved.

Keywords: Message passing; local clocks; potential; networks; distributed algorithms

1   Introduction

We consider message systems consisting of mailboxes (joined by links), and messages that can be created, move from mailbox to mailbox along the joining links and disappear after reaching their destination. Mailboxes have limited capacity, therefore, not all routes through the system are available for messages and some of them have to give way to others. It might happen that some messages are constantly pushed away from their way and never get their targets. To avoid such situations, a rule of message moving, which ensures responsiveness of the system should be defined. Such a rule should guarantee any message appearing in the system to eventually reach its destination. In particular, it should prevent messages from circulating endlessly in the network, or from being constantly blocked by others in a mailbox.

To this end, the notion of potential is introduced. The potential of a message depends on its age and its distance from the target: the younger message and farther from the target, the greater potential. Then the required rule, allowing to perform only moves that decrease the potential of involved messages, is proved to be satisfactory. The potential function can be determined locally, so that the rule can be applied locally, and then the whole system can be viewed as distributed.

To supply the system with information about distances between places needed for potential calculation, mailboxes update their mutual distances if necessary. They are doing it locally and independently of the flow of messages

---

* partially supported by grant KBN 7 T11C 006 20

B. Dunin-Kęplicz and E. Nawarecki (Eds.): CEEMAS 2001, LNAI 2296, pp. 187–196, 2002.
© Springer-Verlag Berlin Heidelberg 2002

through the system. Results of updating (final or intermediate) create information used for messages navigation through the network. Moreover, each mailbox is supplied with a clock, being advanced after some mailbox actions. Clocks indicate local time as non-negative integers; their indications are not subject to any synchronisation mechanisms whatsoever; it is only assumed that all clocks are always progressing.

Activity of the whole message system is uniform (no particular message and no particular mailbox is distinguished), local (any step of the system is determined by the system of a single mailbox and its neighbourhood only), self-stabilising (it can start with an arbitrary initial state), non-deterministic (there is no prescribed order, in which messages are processed), and responsive (any message appearing in the system eventually reaches its destination).

2   Related Works

This work is significantly influenced by [1]. The authors of that work presented a greedy "hot-potato" message routing on a fixed two-dimensional mesh of mailboxes with message buffers of fixed capacity. Also, the used network was synchronous and so this model was quite specific and not very flexible.

The rationale behind this work was to generalise the interesting results achieved in [1], so as the similar algorithm could be defined for almost any kind of network, especially for the networks that work asynchronously, and whose structure fluctuates during the algorithm execution. Such types of networks seem to become more and more commonplace nowadays (e.g. mobile networks) and become the natural environment for the mobile agents.

To this end, the structure of the network has been generalised (from a two-dimensional mesh to any connected graph), so was the mailboxes capacity (from 4 to any integer), and there is no requirement of synchronousness any more.

But, what seems even more important (and is completely new, as compared with [1]), is the distance recognition (signposts) part of the algorithm. In [1], the network was a constant during the algorithm execution, and the distances were known a priori. In this work, we present a model of a network, that can be a good approximation of a real-life network, whose structure can change during the process execution. It is crucial, that the algorithm is able to adapt to a new structure and continue working.

The routing algorithm (and the notion of potential) is also new, although it is quite straightforward in the presented model.

We use the word "self-stabilisation" as independence of algorithm results from its initial state, following [2,3,4].

3   Message Systems

A *message system* consists of a finite set P of *mailboxes*, and a set M (potentially infinite) of *messages*. In the set P of all mailboxes an irreflexive and symmetric relation E (the *neighbourhood* relation in P) is defined. Two mailboxes in this relation are called *neighbours* and each of the two is called a *neighbour* of the other. The set of mailboxes together with the neighbourhood relation form the *network* of the message system. A *path* joining mailbox p' with mailbox p'' is any sequence $(p_0, p_1, \ldots, p_n)$, $n \geq 0$, such that $p_0 = p'$, $p_n = p''$, and p_{i-1}, p_i are neighbours for all $i > 0$; number n is then called the *length* of the path. The set of mailboxes P is said to be connected if for any two mailboxes p', p'' in P there exists a path joining p' with p''. Generally, we assume that the algorithm is meant to work with a connected set of mailboxes (which is quite an obvious requirement), however, the case of a disconnected network is discussed as well.

The *distance* $\delta(p, q)$ in the network between mailboxes p and q is the length of the shortest path joining p with q, if such a path exists, and otherwise undefined. It is clear that the distance between a mailbox and its neighbour is 1. Therefore, if the distance between a mailbox p and mailbox q is n, then the distance between p and a neighbour of q is either $n - 1$, or n, or $n + 1$. Also, it is easy to observe that for any two different mailboxes p, q of the network there is a neighbour r of p such that $\delta(p, q) = \delta(r, q) + 1$.

To each mailbox $p \in P$ an integer c_p (the *capacity* of p) is assigned and to each message $m \in M$ are assigned:

(i) a mailbox $d_m \in P$ (the *destination* of m), and
(ii) an integer $t_m \in \mathcal{N}$ (the *time of birth* of m).

Given two messages, m_1, m_2, if $t_{m_1} < t_{m_2}$, we say that m_1 is *older* than m_2 (and, consequently that m_2 is *younger* than m_1), and if $t_{m_1} = t_{m_2}$, the messages are said to be of the same age.

Let $\mathbf{M} = (P, E, M)$ be a message system, arbitrary but fixed for the rest of the paper, with the set of places P, the neighbourhood relation E, and the set of messages M. A state σ of $\mathbf{M}$ is a triple $(S_\sigma, T_\sigma, B_\sigma)$ of functions:

$$S_\sigma : P \longrightarrow 2^M, \text{ the distribution function,}$$
$$T_\sigma : P \longrightarrow \mathcal{N}, \text{ the clock function,}$$
$$B_\sigma : P \times P \longrightarrow \mathcal{N}, \text{ the signpost table,}$$

such that for all $p, q \in P$

$$p \neq q \Rightarrow S_\sigma(p) \cap S_\sigma(q) = \emptyset \tag{1}$$

(*uniqueness* condition), and

$$|S_\sigma(p)| \leq c_p \tag{2}$$

(*capacity* condition). The set of all possible states is denoted as Σ. For any $p \in P$, $\sigma \in \Sigma$ we call $S_\sigma(p)$ the *contents*, $T_\sigma(p)$ the *local time*, and $B_\sigma(p)$ the *signpost table* of mailbox p at state σ ($B_\sigma(p)$ is a function, which to each $q \in P$ assigns an integer $n \in \mathcal{N}$ such that $B_\sigma(p)(q) = B_\sigma(p, q)$), and for each mailbox $p \in P$, we define its *local state* as $\sigma(p) = (S_\sigma(p), T_\sigma(p), B_\sigma(p))$.

Message m is said to be stored in mailbox p at state σ, if $m \in S_\sigma(p)$; condition (1) guarantees that no message can be stored in two different mailboxes at the same state, condition (2) means that the number of messages stored in a mailbox cannot exceed its capacity at any state. Let $M_\sigma = \{m \mid \exists p : m \in S_\sigma(p)\}$; messages in M_σ are called *active* at state σ. Clearly, the total number of active messages in the system cannot exceed $\sum_{p\in P} c_p$.

Because of the uniqueness condition there exists at most one mailbox containing a given message; it means that for any state σ there exists a partial function, which to each active message assigns the mailbox containing it. This function, denoted by pos_σ, is defined by the equivalence: $\mathrm{pos}_\sigma(m) = p \Leftrightarrow m \in S_\sigma(p)$, and is referred to as the *position* function.

The clock function defines the local clocks situated at each mailbox. Clocks are not supposed to be synchronised: a situation, when different clocks indicate different time is perfectly allowed. Because of that, the relation of being older (younger) has a relative, not absolute, meaning. During the run of the algorithm, the local clocks will be increasing independently of each other.

The signpost table is used to indicate the proper direction of moving messages towards their destinations; its entries are approximations of true distances between mailboxes of the system. The value $B_\sigma(p, q)$ can be viewed as knowledge of the system being in state σ how far mailbox q is from mailbox p; this knowledge, called the *approximate distance* between p and q, will be proved to be more and more accurate in the course of system activity.

Before defining actions of message systems, we need some auxiliary notions. The *height* of message m at state σ of the system is the number

$$h_\sigma(m) = B_\sigma(\mathrm{pos}_\sigma(m), d_m).$$

The height of a message is (an approximation of) the distance between its current position and its destination, as computed for this position at the state σ (it can differ from the real distance as much as the values of approximate distances can differ from the true distances in the network.

By *potential* of message m, active at state $\sigma = (S_\sigma, T_\sigma, B_\sigma)$ we mean the number

$$V_\sigma(m) = 1 - \frac{1}{2 + t_m + h_\sigma(m)}$$

From the above definition it follows that $\frac{1}{2} \le V_\sigma(m) < 1$ for all messages $m \in M$ and states $\sigma \in \Sigma$. Potential of a message decreases together with its height: the smaller is its height, the lower is its potential. Similarly, the younger is the message (i.e. the greater is its time of birth), the greater is potential of m. By potential of set K of messages at state σ we mean the sum

$$V_\sigma(K) = \sum_{m\in K} V_\sigma(m).$$

The number $V_\sigma(S_\sigma(p))$ is then potential of all messages stored in place p at state σ, and the potential of the whole system $\mathbf{M}$ at state σ is a number

$$\mathbf{V}_\sigma = \sum_{p\in P} V_\sigma(S_\sigma(p)).$$

Let $N(p)$ be the set of all neighbours of p. For any mailboxes p, q and any state σ define their *supposed distance* as:

$$B_\sigma^*(p, q) = \begin{cases} 0, \text{ if } p = q, \\ \\ 1 + \min\{B_\sigma(r, q) \mid r \in N(p)\}, \\ \qquad \text{otherwise.} \end{cases}$$

Notice that by definition of B_σ^* we have $B_\sigma = \delta$ if and only if $B_\sigma = B_\sigma^*$. In this case the approximate distance at state σ is the true distance function.

4   Message System Actions

Actions of a message system are binary relations in the set of the system states. Informally speaking, any action defines a state transformation, i.e. transformation of mailboxes contents, of signpost tables, and/or of local times of mailboxes. Such a set does not distinguish any mailbox; in this sense the system is *uniform*. Any action associated to a mailbox neither can change a state of mailboxes outside its neighbourhood, nor the state of the outside mailboxes can influence the result of transformation of the neighbourhood state. In this sense the system is *local*. The following are possible actions of such a system:

(i) Updating the signpost table of a mailbox;
(ii) Activating a message in a mailbox and advancing its local time;
(iii) Moving a message to a neighbour mailbox;
(iv) Exchanging positions of two messages stored in neighbour mailboxes;
(v) Deleting a message from its destination mailbox.

A more detailed description of the message system instructions follows.

1. **Updating.** Let p, q be mailboxes. If their approximate distance is not equal to supposed distance, replace it with the supposed distance value;

2. **Creating** a message. Let p be a mailbox not completely filled. If the local time of p is equal to the birth time of a not yet active message, then activate this message by putting it into p and advance the local clock of p.

3. **Moving** a message. Let m be a message and p be its instantaneous position. If q is a neighbour mailbox of p, which is not completely filled at the moment, then take m out of p and put it into q.

4. **Swapping** messages. Let m', m'' be messages placed in two neighbour mailboxes p', p'', respectively; then replace message m' by m'' in p' and m'' by m' in p'.

5. **Deleting** a message. If the instantaneous position of a message is its destination, remove it from the mailbox (and from the set of active messages).

5   Message System Runs

Denote by R the set of all actions of $\mathbf{M}$. Any $r \in R$ is a binary relation in the set of all states Σ of the system. Observe that $\mathrm{Dom}(r) \cap \mathrm{Rng}(r) = \emptyset$ for each

$r \in R$. Instruction r is said to be *enabled* at state σ, if $\sigma \in \text{Dom}(r)$. If there exists $r \in R$ such that $(\sigma', \sigma'') \in r$ we shall write $\sigma' \to \sigma''$; relation $\to$ will be called the *step relation* of $\mathbf{M}$. An *execution sequence* of $\mathbf{M}$ is any sequence $\boldsymbol{\sigma}$ of its states,

$$\boldsymbol{\sigma} = (\sigma_0, \sigma_1, \ldots, \sigma_n, \ldots),$$

finite or infinite, such that $\sigma_{i-1} \to \sigma_i$ for each $i > 0$.

An instruction r is *pending* in execution sequence $\boldsymbol{\sigma}$, if there is $j \geq 0$, such that for all $k \geq j$ instruction r is enabled at σ_k, i.e. if

$$\{\sigma_j, \sigma_{j+1}, \ldots, \sigma_{j+n}, \ldots\} \subseteq \text{Dom}(r).$$

An execution sequence is *complete*, if it contains no pending instructions. In particular, a finite execution sequence is complete if and only if there is no action enabled at its last state. An execution sequence is *progressive*, if for each $p \in P$ and each $t \in \mathcal{N}$ there is $i \geq 0$, such that $T_{\sigma_i}(p) > t$ (the "clock axiom"). Since the set P of mailboxes is finite, from progressiveness it follows that for each $t \in \mathcal{N}$ there is $i \geq 0$ such that $T_{\sigma_i} > t$, i.e. that for all $p \in P$ it holds $T_{\sigma_i}(p) > t$. Finally, an execution sequence is *gravitational*, if for any step $\sigma_{i-1} \to \sigma_i$ but creation and update, the potential $\mathbf{V}_{\sigma_{i-1}} > \mathbf{V}_{\sigma_i}$. That is, any step (excluding creation and update) in a gravitational execution sequence decreases the total potential of the system.

Any complete, progressive, and gravitational execution sequence of a system is its *run* and the *behaviour* of a system is the set of all its runs.

Let, from now on, $\boldsymbol{\sigma} = (\sigma_0, \sigma_1, \ldots, \sigma_i, \ldots)$ be a complete run of $\mathbf{M}$ and let $\sigma_i = (S_i, T_i, B_i)$ for all $i \geq 0$. Denote also by M_i the set M_{σ_i} (of active messages at σ_i).

6 Message System Behaviour: Distance Updating

In this section we show that if P is connected, then independent of the initial state of the system, after sufficient number of steps the signpost function becomes stabilised and identical with the distance function in the network. We also discuss the case of P not being connected.

A subset $Q \subseteq \Sigma$ is an *invariant* of $\mathbf{M}$, if $\sigma' \in Q \wedge \sigma' \to \sigma'' \Rightarrow \sigma'' \in Q$ for all $\sigma', \sigma'' \in \Sigma$. Clearly, if $(\sigma_0, \sigma_1, \ldots, \sigma_n, \ldots)$ is an execution sequence of a system and Q is its invariant such that $\sigma_i \in Q$, then $\sigma_j \in Q$ for all $j \geq i$.

Define subset Σ_k of Σ as follows:

$$\Sigma_k = \{\sigma \in \Sigma \mid \forall p', p'' \in P :$$
$$(B_\sigma(p', p'') = \delta(p', p'') \leq k \vee B_\sigma(p', p'') \geq k \wedge \delta(p', p'') > k)\}$$

Informally speaking, for any state in Σ_k, the approximate distance is equal to the true distance between any two mailboxes, if their true distance is not greater than k, and the approximate distance between them is not less than k, otherwise. Observe that in case of a network with diameter less than k we have

$\Sigma_k = \Sigma_j$ for all $j \geq k$ (*diameter* of a network is the longest distance between its elements). We have the following theorems.

Theorem 1. If the network of **M** is connected, then there exists $k \geq 0$ such that $B_j(p', p'') = \delta(p', p'')$ for all $j \geq k$ and for all mailboxes p', p'' of **M**.

PROOF. The proof results from the fact that Σ_k is an invariant for any $k \geq 0$. Let the network be connected and N be its diameter. It is not easy to prove that Σ_0 holds. Next, if Σ_k holds for a state of a run and $k < N$, then eventually Σ_{k+1} will hold. Therefore, Σ_N will hold for all sufficiently far states of a run; otherwise, some updating actions would be pending forever. Thich means that for all such j the approximate distance is identical with the true distances in the network.   □

Theorem 2. If mailboxes p, q are separated (the network is disconnected), then for any integer $n \geq 0$ there exists $j \geq 0$ such that $B_j(p, q) > n$ (the value of signpost function for the pair (p, q) infinitely increases).   □

Thus, the updating procedure is not fully efficient if P is disconnected. On the other hand, the distances between mailboxes situated within the same connected part of the network will be counted properly anyway.

It is worthwhile noting that the updating procedure is self-stabilizing in that no particular initial values for $B_0(p, q)$ are assumed: updating procedure can start from arbitrary non-negative integers assigned to initial values of the signpost function. Consequently, if some of the links break, or the updating procedure is disturbed by an external force changing by random one or more values of the signpost function, nothing wrong happens; the updating procedure starts over again and calculates eventually proper distances in the network. In case of disconnection, as soon as the network re-connects, the algorithm becomes fully efficient again.

Observe also that the updating procedure is local. If values of the signpost table $B(p, q)$ for all $q \in V$ are stored in mailbox p, then the calculation of updated version of B needs only information stored in p and the neighbours of p. Thus, updating of $B(p, q)$ is done in the neighbourhood of p only. Notice also that the signpost function, in opposite to the distance function, needs not to be symmetric before it stabilises.

7   Message System Behaviour: Message Passing

In this section we show responsiveness of the introduced message system, namely we prove that any message born in the system eventually reaches its destination.

Lemma 1. Let M be the set of all messages with minimum potential at a certain system state. Then any of these messages is enabled to be swapped, or moved, or deleted, each action with decreasing the system potential.   □

By the above Lemma the message system is guaranteed to be deadlock-free. E.g. two messages with the minimum potential can always be swapped diminishing their joint potential, as shown in the following example.

Consider a network in a state σ with five mailboxes, five links, and five active messages, meeting the following properties: $d_{m_i} = \text{pos}_\sigma(m_{i+1})$ for $i = 1, \ldots, 4$, $d_{m_5} = \text{pos}_\sigma(m_1)$, $t_{m_i} = 0$ for $i = 1, \ldots, 5$, as depicted in Fig. 1.

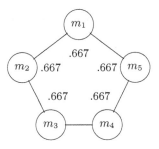

Fig. 1. A network with potential 3.333

Consider then the same network in a state σ' achieved by applying the action **swap**(m_1, m_2) at the state σ. The action is enabled, as m_1 has the minimum potential (as well as all m_i for $i = 2, \ldots, 5$). The result is shown in Fig. 2.

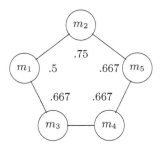

Fig. 2. The same network after **swap**(m_1, m_2); the new potential is 3.25

Theorem 3. Any message active in the message system will be eventually delivered.

PROOF. (A sketch). By contradiction. Let $K \neq \emptyset$ be the set of all messages never delivered, i.e. active in all states of a run. Let K_0 be subset of K with minimum potential. Because of progressiveness of the run, at all sufficiently far states of the run, all active messages not in K_0 will have potential higher than those in K_0 (newborn messages have potential higher than the older ones). Therefore, an instruction concerning some messages in K_0 is executed at a state of the run, since otherwise some instructions would be pending forever, contradicting the assumed completeness of the run. Therefore, joint potential of K_0 will eventually decrease. It means that the joint potential value of K_0 decreases infinitely while the run is progressing. By the definition of potential and because K_0 is a finite set, there is a finite number of joint potential values less than any given number, hence such a decreasing sequence must be finite. Thus, it must terminate with 0. But it is possible only with K_0 equal to the empty set, a contradiction.   □

As it was already stated, when the network disconnects, the mutual distances between mailboxes in different parts of the network start rising infinitely.

On the other hand, the disconnection of the network obviously causes some messages to be undeliverable. Such messages could become obstacles in the flow of other messages that are still deliverable. However, this is not the case. As the distances to unreachable targets are rising, the potential of undeliverable messages is also rising. This way, such messages get lower and lower priority and are no longer an obstacle after a finite number of system steps. They can be seen as postponed. Note, that as soon as the network re-connects, the messages start decreasing their potential and the situation gets back to normal. This is how the system deals with the case of disconnectedness.

8   Application, Experiments, Complexity

The algorithm (possibly with modifications) can be used as a base communication system of any computer network whose structure is fluctuating, the natural application area is mobile networking.

The algoritm can be easily seen (and implemented) by means of a multi-agent system, and in fact was already implemented on PEGAZ Multi-Agent Platform [5], however, a really efficient, very low-level implementation is suggested.

For the experiments, the algorithm was implemented in C++ with no modifications at all. The non-distributed runs (sequences of single actions) were tested on several small graphs. For instance, 25 sequential runs were performed on a graph consisting of 10 mailboxes (each of capacity 1) and 10 links. 10 messages were the initial load (one message per each mailbox), each message's distance from its destination was 3. The distance table was initialised with random values from range [0..900]. For clarity of results, the runs were performed in two phases: distance updating, and message delivery. The minimum, average, and maximum number of steps of the first phase was 180, 204.56, and 232, respectively. The message passing took less steps: 36, 40.12, and 45, respectively.

The scope of this paper does not allow us to present neither proofs nor a detailed discussion of the complexity of the algorithm. They will be given in the full version of the present paper.

9 Conclusions

Never ending system of message passing has been discussed. Message can be created at places of the network, transmitted to neighbour places, and deleted after reaching their destinations. The common rule they must observe is to keep the maximum number of messages stored in one place not exceeding the capacity of the place. To each place, a local clock is assigned.

The signpost table is introduced to be used in the message routing, and the algorithm is defined as a set of instructions that move/swap/create the messages or update the signpost table. The run of the algorithm is required to be complete, i.e. not to contain pending instructions.

Two assumptions are needed for the system validation: the clock axiom that guarantees that any local clock will show arbitrarily late time after a sufficiently many system steps, avoiding in this way "Zeno paradox", and the completeness axiom, preventing system from postponing forever a message permanently authorised to execute a move.

For connected networks (with no places separated), any message present in the system will eventually reach its destination. Any run of the system described above looks as follows. Initially, until the signposts values become stabilised, moves of active messages are more or less chaotic. After stabilisation of distances, which eventually occurs, older messages gain priority over younger ones and (sooner or later) reach their destination and disappear.

The presented algorithm does not include any priorities/rules that could be (under some specific conditions) applied to performing actions. Employing such rules could have a positive impact on the speed of the algorithm.

Possible extensions admitting the lack of network connectedness can be also introduced, employing the timeout detection.

References

1. I. Ben-Aroya, T. Eilam and A. Schuster, Greedy Hot-Potato Routing on the Two-Dimensional Mesh, *Distrib. Comp.* **9** (1995) 3-19
2. J. Abello and S. Dolev, On the Computational Power of Self-Stabilizing Systems, *TCS* **182** (1997) 159-170
3. S. Ghosh, A. Gupta and S. Pemmaraju,
   A Self-Stabilizing Algorithm for the Maximum Flow Problem, *Distrib. Comp.* **10** (1997) 167-180
4. S.-T. Huang and L.-C. Wuu, Self-Stabilizing Token Circulation in Uniform Networks, *Distrib. Comp.* **10** (1997) 181-187
5. D. Wróblewski, Gravitational message passing as a sample distributed algorithm implemented on the PEGAZ agent platform, *ICS PAS Reports* **911** (2000)

An Improved Q-Learning Algorithm Using Synthetic Pheromones

Ndedi Monekosso, Paolo Remagnino, and Adam Szarowicz

Digital Imaging Research Centre
School of Computing and Information Systems
Kingston University, United Kingdom
{n.monekosso, p.remagnino, a.szarowicz}@kingston.ac.uk

Abstract. In this paper we propose an algorithm for multi-agent Q-learning. The algorithm is inspired by the natural behaviour of ants, which deposit pheromone in the environment to communicate. The benefit besides simulating ant behaviour in a colony is to design complex multi-agent systems. Complex behaviour can emerge from relatively simple interacting agents. The proposed Q-learning update equation includes a belief factor. The belief factor reflects the confidence the agent has in the pheromone detected in its environment. Agents communicate implicitly to co-ordinate and co-operate in learning to solve a problem.

Keywords: Machine Learning, Multi-agents, Pheromones, Coordination, Communication

1 Introduction

The ant colony exhibits a collective problem solving ability [5,11]. Complex behaviours can emerge from the interaction of relatively simple behaviour of individuals. A characteristic that multi-agent systems seek to reproduce. The ant colony exhibits among other features, co-operation and co-ordination, and communicate implicitly by depositing pheromone chemicals. The ant foraging for food will deposit a trail of pheromone. The problem is that of learning the shortest path between the nest and the food source whilst minimising energy. The aim of this work is to design an algorithm for multi-agent learning inspired by the search strategies of foraging ants, using synthetic pheromones. In particular we use Q-Learning augmented with a belief factor. The belief factor is a function of the synthetic pheromone concentration on the trail and reflects the extent to which an agent will take into account the information lay down by other agents from the same co-operating group. Reinforcement learning and synthetic pheromone have been combined for action selection [18,27]. The usefulness of the belief factor is that it allows an agent to selectively make use of implicit communication from other agents where the information may not be reliable due to changes in the environment. Incomplete and uncertain information are critical issues in the design of real world systems, the work presented in

B. Dunin-Kęplicz and E. Nawarecki (Eds.): CEEMAS 2001, LNAI 2296, pp. 197–206, 2002.
© Springer-Verlag Berlin Heidelberg 2002

this paper addresses this issue by introduceing the belief factor into the update equation for Q-Learning.

Section 2 presents related work in ant behaviour modelling and ant systems that have applied ant foraging mechanisms to optimisation problems. Section 4 describes the natural behaviour of ants in a colony. Section 5 discusses reinforcement learning, specifically Q-learning, followed in Section 6 by the pheromone-Q algorithm. Experiments and results obtained with this algorithm are described in Sections 7 and 8 respectively. In section 10 future work is discussed. Finally the paper conclude in Section 11.

2   Related Work

The work described in this paper is inspired by ant foraging mechanisms. The aim is to produce complex and useful behaviours from relatively simple behaviours in computational agents. Ant behaviour has been researched both for the understanding of the species but also as an inspiration in developing artificial systems. Ollason, in [20,21], reports a deterministic mathematical model for feeding ants. The model predicts the behaviour of ants moving from one regenerating food source to the next. Anderson [1] extends Ollason's work to simulate a colony of ants feeding from a number of regenerating food sources.

Though not intended for ant behaviour modelling and simulation a methodology inspired by the ant behaviour was developed in [9,13,16]. While foraging for food, certain ant species find the shortest path between a food source and the nest [2]. Some of the mechanisms adopted by foraging ants have been applied to classical NP-hard combinatorial optimisation problems with success. In [12] Ant Colony Optimisation is used to solve the travelling salesman problem, a quadratic assignment problem in [16], the job-shop scheduling problem in [8], communication network routing [7] and the Missionaries and Cannibals problem in [22].

In [15] Gambardella suggests a connection between the ant optimisation algorithm and reinforcement learning (RL) and proposes a family of algorithms (Ant-Q) related to the RL Q-learning. The ant optimisation algorithm is a special case of the Ant-Q family. The merging of Ant foraging mechanisms and reinforcement learning is also described in [18]. Three mechanisms found in ant trail formation were used as exploration strategy in a robot navigation task. In this work as with the Ant-Q algorithm, the information provided by the pheromone is used directtly for the action selection mechanism.

Another work inspired by ant behaviour is reported in [27]. It is applied to a multi-robotic environment where the robots transport objects between different locations. Rather than physically laying a trail of synthetic pheromones, the robots communicate path information via shared memory.

3   Related Work in the Book

In this paper, the collective problem solving ability of ants is modelled to produce a solution to a search problem. From a relatively simple behaviour can emerge a more complex and useful behaviour. The ant system as described in this paper is an instance of mass MAS as described in [14], "a large number of simple computational agents". This work is an implementation of a mass MAS system. In contrast with the work described by [24], the ant agents do not reason about co-agents' belief to achieve cooperation. The ant agents communicate with each other through the environment by depositing synthetic pheromones. In the search problem described, the ant agents act independently performing relatively simple actions e.g. move NORTH, SOUTH, EAST, and WEST. At each step they sample the environment for information (i.e. synthetic pheromone) previously deposited by the other agents inhabiting the environment. This information is assigned a degree of belief. The organisation of the ant agents emerges from these relatively simple actions. The aim is to design a MAS organisation that will solve real (useful) problems. The approach taken to design the simulated MAS system based on real ant behaviour was a top-down approach. [19] describe a bottom-up approach where the local agent behaviour is analysed in order to extract collective behaviours with the aim is to design MAS organisations.

4   Ant Behaviour

Ants are able to find the shortest path between the nest and a food source by an autocatalytic process [3,17]. This process comes about because ants deposit pheromones along the trail as they move along in the search for food or resources to construct the nest. The pheromone evaporates with time nevertheless ants follow a pheromone trail and at a branching point prefer to follow the path with higher concentrations of pheromone. On finding the food source, the ants return laden to the nest depositing more pheromone along the way thus reinforcing the pheromone trail. Ants that have followed the shortest path return quicker to the nest, reinforcing the pheromone trail at a faster rate than those ants that followed an alternative longer route. Further ants arriving at the branching point choose to follow the path with the higher concentrations of pheromone thus reinforcing even further the pheromone and eventually all ants follow the shortest path. The amount of pheromone secreted is a function of an angle between the path and a line joining the food and nest locations [6]. Deneubourg [10] found that some ants make U-turns after a branch, and a greater number would make a U-turn to return to the nest or to follow the shorter path after initially selecting the longer path. This U-turn process further reinforces the laying-down of pheromone on the shortest path.

So far two properties of pheromone secretion were mentioned: aggregation and evaporation [23]. The concentration adds when ants deposit pheromone at the same location, and over time the concentration gradually reduces by evaporation. A third property is diffusion [23]. The pheromone at a location diffuses into neighbouring locations.

5   Reinforcement Learning

Reinforcement Learning (RL) [4], [25] is a machine learning technique that allows an agent to learn by trial and error which action to perform by interacting with the environment. Models of the agent or environment are not required. At each discrete time step, the agent selects an action given the current state and execute the action, causing the environment to move to the next state. The agent receives a reward that reflects the value of the action taken. The objective of the agent is to maximise the sum of rewards received when starting from an initial state and ending in a goal state. One form of RL is Q-Learning [28]. The objective in Q-learning is to generate Q-values (quality values) for each state-action pair. At each time step, the agent observes the state s_t, and takes action a. It then receives a reward r dependent on the new state s_{t+1}. The reward may be discounted into the future, meaning that rewards received n time steps into the future are worth less by a factor γ^n than rewards received in the present. Thus the cumulative discounted reward is given by (1)

$$R = r_t + \gamma r_{t+1} + \gamma^2 r_{t+2} + \cdots + \gamma^n r_{t+n} \tag{1}$$

where $0 \leq \gamma < 1$. The Q-value is updated at each step using the update equation (2) for a non-deterministic Markov Decision Process (MDP)

$$\hat{Q}_n(s_t, a) \longleftarrow (1 - \alpha_n)\hat{Q}_{n-1}(s_t, a) + \\ \alpha_n(r_t + \gamma \cdot max_{a'}\hat{Q}_{n-1}(s_{t+1}, a')) \tag{2}$$

where $\alpha_n = \frac{1}{1+visits_n(s_t,a)}$. Q-learning can be implemented using a look-up table to store the values of Q for a relatively small state space. Neural networks are also used for the Q-function approximation.

6   The Pheromone-Q Learning

The main difference between the Q-learning update equation and the pheromone-Q update equation is the introduction of a belief factor that must also be maximised. The belief factor is a function of synthetic pheromone. The synthetic pheromone ($\Phi(s)$) is a scalar value (where s is a state/cell in a grid) that comprises three components: aggregation, evaporation and diffusion. The pheromone $\Phi(s)$ has two possible discrete values, a value for the pheromone deposited when searching for food and when returning to the nest with food.

The belief factor (B) dictates the extent to which an agent believes in the pheromone that it detects. An agent, during early training episodes, will believe to a lesser degree in the pheromone map because all agents are biased towards exploration. The belief factor is given by (3)

$$B(s_{t+1}, a) = \frac{\Phi(s_{t+1})}{\sum_{\sigma \in N_a} \Phi(\sigma)} \tag{3}$$

where $\Phi(s)$ is the pheromone concentration at a cell, s, in the environment and N_a is the set of neighbouring states for a chosen action a.

The Q-Learning update equation modified with synthetic pheromone is given by (4)

$$\hat{Q}_n(s_t, a) \longleftarrow (1 - \alpha_n)\hat{Q}_{n-1}(s_t, a) +$$
$$\alpha_n(r_t + \gamma \prime \cdot max_{a'}(\hat{Q}_{n-1}(s_{t+1}, a') + \xi B(s_{t+1}, a')) \qquad (4)$$

where the parameter, ξ, is a sigmoid function of time (*epochs* ≥ 0). The value of ξ increases as the number of agents successfully accomplish the task at hand.

7   Methodology

The objective is to evaluate the modified updating equation for Phe-Q and confirm empirically convergence. In addition the Phe-Q performance is compared to Q-Learning. For the experiments reported the agent environment is a $N \times N$, grid where $N = 10, 20, 40$. Each cell has associated a pheromone strength (a scalar value). The agents are placed at a starting cell (the nest) on the grid. The aim is for the agents to locate the 'food' sources occupying one or more cells throughout the grid space and return to the starting cell. The agents move from cell to cell depositing discrete quantities of pheromone in each cell. There are two pheromone values, one associated with search for the food source (outbound pheromone = 1) and the other associated with the return to the nest (return pheromone = 10). The pheromone adds linearly (aggregates) in a cell up to an upper bound, and evaporates at a rate (evaporation rate (φ_a) until there is none remaining if the cell pheromone is not replenished. Each agent has s set of tasks represented by a Q-table. One task is to reach the 'food' location, and the second task is to return to the nest.

The grid size is $N \times N$, more than one agent can occupy a cell. A cell has associated a pheromone strength, $\Phi \in [0, 100]$. Pheromone is de-coupled from the state at the implementation level so that the size of the state space is an $N \times N$. For a small grid, a lookup table is used for the Q-table.

The agent receives a reward of 1.0 on completing the tasks i.e. when it locates the food and returns to the nest. Each experiment consists of a number of agents released into the environment and running in parallel for 500 to 1000 epochs. Each epoch is the time from the agent's release from the nest to the agent's return to the nest.

In the experiments, the search is achieved with pheromone aggregation and evaporation. The outbound pheromone strength is +1.0, and the return pheromone strength is +10.0. While returning to the nest the agents do not 'use' pheromone for guidance. The experiment was run with and without obstacles.

8   Results

To demonstrate empirically convergence of the update equations, the Root Means Square (RMS) of the error between successive Q-values is plotted against epochs (an epoch is a complete cycle of locating food and returning to the nest). The RMS curves for Phe-Q in Figure 1 show convergence, Phe-Q converges faster than Q. For a given grid size, there is a limit to the number of agents for which Phe-Q performs better than Q-Learning with or without obstacles. In a 20x20 grid space, the performance degrades to that of Q-learning with approximately 30 agents. The graph in Figure 2 shows the RMS curves for increasing number of Phe-Q agents maintaining a constant grid size (for clarity only the RMS curves for 5, 40, and 60 agents are shown on the graph). Between 5 and 20 agents, the speeds of convergence are comparable for Phe-Q. Above that number, the trend is slower convergence, a phenomenon that does not occur with Q-learning. The reason for this is explained in the next section.

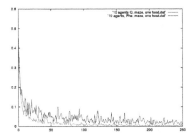 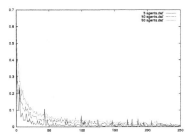

Fig. 1. RMS curve for Phe-Q learning   **Fig. 2.** Performance scaling

The graph in Figure 3 shows the performance with two food sources. The objective was to determine how a food location e.g. that closest to nest, would be favoured by the two types of agents. In Figures 4 and 5, the number of visits per episode (locate food and return) is plotted. Initial results indicate that for a relatively simple 'world' e.g. at least one food source located centrally, both types of agents learn to visit mainly the closest food location as expected but the Q-agent visited it more frequently than the Phe-Q agent. With the closest food location partially hidden and the more distant food location unobstructed, the Q-agent visited the hidden food source with similar frequency as before while the Phe-Q agent visited the hidden food source less frequently as shown in Figure 5. The Phe-Q agents converge faster with several food sources.

9   Discussion

The synthetic pheromone guides the agents. It is implicit communication. At the implementation level, a pheromone map is produced. This map is de-coupled from the grid 'world' thus reducing the state space. The information exchange via pheromone enables the agents to learn faster as demonstrated by faster convergence. Phe-Q was compared with Q-learning, in both cases using the greedy

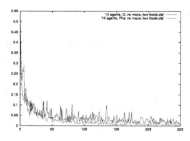

Fig. 3. Two competing food sources

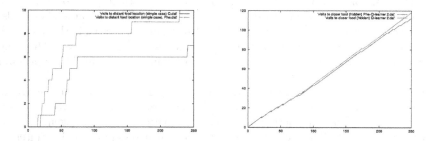

Fig. 4. Visits to unobstructed but distant **Fig. 5.** Visits to hidden, closer food source food

and Boltzmann action selection mechanisms. Phe-Q using Boltzmann was seen to perform better than all three other combinations. There is however a price to be paid for this information sharing. Too much information i.e. too high a pheromone deposition rate or too low a pheromone evaporation rate causes not unexpectedly poorer results especially in the earlier learning stages. Agents are 'mislead' by other exploring agents. However it was seen that the agents were not highly sensitive to the degree of pheromone information belief. In addition, it was expected that the agent ant may be 'deceived' by its own pheromone, influenced by pheromone just previously deposited. It was anticipated that this could lead to cycling. However the higher exploration rates in the early learning phases prevents cycling from becoming a problem.

Whereas with non-interacting Q-learning agents, the convergence speed is not expected to and does not vary with number of agents, with Phe-Q learning it was seen that there is an upper limit to the number of agents searching a space while maintaining faster convergence (with respect to Q-learning). Too high a number not slows down learning (convergence). The pheromone deposited by large numbers of exploring agents 'mislead' agents. In addition, with a high number of agents the solution also becomes computationally intensive.

10   Future Work

Phe-Q will be compared to other reinforcement learning techniques specifically elegibility traces. An advantage of a multi-agent system compared to a single monolithic agent is the emergence of a more 'complex' behaviour [26]. In this particular case it is required to solve a problem faster with multiple agents. The more complex the problem, the greater the benefits of the multi-agent solution. It remains to be seen if the performance of Phe-Q is better than standard Q-learning on more complex maze problems. In particular, adaptability will be investigated with food sources that are replenished.

Values for are several variables to be fine tuned in order to optimise the problem solving capability of the Phe-Q agent. Particularly with respect to pheromone concentrations, dropping rates, evaporation rates, and diffusion rates across cells. Though the latter was not implemented for the results presented in this paper. A means for automating the parameter fine tuning will be investigated. This may be achieved by reverse engineering the problem in order to find the optimum values.

An issue currently under investigation is that of agent trust. So far the agents have believed the shared information. The authors are looking into deception whereby agents use synthetic pheromone information to deceive agents inhabiting the 'world'. This work will lead to modelling deception and countering deception.

11   Conclusions

The work described in this paper set out to investigate the use of synthetic pheromone for implicit communication to speed up multi-agent learning. Rather than using pheromone information directly for action selection, each agent calculates a belief value for the information based on pheromone concentration in the four surrounding cells. The belief is maximised together with the Q-value. This technique, Phe-Q learning, was shown to converge faster than Q-learning for searching for food locations in virtual spaces with varying degrees of complexity (obstacles). However with two food sources, Q-agents had a preference for the closest source almost to the exclusion of the furthest food source, irrespective of whether the closer food source was hidden or not, in the process taking more time to learn the solution.

References

1. C. Anderson, P.G. Blacwell, and C. Cannings. Simulating ants that forage by expectation. In *Proc. 4Th Conf. on Artificial Life*, pages 531–538, 1997.
2. R. Beckers, J. L. Deneubourg, S. Goss, and J. M. Pasteels. Collective decision making through food recruitment. *Ins. Soc.*, 37:258–267, 1990.
3. R. Beckers, J.L. Deneubourg, and S. Goss. Trails and u-turns in the selection of the shortest path by the ant lasius niger. *Journal of Theoretical Biology*, 159:397–4151, 1992.

4. D.P. Bertsekas and J.N. Tsitsiklis. *Neuro-Dynamic Programming*. Athena Scientific, 1996.
5. E. Bonabeau, M. Dorigo, and G. Theraulaz. *Swarm intelligence, From Natural to Artificial Systems*. Oxford University Press, 1999.
6. M. C. Cammaerts-Tricot. Piste et pheromone attraction chez la fourmi myrmica ruba. *Journal of Computational Physiology*, 88:373–382, 1974.
7. G. Di Caro and M. Dorigo. Antnet: a mobile agents approach to adaptive routing.
8. A. Colorni, M. Dorigo, and V. Maniezzo. Ant system for job-shop scheduling. *Belgian Journal of OR, statistics and computer science*, 34:39–53, 1993.
9. A. Colorni, M. Dorigo, and G. Theraulaz. Distributed optimzation by ant colonies. In *Proceedings First European Conf. on Artificial Life*, pages 134–142, 1991.
10. J.L. Deneubourg, R. Beckers, and S. Goss. Trails and u-turns in the selection of a path by the ant lasius niger. *Journal of Theoretical Biology*, 159:397–415, 1992.
11. J.L. Deneubourg and S. Goss. Collective patterns and decision making. *Ethol. Ecol. and Evol.*, 1:295–311, 1993.
12. M. Dorigo and L. M. Gambardella. Ant colony system: A cooperative learning approach to the travelling salesman problem. *IEEE Trans. on Evol. Comp.*, 1:53–66, 1997.
13. M. Dorigo, V. Maniezzo, and A. Colorni. The ant system: Optimization by a colony of cooperatin agents. *IEEE Trans. on Systems, Man, and Cybernetics*, 26:1–13, 1996.
14. M. Kisiel-Dorohinicki E. Nawarecki, G. Dobrowolski. Organisations in the particular class of multi-agent systems. In *in this volume*, 2001.
15. L. M. Gambardella and M. Dorigo. Ant-q: A reinforcement learning approach to the traveling salesman problem. In *Proc. 12Th ICML*, pages 252–260, 1995.
16. L. M. Gambardella, E. D. Taillard, and M. Dorigo. Ant colonies for the qap. *Journal of Operational Research society*, 1998.
17. S. Goss, S. Aron, J.L. Deneubourg, and J. M. Pasteels. Self-organized shorcuts in the argentine ants. *Naturwissenschaften*, pages 579–581, 1989.
18. L. R. Leerink, S. R. Schultz, and M. A. Jabri. A reinforcement learning exploration strategy based on ant foraging mechanisms. In *Proc. 6Th Australian Conference on Neural Nets*, 1995.
19. J-P. Sansonnet N. Sabouret. Learning collective behaviour from local interaction. In *in this volume*, 2001.
20. J.G. Ollason. Learning to forage - optimally? *Theoretical Population Biology*, 18:44–56, 1980.
21. J.G. Ollason. Learning to forage in a regenerating patchy environment: can it fail to be optimal? *Theoretical Population Biology*, 31:13–32, 1987.
22. H. Van Dyke Parunak and S. Brueckner. Ant-like missionnaries and cannibals: Synthetic pheromones for distributed motion control. In *Proc. of ICMAS'00*, 2000.
23. H. Van Dyke Parunak, S. Brueckner, J. Sauter, and J. Posdamer. Mechanisms and military applications for synthetic pheromones. In *Proc. 5Th International Conference Autonomous Agents, Montreal, Canada*, 2001.
24. L. Sheremetov R. Romero Cortes. Model of cooperation in multi-agent systems with fuzzy coalitions. In *in this volume*, 2001.
25. R. S. Sutton and A.G. Barto. *Reinforcement Learning*. MIT Press, 1998.
26. Ming Tan. Multi-agent reinforcement learning: Independent vs. cooperative agents. In *Proceedings of the Tenth International Conference on Machine Learning*, pages 330–337, 1993.

27. R. T. Vaughan, K. Stoy, G. S. Sukhatme, and M. J. Mataric. Whistling in the dark: Cooperative trail following in uncertain localization space. In *Proc. 4Th International Conference on Autonomous Agents, Barcelona, Spain*, 2000.
28. C. J. C. H. Watkins. *Learning with delayed rewards*. PhD thesis, University of Cambridge, 1989.

Organisations in the Particular Class of Multi-agent Systems

Edward Nawarecki, Marek Kisiel-Dorohinicki, and Grzegorz Dobrowolski

Department of Computer Science
University of Mining and Metallurgy, Kraków, Poland
{nawar,doroh,grzela}@agh.edu.pl

Abstract. The paper deals with the problem of organisation with respect to mass multi-agent systems (mMAS). The central question is how to influence the system so that the emerged organisation is conducive to its effective operation. The analysis is supported by a case study on management of a number of agents in an evolutionary multi-agent system (EMAS).

1 Introduction

The notion of *organisation* appeared in literature about multi-agent systems not long ago. Precursors of research on a phenomenon of organised and (self-)organised agents [1,7] most often introduced the notion intuitively as representing some ability or form of adaptation of the system to fulfil specific — maybe changing — tasks. Following this way of thinking, one can imagine that the organisation implies the manner (strategy) of how a multi-agent system will realise functions assigned to it. Then a question arises how to influence the system so that the emerged organisation is conducive to its effective operation.

Possible organisations of a multi-agent system depend on a class of systems under consideration, and a study on the above-sketched problem can turn out to be very difficult in a general case.

The paper deals with the problem of organisation with respect to a chosen class of multi-agent systems (MAS), called the mass ones, or in short mMAS [6]. These systems are marked by special features that result from the fact that they consist of a relatively large number of rather simple computational agents. The systems essentially differ from typical MAS that most often operate in the net. The field of application of mMAS can be mainly:

- simulation of problems that are distinguished due to their granularity in the sense of existence of a large number of similar objects that manifest some kind of autonomy and
- soft computing restricted to problems that can be reduced to searching some space for elements of the given features where objects similar to those mentioned above are used as a means for the search.

Possible applications from the latter sub-field make the considered systems close to evolutionary computation. In fact, one can find similarities also with respect to functionality and internal structure.

B. Dunin-Kęplicz and E. Nawarecki (Eds.): CEEMAS 2001, LNAI 2296, pp. 207–216, 2002.

In most agent systems, and particularly in mMAS, the behaviour of the whole system cannot be directly derived from the behaviour of a single agent. This may be considered as a subcase of the micro-macro link problem [8], i.e. the problem of the relation between the behaviour of a system and that of its constituents — this problem is more general and is discussed also in social theory and cognitive science [9]. That is why, for mMAS one may need a specific approach to analysis and design. On the one hand, processes and activities concerning individual agents should be described, yet this description may (in fact must) be incomplete. On the other hand, global effects of autonomous (inter-)actions of these elements should be expressed as population-level parameters.

A core idea of the paper is to bridge those two positions. It can be done with the help of the especially formed notion of organisation. As an effect of mechanisms implemented in mMAS, some organisation arises at the micro level that occurs to be a decisive factor for fulfilment of the system global goal. In turn, manners of how organisation can be influenced and observed becomes important for the discussed class of systems.

The paper is organised as follows. Basic notions about mMAS opens considerations in section 2. It is supported by a sketch of the formal model of section 3 that gives foundation for a concept of organisation of such a system. The next section 4 shortly introduces EMAS as a particular realisation of mMAS using evolutionary mechanisms of generation and removal of agents. The system applied to optimisation in the multi-objective case produces an example of how organisation can be understood, influenced and observed in the discussed type of multi-agent systems.

2   Mass Multi-agent Systems

A **mass multi-agent system** consists of a relatively large number of agents which are often not so computationally complicated. The operation of mMAS is aimed at a well-defined external global goal which is also the utilitarian one of the system design, implementation and run. The goal emerges together with the organisation that is realised among agents (all or but a part of) of the system as a result of the performed actions. Because of both computational simplicity and a huge number of agents, the influence of a single one on the overall system operation, its organisation and, finally, the global goal may be neglected. Although it is not required in general, agents of mMAS are often identical in the sense of an algorithm and built-in actions.

The above description of mMAS leads to the following observations:

- mMAS must be designed (synthesised) or analysed simultaneously at two levels:

  macro — of the system, agent population, their organisation, the global goal, and
  micro — of single agents, built-in actions (mechanisms), the influence of agents on themselves and the environment, and *vice versa*;
- the basic and almost the only way to affect the behaviour of mMAS (global goal) is an adequate design of agents' (inter)actions and their relations to the environment so that desirable organisation can arise;
- during a mMAS run, only indirect management of agents is possible, that is via the environment (providing some resources or information).

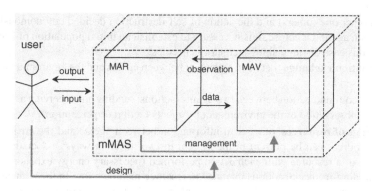

Fig. 1. Schema of utilisation of mMAS

The full schema of possible interactions (including a user) in the case of utilisation of mMAS has been proposed in [6]. It is based on decomposition of an agent system into *virtual* (MAV) and *real* (MAR) layers as figure 1 shows.

MAV represents the mMAS itself, i.e. the agents (inter-)acting in the environment. Each agent tries to achieve its local goal with the use of predefined built-in actions (mechanisms). Based on the information that comes also from the outside — depicted in figure 1 by *data* — the agent chooses its locally best strategies to realise.

Since an agent system should realise some global utilitarian goal, MAV needs a kind of interface to a user (the real world), which is accomplished by MAR layer. Firstly, the information describing the actual state of the real world or needs of the user — *input* — should be translated for the sake of the system (agents). Secondly, the state of the system, which represents a solution to the problem should be translated into the form useful in the application domain — *output*. What is more, MAR layer should be able to affect the behaviour of the agents (MAV layer).

The so-called *V-R decomposition* gives clear interrelations between macro and micro levels putting them into MAR and MAV accordingly. It also finally constitutes a role of a user that actively interacting with the system closes the main information loop at run-time and can manage the system by implementing and tuning the chosen mechanisms before it starts — *design*.

To fulfil the characteristic of mass multi-agent systems, it is necessary to present the basic mechanisms that can be incorporated in such a system. In general, there are mechanisms typical of multi-agent systems defined in an environment [7], but their detailed implementation can take advantage of results of other disciplines. The implementation of a mechanism means here equiping agents with appropriate set of actions and, if it is necessary, extending the environment with a corresponding feature or structure. In a concrete system implemented mechanisms can be chosen from among the set presented below.

Generation and removal of agents. The mechanism corresponds to a type of open multi-agent systems in which a number of agents changes during the operation. In mMAS it is an effect of the action of generation of a new agent performed by another one (others) and the action of self-destruction decided autonomously by a given agent. Of course, it is necessary to establish an initial population of agents — in this case distinguishing a creator is needless.

Information exchange between agents, or between agents and the environmentmay be realised as:

- communication between two agents (actions: sending and receiving a message),
- observation of the environment by agents (action of perception).

Exchange of resources other than information between agents and the environment. Resources can be present in the system in two different ways: associating a portion of a resource with each action performed (necessary energy expenditure) and building-in special actions intended to resource manipulation. In the both cases the environment must include a structure allowing for balancing of the resource.

Migration of agents. The mechanism needs a structure embedded in the environment that reflects spatial phenomena of mMAS (e.g. a graph) and can be a base for migration. The action of the mechanism moves an agent to a new location. Sometimes direct perception of co-ordinates in the space is also implemented.

The majority of the above mechanisms (actions) require the introduction of notions of agent and environment states. Then the completion of an action changes a corresponding state, e.g. communication (perception) changes a state of a receiver (observer). Many actions change the environment state (virtual effect of an action) that, in turn, can be observed by agents.

How can the above mechanisms be realised in a particular mMAS? A very interesting case seems to be an evolutionary multi-agent system (EMAS), where the mechanism of generation and removal of agents is built on the base of adequately combined evolutionary operators. Designed in this way EMAS (with other mechanisms somehow implemented) can turn out to be fruitful, especially for the second field of application — soft computing. The idea finds its justification also in an opinion popular among experts in the field about purposefulness of combining known methods [2]. It is because very often such hybrids occur to be more effective than the components alone.

3   Modelling Organisations in mMAS

Below a model of a mass agent system is proposed. The model is based on fundamentals of M-Agent architecture and may be extended to support various types of agent systems (for further reference see e.g. [3]). The notation uses lower-case symbols to denote single objects and capital letters to denote sets of objects; subscripts are used to distinguish particular elements only if it is indispensable in the current context.

A multi-agent system consists of a set of *agents* ($ag \in Ag$, $card\,Ag = N$) and some *environment* (env) they operate in:

$$mas \equiv \langle Ag, env \rangle \tag{1}$$

The environment may have spatial structure and contain some *information* and/or *resources*, which may be observed by agents.

The functionality of i-th agent is defined by a set of *actions* (act $\in$ Act$_i$) it is able to perform depending on its *state* (stat$_i$):

$$ag_i \equiv \langle Act_i, stat_i \rangle \tag{2}$$

An action is an atomic (indivisible) activity, which may be executed by an agent in the system. The set of all actions is denoted by Act (Act$_i$ $\subset$ Act, card Act $= M$). An effective action is an action act performed by agent ag in time t: (ag, act, t) $\in$ Ag $\times$ Act $\times$ T.

To simplify further considerations let us denote the space of possible states of the system, the environment, and i-th agent by $\mathcal{X}$(mas), $\mathcal{X}$(env), and $\mathcal{X}$(stat$_i$) accordingly. Of course, the state of the system consists of the state of the environment and states of all agents and:

$$\mathcal{X}(mas) = \mathcal{X}(env) \times \left(\overset{N}{\underset{i=1}{\times}} \mathcal{X}(stat_i) \right) \tag{3}$$

If a typical mMAS consists of agents of the same type, the spaces of possible states are the same for all agents, i.e. $\forall i = 1, 2, \ldots, N \mathcal{X}(stat_i) = \mathcal{X}(stat)$ and:

$$\mathcal{X}(mas) = \mathcal{X}(env) \times \mathcal{X}(stat)^N \tag{4}$$

Realisation of particular actions changes not only internal states of acting agents but also states of other agents and the state of the environment:

$$act : \quad \mathcal{X}(mas) \rightarrow \mathcal{X}(mas) \tag{5}$$

It must be stressed here that in general the state of the system (environment and agents) represents the global utilitarian goal of the system — some problem to be solved and its solution. The agents' states or results of their actions recorded in the environment constitute a base for formulation of a solution in the real world terms.

Let us introduce the notion of *organisation*. For mMAS it can be done indirectly only through results of (specific) effective actions performed by (selected) agents in a given time period:

$$org \equiv \{(ag, act, t) : \quad ag \in Ag, act \in Act, t \in (t_1, t_2)\} \tag{6}$$

The results — the emerged organisation cannot be precisely observed by the user because of a huge amount of the resulting information. What may be observed is only some representation of the state of the whole system $\omega \in \Omega$ available via some heuristics Υ (depicted as "observation" on fig. 1):

$$\Upsilon : \quad \mathcal{X}(mas) \rightarrow \Omega \tag{7}$$

During the system activity the value of $\omega \in \Omega$ represents some global effect of the emerged organisation in mMAS and should allow for estimation of the quality of the result(s) obtained.

As we cannot influence every single action, the management in mMAS may only be achieved through the introduction of preferences or indications for actions to be executed by agents depending on their state. It is proposed to describe these preferences in terms of *strategies* defined by distributions of probabilities of individual actions:

$$\mathsf{st} \equiv \langle p_{\mathsf{act}_1}(stat), p_{\mathsf{act}_2}, \dots, p_{\mathsf{act}_M} \rangle \tag{8}$$

Assuming that the state of the system is observed only in certain time points $t_0, t_1, \dots, t_{k-1}, t_k$ (e.g. after a fixed number of actions performed), the dynamics of mMAS may be considered as a step-by-step process. At some time t_k this process may be illustrated as:

$$
\begin{array}{ccccccc}
\dots & \xrightarrow{\mathsf{org}(t_{k-1})} & \mathsf{mas}(t_{k-1}) & \xrightarrow{\mathsf{org}(t_k)} & \mathsf{mas}(t_k) & \xrightarrow{\mathsf{st}^*} & \mathsf{mas}^* \\
 & & \downarrow r & & \downarrow r & & \downarrow r \\
\dots & & \omega(t_{k-1}) & & \omega(t_k) & & \omega^*
\end{array} \tag{9}
$$

where: $\mathsf{org}(t_{k-1}), \mathsf{org}(t_k)$ – organisation emerged in $(k-1)$-th and k-th step of system operation,

st^* – a strategy to be applied in the next step, which should induce the organisation of the system leading to desirable global effect ω^*.

To recapitulate, the postulates concerning global (macro) characteristics of mMAS can only be fulfilled via (parametric) changes of existing micro-level mechanisms or the introduction of some new ones, and thus influencing the strategy to be realised by the system in the next step(s) of its operation (st^*).

4   A Case Study on Organisation of EMAS

The key idea of an evolutionary multi-agent system is the incorporation of evolutionary paradigms into mMAS at a population level [4]. It means that besides interaction mechanisms typical for MAS (such as communication) agents are able to reproduce (generate new agents), and may die (be eliminated from the system). It ought to be stressed that EMAS is a kind of mMAS, and the whole discussion of the previous sections, including the model presented, refers also to them.

Let us consider a generic optimisation problem, i.e. searching over some space of attainable solutions D according to some criteria (utility, goal, fitness) – a typical yet not the only application of EMAS. In the case [5] the state of an agent reflects directly an attainable point (below denoted by $x \in D$) that can be a partial solution to the problem. If so, the states of such agents constitute the approximation of the Pareto frontier for a given multicriteria optimisation problem: $\mathcal{P} \subset \mathbb{R}^Z$, where Z is the dimension of the search space.

At the same time a decisive factor of the agent's activity in **EMAS** is its fitness, expressed by the amount of a possessed non-renewable resource called *life energy* (eng). The state of the agent in **EMAS** may be thus defined as a pair:

$$\text{stat} = \langle x, \text{eng} \rangle \tag{10}$$

At the very beginning of the evolution process each agent is given the same amount of energy $\text{eng}_{ag_i}(t_0) = \text{eng}_0 > 0$. The energy is gained and lost when agents execute actions. In general, an increase in energy is a reward for "good" behaviour of an agent, a decrease – a penalty for "bad" behaviour. In fact, an agent *looses* energy performing any action (this is the cost of doing anything), and the energy *is given* to an agent when its behaviour proves useful for the environment or other agents (of course this should depend on x):

$$\text{eng}_{ag}(t_{k+1}) = \text{eng}_{ag}(t_k) + \Delta\text{eng}_{ag}^{+}(t_k) - \Delta\text{eng}_{ag}^{-}(t_k) \tag{11}$$

where: t_{k+1}, t_k – moments in time, when the state of the system is observed,
$\Delta\text{eng}_{ag}^{+}(t_k)$ – total energy gained by agent ag in time period (t_k, t_{k+1}),
$\Delta\text{eng}_{ag}^{-}(t_k)$ – total energy lost by agent ag in time period (t_k, t_{k+1}).

At the same time energy possessed by an agent should determine its ability to execute actions. Thus a strategy of selection should be defined so that high energy level should increase the probability of reproduction – generation of offspring agents: $p_{rp} = p_{rp}(\text{eng})$, and low energy level should increase the probability of death – elimination of an agent: $p_{die} = p_{die}(\text{eng})$:

$$\text{st}^{*} = \langle p_{rp}(\text{eng}), p_{die}(\text{eng}) \rangle \tag{12}$$

Typically there are two factors describing **EMAS** in macro scale (i.e. the global effect of its operation): the actual solution to the problem and total number of agents in the population. The first one may be used to estimate the quality of the system in the problem domain, the second one – the quality of the solving process. The characteristic feature of **EMAS** is that selection (reproduction and elimination) causes dynamic changes in the number of agents, which should be reflected in the management mechanisms. In general, increasing the number of agents improves the ability of the system to perform its tasks, but at the same time may make the whole system work inefficiently (e.g. because of excessive load of executed actions) or even prove impractical in real applications.

Let us discuss organisation of the presented system. From the point of view of the global goal as well as the general efficiency requirements the formation of a desirable organisation ought to be monitored according to:

$$\omega = \langle \mathcal{P}, N \rangle \tag{13}$$

The system can be regarded as a *well-organised* one if the *acceptable* approximations of the Pareto frontier $\mathcal{P}(t)$ are achieved by *resonably* numerous populations of agents.

The dynamics of successive approximations of the Pareto frontier $\mathcal{P}(t)$ in given time intervals Δt is presented on fig. 2. The dynamics is characterised in terms of convergence rate defined as an average distance of new non-dominated solutions $x \in \mathcal{P}(t+\Delta t)$ from

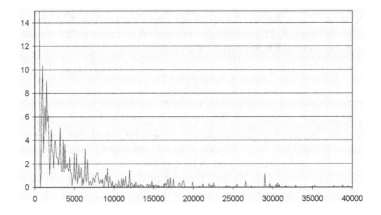

Fig. 2. Successive approximations of the Pareto frontier

the previous approximation $\mathcal{P}(t)$. The distance of a particular solution x from the set $\mathcal{P}$ is defined as the least Euclidean distance from elements of $\mathcal{P}$ in the evaluation space:

$$d(\boldsymbol{x}, \mathcal{P}) = \min_{\boldsymbol{x}^{\mathcal{P}} \in \mathcal{P}} \sqrt{\sum_{i=1}^{M} \left(f_i(\boldsymbol{x}) - f_i(\boldsymbol{x}^{\mathcal{P}})\right)^2} \tag{14}$$

As one may expect the distance between successive approximations is quite big at the beginning of the process, and decreases during the further operation of the system.

In the discussed system self-management of the number of agents was realised through closed circulation of energy, which makes total energy possessed by all agents constant during the whole run. Due to this assumption each change in the agent's energy should be reflected by an appropriate change in energy of another agent or the environment:

- energetic cost of performed actions $\Delta\mathrm{eng}_{ag}^-$ is transferred to the environment,
- energetic reward for a (successful) execution of actions $\Delta\mathrm{eng}_{ag}^+$ is given to the agent from the environment or from another agent,
- an agent created in reprodution process obtains energy from its parents or the environment,
- energy of a dead agent is transferred to another agent or the environment.

If the environment takes part in the energetic transitions:

$$\mathrm{eng}_{env}(t_{k+1}) = \mathrm{eng}_{env}(t_k) + \sum_{ag \in Ag} \Delta\mathrm{eng}_{ag}^-(t_k) - \sum_{ag \in Ag} \Delta\mathrm{eng}_{ag}^+(t_k) +$$
$$+ \sum_{ag \in Ag^{die}} \mathrm{eng}_{ag}(t_k) - \sum_{ag \in Ag^{rp}} \mathrm{eng}_{ag}(t_k) \tag{15}$$

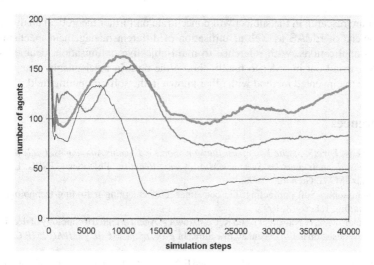

Fig. 3. The number of agents in EMAS for three different multicriteria optimisation problems

where: Ag^{die} – the agents died in time period (t_k, t_{k+1}),
 Ag^{rp} – the agents reproduced in time period (t_k, t_{k+1}).

Fig. 3 shows desirable characteristics of dynamics of the population in case of EMAS for multicriteria optimisation. The fall in the number of agents at the beginning of the process means destruction of the worst agents. Then the new population is created based on the remaining individuals as they are able to gain more energy, and the size of the population grows.

5 Concluding Remarks

In the paper a short characteristics of mMAS and its special mutation called evolutionary multi-agent system (EMAS) is presented. The presentation of the newly proposed types of MAS are supported by a formal model that allows for description of built-in mechanisms of *evolutionary* as well as *agent* origin that create a base for agent functioning and, in turn, spontaneous organisation arising.

It is shown that attaining some external utilitarian goal of such a system and assuring effectiveness of that process can be achieved merely by applying the specific management that indirectly influences the organisation of the system. If the mechanisms are appropriately stimulated, desirable organisation forms and, in consequence, are able to produce useful outcome of the system.

Applicability of the presented ideas is illustrated using EMAS designed and implemented to search for the approximation of the Pareto frontier for a given multi-objective optimisation problem. The results obtained for several testing examples confirm legitimacy of the general approach and effectiveness of the proposed scheme of management.

Future research in the subject will concentrate on further theoretical analysis of the phenomena of **EMAS** as well as utilisation of different management mechanisms in various applications. With reference to multi-objective optimisation, detailed studies will be carried out in order to finally choose the built-in mechanisms, tune them and compare the invented method with other known in the soft-computing field.

References

1. C. Baeijs. *Fonctionnalité Emergente dans une Société d'Agents Autonomes. Etude des Aspects Organisationnels dans les Systèmes Multi-Agents Réactifs.* PhD thesis, INPG, Laboratoire Leibniz IMAG, Grenoble, 1998.
2. P. Bonissone. Soft computing: the convergence of emerging reasoning technologies. *Soft Computing*, 1(1):6–18, 1997.
3. E. Cetnarowicz, E. Nawarecki, and K. Cetnarowicz. Agent oriented technology of decentralized systems based on the M-Agent architecture. In *Proc. of the MCPL'97, IFAC/IFIP Conference*, 1997.
4. K. Cetnarowicz, M. Kisiel-Dorohinicki, and E. Nawarecki. The application of evolution process in multi-agent world (MAW) to the prediction system. In M. Tokoro, editor, *Proc. of the 2nd Int. Conf. on Multi-Agent Systems (ICMAS'96)*. AAAI Press, 1996.
5. G. Dobrowolski, M. Kisiel-Dorohinicki, and E. Nawarecki. Evolutionary multi-agent system in multiobjective optimisation. In M. Hamza, editor, *Proc. of the IASTED Int. Symp.: Applied Informatics*. IASTED/ACTA Press, 2001.
6. G. Dobrowolski, M. Kisiel-Dorohinicki, and E. Nawarecki. Some approach to design and realisation of mass multi-agent systems. In R. Schaefer and S. Sędziwy, editors, *Advances in Multi-Agent Systems*. Jagiellonian University, 2001.
7. J. Ferber. *Multi-Agent Systems. An Introduction to Distributed Artificial Intelligence.* Addison-Wesley, 1999.
8. J. Ferber, O. Labbani, J.-P. Muller, and A. Bourjault. Formalising emergent collective behaviours: Preliminary report. In *Proc. of Int. Workshop on Distributed Artificial Intelligence and Multi-Agent Systems (DAIMAS'97)*, St Petersburg, Russia, 1997.
9. H. J. E. Verhagen and R. A. Smit. Modelling social agents in a multiagent world. In *Position Papers of the 7th European Workshop on Modelling Autonomous Agents in a Multi-Agent World (MAAMAW'96)*, Technical Report 96-1. Vrije Universiteit Brussel, Artificial Intelligence Laboratory, 1996.

UML for Behavior-Oriented Multi-agent Simulations

Christoph Oechslein, Franziska Klügl, Rainer Herrler, and Frank Puppe

Department for Artificial Intelligence,
University of Würzburg
Am Hubland, 97074 Würzburg
{oechslein,kluegl,herrler,puppe}@informatik.uni-wuerzburg.de

Abstract. Developing multi-agent simulations seems to be rather straight forward, as active entities in the original correspond to active agents in the model. Thus plausible behaviors can be produced rather easily. However, for real world applications they must satisfy some requirements concerning verification, validation and reproducibility. Using a standard framework for designing a multi-agent model one can gain further advantages like fast learnability, wide understandability and possible transfer.

In this paper we show how UML can be used to specify behavior-oriented multi-agent models. Therefore we focus on activity graphs and the representation of different forms of interactions in these graphs.

1 Motivation

A multi-agent model captures the behavior of a system on the level of the active entities and maps them onto simulated active entities. Thus, on a rather coarse grain level of analysis, it is far more intuitive to describe the model in terms of agents and roles, using goals or activities, than to abstract it into a set of formulas. However, for executable simulations the concrete refinement and implementation exhibits properties that are rather difficult to deal with. The step between the model concept and the running experiment is by no way trivial:

- The modeler has to bridge the gap between top-down analysis and bottom-up implementation.
- Concurrent interactions form a central part of multi-agent systems. However, their concrete implementation is rather tricky.
- Complex agent behavior in sophisticated environments leads to rather large models that are effortful to design and implement in a consistent way.
- A huge amount of parameter has to be fixed for an executable simulation.

The consequence is that tools and frameworks are essential for the applicability of multi-agent simulation as a method for analyzing systems. The ideal framework for modeling would be easy to learn, generates understandable representation, provides all necessary primitives and constructors, and scales for concrete domains. In addition to these methodological points, the representation of a model

B. Dunin-Kęplicz and E. Nawarecki (Eds.): CEEMAS 2001, LNAI 2296, pp. 217–226, 2002.
© Springer-Verlag Berlin Heidelberg 2002

based on a framework should be clear and understandable to a wide group of people working in the same domain. This leads to the overall hope that models in multi-agent simulation can also satisfy the strong requirements concerning verification and validation that traditional simulation models are exposed to.

A prominent example for an already established framework is UML ("Unified Modeling Language" [1]). Besides multiple diagram types for the specification of structure and dynamics, UML provides with OCL ("Object Constraint Language") a formal language for attaching additional information, like invariants, constraints, etc. to the graphical specification.

In the following we therefore want to introduce behavior-oriented multi-agent models in the next section. After a short survey of existing frameworks in the area of agent-oriented simulation and software-engineering we are presenting the application of UML for our problem. This paper ends with a conclusion and short sketch of further works.

2   Behavior-Oriented Multi-agent Simulation

A multi-agent model in general can be seen as a simulated multi-agent system that exists in a simulated environment [2]. This is a natural form of modeling, especially for societies, as active entities in the original system are also interpreted as active ones in the model.

Existing multi-agent models focus on different aspects of a society from the development of dependence networks based on agents beliefs to a huge amount of massively interacting simple entities. Instead of trying to develop a plausible framework for human reasoning in interacting groups or organizations, we restrict ourselves to models that are simple enough to be validate-able, but on the other side capture rather sophisticated behaviors at the agent level. We call these multi-agent models *behavior-oriented* as they do not focus on the internal reasoning processes based on beliefs, goals or desires, but on the agents behavior and the effects of their actions and interactions. This focus is motivated by our primary application domain: the simulation of social insects; However, several other applications show the broad applicability of our approach.

Behavior-oriented multi-agent models follow two main concepts that help to structure the complete multi-agent simulation supporting extensive models with non-trivial behaviors and a huge amount of entities: The agent body as a set of sorted state variables and rule-based behavior representation that is augmented by structures like primitive and abstract activities.

Associating task fulfilment with activities and incorporating organizational concepts like roles additionally facilitates the development of complex society models. Although these concepts are already implemented into a modeling and simulation environment, called SeSAm ("Shell for Simulated Multi-Agent Systems" [3]), this framework is based on a proprietary specification language. This leads to the problem that our work still lacks a more generally applicable method for developing multi-agent simulations. Using a standard framework will have the additional advantage of generating models that are more likely to be reproducible by a modeler familiar with that standard.

Our overall goal is hereby to support the construction of models that satisfy the high standards of quality – concerning validation and verification – in standard simulation models. Using a standard framework for the step between concept and implementation is a major part of a viable solution.

3   Related Work: Modeling Frameworks and Formalisms

There are already lots of frameworks, tools, and languages for multi agent simulation. Approaches range from schemata and systems originating in the simulation area to languages for modeling multi-agent systems developed in Distributed Artificial Intelligence (for a more complete survey, see [2]).

3.1   Existing Frameworks Developed in the Simulation Area

Multi-agent simulation can be seen as an enhancement of standard individual oriented simulation: Agents can be taken as equipped with more sophisticated behavior in comparison to the individuals in process-oriented models or cellular automatons. In the line of this interpretation the approaches from agent-oriented simulation tackle more the management of the internal processes and internal agent structures. Frameworks like AgedDEVS ("agent-oriented DEVS" [4]) or PECS ("Physis, Emotion, Cognition, Social Status" [5]) provide schemata for the internal state structure of an agent. They are comparable to "traditional" agent architectures [6], but refer to sets of state variables. Another level of support can be found in modeling and simulation environments: e.g. in AgentSheets [7] (*www.agentsheets.com*) and its visual programming or in Swarm [8] (*www.swarm.org*) and its focus on animation and evaluation tools. The latter tackle just the concrete implementation problem and not the gap between concept and implementation.

3.2   From Agent-Oriented Software Engineering

Frameworks for building multi-agent systems are also a central issue in the area of agent-oriented software-engineering. Existing schemata provide support on different levels and for different stages of development. Methods like GAIA [9] or MAS-CommonKADS [10] concentrate on the analysis and design task by providing means for capturing views onto and models of the agent system in a top-down manner. The actual implementation is not tackled; the user is directed to use standard frameworks, like UML.

On the other hand, declarative languages and schemata for the specification of multi-agent systems exist. These start bottom-up from the agents and their behavior. If these specifications are executable – like in ConcurrentMetateM [11] – these languages can be used for simulation as well. In the area of social simulation, an analogous parallel rule-interpreting system, SDML ("Strictly Declarative Modeling Language" [12]), was developed. However, the problem is that these frameworks operate just on the complete agent level – there is no support for structuring actions and interactions. The behavior of the agents itself is formulated using an unstructured set of rules.

A specification language that is meant to bridge the gap between theoretical models and implemented systems is the Z-Framework of M. Luck et al. [13]. The Z schemata of "object", "agent" or "autonomous agents" are more and more extended to capture different forms and components of agent architectures or organizational structures like dependence networks [14]. The major criticism of this approach is its drawbacks in the formulation of dynamic aspects. However, the major advantage is the direct transformation into object-oriented class structures for the single agents.

Agent-oriented software engineering in general can be seen as an extension of object-oriented analysis, design and implementation. Thus the usage or even enhancement of standard object-oriented techniques is a proximate idea. In the area of social simulation a suggestion was made for a general framework for multi-agent simulation in social science, called Massif [15]. This framework uses (standard) UML sequence diagrams for describing interactions. Agent UML [16] on the other side focusses on the enhancement of these sequence diagrams as they are not apt for representing more sophisticated interaction protocols due to their message-based structure. Agent UML provides additional means for specifying negotiations with multiple, concurrently active participants. But for the purpose of designing behavior-oriented multi-agent simulations standard UML is almost satisfying, as we want to show in the following sections.

4   Using UML for Multi-agent Simulations

4.1   Class Diagrams

A class diagram for an agent class shows the external view on this kind of agent. The external view is divided into the accessible part of the agent memory, i.e. the state variables that are perceivable for other agents, and the interaction methods. The methods are named and contain its interaction partner, which for example is the special class *Environment*, as arguments. Methods specifying interactions can also be documented using the activity graph associated with that agent class. For completely describing the interaction situation the diagrams of the other agents, that participate in the interaction situation, are needed.

4.2   Activity Graphs

General Components. An activity graph in UML shows the behavior depicted as activity flow of objects in an object-oriented program. The main nodes in an activity graph are actions or activities. The latter are compositions of actions. Additionally there exist state nodes that are known from the UML state graph. State graphs can be seen as a specialization of an activity graph and are used in UML for describing state changes of a single object in contrast to activity changes concerning many objects in an activity graph. Other nodes are signal receiving and sending nodes. These nodes are important for modeling interactions and are explained later in more detail.

Transitions between nodes are defined based any form of conditions. One frequently used condition for a transition from an activity consists of the termination of this activity together with the activation of another state or activity. The modeler may use a rhombus node to show that there is an explicit decision in determining the next state or activity.

Activity Graphs for Multi-agent Models. As in the design of a multi-agent system in general, one can use activity graphs for describing the activity flow of one or more simulated agent classes. The transitions are conditions on external perceptions and internal state values (also goals, desires, and intensions if the agent architecture uses such concepts).

If there is more than one transition from a node, but the associated conditions form a crucial part of the model, then an explicit decision node should be used. As we observed in most of our applications, domain experts are using state-like behaviors (e.g. the IDLE "behavior") in their model to capture e.g. waiting. These can be better represented by state nodes.

There exist two special nodes: the start node and the end node. The agent starts its behavior at the start node, which entails no actions or activities and no incoming transitions. A filled circle depicts this start node. In an analogous way the end node is a dead end for the behavior of the agent, i.e. it has no outgoing transitions and can be interpreted as the terminating state of the agent. The end node is a filled circle surrounded by another unfilled circle.

This usage of UML activity graphs is straightforward, not only for describing the modeled behavior but also for generating the executable code of this agent. However, relationships and interaction between agents have to be explicitly shown. These involve agent-agent and agent-environment interactions. Thus a combination of activity graphs is necessary. How this is be managed is shown in the following.

Interaction Types. Until now relationships between the behavior of several agents are hidden in activities in different graphs. In the following we are examining possible interaction types and suggest how these interactions can be expressed in (standard) activity graphs:

In general possible interaction forms are direct or indirect (via the environment) interactions. For combining activity graphs a further distinctions is necessary: whether the receiver may be another instance of the same agent class or an instance of another agent class or a combination of these. Thus an interaction may have one of the following forms:

a) *Object flow* is the prominent method for indirect interactions. One agent creates a resource object, that is perceived by other agents, that in consequence adapt their behavior due to the modified environmental configuration. If a pheromone trail is implemented by pheromone resource objects, then depositing and following of trails corresponds to exactly this kind of interaction.

b) *Agent creation* is an important component of dynamic, variable structure model. An example is the production of offsprings frequently used in biological models.

c) *Manipulation of public instance variables* is the most technical form. It exhibits three subtypes: The sending agent modifies values either of itself, of a direct receiver or an intermediary. The first kind represents some sort of indirect broadcast, the sender changes its shape for the agents that are able to perceive it. Manipulating the variables of a receiver corresponds to directed interaction. If the changes concern variables of the environment we can observe a special case. It can be both directed and broadcast-like depending whether the environment serves as a communication medium or not.

d) The standard form of interaction is the synchronous and directed *sending and receiving of messages*. This can be part of complex negotiation protocols. A special form is broadcast communication in an explizit and synchronous form.

These four kind of interactions can be represented in activity graphs based on sending and receiving nodes:

Specification of Interaction in Activity Graphs. UML provides a facility for describing these interactions via signal sending and receiving nodes in activity graphs. Inserting these nodes into an activity graph is straightforward, but additional information concerning the concrete interaction might be necessary. Adding this enhanced specification to the sending-receiving node combination is sophisticated and depends on the interaction type. To clarify the sender and the receiver we draw a link between these two nodes and attach an additional node to this link. This is an optional procedure in UML but we want to restrict ourselves to establish a transparent representation. In detail the form of this additional node depends on the interaction types (see figure 1 for an illustration):

a) Object flow in general is specified by signal sending and receiving nodes and a link that is annotated by the class diagram of the "exchanged" objects.

b) Agent creation is represented by a link between the sender node and the start node of the new agent's activity graph. This is a special case since no receiver node is addressable for the created agent.

c) For variable manipulation we propose to augment the link with a documentation node that contains the necessary information about the sender, the receiver and the involved variable. Unfortunately a documentation node in standard UML just contains of unstructured text. An additional node type may be more appropriate. As we are restricting ourself here to standard UML, we postpone suggestions about additional node types to other papers.

d) Interaction via direct messages can be specified by both object flow links or documentation annotated links. This depends on the complexity of the message. Details of this kind of interaction are better specified using sequence diagrams.

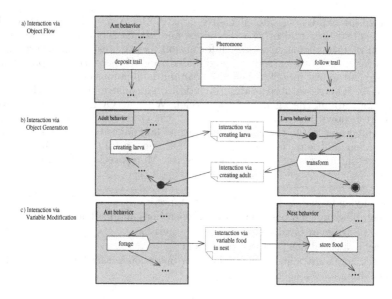

Fig. 1. Specifying Different Interactions Types in UML.

4.3 Sequence Diagram

In sequence diagram the message passing between objects is described. On the x-axis the participants of the interaction situation are listed, the y-axis is the timeline. For direct interactions, *Agent UML* [16] proposes enhancements to UML for sending a message to a few concurrently active agents. The overall aim of Agent UML is to provide a framework for sophisticated (reusable) negotiations. In behavior-oriented multi-agent simulations this kind of interactions may be rarely found due to the focus on agent behavior and not on sophisticated internal reasoning processes which are prerequisites for complex negotiation abilities.

Moreover, most of the interactions in such simulations take the form of indirect ones, that means the happen via coordinated changes in the environment ("stigmercy" [17]). Asynchrony and undirectedness are therefore important features of this kind of interaction. Thus sequence diagram are not well suited. Nevertheless, for documenting a typical path of interaction they are useful. But, a modeler using sequence diagrams in this case should keep in mind that both, participants and the concrete sequence of primitive interactions, are just examples and not fixed and complete specifications of protocols.

Without a specific protocol for the interactions it is useful to formulate invariants and constraints on the system that contains these interactions. UML also provides a facility: OCL.

4.4 Object Constraint Language (OCL)

An often overlooked feature in UML is the possibility to augment UML diagrams with OCL expressions. OCL ("Object Constraint Language" [18,19]) is a formal language for expressing side effect-free constraints. A modeler can use OCL to specify constraints and other expressions and attach them to his models, with the aim of formalizing necessary information for e.g. testing and verifying his simulations. OCL was introduced and added to UML because a graphical specification, like a class model, is not precise and unambiguous enough for specifying all details. There is a need to describe additional constraints about the objects, even more about the agents in the model. Without OCL constraints have to be written down in natural language with the consequences of its ambiguities and impreciseness. On the other hand, formal languages tend to be hard to read due to their mathematical background. OCL tries to fill this gap: It is a formal language and it is easy to read and to write. More precisely OCL can be used for ...

- specifying invariants for classes or stereotypes,
- describing pre- and post conditions on operations and methods,
- describing guards and event triggers (or transitions),
- tracing associations in object graphs and
- specifying constraints on operations, an operation constraint can be read as a definition for the operation.

These application areas are specially relevant for describing indirect and asynchrone interactions in a multi-agent simulation. Moreover, this kind of declarative and explicit information about the interacting system as a whole and its components is special useful since a procedural definition of interactions is lacking.

One can identify two different kinds of invariants: local and global. An invariant for one class is called a local invariant independent from the number of participating agents. If instances from different class are involved, we call it a global invariant. For an example see figure 2a.

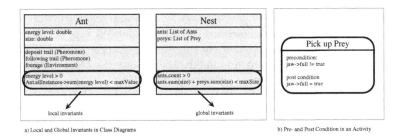

a) Local and Global Invariants in Class Diagrams   b) Pre- and Post Condition in an Activity

Fig. 2. Using OCL for multi-agent model.

Another important application is the assignment of pre- and post conditions to activities. Figure 2b shows an example. Other ways of applying OCL are also useful. OCL is the language for formulating the conditions of the transitions in an activity graphs described above. In an analogous way every side effect-free computation can be specified using OCL.

Although OCL provides no completely precise semantics, it is possible to restrict the power of this language for making it executable. Analyzing the applicability and usefulness in concrete applications of behavior-oriented multi-agent simulations, remains a main part of our future work. We are now working on a environment for designing and implementing executable simulations that is based on the concepts described here.

5   Conclusion and Further Work

In this paper we examined how to use standard UML for specifying behavior-oriented multi-agent simulations. This kind of multi-agent models are characterized by a focus on behavior and interactions of agents in a simulated environment.

Activity graphs are the prominent mean for formalizing behavior of many interacting agents. In general they are used for specifying behavior, here the activity flow of an agent or an agent class. However, in standard UML interactions are not explicitly tackled, since they are mostly hidden in several activity nodes, not directly connected with standard arrows. For multi-agent simulations this is a drawback as interactions form the central part. Based on some not widely used features in UML we presented a viable solution for the representation of interactions. For this we identified four major types of interactions in behavior-oriented multi-agent simulations. Based on sending and receiving nodes with augmented links, all four can be specified. The augmentation consists of additional nodes: single class diagrams or documentation nodes. The latter is a starting point for our future work as instead of using unstructured text information, a structured node would improve the description of the interaction.

UML provides another very important feature, namely the OCL. The formal expression language is both, precise and unambiguous. Thus it can be used to describe important facets of the model, to reduce the gap between modeling language and concrete implementation.

After an extensive phase of evaluation of this suggestions using real world applications, we want to show in our future work that using UML for multi-agent simulations improves the quality of model description. Thus we hope that it enables a modeler to build and execute multi-agent simulations with the same high standard of validation and verification as it is propagated in standard simulation models.

Acknowledgement. We would like to thank Dr. Jürgen Liebig and Anna Dornhaus from the Biozentrum at the University of Würzburg for their comments while applying the presented concepts. This research is partially funded by the DFG (German Research Foundation) in SFB 554 (Project C4) and SPP 1083.

References

1. G. Booch, I. Jacobson, J. Rumbaugh, and J. Rumbaugh. *The Unified Modeling Language User Guide.* The Addison-Wesley Object Technology Series. Addison Wesley, 1998.

2. F. Klügl. *Multi-Agent Simulation – Concept, Tools, Application (in German)*. Addison Wesley, 2001.
3. F. Klügl. *Activity-based Behavior Modeling and its Support for Multi-Agent Simulation (in German)*. PhD thesis, Universität Würzburg, 2000.
4. A. M. Uhrmacher. Object-oriented and agent-oriented simulation: Implications for social science application. In K. G. Troitzsch, U. Mueller, G. N. Gilbert, and J. E. Doran, editors, *Social Science Microsimulation*, chapter 20, pages 432–447. Springer, 1996.
5. C. Urban. Pecs: A reference model for the simulation of multi-agent systems. In R. Suleiman, K. G. Troitzsch, and G. N. Gilbert, editors, *Tools and Techniques for Social Science Simulation*. Physica-Verlag, Heidelberg, 2000.
6. J. P. Müller. Architectures and applications of intelligent agents: A survey. *Knowledge Engineering Review*, 13(4):353–380, 1999.
7. A. Repenning. Agentsheets: an interactive simulation environment with end-user programmable agents. In *Proceedings of INTERACTION 2000, Tokyo, Japan*, 2000.
8. N. Minar, R. Burkhart, C. Langton, and M. Askenazi. The swarm simulation system: A toolkit for building multi-agent simulation. http://www.santafe.edu/projects/swarm/, 1996.
9. M. Wooldridge, N. R. Jennings, and D. Kinny. A methodology for agent-oriented analysis and design. In *Proceedings of the 3rd Internation Conference on Autonomous Agents,1999*. ACM Press, 1999.
10. C. Iglesias, M. Garijo, and J. C. Gonzales. A survey of agent-oriented methodologies. In J. P. Müller, M. Singh, and A. S. Rao, editors, *Intelligent Agents V: Proceedings of the ATAL'98*, volume 1555 of *LNAI*. Springer, 1999.
11. M. Fisher. Representing and executing agent-based systems. In M. Wooldridge and N. R. Jennings, editors, *Intelligent Agents: Proceedings of the ATAL'94*, volume 890 of *LNAI*, pages 307–323. Springer, 1995.
12. S. Moss, H. Gaylard, S. Wallis, and B. Edmonds. Sdml: A multi-agent language for organizational modelling. CPM-Report 16, Centre for Policy Modelling, 1997.
13. M. Luck, N. Griffiths, and M. d'Inverno. From agent theory to agent construction. In J. P. Müller, M. J. Wooldridge, and N. R. Jennings, editors, *Intelligent Agents III (= Proceedings of ATAL'96)*, volume 1193 of *Lecture Notes in Artificial Intelligence*, pages 49–63. Springer, 1997.
14. F. Lopez y Lopez, M. Luck, and M. d'Inverno. A framework for agent architecture, dependence, norms and obligations. In *(Pre-)Proceedings of the MAAMAW'2001*, 2001.
15. E. Mentges. Concepts for an agent-based framework for interdisciplinary social science simulation. *Journal of Artificial Societies and Social Simulation*, 2(2), 1999.
16. J. Odell, H. van Dyke Parunak, and B. Bauer. Extending uml for agents. In *Proceedings of Agent-Oriented Information Systems 2000, Workshop at the AAAI 2000*, 2000.
17. E. Bonabeau, M. Dorigo, and G. Theraulaz. *Swarm Intelligence - From Natural to Artificial Systems*. Santa Fe Institute Studies in the Sciences of Complexity. Oxford University Press, Oxford, 1999.
18. OMG. *Object Constraint Language Specification*. http://www.omg.org/cgi-bin/doc?ad/97-08-08, 1997.
19. J. B. Warmer and A. G. Kleppe. *The Object Constraint Language : Precise Modeling With Uml*. The Addison-Wesley Object Technology Series. Addison Wesley, 1999.

Robot Disassembly Process Using Multi-agent System

Ales Pavliska and Vilem Srovnal

Department of Measurement and Control
Faculty of Electrical Engineering and Computer Science
VSB - Technical University of Ostrava
17.listopadu 15, Ostrava, 70833, Czech Republic
`ales.pavliska@email.cz`, `vilem.srovnal@vsb.cz`

Abstract. Increased industrialization and new markets have led to an accumulation of used technical consumer goods, which results in greater exploitation of raw materials, energy and landfill sites. In order to reduce the use of natural resources conserve precious energy and limit the increase in waste volume. The linear progression from production through consummation and finally to landfill sites must be stopped either by the product reuse, the parts reuse or the material recycling. The application of disassembly techniques is the first step towards this prevention of waste. These techniques form a reliable and clean approach: "noble" or high-graded recycling. This paper presents a multi agent system for disassembly process, which is implemented in a computer-aided application for supervising of the disassembling system: the Interactive Intelligent Interface for Disassembling System.

Keywords: Multi agent system, Recycling, Disassembly planning, Supervision, Disassembly process

1 Introduction

Global competition and rapidly changing customer requirements are forcing major changes in the production styles and configuration of manufacturing organizations. Increasingly, traditional centralized and sequential manufacturing planning, scheduling, and control mechanisms are being found insufficiently flexible to respond to changing production styles and highly dynamic variations in product requirements. The traditional approaches limit the expandability and reconfiguration capabilities of the manufacturing systems. The traditional centralized hierarchical organization may also result in much of the system being shut down by a single point of failure, as well as plan fragility and increased response overheads.

Agent technology provides a natural way to overcome such problems, and to design and implement distributed intelligent manufacturing environments. It has been considered as an important approach for developing those industrial distributed systems. The agent technology could be applied to manufactur-

B. Dunin-Kęplicz and E. Nawarecki (Eds.): CEEMAS 2001, LNAI 2296, pp. 227–233, 2002.

ing enterprise integration, supply chain management, manufacturing planning, scheduling and control and materials handling [1].

This paper contains the work carried out to create the man-machine interface for supervision of disassembling system, where disassembly process is provided by multi agent system. Section 2 deals with the whole 3IDS (Interactive Intelligent Interface for Disassembling System) project realization. Section 3 presents the internal realization of multi agent environment.

2   The Interactive Intelligent Interface for Disassembling System

The 3IDS is a project for supervising of disassembly process. The 3IDS project enables to select an end-of-life product, to analyze its sequences, to choose the best one, to control and to monitor a disassembly process using multi agent system.

The 3IDS project represents a section of the disassembling system. Whole disassembling system could be divided into three main sections: the CAD model, the Supervising cell (3IDS) and the Disassembling cell. The CAD model represents a difficult step in a disassembly planning system. The CAD models are used for a fully automated analysis of contacts among the parts evaluated along the axes XYZ of the CAD reference system. Data, together with the description of the connections, are transferred to a numerical contact-relation model to be easier handled by the second section of the disassembling system. The contact-relation model expresses the types of contact-relationships between parts of the product [3]. These models are input of the 3IDS project. Disassembling cell represents the core of disassembling system. It contains robots with specialized tools and operators. In this case, system is designed for using of one operator and one robot. This disassembling cell could be also simulated, for example in Robcad application from Technomatix.

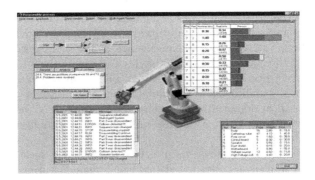

Fig. 1. Sequence diagram for action modifying

The 3IDS project composes of two main areas: Analyze sequences and Disassembly process (fig. 1). The first one is very complex project part, which takes in plenty of tools for searching the best disassembling sequence for selected end-of-life product. The output is an optimal dismantling sequence described by a numbered list of parts. The second one provides to simulate the final product disassembly. It works in three modes: Manual mode, where MAS is not used, and two Automatic modes that use MAS for disassembling.

3 Multi Agent System Realization

In the 3IDS project, the multi agent system (MAS) is designed to work based on a predicted scenario. It's designed to deal with decision making in a disassembly process by choosing the best disassembling sequence, when a non-expected collision is occurred. Otherwise, it disassembles systematically parts from just selected product sequence. The disassembling sequence is an ordered sequence of product parts to be disassembled.

The MAS is realized in two different modes: the Semi-automatic mode and the Fully- automatic mode. If a collision is occurred, the MAS will try to replace the current disassembling sequence from its last disassembled part to its end with another fraction. A fraction is a part of whole sequence. If the MAS finds more than one possible fraction, it will choose the fraction which first part best corresponds to adjusted criteria. The supervisor sets these criteria in the main menu of the Disassembly process window (fig. 1). There are five different criterion types: the disassembly cost, the part value, the benefit price, the part weight and the disassembling time estimation. For each type, the MAS could look for the highest value or the lowest value in dependence on the supervisor's setting. If the MAS doesn't find any possible fraction, then its next behavior will depend on the adjusted mode. If the Semi-automatic mode is set, it asks supervisor for help how to continue. If the Fully-automatic mode is set, the supervisor agent is implemented and he calls the operator to try to continue on disassembly of the current part at the place, where the robot ended with a collision. However, if the operator doesn't succeed, the supervisor agent has to cancel current disassembly process.

3.1 General Structure

The general structure of the MAS consists of four logical units [2]:

Data structures are the set of structures, which contains input and preprocessed data. System receives the set of possible sequences to disassembly and their economical specifications.

Decision making is the set of agents, which has references to data structures and which dynamically choose the best step from the set of sequences to perform some operations depending on the end-of-life product state and the current situation. The Decision unit has to determine which operation is the best. If some operation fails, it has to decide what another operation could be performed or that the intervention of the operator or the supervisor is needed.

Controllers are the set of agents that can interact with a robot or an operator. The Controller agents execute the operations, which was chosen by the Decision making unit. They are used for executing of an action of Robot and Operator objects.

Supervisor is a person who interacts with the system and controls it. To perform some actions on the product he can use his agent (Supervisor agent) to "tell" him execute some actions.

3.2   Decision Making Unit

There are three types of agents in the decision-making unit (fig. 2):

- Decision
- Operation
- Action

Decision agent is one agent, which makes decision basing on the information from operation agents. This agent has its current state. On the beginning, its state is the selected dismantling sequence. Every step the agent updates its current state. On a collision in a disassembly process, this agent creates operation agents for all possible operations. To decide which operation is the best to perform on the current state, the decision agent asks the operation agents (calling Negotiate method). The decision agent chooses the operation agent, which returns the best-fit value.

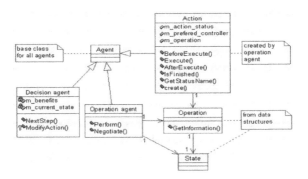

Fig. 2. Class structure of agents in the decision-making unit

Operation agent is the agent, which is created for each possible operation. This agent has a method Negotiate, which returns a numerical value of the economical specification of the first potential operation in the state, which could be performed by the operation agent.

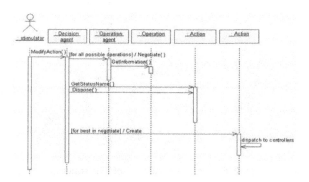

Fig. 3. Sequence diagram for action modifying

Action agent is the agent, which is created after making a decision. It is created to perform a chosen operation. It is a mobile agent and it can be dispatched between two units: the decision making unit and the controllers unit. If the controller has a problem with executing the action, the action agent is dispatched back to the decision unit. In this case, another decision has to be made or the action agent has to be canceled.

3.3   Controllers Unit

There are three agents in controllers unit (fig. 3):

- Station controller agent
- Supervisor agent
- Operator agent

All those agents are extended from its base class: the controller agent. There are also two objects in this unit: the Robot and the Operator. The agents from the controllers unit control those objects.

Each controller agent is stimulated by the system. Each free (not busy) controller agent (rather its specialization) searches for an action agent in the agents' container. If the action agent exists and waits for its realization and if the controller agent is able to execute this action (fig. 5), then the controller agent tries to execute it. If the action was successfully executed, the action agent is disposed. Then the decision unit will create the next action agent, which will represent another operation. If execution was failed, the action agent is not disposed. It is dispatched back to the decision unit and it is there processed (it is analyzed, disposed and the new action agent is created if necessary).

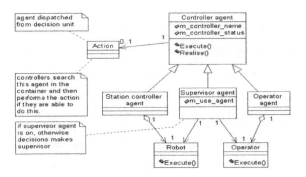

Fig. 4. Class structure of controllers

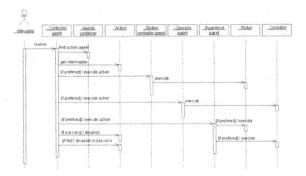

Fig. 5. Sequence diagram for action execution

4   Conclusion

This paper describes a recycling platform, which implements the "noble recycling" concept for technical end-of-life products. It concentrates on the description of multi agent system, which is used in the 3IDS project to increase the reactivity of disassembly process. All project algorithms are implemented using MS Visual C++ 6.00 basing on Unified Modelling Language (UML) model.

There are few elements of the system, which might be further worked out. The most important element of further work will be the connection with real or simulated disassembling cell. Simulation could be effected in Robcad environment from Technomatix. Within the "Rester propre" project, research works proceed just in Robcad environment to simulate whole disassembling cell containing a robot, an operator and an end-of-life product. (The Rester propre project has originated on Institut National Polytechnique de Grenoble in Laboratoire d'Automatique de Grenoble. It deals with supervision and control systems in high-graded recycling.) For materialize, the agents' environment upgrading is needed. Robot object is currently an abstract object, which simulates execution of some actions. In the future, this object has to be replaced by a real robot object, which will translate all information from the action agent to a language of the robot and passes it to this robot.

The 3IDS project was finished on VSB Technical University of Ostrava, Department of Measurement and Control. The Ministry of Education of the Czech Republic supplied the results of the project CEZ:J17/98:272400013 with subvention.

References

1. Shen,W., Norrie,D.H.: Agent-Based system for intelligent manufacturing: A state of the art survey. Knowledge and Information Systems, an International Journal, 1(2), 129-156, http://imsg.enme.ucalgary.ca/publication/abm.htm, University of Calgary, Canada, 1999
2. Kwiatkowski,K., Skaf,A.: Decision making system for disassembling process. Laboratoire d'Automatique de Grenoble - INPG, France, 2000
3. Dini,G., Failli,F., Santochi,M.: A disassembly planning software system for the optimization of recycling process. Department of Production Engineering - University of Pisa, Italia, 1999
4. Chevron,D., Drevon,S., Binder,Z.: Design and implementation of a man-machine interface for disassembling cell. Laboratoire d'Automatique de Grenoble - INPG, Grenoble, France, 1997
5. Cetnarowicz, K., Kozlak, J.: Multi-Agent System For Flexible Manufacturnig Systems Management. In: Pre-Proceeding International Workshop CEEMAS'01. AGH Krakow 2001, ISBN 83-915953-0-7, p.41-50
6. Nawarecki, E., Kisiel-Dorohinicki, M., Dobrowolski, G.: Organisations in the Particular Class of Multi-agent systems. In: Pre-Proceeding International Workshop CEEMAS'01. AGH Krakow 2001, ISBN 83-915953-0-7, p.181-190

CPlanT: An Acquaintance Model-Based Coalition Formation Multi-agent System

Michal Pechoucek, Vladimir Marik, and Jaroslav Barta

Gerstner Laboratory, Czech Technical University in Prague
{pechouc|marik}@labe.felk.cvut.cz

Abstract. This article will describe the CPlanT multi-agent system that has been designed in order to suggest and test alternative approaches to coalition formation. The system has been implemented for planning the Operations Other Than War (OOTW) coalition, which is the domain with a strong emphasis put on maintaining privacy of communicated information among collaborating actors – agents and important level of autonomy of their decision making. The paper presents a concept of an *acquaintance model* as computational models of agents' mutual awareness. In the acquaintance model the agents administer and maintain different types social knowledge that are exploited in the coalition formation process.

1 War Avoidance Operations

The application domain of this coalition formation research belongs to the area of **war avoidance operations** such as peace-keeping, peace-enforcing, non-combatant evacuation or disaster relief operations. Unlike in classical war operations, where the technology of control is strictly hierarchical, **operations other than war** (OOTW) are very likely to be based on cooperation of a number of different, quasi-volunteered, vaguely organized groups of people, non-governmental organizations (NGO's), institutions providing humanitarian aid but also army troops and official governmental initiatives.

Collaborative, unlike hierarchical, approach to operation planning allows greater deal of flexibility and dynamics in grouping optimal parties playing an active role in the operation. New entities shall be free to join autonomously and involve themselves in planning with respect to their capabilities. Therefore any organization framework must be essentially "open". OOTW have, according to [12], multiple perspective on plan evaluation as there does not need to be one shared goal or a single metrics of the operation (such as political, economical, humanitarian). From the same reason the goals across the community of entities involved in a possible coalition may be in conflict. Even if the community members share the same goal it can be easily misunderstood due to different cultural backgrounds.

The main reason why we can hardly plan operations involving different NGO's by a central authority results from their **reluctance to provide information** about their intentions, goals and resources. Consequently, besides difficulties related to planning and negotiation we have to face the problems how to assure sharing detailed information. Many institutions will be ready to share resources and information within

B. Dunin-Kęplicz and E. Nawarecki (Eds.): CEEMAS 2001, LNAI 2296, pp. 234–241, 2002.

some well specified community, whereas they will refuse to register their full capabilities and plans with a central planning system and will not follow centralized commands. They may agree to participate in executing a plan, in forming of which they played an active role.

Actual information may become **unavailable** also due to **unreliable** communication channels. It may happen that a collaborative entity gets cut off the communication links for certain period of time and the rest of the community still wishes to be able to form/execute plan relying upon a missing player (and the same vice-versa). For this reason, each participating entity shall be able to maintain approximate model of the collaborating members of the coalition.

2   Coalition Planning

Naturally, a paradigm of multi-agent systems, a community of heterogeneous, autonomous, proactive and collaborative agents, suits the domain of coalition planning. Firstly, let us put down several terms that will be used throughout this study. As a **multi-agent community** we understand the whole collection of agents participating in the above-described OOTW (quasi-volunteered, vaguely organized groups of people, non-governmental organizations, institutions providing humanitarian aid, army troops or official governmental initiatives). Throughout the paper we will refer to a **coalition** as a set of agents (an agreement) who agreed to fulfill a single, well-specified goal. Agents thus commit themselves to collaboration with respect to the in-coalition-shared goal. An agent may participate in multiple coalitions. Unlike an alliance (see below), a coalition is usually regarded as a short-term agreement between collaborative agents. As a **coalition formation/planning** we understand the process of finding a coalition of agents who may participate in achieving the respective goal [10], [11]. As an **alliance** we understand a collection of agents that share general humanitarian objectives and all agree to form possible coalitions. Moreover, the alliance members decided to share detailed information about their status, resources they may provide and their collaboration preferences. The alliance is regarded as a long-term cooperation agreement among the agents.

Classical methods to coalition formation rely on game-theoretic models, where possible alternatives of how the coalition may be formed and how beneficial that will be for the community and the participating agents are investigated. The space of all possible alternatives is called a **coalition structure**. Sometimes it is assumed each value of the community to be independent from nonmembers' actions (Characteristic Function Game – CFG), where agents may face positive externalities (e.g. in a form of overlapping goals) or negative externalities (e.g. shared resources). The coalition structure is usually searched by a central agent – a coordinator, or collaboratively by the community members. Searching a coalition structure is usually a computationally explosive problem and is hard to be implemented in many real life problems. We suggest pruning the coalition structure by exploiting the agents' social knowledge that will exclude specific branches of the structure and will guide the search.

However, a more important contribution of this research effort is rooted in suggesting a framework for agents to form coalitions autonomously, collaboratively and without any central facilitating component. Unlike in classical coalition formation problems, the quality of a coalition in OOTW operations is not given only by a function of different utilities (such as collaboration cost, task completion time, number of collaborating agents) but also by the amount of private information that agents had to reveal. We will show how the agents' acquaintance models may help forming a coalition among autonomous agents and at the same time minimize the amount of disclosed information.

3   CPlanT Multi-agent System

We will model collective behavior of the multi-agent community by a CPlanT multi-agent system. The CPlanT architecture consists of several specific classes of agents:

- **Resource Agents** (R-agents) represent the in-place resources that are inevitable for delivering humanitarian aid, such as roads, airports, seaports but also subcontracted shipping agencies. Unlike below-defined H-agents, the R-agents are regarded as passive and they do not initiate any kind of humanitarian effort.
- **In-need Agents** (In-agents) are critical bodies in the entire simulation. They will represent the centers of conflict that call for help (e.g. cities, villages, etc.).
- **Coordination Agents** (C-agents) are specific types of matchmaking agents that monitor the In-agents' call for help, contract other countries' C-agents, who broadcast the call within humanitarian agencies. In many cases the C-agents also wish to coordinate the flow of humanitarian aid towards the In-agents.
- **Humanitarian Agents** (H-agents), who are computational representations of the participating humanitarian agencies. Like the R-agents, H-agents provide humanitarian aid. Therefore, one may regard the H-agent as a subclass of R-agents. However the H-agents are proactive and they initiate providing the respective humanitarian aid.

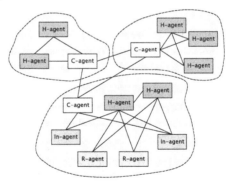

Fig. 1. CPlanT Multi-Agent Architecture

Though the coalition formation problem is much wider and involves forming coalition together with all the other participating agents, we will investigate coalition formation among the H-agents.

3.1   H-Agent Knowledge Architecture

The H-agent may participate in one or more alliances and at the same time he may be actively involved in a coalition of agents cooperating in fulfilling a shared task. Computational and communication complexity of the above defined coalition formation problem, depends on the amount of pre-prepared information the agents administer one about the other and on the sophistication of the agents meta-reasoning mechanisms (as a meta-reasoning we understand agent's capability to reason about the other agent's reasoning processes). We suggest three levels of agent's knowledge representation:

Public Knowledge is shared within the entire multi-agent community. This class of knowledge is freely accessible within the community. As public knowledge we understand agents name, type of the organization the agent represents, general objective of the agent's activity, country where the agent is registered, agent's human-human contact (fax number, email), the human-agent type of contact (http address) and finally the agent-agent type of contact (the IP address, incoming port, ACL)

Alliance-Accessible Knowledge is shared within a specific alliance. We do not assume the knowledge to be shared within the overlapping alliances. Members of an alliance will primarily share information about free availability of their resources and respective position. This resource-oriented type of knowledge may be further distinguished as material resources, human resources and transport resources.

Private Knowledge is owned and administered by the agent himself. Though the agents are expected to share private information neither within an alliance nor within a coalition, provided they find it useful, they may communicate some pieces of the private information upon a request. As an instance of private knowledge we can consider mainly specific status of the resources the agent administers, future plans and allocation of resources, his past performance, agent's collaboration preferences and restrictions, and agent's planning and scheduling algorithms.

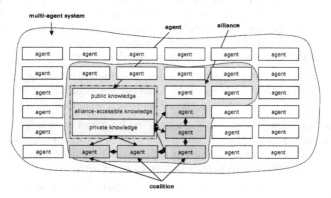

Fig. 2. Concept of the Alliance and the Coalition

The multi-agent community will operate in three separate phases: (i) **registration phase**, when a new-coming agent registers within the multi-agent community, (ii) **alliance formation**, when the agents will analyse the information they have about the members of the multi-agent system and will attempt to form alliances and (iii)

coalition formation phase, when the agents group together not according to a similar mission objective and but with respect to a single, well specified task that needs to be accomplished.

3.2 Agents' Acquaintance Model

The main research challenge of this project is to design an appropriate H-agents' acquaintance model. An acquaintance model represents agent's awareness about other members of the community. Utilisation of an agents acquaintance model will allow fast and efficient coalition formation while it will keep an important part of the agent's knowledge private and inaccessible to unauthorised agents. Apart from ensuring the agents' knowledge privacy, we use the acquaintance models in order to allow an agent to reason about the other agents while it is disconnected from the rest of the community. Similarly the other alliance members may form plans that rely upon the missing agent as they keep much of the knowledge about such agent in their acquaintance models.

There have been many different acquaintance models designed for various purposes. The concept of the **tri-base acquaintance model** (3bA model) has been successfully applied in the domain of production planning [4] and in providing safety and efficiency improvements of the communication traffic in multi-agent systems 7. A similar approach has been applied to the problem of multi-level optimisation in multi-agent systems. A general meta-reasoning acquaintance model (MRAM) has been designed for implementing meta-agents and instantiating reflexivity in a multi-agent system 5.

The humanitarian relief operations acquaintance model for shall contain four key knowledge-bases (based on our experience with 3bA and MRAM):

– **self-belief-base** (stored in the knowledge wrapper) stores the knowledge the agent knows about himself and may want to make accessible to all or some of agents. As there are accessibility relations to each piece of knowledge in the self-belief-base (specifying who can manipulate/access the respective knowledge), all three types of knowledge (private knowledge, alliance-accessible knowledge and public knowledge) may be stored in a single knowledge structure.

– **community-belief-base** (stored in the communication wrapper) contains the communication-like, technical public knowledge about all members of the multi-agent systems (e.g. symbolic name, IP addresses, communication means, type, ...)

– **social-belief-base** (stored in the agents' body) stores knowledge about the other agents. In the ground-belief-table it stores the accessible fraction of someone else self-belief-base and in the assumed-belief-table it maintains new hypothesis about other agents operation that has been formed by the agent.

– **task-base** (stored in the agents' body) is a collection of pre-planned coalitions that the agent may coordinate or participate in with respect to different tasks. Planned coalitions are constructed from the information stored in other parts of the agents acquaintance model.

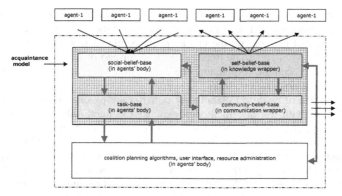

Fig. 3. Suggested Acquaintance Model Architecture

The agents' social neighbourhood – structure of various alliances – is expected to change dynamically. Even already planned coalitions may require acute re-planning and resources reconfiguration as the environment changes, the respective crises dynamically evolve or even the agents may leave the coalition for many different reasons. Logical clustering of knowledge about services the agents may provide and its appropriate maintenance will transform an important amount of computation from the time of request to the agent's idle times. An important issue is the problem of maintaining the knowledge an agent may have about the others. We have implemented **subscription-based knowledge maintenance**. Once an agent appends a record about another agent to its social-belief-base it subscribes this collaborating agent for future updates. Upon a change of a required resource the subscribed agents informs its subscriber.

Let us distinguish the process of forming a coalition from the process of planning a coalition. As the process of **coalition planning** we will understand agent's reasoning about possible candidate for membership in the planned coalition. The planning agent can either broadcast a call for cooperation and select the best possible proposal or he can directly analyse the social knowledge it keeps in its acquaintance model. **Coalition formation** is the process of closing an agreement among candidates for membership in a planned coalition. Usually the planning/coordinating agent contracts the respective collaborators. Once the coalition is formed the **coalition activity** may start. The **quality** of the coalition is the factor of how suitable will be the coalition for accomplishing the shared objective while minimising the amount of disclosed information.

The coordinating agent may be (i) either asked to form a coalition and immediately initiate task implementation within the coalition members in order to accomplish the shared objective (both coalition planning and formation in the **coalition formation phase**) (ii) or he will maintain certain number of patterns of the coalition structures (**coalition planning phase**) by combination of which he will form an accurate coalition in a reasonable amount of time (coalition formation phase). Practically, agents will maintain a collection of suggested coalitions in their task-base. As the involved agents will change their status throughout the time, the suggested coalitions will be changing in quality. The agent's activity of keeping the task-base knowledge up-to-date and consistent with changes in the social belief-base is called **coalition re-planning**. Upon each update in the social-belief-base the agent has to check quality of the coalition that depends on the given update or plan a new coalition if the already planned coalition proves to be impossible to be formed or with the quality lower than acceptable. For accurate re-planning the agents may keep in their state-bases several alternative coalitions for one task.

The problem of coalition planning is rather complex one. Many researchers have experimented with various methodologies. In Gerstner Laboratory we have been investigating behaviour of two types of algorithms that reduce the state-space of possible coalitions 1. By using distributed branch-and-bounds algorithm, we manage to decompose the problem of searching for the optimal coalition within possible candidates. The agents jointly find an optimal coalition. The other algorithm is based on parallel state-space search. Though we have proved linear complexity of the single agent problem solving, the found coalition is not guaranteed to be optimal. Nevertheless, the experiments shown that the solutions found by the fast algorithm are very close to the optimum (see Figure 4 for comparison).

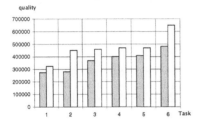 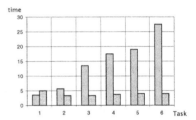

Fig. 4. Comparison of the optimal and linear coalition formation algorithms in terms of quality of the formed coalition (left graph) and in terms of time requirements for the coalition formation process

3.3   Form of Acquaintance Knowledge

An interesting problem concerns the type and structure of the knowledge that is advertise throughout the maintenance phase in the agents' acquaintance model. Owing to the collaborative property of the respective coalition, the coalition members shall assist the coordinating agent in his coalition planning activity by supplying him with the most accurate approximation of their resources. This approximation shall be communicated to the coalition leader in order to keep his acquaintance model as accurate as possible.

In many acquaintance models implementations the respective social knowledge structure (of an agent A) is represented as a simple set:

$$sk_{min} = \{\langle B, \{resource, cost, delivery\text{-}time\}\rangle\}_{B \in \mu(A)},$$

where B is an agent (resource provider) monitored by agent A (coalition leader), thus member of agent's A monitoring neighborhood $\mu(A)$ [5].

However this knowledge structure does not bear the complex information about already contracted resources. Such a knowledge structure shall contain information about resource allocation of each possible requested amount of resources:

$$sk_{max} = \{\langle B, \{resource, m, cost, delivery\text{-}time\}\rangle\}_{B \in \mu(A), m \in N},$$

where m is an amount of resources that can be delivered. The most appropriate form of the social knowledge structure sk will need little computational resources for representation and at the same time will sufficiently approximate the respective resource allocation. In a way we are trying to find a middle ground between sk_{min} and sk_{max} .

4   Conclusion

The above specified principles and ideas are currently tested and implemented on a subset of the OOTW types of operations – humanitarian relief (HR) operations. For this purpose we have designed and implemented a hypothetical humanitarian scenario in a fictious country – Sufferterra (inspired by 89). The scenario knowledge has been encoded in the XML files and the computational model of the scenario has been implemented in Allegro Common Lisp. This project was supported by AFOSR/European Office of Aerospace Research and Development under contract number F61775-00-WE043.

References

1. Barta J., Pechoucek M., Stepankova O.: Object Oriented Approach to Coalition Forming. GL 2000/100 - *Technical Report of The Gerstner Lab* CTU Prague & FAW Linz, Hagenberg - Praha - Wien, 2000
2. Dix J., Subrahmanian V.S., Pick G.: Meta Agent Programs. *Journal of Logic Programming*, 46(1-2):1-60, 2000.
3. Jennings, N., Agent Based Computing: Promises and Perils, Computer and Thought Award Lecture, *Int. Conference on Artificial Intelligence*, Stockholm, August 1999
4. Marik V., Pechoucek M., Lazansky J., Roche, C.: *PVS'98 Agents: Structures, Models and Production Planning Application*. In: Robotics and Autonomous Systems, vol. 27, No. 1-2, Elsevier, 1999, pp.29-44. ISSN 0921-8890
5. Pechoucek, M., Marik, V., Stepankova O.: Towards Reducing Communication Traffic In Multi-Agent Systems, *Journal of Applied System Studies*, CIS Publishing, UK, 2001.
6. Pechoucek, M., Norrie, D.: Knowledge Structures for Reflective Multi-Agent Systems: On reasoning about other agents, registered as Report no.: 538, Department of Mechanical and Manufacturing Engineering, University of Calgary, Alberta, Canada, December 2000
7. Pechoucek M., Stepankova O. Marik V.: Saving Communication in Multi-Agent Systems with Tri-base Acquaintance Models and Machine Learning - *Project Report of US Air Force Research Contract*, project contract no.: F61775-99-WE099, August 2000
8. Rathmell R. A.: A Coalition Force Scenario 'Binni – Gateway to the Golden Bowl of Africa', *Defence Evaluation Research Agency*, 1999
9. Reece, G. A. and Tate, A. (March 1993) The Pacifica NEO Scenario. Technical Report ARPA-RL/O-Plan2/TR/3. AIAI, University of Edinburgh, Scotland, 1993
10. Sandholm W. Distributed Rational Decision Making, In Multi-Agent Systems: *Modern Approach to Distributed Artificial Intelligence*, The MIT Press, Cambridge, 1999
11. Shehory O. and Kraus S., Methods for Task Allocation via Agent Coalition Formation, *Artificial Intelligence*, vol. 101 (1-2), pp. 165-200, 1998
12. Walker, E. C. T., Panel Report: Coalition Planning for Operations Other Than War, *Workshop at AIAI*, Edinburgh, Spring 1999

Efficient Model Checking of Causal-Knowledge Protocols[*]

Wojciech Penczek

Institute of Computer Science
Polish Academy of Sciences, Warsaw, Poland
and Akademia Podlaska
Institute of Informatics, Siedlce, Poland
penczek@ipipan.waw.pl

Abstract. A model checking algorithm for proving correctness of causal knowledge protocols for multi-agent systems is given. Protocols are specified in an extension of the temporal logic of causal knowledge [18]. The temporal language is interpreted over labelled prime event structures. The epistemic operators correspond to knowledge and goals, whereas the temporal modalities correspond to the immediate causality and causality. The model checking algorithm is translated to the model checking problem for LTL or ACTL. This enables a further translation to the SAT-problem, using the technique of the bounded model checking.

1 Introduction

The classical definition of knowledge and semantics of knowledge-based programs are built on global states and global time, see [6,5]. The consequence of that definition is logical omniscience of the agents, which is frequently regarded as a drawback, especially if the agents are modeled to take decisions in real time. An alternative proposal to the classical notion of knowledge [19,17,18] is based on partial order structures of local states, called event structures [20,16]. Knowledge is acquired by the agents via communication with local interactions. Each agent has (causal) knowledge about the most recent events of the other agents. This approach captures the changes in state due to actions, which is crucial for successful modeling of knowledge, but quite rarely incorporated by global state logical formalisms (due to undecidability [19]). In addition to the advantage of having a very intuitive and "practical" notion of knowledge, there are two more important reasons for investigating knowledge in the framework of partial order models of local states. Firstly, there is no distinction between computations that are equivalent with respect to the ordering of independent operations, which makes it a natural framework. Secondly, local state based interpretations allow for using efficient methods of alleviating the state explosion problem in verification [17].

---

[*] Partly supported by the State Committee for Scientific Research under the grant No. 7T11C 006 20

B. Dunin-Kęplicz and E. Nawarecki (Eds.): CEEMAS 2001, LNAI 2296, pp. 242–252, 2002.

Model checking is one of the most successful methods of automatic verification of program properties. A model-checking algorithm decides whether a finite-state distributed system satisfies its specification, given as a formula of a temporal logic [3,8]. In this paper we address a model checking problem for an extension of the temporal logic of causal knowledge on local states, suggested in [18]. The logics is used to specify causal knowledge based protocols for multi-agent systems. The agents acquire their knowledge gradually by getting informations from other agents during execution of synchronization actions and take decisions depending on their knowledge.

We start with defining labelled prime event structures (lpes) to represent behaviours of multi agent systems in terms of executed events and their relationships. Since our modal language is to be interpreted over local state occurrences (lso's) rather than over events, for each lpes we define the corresponding lso-structure, which serves as a frame. Lso-structures (typically infinite) are generated by finite deterministic asynchronous automata $\mathcal{A}$ using trace semantics. In order to define a model checking algorithm over an lso-structure, we need to find its finite quotient structure, which preserves the formulas of our language. This problem is solved by using a gossip automaton, which keeps track about the latest information the agents have about each other. The global state space of the product of the gossip automaton and the automaton $\mathcal{A}$ is a required finite quotient structure.

The main contribution of this paper relies on defining a model checking algorithm for proving correctness of causal knowledge protocols w.r.t. the goals of the agents. Moreover, our algorithm is defined in such a way that it can be translated to the model checking problem for LTL or ACTL [3,8]. This enables a further translation to the SAT-problem using a very promising technique of the bounded model checking [1,21]. The rest of the paper is organized as follows. In section 2 labelled branching synchronization structures are introduced. Modal logic of causal knowledge is defined in section 3. Model checking is explained in section 4. Translation to the SAT-problem is discussed in section 5. In section 6 we discuss a related work.

2 Labelled Branching Synchronization Structures

Our formal theory of Multi Agent Systems (MASs) uses an event-based approach. Event structures have been successfully applied in the theory of distributed systems [20] and several temporal logics have adopted them as frames [9,16,18]. Next, we present a formal definition of an event structure.

Definition 1. *A **labelled prime event structure** (lpes, for short) is a 5-tuple $\mathcal{ES} = (E, A, \rightarrow, \#, l)$, where*

1. *E is a finite set, called the set of events or action occurrences,*
2. *A is a finite set, called the set of actions,*
3. *$\rightarrow \subseteq E \times E$ is an irreflexive, acyclic relation, called the immediate causality relation between the events such that $\downarrow e \stackrel{def}{=} \{e' \in E \mid e' \rightarrow^* e\}$ is finite for each $e \in E$, where $\rightarrow^*$ is the reflexive and transitive closure of $\rightarrow$,*

4. $\# \subseteq E \times E$ *is a symmetric, irreflexive relation, called the* conflict relation, *such that* $\# \circ \rightarrow^* \subseteq \#$ *(called the* conflict preservation*),*
5. $l : E \longrightarrow A$ *is a function, called the* labelling function

Two events e, e', which are not in $\rightarrow^*$ nor in $\#$ are concurrent, denoted $e\|e'$. The conflict preservation condition specifies that the conflict of two events is inherited by all the events in their causal futures. The labeling function l indicates for each event which action is executed, i.e., $l(e) = a$ means that an event e is an occurrence of the action a. Each action belongs to a set of agents, denoted $agent(a) = \{i \in N \mid a \in l(E_i)\}$. The relations $\rightarrow$ and $\#$ capture the causality and conflict relationship between events, respectively. Two events are in conflict if they cannot occur in the same run.

Let N be a natural number denoting the number of agents. We assume that $E = \bigcup_{i=1}^{N} E_i$, where E_i is a set of the events of agent i for $1 \leq i \leq N$. An event e is called *joint* if it belongs to at least two different sets E_i. We assume that if $e \rightarrow e'$, then $agent(e) \cap agent(e') \neq \emptyset$.

Let $agent(e) = \{i \in N \mid e \in E_i\}$ and $E_N \overset{def}{=} \{(e, i) \in E \times N \mid i \in agent(e)\}$ denote the set of *local state occurrences* (lso's, for short), i.e., (e, i) represents the lso of the agent i reached after executing the event e. Since our language is to be interpreted over lso's rather than over events, for each lpes we define the corresponding lso-structure.

Definition 2. *Let* $\mathcal{ES} = (E, A, \rightarrow', \#', l')$ *be an lpes. The* **lso structure** *corresponding to* $\mathcal{ES}$ *is defined as* $\mathcal{S} = (E_N, A, \rightarrow, \#, l)$, *where*

1. $(e, i) \rightarrow (e', j)$ *iff* $e \rightarrow' e'$ *and* $i \in agent(e')$,
2. $(e, i) \# (e', j)$ *iff* $e\#'e'$,
3. $l : E_N \longrightarrow A$ *such that* $l(e, i) = l'(e)$, *for* $e \in E$.

Two lso's $s, s' \in E_N$, which are not in $\rightarrow^*$ nor in $\#$ are concurrent, denoted $s\|s'$.

The above definition needs some explanation. Intuitively, for two lso's $(e, i) \rightarrow (e', j)$ if (e, i) is one of the starting lso's of event e'. Intuitively, two lso's are concurrent if they can be reached by the system at the same time. According to the definition two lso's $(e, i), (e', j)$ are in the relation $\|$ if they correspond either to the same event (then $e = e'$) or to concurrent events, or to causally related events e, e' and $(e, i), (e', j)$ are not comparable by $\rightarrow^*$. Notice that $e \rightarrow'^* e'$ iff $(\exists k, j \in N) : (e, k) \rightarrow^* (e', j))$.

Consider the lso structure corresponding to the two synchronizing agent system represented by the Petri Net in Figure 1. We have added two starting lso's corresponding to an artificial action @ putting tokens to the places 1 and 2. The agents can synchronize by executing the joint action e. The immediate causality relation is marked by the arrows, the concurrency relation by the dotted lines, whereas the conflict relation is not marked.

Our present aim is to incorporate into the formalism the notions of agent's **knowledge** and **goals**. The first step towards this aim is to define runs of lpes's.

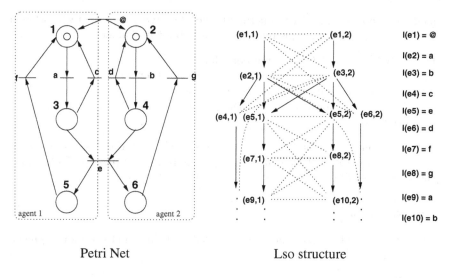

Petri Net   Lso structure

Fig. 1. Petri Net together with the corresponding lso-structure

A run plays a role of "reality", i.e., it describes one of the possible "real" full behaviours of the agents.

Definition 3. *Let* $\mathcal{S} = (E_N, A, \rightarrow, \#, l)$ *be an lso-structure. A maximal, conflict-free substructure* $\mathcal{R} = (R, A, \rightarrow_r, \emptyset, l_r)$ *of* $\mathcal{S}$ *is a* **run**, *where* $R \subseteq E_N$, $\rightarrow_r \subseteq \rightarrow$, *and* $l_r = l|_R$. *The set of all runs of the lso-structure is denoted by* $\mathcal{R}_\mathcal{S}$.

Notice that $R_1 = \{(e, 1), (e, 2) \mid l(e) \in \{@, a, b, c, d\}\}$ and $R_2 = \{(e, 1), (e, 2) \mid l(e) \in \{@, a, b, e, f, g\}\}$ are examples of the set of states of two runs of the above lso-structure.

3   Modal Logic for MAS

In this section we introduce the language of modal logic for reasoning about MASs. The language is interpreted over abstract models, based on lso-structures extended with selected runs. Then, we show how to restrict the class of models to these corresponding to our knowledge protocols. We use temporal operators corresponding to the relations $\rightarrow$ and $\rightarrow^*$.

3.1   Syntax

Let $PV = \{p_1, p_2, \ldots\} \cup \{q_i \mid i \in N\} \cup \{q_a \mid a \in A\}$ be a countable set of propositional variables including propositions corresponding to the agents' numbers and actions, $B \subseteq A$ be a set of actions, and $b \in A$.

   The logical connectives $\neg$ and $\wedge$, as well as modalities $\Box$ (causally always), $\otimes_B$ (all causally next w.r.t. B), do_b (next step in the run along b), and epistemic modalities *Know* (knowledge operator), and *Goal* (goal operator) will be used. The set of temporal and epistemic formulas is built up inductively:

E1. every member of PV is a temporal formula,

E2. if α and β are temporal (epistemic) formulas, then so are $\neg\alpha$ and $\alpha \wedge \beta$,

E3. if α is a temporal (epistemic) formula, then so are $\Box\,\alpha$, $^{\otimes}{}_B\,\alpha$, and $do_b(\alpha)$,

K4. if α is a temporal formula, then $Know_i(\alpha)$ and $Goal_i(\alpha)$ are epistemic formulas.

Notice that epistemic modalities cannot be nested. With this restriction we can still define knowledge based protocols and keep the complexity of the model checking algorithm one exponential in the size of the model.

3.2 Semantics

Frames are based on lso-structures extended with runs and the indistinguishability relation.

Definition 4 ((frame)).
   Let $\mathcal{S} = (S, A, \rightarrow, \#, l)$ be the lso-structure corresponding to an lpes. A structure $F_\mathcal{R} = (\mathcal{S}, R, KNOW)$ is a frame, where

- R is the set of states of a run $\mathcal{R}$ of $\mathcal{S}$,
- $KNOW : S \longrightarrow 2^S$ is a function, defined as follows:
  $KNOW((e, i)) = \{(e', j) \in S \mid e'$ is the maximal j-event in the causal past of e; $1 \leq j \leq N\}$ -
  the most recent causal knowledge, *agent i knows the most recent lso's of the other agents occurring in his past.*

Notice that the knowledge about the most recent lso of an agent j could be acquired either by direct synchronization with the agent j or by a synchronization with another agent who has had this knowledge.

Definition 5. *A model is a tuple $\mathcal{M}_\mathcal{R} = (F_\mathcal{R}, V)$, where $F_\mathcal{R}$ is a frame and $V : S \longrightarrow 2^{PV}$ is a valuation function such that*

- $q_i \in V((e, i))$, for each $(e, i) \in S$ and $q_i \in PV$,
- $q_a \in V((e, i))$, for each $(e, i) \in S$ with $l(e, i) = a$ and $a \in PV$.

Let $\mathcal{M}_\mathcal{R} = (F_\mathcal{R}, V)$ be a model, $s = (e, i) \in S$ be a state, and α be a formula. $\mathcal{M}_R, s \models \alpha$ denotes that the formula α is true at the state s in the model $\mathcal{M}_\mathcal{R}$ ($\mathcal{M}_\mathcal{R}$ is omitted, if it is implicitly understood). $\mathcal{M}_\mathcal{R} \models \alpha$ denotes that the formula α is true at all the minimal states in $\mathcal{M}_\mathcal{R}$. $\mathcal{S} \models \alpha$ denotes that the formula α holds in all the models $\mathcal{M}_R$ for $\mathcal{S}$ with $R \in \mathcal{R}$.

   Let S_i denote the set of states of agent i, i.e., of the form (e, i). The notion of $s \models \alpha$ for $s = (e, i) \in S$ is defined inductively:

E1. $s \models p$ iff $p \in V(s)$, for $p \in PV$,

E2. $s \models \neg\alpha$ iff not $s \models \alpha$,

$\quad s \models \alpha \wedge \beta$ iff $s \models \alpha$ and $s \models \beta$,

E3. $s \models \Box\,\alpha$ iff $(\forall s' \in S)\ (s \to^* s'$ implies $s' \models \alpha)$,

$\quad s \models \otimes_B \alpha$ iff $(\forall s' \in S)\ ((s \to s'$ and $V(s') \cap \{p_b \mid b \in B\} \neq \emptyset)$ implies $s' \models \alpha)$,

$\quad s \models do_b(\alpha)$ iff $s \in R$ implies $(\exists s' \in R)\ (s \to s',\ q_b \in V(s')$ and $s' \models \alpha)$,

K. $s \models Know_i(\alpha)$ iff $s \in S_i$ implies $(\forall s' \in KNOW(s))\ s' \models \alpha$.

G. $s \models Goal_i(\alpha)$ iff $s \in S_i$ implies $(\exists s' \in R \cap S_i)\ s \to^* s'$ and $s' \models \alpha$.

3.3 Knowledge-Based (KB) Protocols

Each agent is supposed to follow its knowledge-based protocol:

- **Protocol for agent i:**
  $Protocol_i = \bigwedge_j (Know_i(\alpha_j) \wedge \beta_j) \Rightarrow \bigvee_{b \in B_j} do_b(true)$, where
  α_j, β_j are temporal formulas and $B_j \subseteq A_i = \{a \mid i \in agent(a)\}$.
  The protocol specifies, which actions should be executed by agent i provided given knowledge about other agents and its local states.

Then, we specify that if the agents follow their knowledge protocols, then they reach their goals.

- **Correctness w.r.t. the goals of the MAS:**
  $\psi_c = (\bigwedge_{i \in N} \Box(q_i \Rightarrow Protocol_i)) \Rightarrow (\bigwedge_{i \in N} q_i \Rightarrow Goal_i(\varphi_i))$

4   Model Checking of Protocol Correctness

In this section we outline how to verify that MAS $\mathcal{S}$ behaves correctly, i.e., $\mathcal{S} \models \psi_c$. We assume that a finite representation of our models $\mathcal{M}_R$ of MAS is given by a deterministic asynchronous automaton [13], denoted $\mathcal{A}$, and extended with a valuation function V. For the automaton $\mathcal{A}$ we give its trace semantics, which is then used to extract the corresponding event structure (the complete construction can be found in [16,17]) and consequently the corresponding lso-structure, as shown in the former section.

Our aim is to define a finite quotient structure of models $\mathcal{M}_R$, which preserves the formulas of our language. It has been shown in [13] that it is possible to define constructively a deterministic asynchronous automaton (called gossip), which keeps track about the latest information the agents have about each other. This automaton is necessary in order to define an equivalence relation over configurations, which preserves the (unnested) knowledge formulas. Therefore, the quotient structure is obtained as the global state space of the automaton $\mathcal{B}$ being a product of $\mathcal{A}$ and the gossip automaton $\mathcal{G}$. This structure preserves **all** the temporal and unnested knowledge formulas of our language. Then, for each protocol $Protocol_i$, we mark green all the transitions in $\mathcal{B}$, which are consistent with the actions of the protocol. This is possible because the protocols use as premises unnested epistemic formulas, which are preserved by $\mathcal{B}$. Next, we check whether each sequence of states and green transitions (representing a run) in

$\mathcal{G}$ intersects a state with the i-local component satisfing φ_i for each $i \in N$. If so, then each green-labeled run is successful, which proves ψ_c. The detailed construction follows. We abuse the symbol N using it for both the natural number or the set $\{1, ..., N\}$, which is always clear from the context.

Definition 6. *An asynchronous automaton (AA) over a distributed alphabet* $(A_1, \ldots, A_N)$ *is a tuple* $\mathcal{A} = (\{S_i\}_{i \in N}, \{\xrightarrow{a}\}_{a \in A}, S_0, \{S_i^F\}_{i \in N})$, *where*

- S_i *is a set of local states of process i,*
- $\xrightarrow{a} \subseteq S_{agent(a)} \times S_{agent(a)}$, *where* $S_{agent(a)} = \Pi_{i \in agent(a)} S_i$,
- $S_0 \subseteq G_{\mathcal{A}} = \Pi_{i \in N} S_i$ *is the set of initial states,*
- $S_i^F \subseteq S_i$ *is the set of final states of process i, for each $i \in N$.*

We deal with deterministic AA's such that $S_i^F = S_i$ for each $i \in N$, and extended with valuation functions $V : G_{\mathcal{A}} \to 2^{PV}$.

For a global state $g \in G_{\mathcal{A}}$ and $K \subseteq N$ by $g \mid_K$ we mean the projection of g to the local states of processes in K. Let $\Rightarrow_{\mathcal{A}} \subseteq G_{\mathcal{A}} \times A \times G_{\mathcal{A}}$ be the transition relation in the global state space $G_{\mathcal{A}}$ defined as follows: $g \xRightarrow{a}_{\mathcal{A}} g'$ iff $(g \mid_{agent(a)}, g' \mid_{agent(a)}) \in \xrightarrow{a}$ and $g \mid_{N \setminus agent(a)} = g' \mid_{N \setminus agent(a)}$.

An *execution sequence* $w = a_0 \ldots a_n \in A^*$ of $\mathcal{A}$ is a finite sequence of actions s.t. there is a sequence of global states and actions $\xi = g_0 a_0 g_1 a_1 g_2 \ldots a_{n-1} g_n$ of $\mathcal{A}$ with $g_0 \in S_0$, $g_n \in \Pi_{i \in N} S_i^F$, and $g_i \xRightarrow{a_i}_{\mathcal{A}} g_{i+1}$, for each $i < n$. A word w is said to be *accepted* by $\mathcal{A}$ if w is an execution sequence of $\mathcal{A}$.

In order to define the lso-structure semantics of the automaton $\mathcal{A}$, we first define the configuration structure $CS = (C_{\mathcal{A}}, \to)$ corresponding to $\mathcal{A}$. Then, the lpes and the lso-structure is induced by CS. Since $\mathcal{A}$ is deterministic, the configurations of CS can be represented by Mazurkiewicz traces [12].

4.1 Trace Semantics of AA's

By an *independence alphabet* we mean any ordered pair (A, I), where $I = \{(a, b) \in A \times A \mid (\forall i \in N) \{a, b\} \not\subseteq A_i\}$. Define $\equiv$ as the least congruence in the (standard) string monoid $(A^*, \circ, \epsilon)$ such that $(a, b) \in I \Rightarrow ab \equiv ba$, for all $a, b \in \Sigma$ i.e., $w \equiv w'$, if there is a finite sequence of strings $w_1, \ldots, w_n$ such that $w_1 = w$, $w_n = w'$, and for each $i < n$, $w_i = uabv$, $w_{i+1} = ubav$, for some $(a, b) \in I$ and $u, v \in A^*$. Equivalence classes of $\equiv$ are called *traces* over (A, I). The trace generated by a string w is denoted by $[w]$. We use the following notation: $[A^*] = \{[w] \mid w \in A^*\}$. Concatenation of traces $[w], [v]$, denoted $[w][v]$, is defined as $[wv]$. The *successor* relation $\to$ in $[A^*]$ is defined as follows: $[w_1] \to [w_2]$ iff there is $a \in A$ such that $[w_1][a] = [w_2]$.

Definition 7. *The structure* $CS = (C_{\mathcal{A}}, \to)$ *is a configuration structure of the automaton $\mathcal{A}$, where*

- $[w] \in C_{\mathcal{A}}$ *iff w is an execution sequence of $\mathcal{A}$,*
- $\to$ *is the trace successor relation in $C_{\mathcal{A}}$.*

Configuration $[w]$ *is i-local iff for each* $w' \in A^*$ *with* $[w] = [w']$ *there is* $a \in A_i$ *and* $w'' \in A^*$ *such that* $w' = w''a$.

The definition of the lpes and the lso-structure corresponding to $\mathcal{A}$ can be obtained from CS. When we represent configurations by traces, the same configurations can belong to different AA's. Therefore, we adopt the convention that $M_{\mathcal{A}}(c)$ denotes the global state in automaton $\mathcal{A}$ corresponding to the configuration c. Let $Max([w]) = \{a \mid [w] = [w'a] \text{ for some } w' \in A^*\}$, $\downarrow^i [w]$ be the maximal i-local configuration $[w']$ such that $[w'] \rightarrow^* [w]$, and $agent([w]) = \{i \in N \mid [w] \text{ is } i\text{-local}\}$. Moreover, by $c \equiv_l c'$ in $\mathcal{A}$ we mean that $f_i^{\mathcal{A}}(c) = f_i^{\mathcal{A}}(c')$, where

- $f_g^{\mathcal{A}} : C_{\mathcal{A}} \longrightarrow G_{\mathcal{A}} \times 2^A$ such that $f_g^{\mathcal{A}}(c) = (M_{\mathcal{A}}(c), Max(c))$,
- $f_l^{\mathcal{A}} : C_{\mathcal{A}} \longrightarrow \Pi_{i=0}^{N}(G_{\mathcal{A}} \times 2^A)$ with $f_l^{\mathcal{A}}(c) = (f_g^{\mathcal{A}}(c), f_g^{\mathcal{A}}(\downarrow^1(c)), \dots, f_g^{\mathcal{A}}(\downarrow^N(c)))$.

It has been shown in [17] that the equivalence $\equiv_l$ preserves the temporal and (unnested) knowledge formulas of our language.

Let $\mathcal{A}$ be an AA. For each $i, j \in N$ define the functions:

- $latest_{i \rightarrow j} : C_{\mathcal{A}} \longrightarrow \bigcup_{a \in A}\{\xrightarrow{a}\}$ is defined as follows: $latest_{i \rightarrow j}(c) = (S, S')$ iff (S, S') is the latest transition executed by agent j in $\downarrow^i c$, i.e., if $\downarrow^j \downarrow^i c =\downarrow e$, then event e corresponds to the transition (S, S').
- $latest_i : C_{\mathcal{A}} \longrightarrow 2^N$ is defined as follows: $latest_i(c) = K$ iff $\downarrow^i \downarrow^l (c) \subseteq \downarrow^i \downarrow^k (c)$, for each $l \in N$ and $k \in K$.

Intuitively, $latest_{i \rightarrow j}(c)$ gives the most recent transition in which agent j participated in the i-history of c, i.e., in $\downarrow^i c$, whereas $latest_i(c)$ gives the set of agents, which have the most recent information about agent i.

Theorem 1 ([13]). *There exists a deterministic asynchronous automaton, called Gossip automaton,* $\mathcal{G} = (\{T_i\}_{i \in N}, \{\xrightarrow{a}\}_{a \in A}, T_0, \{T_i^F\}_{i \in N})$ *such that:*

- $T_i^F = T_i$, *for all* $i \in N$,
- $\mathcal{G}$ *accepts all the words of* A^*,
- *There are effectively computable functions:*
  $gossip : T_1 \times \dots \times T_N \times N \times N \longrightarrow \bigcup_{a \in A}\{\xrightarrow{a}\}$ *such that for each* $c \in [A^*]$ *and every* $i, j \in N$, $latest_{i \rightarrow j}(c) = gossip(t_1, \dots, t_N, i, j)$, *where* $M_{\mathcal{G}}(c) = (t_1, \dots, t_N)$.
  $gossip1 : T_1 \times \dots \times T_N \times N \longrightarrow 2^N$ *such that for each* $c \in [A^*]$ *and every* $i \in N$, $latest_i(c) = gossip1(t_1, \dots, t_N, i)$, *where* $M_{\mathcal{G}}(c) = (t_1, \dots, t_N)$.

Each agent in the gossip automaton has $2^{O(N^2 log N)}$ local states. Moreover, the functions $gossip$ and $gossip1$ can be computed in time, which is polynomial in the size of N.

Consider the asynchronous automaton $\mathcal{B}$, which is the product of the automaton $\mathcal{A}$ and the automaton $\mathcal{G}$. We assume that all the local states of $\mathcal{A}$ are final. This is also the case for $\mathcal{G}$. Then, each state of the global state space of $\mathcal{B}$ is of the following form $(l_1, \dots, l_N, t_1, \dots, t_N)$, where $l_i \in S_i$ and $t_i \in T_i$, for $i \in N$. The transition relation $\Rightarrow_{\mathcal{B}}$ is defined as follows:

$(l_1, \ldots, l_N, t_1, \ldots, t_N) \overset{a}{\Rightarrow}_B (l'_1, \ldots, l'_N, t'_1, \ldots, t'_N)$ iff $(l_1, \ldots, l_N) \overset{a}{\Rightarrow}_A (l'_1, \ldots, l'_N)$ and $(t_1, \ldots, t_N) \overset{a}{\Rightarrow}_G (t'_1, \ldots, t'_N)$. Notice that automaton B accepts exactly all the words accepted by A. Proofs of the following theorems are omitted because of a lack of space.

Theorem 2. *Let $c, c' \in C_A$. If $M_B(c) = M_B(c')$, then $c \equiv_l c'$ in A.*

Therefore, model checking can be performed over the structure $F_M = (W, \rightarrow, V)$, where

- $W = \{(M_B(c), i) \mid i \in agent(c)$ for c being local, and $i = *$, otherwise$\}$,
- $(M_B(c), i) \overset{a}{\rightarrow} (M_B(c'), j)$ iff $M_B(c) \overset{a}{\Rightarrow}_B M_B(c')$,
- $V : W \longrightarrow 2^{PV'}$, where PV' is equal to the set of propositions used in ψ_c, $p_j \in V(M_B(c), i)$ iff $p_j \in V(M_A(c))$ and $q_i \in V(M_B(c), i)$ for $i \in N$, and if $(M_B(c), i) \overset{a}{\rightarrow} (M_B(c'), j)$, then $q_a \in V(M_B(c), j)$ for $j \in N$.

Theorem 3. *The model checking algorithm for formula ψ_c over automaton A of N-agents is of the complexity $((|\psi_c| - m) + m \times |A|) \times |G_A|^N \times 2^{O(N^3 \log N)}$, where $|G_A|$ is the size of the global state space of A and m is the number of the subformulas of $\{\varphi_1, \ldots, \varphi_N\}$ of the form $\otimes \phi$.*

5   Bounded Model Checking

State explosion is the main obstacle in practical applications of model checking algorithms. Unfortunately, G_A can be of prohibitive size. Therefore, it is important to offer methods, which can perform model checking on a part of the state space. One of such methods is a bounded model checking (BMC). BMC based on SAT-checking has been recently introduced as a complementary technique to BDD-based symbolic model checking. The basic idea is to search for a counterexample of a particular length $k > 0$ and to generate a propositional formula that is satisfiable iff such a counterexample exists. This new technique has been introduced for LTL [1] and for ACTL [21].

We have translated our model checking problem to verification that formulas φ_i hold over the selected fair sequences of states. Therefore, we have a translation to model checking formula $\bigwedge_{i \in N} \forall \diamond \varphi_i$, which is an LTL formula if $\varphi_i \in PV$, or ACTL formula if φ_i uses only universal quantifiers (without negation). This enables to use the technique of BMC and generating a propositional formula $[F_M] \wedge [\psi_c]$, which is satisfiable iff $S \models \psi_c$.

6   Related Work

So far model checking algorithms have been given for several modal logics of multi-agent systems interpreted on global states [5,2]. The first model checking algorithm for a temporal logic of knowledge on local states has been suggested by Ramanujam [19]. Our frames are defined as labelled prime event structures including branching runs of Petri Nets [4]. In this respect they are close to the models used in [9]. Modal logic of causal knowledge was introduced in [18]. The technique of applying the Gossip automaton was used for the first time for model checking of a branching time temporal logic in [17]. It had been also successfully applied for partial order temporal logics of linear time for traces [14].

References

1. A. Biere and A. Cimatti and E. Clarke and Y. Zhu, Symbolic model checking without BDDs, Proc. of DAT'99, 1999.
2. M. Benerecetti, F. Giunchiglia, L. Serafini, Model checking multiagent systems, Proc. of ATAL'98, pp. 107–120, 1998.
3. E. M. Clarke, E. A. Emerson, and A. P. Sistla. Automatic verification of finite state concurrent systems using temporal logic specifications: A practical approach. *ACM Transactions on Programming Languages and Systems*, 8(2), pp. 244–263, 1986.
4. J. Esparza, S. Romer, and W. Vogler, An improvement of McMillan's unfolding algorithm, Proc. of TACAS'96, LNCS 1055, pp. 87–106, 1996.
5. R. Fagin, J.Y. Halpern, Y. Moses, M.Y. Vardi, "Knowledge-based programs", Distributed Computing 10, pp.199–225, 1997.
6. R. Fagin, J.Y. Halpern, Y. Moses, and M.Y. Vardi. *Reasoning about knowledge*, MIT Press, 1995.
7. J. Halpern, and Y. Moses, Knowledge and Common Knowledge in a Distributed Environment, *JACM*, Vol. 37 (3), pp. 549–587, 1990.
8. O. Lichtenstein, A. Pnueli, Checking that finite-state concurrent programs satisfy their linear specification. *Proc. 11th ACM POPL*, pp. 97–107, 1984.
9. K. Lodaya, R. Ramanujam, P.S. Thiagarajan, "Temporal logic for communicating sequential agents: I", Int. J. Found. Comp. Sci., vol. 3(2), pp. 117–159, 1992.
10. K. Lodaya, K. Parikh, R. Ramanujam, P.S. Thiagarajan, A logical study of distributed transition systems, Information and Computation, vol. 19, (1), pp. 91–118, 1995.
11. R.E. Ladner and J.H. Reif, The logic of distributed protocols, Proc. of TARK 1986, pp. 207-221, 1996.
12. A. Mazurkiewicz, Basic notions of trace theory, LNCS 354, pp. 285–363, 1988.
13. M. Mukund and M. Sohoni. Keeping track of the latest gossip: Bounded timestamps suffice, *FST&TCS'93, LNCS* **761**, pp. 388-199, 1993.
14. M. Mukund and P.S. Thiagarajan. Linear time temporal logics over Mazurkiewicz traces, LNCS 1113, pp. 62–92, 1996.
15. M. Huhn, P. Niebert, and F. Wallner, "Model checking logics for communicating sequential agents", submitted for publication.
16. W. Penczek. Model checking for a Subclass of Event Structures, LNCS 1217, Proc. of TACAS'97, pp. 145–164, 1997.
17. W. Penczek and S. Ambroszkiewicz, Model checking of local knowledge formulas, Proc. of FCT'99 Workshop on Distributed Systems, Vol. 28 in Electronic Notes in Theoretical Computer Science, 1999.
18. W. Penczek. A temporal approach to causal knowledge, Logic Journal of the IGPL, Vol. 8, Issue 1, pp. 87–99, 2000.
19. R. Ramanujam. Local knowledge assertions in a changing world. In *Proc. of the Sixth Conference TARK 1996, Theoretical Aspects of Rationality and Knowledge*, Y. Shoham editor, pp. 1-14, Morgan-Kaufmann 1996.

20. Winskel, G., An Introduction to Event Structures, LNCS 354, Springer-Verlag, pp. 364-397, 1989.
21. W. Penczek, B. Woźna, Towards bounded model checking for timed automata, Proc. of CS&P, Warsaw, 2001.

Volcano, a Vowels-Oriented Multi-agent Platform

Pierre-Michel Ricordel and Yves Demazeau

MAGMA, LEIBNIZ lab., 46, Ave. Félix Viallet,
38000 Grenoble, France
{Pierre-Michel.Ricordel, Yves.Demazeau}@imag.fr
http://www-leibniz.imag.fr/MAGMA/

Abstract. In this paper we present a new multi-agent platform, called Volcano, based on the Vowels decomposition paradigm. The application of this paradigm to a building platform allows higher flexibility, better reuse, and reduces development costs. The entire building process is covered, from analysis to deployment.

1 Introduction

Multi-agent systems (MAS) are very complex software, where both high-level concepts (such as autonomy, coordination, ...) and low-level techniques (such as code mobility or embedding in robotic devices, ...) are involved. Naturally, this big complexity leads to big difficulties in building such systems. Efficient tools are needed to assist the building of multi-agent systems. In this paper we present a new multi-agent platform, based on the Vowels decomposition paradigm. In the first section, we define what a multi-agent platform is, and we present the Vowels paradigm. Then we present an overview of the building process, that we detail in section 4 for the analysis and design, 5 for the development and 7 for the deployment. In section 6 we present a description language used to join the development and deployment stages. Finally, we conclude in section 8.

2 Context

2.1 Multi-agent Platforms

Multi-Agent Systems are very complex software. Building such complex system software requires using adequate engineering methods. A multi-agent platform is a tool designed to help the building of multi-agent systems. This includes both methodological tools and software tools. Previous research [5] has shown that existing platforms do not cover all the methodological aspects of multi-agent building, and have conceptual granularity problems. Indeed those platforms propose either a low-level approach, that requires a lot of code to build complex multi-agent systems, or a high-level approach, that solves the previous problem, but poses serious problems because of the steep learning curve required to use

B. Dunin-Kęplicz and E. Nawarecki (Eds.): CEEMAS 2001, LNAI 2296, pp. 253–262, 2002.

them, as well as a general lack of flexibility. An ideal platform must provide the balance between these factors, it must be easy to use, manage high-level concepts, and be flexible enough to be used to build any kind of multi-agent system. Such a platform must support all the building stages, from the description of the problem, to the execution of the multi-agent system.

2.2   The Vowels Paradigm

The four basic bricks of the Vowels paradigm [1] are the Agents, the Environment, the Interactions and the Organisations (A, E, I, O). This vision is driving our Vowels methodology, from analysis to deployment. Agents range from simple fine-grained automata to complex coarse-grained knowledge-based systems. The environments are most usually spatialised but there is no constraint about them. Interaction structures and languages range from physics-based interactions to speech acts. Organisations range from static to dynamic ones, and follow any kind of structure from hierarchies to markets.

In addition to these bricks, Vowels is guided by three principles. The first one is the declarative principle. As we have just seen it, and from a declarative point of view, a multi-agent system will be composed of several agents, an environment, a set of possible interactions, and possibly at least one organisation. From a more computational point of view, the functions which are performed by the multi-agent system are including the ones of the agents enriched by the ones which result from the added value generated by the multi-agent system itself, usually known as collective intelligence. This is the functional principle. Finally, to capture the spirit of what Multi-Agent Oriented Programming could really be, multi-agent systems should be possibly considered as multi-agent entities at a higher level of abstraction. This final principle is called the recursion principle.

According to the Vowels paradigm, for a given problem to solve (or a system to simulate) in a given domain, the user chooses the agent models, the environment model, the interactions models, and the organisation models to be instantiated, as well as their dynamics along the three Vowels principles, in order to generate computational and deployable multi-agent systems.

3   Overview

Volcano is a Vowels-oriented multi-agent platform designed to assist the building process with both methodological and software tools, for a variety of applications and domains, since the Vowels decomposition is application-neutral. The multi-agent systems produced can range from a swarm of simple reactive agents to small groups of complex cognitive agents. Numerous pre-existing and future Agent, Environment, Interaction or Organisation models should be integrable in the platform. Reuse and ease of use are also an important concern.

The building process is decomposed into four stages. Traditionally, software engineering distinguishes three building stages: Analysis, Design and Development. We believe that for systems like Multi-Agent Systems this is not sufficient, and that describing the entire MAS creation process, from early design to a running application, we have to distinguish a fourth stage after the development stage, called deployment. The figure 1 summarises this process, which will be later described.

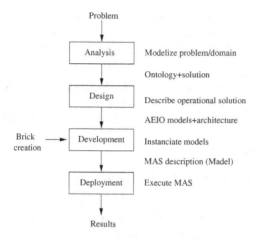

Fig. 1. The four building stages

4   Analysis and Design

In this section, we shortly describe the first two building stages. We did not develop these former steps, since the emphasis in this paper is on the two latter stages. Further information about the analysis and design stages can be found in [2].

4.1   Analysis

The main goal of the Analysis stage is to model the problem, which means to separate the domain in which the problem lies, and the fundamental problem class that has to be solved. This leads to two outputs:

- A domain ontology, which describes the information that is used in the formulation of the problem and the solution,
- A problem definition, and a precise solution of this problem, independently of the means of realisation.

This kind of analysis is classic, and existing analysis methods can be used or adapted to obtain these results. This stage does not requires any software tools to be completed.

4.2   Design

The design stage consists of making operational choices for the implementation of the application, taking into account the means of realisation. In the Vowels context, this includes:

- The choice of the orientation of the application (on which vowel is the emphasis : Agent, Environment, Interaction or Organisation),
- The choice of the models that will be used for each vowel in the application,
- The mode of interconnection between the vowels.

We plan to use design patterns to simplify the design process by reusing designs across projects [3,6]. A UML extension may be used to describe the output of the design stage. This extension could be part of the AgentUML project [4].

5   Development

5.1   Overview of the Development Process

The development stage consists of the realisation of a functional application from the design specifications. In the Vowels context, this means to *instantiate* the chosen models, as well as their interconnections.

Examples of model instantiation can be the filling of a BDI Agent model with behavioural rules and initial beliefs, the definition of protocols for an Interaction model, the definition of the world physics laws and initial state for an Environment model, or the definition of roles and organisational links for an Organisational model. Depending on the model, these instantiations can range from low-level to high-level paradigms, from simple checkbox checking to complex code production.

This construction approach is very similar to the component paradigm. However, there are important differences between the two :

The A, E, I, O elements are called *bricks*, and as shown in Figure 2 these bricks are not atomic components, they are composed of several *parts*, and these parts are distributed across the multi-agent system when it is deployed. A brick can be composed of one or more from three kinds of parts: a *distributed component* (DC), which will be duplicated as an element of the individuals [1] composing the deployed MAS, a *global service* (GS), which is an optional part of software needed for the operation of the deployed brick, for example a message routers for an interaction brick, and an *editor* (ED) which is an instantiation helper, used only at the development stage. The number of distributed components, global services and editors may vary depending on the needs of the implemented model. For example, in Figure 2, the Agent brick is composed of a distributed component (an agent engine) and an editor (to edit the comportemental rules), but does not have a global service. The Interaction brick is composed of a distributed component that processes the message and follows the protocols, two

---

[1] The term *individual* is used to designate an agent as an autonomous process, not to mistake with the Agent brick.

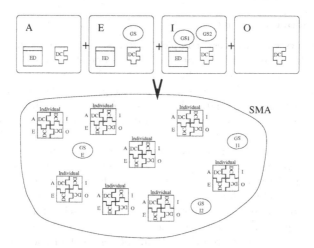

Fig. 2. The composition of a MAS from four bricks

global naming services (e.g. a name server and a message router), and a protocol editor. The Organisation brick is a very simple one with only a distributed component (e.g. an emergent spatial organisation brick), and the Environment brick contains a distributed component, an environment server and an environment editor.

Bricks are also interconnected through special bricks called *wrappers* (not shown on Figure 2 for clarity), in opposition to classic components which are generally directly interconnected. The role of the wrappers is to absorb the unavoidable incompatibilities between models. They add a lot of flexibility to the model, but they may be difficult to build. As the bricks, they are compound objects, as they handle incompatibilities at the individual level (between distributed components), but also, when necessary, between global services (for example if a message router has to know the agents' location from the environment server). There are at most six wrappers to interconnect four bricks, since there are six possible dual relations between four elements. Depending on the bricks that are attached, sometimes simple generic wrappers can be used (e.g. message translators), but generally they are more complex and have to be hard-coded. This is the price for flexibility.

Finally, another difference between the component approach and our approach is that there are four types of bricks: Agent, Environment, Interaction and Organisation. Components generally do not have this kind of strong typing.

However, we must note that distributed components (from bricks and wrappers) are genuine components, and that all the individuals are assembled with these components. The current Java implementation of Volcano therefore uses the JavaBean component architecture as the distributed component architecture.

5.2 Developer Interface

Multi-agent systems are very complex systems, so are the different building stages of such systems. The development stage is one of the more complex stages, since it involves a lot of technical knowledge, and the distributed nature of multi-agent systems leads to difficulties for the developer(s) to master all the aspects of the application. Additionally, the development stage traditionally makes an extensive use of software tools, such as compilers or more evolved Integrated Development Environment (IDE). Consequently, a good multi-agent development tool has to provide a comprehensive Graphical User Interface (GUI) to help the developer in his task. Hopefully, the Vowels decomposition provides a support to decompose a multi-agent system into four fairly independent aspects, namely Agents, Environment, Interaction and Organisation, thus reducing the complexity. In Volcano, a stylised representation of the four bricks and their six possible interface wrappers are represented, the developer can edit them by clicking on the appropriate part of the representation. Different colour codes allow the visualisation of the progress of the development. Proactive help, such as assistants that guide the developer through the development process, or pinpoint missing parts or possible incoherence can also enhance the ease of development. This kind of assistance may help to reduce the steep learning curve generally observed in evolved multi-agent platforms [5].

5.3 Brick Development

An important part in the development process is the possibility to build a new brick when it is necessary. For example, if there is no implemented brick model adequate to solve the problem, then the adequate model has to be implemented as a new brick. This brick, if made generic enough, will then enrich the model collection and be used in other subsequent projects. The freedom to create new bricks and integrate them into the platform enhances the flexibility and the scope of the tool. Also, a big level of reuse is obtained, since the new bricks are capitalised and enrich the platform.

A new brick has to be designed as generic as possible, using distributed components, global services and editors according to the needs of the new model which is implemented. The distributed components have to follow strict rules of interfacing to interact with other distributed components. The quality of the user interfaces of the editors is also very important since the ease of use of this brick depends upon it. Experience showed that existing implementation of models can be easily converted into bricks.

6 Between Development and Deployment: Madel, a Multi-agent Description Language

6.1 Definition

In order to deal with complex structures such as bricks or multi-agent systems, the platform needs to use a formalism to represent these structures. This formalism enhances the flexibility of the platform and simplifies its implementation.

As we will see later, this formalism plays also an important role for the deployment stage. Very few similar formalism exists in the MAS domain. The most interesting works on this topic are found in the domain of Software Architecture, specifically the Architecture Description Languages (ADL). ADLs, such as UniCon [7], are languages used to describe and to deploy complex applications composed of large-grained software component. But standard ADLs are not adapted to the needs of Volcano, so we designed a simplified and specific language called Madel (Multi-Agent DEscription Language) that borrows some elements from UniCon, and adds other specific elements. This language is specific to the platform, and is not a real generic ADL, in order to keep it simple and well suited to the platform. It is a purely descriptive language, and does not embody runnable code. It can describe the main parts of the system under construction. A very simplified (and incomplete) syntax of Madel is:

Description ::= (Block | Instance | Individual)*

Descriptions include Blocks, Instances of parts of blocks, and Individuals composed of instances of distributed components.

Block ::= B_ident (Brick | Wrapper)
Brick ::= Type Part*
Wrapper ::= Type Part*

A block can be either a Brick or a Wrapper, each composed of a type definition and several parts. A Brick can be either of type Agent, Environment, Interaction or Organisation, and a Wrapper can be specialised for certain combinations of bricks (for example Agent-Interaction), or can be generic.

Part ::= Distributed_Component | Global_Service | Editor

A part can be either a Distributed Component, a Global Service, or an Editor, as described below :

Distributed_Component ::= P_ident Property* Event* Implementation

A Distributed component is composed of an identifier, a list of editable properties that have to be instantiated, a list of generated and catched events, and a set providing low-level implementation information used for the deployment of the component.

Global_Service ::= P_ident Property* Implementation

A Global service is composed of an identifier, a list of editable properties that have to be instantiated, and a set of low-level implementation information used for the deployment of the service.

Editor ::= E_ident Property* Implementation

An Editor is composed of an identifier, the list of properties which this editor can edit, and a set of low-level implementation information used be the development tool to call the editor.

Instance ::= Inst_ident B_ident.P_ident Value*

An instance is composed of an identifier, a reference to the part that is instantiated by this instance (the block identifier and the part identifier), and the values
of the instantiated properties.

Individual ::= Ind_ident Link*
Link ::= Inst_ident-Inst_ident-Inst_ident

An individual is composed of an identifier and a list of the links between distributed part instances. A link is a relation between three instances of distributed
component, coming respectively from a Brick, a Wrapper and another Brick. The
definition of the links implicitly defines the distributed components' instances
that compose the individuals.

This syntax is loose and permissive in order to maintain expressivity as
much as possible, since the objects described, the multi-agent systems parts,
can be very complex and may have unplanned structures. Further extensions
are planned, such as expressing low and high level constraints between modules,
or integrating documentation into the description.

6.2 Usage

Depending on the context where the Madel description is parsed, several verifications have to be performed. More precisely, a Madel description can describe
the following objects, depending on the context:

- A ready-to-use Brick or Wrapper. This description accompanies a brick or a
  wrapper package, and is used by the development tool to manage the package. This description is only composed of a Block statement, and includes no
  Instance or Individual descriptions. The development tool uses this package
  to determine the content of the brick, what are the properties to instanciate, how to instanciate them (with the editors included), and what are the
  constraints to satisfy.
- A partially completed multi-agent system. This describes a multi-agent system under construction, with one or more Block description (which are just
  copies of the madel description of the block's package), Instance descriptions
  and Individual descriptions. The development tool uses this kind of Madel
  description all along the multi-agent system construction, as an internal representation of the project. The declared blocks have to be compatible (no
  compatibility constraints violated), the instances have to be related to the
  declared blocks and the individuals have to be well formed (no illegal links)
  and composed of legal instances.
- A complete multi-agent system. It is composed of blocks, instances and individuals descriptions. This description is produced by the development tool
  at the end of the development process, and is used by the deployment tool
  to deploy the multi-agent system. The blocks have to be compatible, the
  instances have to be related to the declared blocks, and have to be complete (all properties instanciated), the individuals have to be well formed

and composed of legal instances. More challenging, the individual collection associated with the global services has to form a valid multi-agent system, and must give the correct solution to the initial problem. If the first point (validation) is partially addressed by syntactic and semantic checks on the Madel file and extensive use of constraints, the second (verification) is still raising very difficult issues.

Generally, the Madel descriptions are not edited by hand. The development tool parses and generates Madel descriptions, according to the developer's interactions with the tool.

7   Deployment

7.1   Deploying a Multi-agent System

Deployment is the last stage of the process, where the developed multi-agent system is deployed on an execution platform, eventually distributed. In the Vowels context, this means that the bricks are composed, instantiated and the final multi-agent system, composed of individuals, runs and computes a valid solution to the initially given problem. Additionally, a deployment system must be able to maintain the multi-agent system, by adding, replacing or terminating individuals, to visualise and trace the system for performance benchmarking or debugging purpose, and eventually to gather and display the results to the user if necessary. However, automating the deployment stage is a difficult problem.

7.2   Deployment with Madel

Using Madel eases this deployment automation. Indeed, at the end of the development stage, a Madel description of a complete multi-agent system is available. The deployment tool parses the description, instanciates and launches the global services, creates the distributed components instances, links them into individuals, and start their execution. The Implementation sections of the Madel file are very important at this stage since they contain low-level details such as file paths, entry points and launch scripts. The deployment tool is independent of the development tool, and can provide more or less advanced deployment services, such as distribution, mobility, integration in a specific middleware, monitoring or debugging of the system. Thus, the deployment-specific aspects of the multi-agent system are managed during deployment, and not during development as it is usually the case.

8   Conclusion

The results of the Volcano platform are very promising. Indeed, given the criteria of evaluation proposed in [5], the Volcano platform manages the four stages of multi-agent systems, and avoids the two main pitfalls encountered in multi-agent platforms: the restriction to a single agent model, and the lack of pre-built models which leads to low code reuse. The ability to add, mix and reuse models of different aspects of multi-agent systems (Agent, Environment, Interaction, Organisation) is unique to this platform. The gains are both a high level of reuse, and the high abstraction level of the manipulated concepts. The brick architecture, mixing centralised and distributed parts, loosely connected by specific wrappers allows the integration and reutilisation of a large range of multi-agent models. Moreover, the Vowels decomposition paradigm, known for its good pedagogical properties, and the care taken to the graphical interface, facilitates the use of the platform, despite its high-level of abstraction. Finally, the Madel language, describing explicitly the multi-agent system, plays a major role both at the development and deployment stages, decoupling the two phases.

However, the Vowels paradigm and the Volcano platform still poses several interesting but unsolved theoretical and practical problems, such as domain embedding and reuse strategies of bricks, multi-agent systems dynamics, heterogeneity, multi-agent systems validation or networked deployment. The platform, still in its early stages of development, helps us to explore the rich domain of multi-agent engineering.

References

1. Demazeau, Y.: From Interactions to Collective Behaviour in Agent-Based Systems. In: Proceedings of the First European Conference on Cognitive Science, Saint-Malo, France, (1995) 117–132
2. Demazeau, Y., Occello, M., Baeijs C., Ricordel, P.-M.: Systems Development as Societies of Agents. In: Cuena, J., Demazeau, Y., Garcia, A., Treur, J. (eds.): Knowledge Engineering and Agent Technology. IOS Series on Frontiers in Artificial Intelligence and Applications (2001)
3. Kendall, E., Malkoun, M.: Design Patterns for the Development of Multi-Agent Systems. In: Zhang, C., Lukose, D. (eds.): Multi-Agent Systems: Methodologies and applications. Proceedings of Second Australian Workshop on DAI, LNAI 1286 (1996) 17–32
4. Odell, J., Van Dyke Parunal, H., Bauer B.: Extending UML for Agents. Proceedings of the Second International Bi-Conference Workshop on Agent-Oriented Information Systems (AOIS'2000) at AAAI 2000
5. Ricordel, P.-M., Demazeau, Y.: From Analysis to Deployment: a Multi-Agent Platform Survey. In Omicini, A., Tolksdorf, R., Zambonelli, F. (eds.): Engineering Societies in the Agents World, First International Workshop, ESAW 2000. LNAI 1972 (2000) 93–150
6. Sauvage, S.: MAS Oriented Patterns. (in this volume).
7. Shaw, M., DeLine, R., Klein, D., Ross, T., Young, D., Zelesnik, G.: Abstractions for Software Architectures and Tools to Support Them. IEEE Transactions on Software Engineering, 21(4): 356-372, April 1995

Model of Cooperation in Multi-agent Systems with Fuzzy Coalitions

José C. Romero Cortés[1,2] and Leonid B. Sheremetov[1,3]

[1] Center for Computing Research of the National Technical University, (CIC-IPN), Mexico
[2] Universidad Autónoma Metropolitana, México
[3] St. Petersburg Institute for Informatics and Automation of the Russian Academy of Sciences (SPIIRAS), Russia
rcjc@correo.azc.uam.mx, sher@cic.ipn.mx

Abstract. Agent-based computing is a new paradigm to build complex distributed computer systems. The article explores one of the key issues of agent-based computing - the problem of interactions in multi-agent systems (MAS) in dynamic organizational context. Particularly, the article describes an approach to the problem of coalition forming based on fuzzy coalition games with associated core, as well as fuzzy linear programming and genetic algorithms for the game solution search. The proposed approach enables coalition forming based on the fuzzy game theory and permits to change the way of MAS programming from the predefined ad-hoc architectures to dynamic flexible and agile systems with dynamic configurations developed on-line by the MAS itself. The proposed model is applied for the coalition forming for management of supply chain networks.

1 Introduction

Agents, high-level interactions and organizational relationships are considered as essential concepts of agent-based computing [6, 9, 10]. To cope with the variety of interactions in dynamic organizational context, agent researchers have devised protocols that enable organizational groupings to be formed; specified mechanisms to ensure groupings act together in a coherent fashion; and developed structures to characterize the macro behaviour of collectives. Nevertheless, when it comes to developing MAS systems with currently available techniques a problem that interactions between the various agents are too rigidly defined still exist. For real applications, such as management processes in supply chain networks (SCN) [4, 8], agents operate within the dynamic organizational context and have to make decisions about the nature and scope of interactions at run time, so it is imperative that this key shaping factor is taken into account while developing models of interaction supporting cooperative activity of agents.

This article describes an approach that enables coalition forming based on the fuzzy game theory. The theory of games in deterministic coalitions has been treated by numerous authors [14, 20], nevertheless, it is more natural to form coalitions as a product of negotiation that occur in a fuzzy environment [1, 3, 12]. The main problem in application of this approach in MAS, even in deterministic case [16], is a difficulty

B. Dunin-Kęplicz and E. Nawarecki (Eds.): CEEMAS 2001, LNAI 2296, pp. 263–272, 2002.
© Springer-Verlag Berlin Heidelberg 2002

of analytical solution of a game. The problem of formation of fuzzy coalitions in the context of the theory of games is formulated in this article under two approaches: (i) based in the fuzzy core; (ii) using fuzzy linear programming. In both cases, for simplicity linear membership functions are assumed. In addition, methods for solution are given based on genetic algorithms and conventional algorithms of linear programming permitting simplify significantly a problem of the game solution search. Finally, the proposed model is applied for the coalition forming for SCN management.

2   Fuzzy Coalition Games Model

The common idea in all distributed artificial intelligence contributions is that agents cooperate during problem solving and hence the basic goal behind cooperation is *reaching a consensus*. The cooperation like function of utility, is motivated by the endeavour of agents to increase their individual benefits by means of coordinated activities [11, 18]. The theory of games with coalitions offers results showing the general form of possible cooperation and conditions under which this is obtained. In many cases, a broad class of attainable patterns of cooperation and of distributions of the final payments exists, and it is important to exactly suggest one of them like the best one or the most unbiassed. Coalition formation generally takes part before the application of coordinated strategies when agents have only a vague idea about the expected gains of the coalitions, so distribution of the gains can be vague, imprecise, and uncertain. Using the theory of the fuzzy sets and the theory of games in coalitions it is possible to study the vagueness and to follow the way from the input of the vague idea about the gains via the bargaining process to the output corresponding to the possibilities of the vagueness of the distributions of the individual gains.

Considering the nature of the application domain, the approach developed in this article is debt to Milan Mares [12, 13] and is based on fuzzy coalition game of integer players with full involvement. Let I be the players set with: $I = \{1, 2, ..., n\}$, where n can be finite or infinite. Then the set of possible coalitions is the power set:

$$2^I = \{\phi, \{1\}, \{2\}, ... \{n\}, \{1, 2\}, ..., \{n-1, n\}, \{1, 2, 3\}, ..., \{n-2, n-1, n\}, ..., \{1, 2, ...n\}\} \quad (1)$$

A structure of n coalitions $K_1, ..., K_m$ is: $\kappa = \{K_1, ..., K_m\}$

The crisp coalition game is defined as a pair (I, v), where I is nonempty and finite set of players, subsets of I are called coalitions, and v is called a characteristic function of the game, which is a mapping: $v : 2^I \rightarrow R$, then $v(K) \in R$, $\forall K \subset I$, with $v(\phi) = 0$ and $v(K) \geq 0$ for any $K \subset I$. The game (I, v) is super-additive, for any $K, L \subset I$ with $K \cap L = \phi$, if the inequality $v(K \cup L) \geq v(K) + v(L)$ holds. The real vector $x = (x_i)_{i \in I} \in R^I$ is called an imputation, and it is accessible for a coalition, $K \subset I \Leftrightarrow \sum_{i \in K} X_i \leq v(K)$. It should be mentioned that our game is of non-zero sum, so the standard form of the imputation definition is not applied in our case.

Definition.- The core of the game (I, v) is defined as a set of imputations:

$$C = \left\{ x = (x_i)_{i \in I} : \sum_{i \in I} x_i \leq v(I), \forall K \subset I : \sum_{i \in K} x_i \geq v(K) \right\} \qquad (2)$$

where C (nonempty) is the set of possible distributions of the total payment achievable by the coalition of all players, this is accessible for the coalition of all players and none of coalitions can offer to its members uniformly more than what they obtain accepting some imputation from the core. The first argument of C, unlike the conventional definition of the core in the case of cooperative game with transferable utilities, or TU-game [18], indicates that the payments for the great coalition are less than the characteristic of I. This restriction is added by the nature of the problem at hand. The second argument are the imputations relative to each coalition.

The fuzzy core for this game is defined as an extension of crisp core in [13]. Let (I, v) be a crisp coalition game and let $w : 2^I \rightarrow R^+$ be a mapping connecting every coalition $K \subset I$ with a fuzzy quantity $w(K) \in R^+$, called characteristic function of the game, with membership function $\lambda_k : R \rightarrow [0,1]$, where $v(K)$ is the modal value of $w(K)$ with $w(\phi) = 0$. Then (I, w) is called a fuzzy coalition game and is a fuzzy extension of (I, v). In this case, the fuzzy core C_F has the following membership function:

$$\gamma_{c_F}(x) = \min_{K \subset I} [v \succ= (w(I), \left\langle \sum_{i \in I} x_i \right\rangle), v \succ= (\left\langle \sum_{i \in K} x_i \right\rangle, w(K)))] \qquad (3)$$

where: $v \succ= (w(I), \left\langle \sum_{i \in I} x_i \right\rangle)$, with the preference $\succ=$ as a weak order fuzzy relation with membership function $v \succ=: R \times R \rightarrow [0,1]$.

This definition differs significantly from the approach of cooperative fuzzy games with scalable players proposed in [1, 19], where coalitions involve fractions of players. In that case, the fuzzy core of a fuzzy game (I, v, Λ) with positively homogeneous v is equal to the subdifferential $\partial v(\Lambda)$ of v at Λ, which is not the case for our problem with integer full-involved players. Moreover, the fuzzy nature of the coalitions as they are defined in [1], is based mainly on the partial participation of the players in the game. In our case, a fuzzy coalition generates the membership function of the players' payments, which are fuzzy.

The class of games with nonempty core is also a fuzzy subset of the class of coalition games and in some games the core is achievable, however in others the agreement occurs with some degree of possibility. In the latter case, the possibility of such agreement is full excluded. The possibility that $C_F \neq \phi$ for the game (I, w) is given by:

$$\gamma_{C_F}(I, w) = \sup(\gamma_{C_F}(x)) : x \in R^I) \tag{4}$$

To assure that $C_F \neq \phi$, we have that if the characteristics of the game (I, w) are fuzzy quantities then:

1. The possibility that the game (I, w) is superadditive is given by:

$$\sigma(I, w) = min(v_{\succ\approx}(\omega(K \cup L), \omega(K) \oplus \omega(K) : with \ K \cap L = \phi, \ K, L \subset I)$$

2. The possibility that the game (I, w) is convex is given by:

$$\delta(I, w) = min(v_{\succ\approx}(\omega(K \cup L) \oplus \omega(K \cap L), \omega(K) \oplus \omega(K) : K, L \subset I)$$

It is evident from 1) and 2) that $\delta(I, w) \leq \sigma(I, w)$, and if (I, v) is convex then $\gamma_{C_F}(I, w) = 1$. If (I, w) is an extension of (I, v) with $\mu_K(x)$ increasing for $x < v(K)$ and decreasing for $x > v(K)$ for $K \subset I$ y $x \ni \mu_K(x) \neq 0$ then:

$$\gamma_{C_F}(I, w) \geq \delta(I, \omega) \tag{5}$$

From (5), if (I, w) is convex then the game has a solution, that is $C_F \neq \phi$.

The fuzziness is a fundamental component of realistic models of cooperation, which can be considered from the following two points: (i) when a simultaneous participation of players in several coalitions, similar to TU-games, takes place, and (ii) when fuzziness is in a preliminary shape or is a priori expressed by players and coalitions about their prospective earnings. Considered approach is more oriented on the second case. This focus of coalitions formation can be supplemented by knowledge administration, individual one as well as of a group.

3   Fuzzy Coalition Game Example and Solution Techniques

Let us consider one example of a game defined above. In order to show how the solution methods proposed below work, we shall consider first the same example discussed in [13], for which the analytical solution exists. Consider a fuzzy game (I, w) with $I = \{1,2\}$, where for some $(x_1, x_2) \in R^2$ we have:

$$\mu_{\{1\}}(x_1,x_2) = \begin{cases} 1 & for \quad x_1 \le 4 \\ 0 & for \quad x_1 \ge 6 \\ 3 - x_1/2 & for \quad x_1 \in (4,6) \end{cases}, \mu_{\{2\}}(x_1,x_2) = \begin{cases} 1 & for \quad x_2 \le 6 \\ 0 & for \quad x_2 \ge 10 \\ .5 & for \quad x_2 \in [7,9] \\ 4 - x_2/2 & for \quad x_2 \in (6,7) \\ 5 - x_2/2 & for \quad x_2 \in (9,10) \end{cases}$$

$$\mu_I(x_1,x_2) = \begin{cases} 1 & for \quad x_1 + x_2 \le 8 \\ 0 & for \quad x_1 + x_2 \ge 16 \\ 2 - (x_1 + x_2)/8 & for \quad x_1 + x_2 \in (8,16) \end{cases}$$

Although the membership functions in our case are linear (triangular and pyramidal forms) [3], it is a complicated task to find the analytical solution of the fuzzy game (I,w). For example, the Pareto optimal and the superoptimal solutions are fuzzy sets in the plane with imputation $(x_1,x_2) = (4,6)$ which occurs with a possibility of 0.75:

$$\gamma_{C_F}(I,w) = \sup(\mu_{C_F}(x_1 = 4, x_2 = 6)) = .75$$

3.1 Solution Technique Using Genetic Algorithms

Due to the complexity of the problem of analytical (exact) solution, it is proposed in this article to apply heuristic techniques and to find an approximate one. In our case, we apply the soft computing techniques using genetic algorithms in a context of fuzzy logic; this is equivalent to a binary codified fuzzy core with adjustment fusion of the supreme of the minimums of membership functions. We fixed the rates of mutation and crossover in the typical values of 6 and 50% respectively, with a size of population of 50 organisms, time convergence parameters and number of iterations are also fixed [15].

In order to obtain the solution, we use the legacy software *Evolver* from Microsoft, which requires of the formulation of the problem in an *Excel* spreadsheet [2]. For this, it is necessary to store a supreme of the minimums as a formulae in one cell, and to store variables and the arguments of fuzzy core in the others. In addition, initial values of the parameters of the genetic algorithm are provided. It is also required to give any initial solution that can or not be a feasible one, this is an arbitrary imputation. As it is shown in figure 1, the solution very close to the analytical one is obtained with this algorithm. The curve of the evolution of fuzzy core can also be observed, as well as the variable and the supreme that have already arrived at convergence levels.

As it can be observed in figure 1, the cell A1 shows the possibility of the imputation (4.0098, 6.0412) in iteration 2659 which is of 0.743625. The criterion of termination of the algorithm was 2000 minutes, nevertheless the shown solution required only 3 minutes. The mathematical effort is reduced enormously, although for real cases where a number of players and therefore of coalitions is large, it is necessary to simulate a great number of games of fuzzy coalitions and to see what happens to the percentage of successes. We shall consider another more real example in the following section.

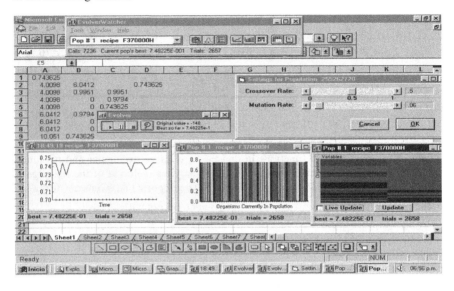

Fig. 1. Solution of the game, evolution of objective function, rates of mutation and crossover and levels of the variables in convergence iteration.

3.2 Solution Technique Using Fuzzy Linear Programming

There are other approaches to this problem, although many of them do not have such a mathematical support as the case of the core. For instance, the problem also can be formulated in terms of the linear programming according to:

$$Min\ Z = CX \lessapprox Z_o, s.a : AX \lessapprox b, X \geq 0, \tag{6}$$

where X is the vector of imputations, b is the vector of modal values of the characteristic functions, A and C have 1´s in their entries; the objective and the constrains are fuzzy indicated by ~.

This problem is similar to the core problem, it is even more easy to formulate and to solve using conventional algorithms as the simplex method. Besides, using this approach, the solution gives additional information, for example the dual problem permits us to make sensitivity analysis and to know what coalitions contribute more to the game, how much must b change to obtain degrees of possibility close to 1, etc.

An example using this model follows, where the membership functions of the characteristic functions $w(j)$ are straight lines according to Table 1:

$$Min\ \ Z = \sum_{i=1}^{4} x_i \lesssim w(I)\ such\ that\ :\quad \begin{aligned} & x_1 + x_3 \gtrsim w(1),\ x_1 + x_4 \gtrsim w(2),\ x_2 + x_3 \gtrsim w(3) \\ & x_2 + x_4 \gtrsim w(4),\ x_j \geq 0, j = 1,2,3,4 \end{aligned}$$

Table 1. Membership functions of the characteristic functions:

Membership function	First point	Second point	Membership function	First point	Second point
$\mu_{w(I)}$	(0,1)	(25,0)	$\mu_{w(3)}$	(0,1)	(12,0)
$\mu_{w(1)}$	(0,1)	(8,0)	$\mu_{w(4)}$	(0,1)	(22,0)
$\mu_{w(2)}$	(0,1)	(10,0)			

The solution is:

$$\lambda^\circ = 0.98 \quad x^\circ_1 = 3.75 \quad x^\circ_2 = 1.89 \quad x^\circ_3 = 1.61 \quad x^\circ_4 = 3.25$$

$$t^o_0 = .5 \quad t^\circ_{13} = .16 \quad t^\circ_{14} = 0 \quad t^\circ_{23} = 0 \quad t^\circ_{24} = .14$$

$$\mu^o_{w(I)} = 0.98, \mu^o_{w(1)} = 1, \mu^o_{w(2)} = 1, \mu^o_{w(3)} = 0.9936, \mu^o_{w(4)} = .98$$

where λ^0 is the degree of possibility associated with the objective function and t^0_{ij} are the deviations of the fuzzy quantities or the right hand sides of the problem.

Coalition gains can be calculated by summing the respective payoffs of each player. Computations associated with the possibility degrees can be realized in the same way.

4 Application Domain and MAS Implementation Details

We consider the forming of virtual SCN as an application domain. Agents in SCN negotiate and form coalitions to reach common objectives. According to this conceptualization, a typical supply chain MAS is composed of the following two types of agents [5]: Supply Chain Advisor (SCA) for each member of the chain and Group Supply Chain Advisor (GSCA). The MAS resides on the Agent Platform (AP) [17]. Domain agents have the access to the standardized problem solving techniques (SCN management methods, genetic programming, linear programming, etc.) implemented as modules of legacy software through the Wrapper Agent.

The layered structure of the SCN is defined according to the roles, each player can play and is behind the scope of this article. Here we define the algorithm of coalition forming process based on the above described methodology, which permits to form the instances of the SCN selecting the most appropriate participants from each layer. One commodity scheme is considered for simplicity. The whole negotiation scheme is supported by the FIPA Iterative Contract Net Protocol [7].

We shall illustrate the algorithm with another example with four players and five coalitions, where only approximate solution using genetic algorithms can be obtained:

$$\mu_{\{1,3\}}(x_1, x_2, x_3, x_4) = \begin{cases} -28/12 + 1/12(x_1 + x_3), & for\ x_1 + x_3 \in [28,40] \\ 0, otherwise. \end{cases}$$

$$\mu_{\{1,4\}}(x_1, x_2, x_3, x_4) = \begin{cases} -30/18 + 1/18(x_1 + x_4), & for\ x_1 + x_4 \in [30,48] \\ 0, otherwise. \end{cases}$$

$$\mu_{\{2,3\}}(x_1,x_2,x_3,x_4) = \begin{cases} -35/14+1/14(x_2+x_3), & for\ x_2+x_3 \in [35,49] \\ 0, otherwise. \end{cases}$$

$$\mu_{\{2,4\}}(x_1,x_2,x_3,x_4) = \begin{cases} -25/15+1/15(x_2+x_4), & for\ x_2+x_4 \in [25,40] \\ 0, otherwise. \end{cases}$$

$$\mu_{\{1,2,3,4\}}(x_1,x_2,x_3,x_4) = \begin{cases} 3-1/30(x_1+x_2+x_3+x_4), & for\ x_1+x_2+x_3+x_4 \in [60,90] \\ 0, otherwise. \end{cases}$$

1. When a new demand occurs, it is transmitted by the GSCA to all possible players according to the product specification (individual companies, subcoalitions, etc.). Each SCA associated with each player facilitates the construction of the membership function of fuzzy payments that he expects to achieve for this demand, displaying a template menu of possible typical membership functions, so that each player selects one of these and fixes the values of the parameters.

2. New coalitions are formed based on the product specification as a result of negotiations between the players. The interaction of the players generates the distribution of fuzzy payments expected by each coalition. This distribution takes into account the membership functions of fuzzy payments constructed as a sum of the expressed individual fuzzy payments generated at the previous step. We suppose for simplicity of the example that at this stage, coalitions don't have redundancy of players (i.e. enterprises bidding for the same sub-product). On the other hand, redundancy between coalitions can exist; the GSCA forms a game based on minor modal value principle (ordering by payments) or all coalitions participate in the game. Accomplishing this, the GSCA finally constructs a fuzzy core of the game.

3. The GSCA accesses the legacy software (Evolver o LPS in our case) via Wrapper Agent to obtain solution of the game, i.e. the imputation that maximizes the possibility of its occurrence. For a convex game, at least one solution exists, so applying genetic algorithm technique we can obtain different solutions at this stage. The best one is selected after a number of iterations. Initial conditions are defined fixing the convergence parameters, in the example we have established initial solution in 16, 17, 19, 17 for each player and the payments for each coalition in 35, 33, 36, 34, 69 respectively with a 0.0714 possibility. The convergence of the algorithm was reached in iteration number 677.

4.-The GSCA scatters the solution to each coalition so that it is analyzed (fig. 2) and in the case of being accepted, it is implemented in the SCN. So, at this step, the GSCA defines the interrelations between groups or coalitions (nodes of the network) obtaining this way a SCN. In the opposite case, when the solution is not accepted, the associated membership functions of individual and coalition fuzzy payments are to be revised; this is equivalent to repeat the process of the previous steps. The latter case also includes the situation when fuzzy core is empty.

5   Conclusions and Future Work

Rational agents decide to cooperate with others (forming fuzzy coalitions) and coordinate their actions to reach expected results. This is obtained involving the theory of games in MAS research, where rationality is explored while agents cooperate reasoning about beliefs of other agents based on the fuzzy utilities derived from their interactions. This is the main difference of the proposed approach from the models of beliefs of other agents based on the explicit logic and permits to change the way of MAS programming from the predefined ad-hoc architectures to dynamic flexible and agile systems with dynamic configurations developed on-line by the MAS itself.

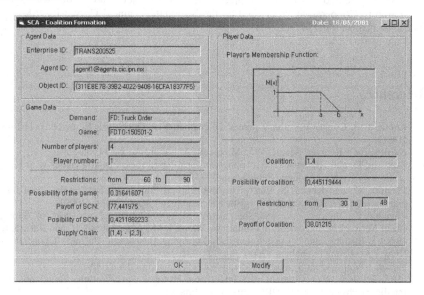

Fig. 2. SCA interface: solution of a game

In the SCN example, SCA agents form a dynamic network of flexible problem solvers able to dynamically create the organizational structure. The flexible interaction structure is guaranteed by the AP. Being applied to dynamic, vague and uncertain environments, where action strategies result from bargaining as far as the alliances are formed, the proposed approach produces better utility for groups and individuals with high possibility that this happens. This scheme breaks with the traditional paradigms of organization, hierarchic or matrix ones, and has the distinguishing point and an advantage in that it takes into account the convenience of the enterprise to participate in groups and allows fast adaptations that respond to enterprise dynamics.

In the ongoing work, the fuzzy core with nonlinear membership functions is studied. With the fuzzy nonlinear programming approach, it will be interesting to make sensitivity analysis to determinate the most important coalitions in relation to their contribution to the value of the game and to what extent the values of the characteristic and membership functions change, that is, the right hand sides of the constraints, in order to obtain higher degrees of possibility. Finally, we will try to apply the methodology integrating this MAS into the enterprises framework. Current experiments are also focused on the development and testing of the management functions of SCA, as well as on further investigation of the interoperability issues with software modules that provide additional services for agents.

Acknowledgements. Partial support for this research work has been provided by the CONACyT, Mexico within the project 31851-A "Models and Tools for Agent Interaction in Cooperative MAS" and by the National Technical University, Mexico, within the project 980739.

References

1. Aubin, J. P. Cooperative fuzzy games. Mathematics of Operations Research, 6(1):1-13, (1981).
2. Axcélis, Inc´s Evolver. Seattle, WA. Microsoft, Aldus and Adobe. (1995).
3. Butnariu, D. and Klement, E. P., Triangular norm-based measures and games with fuzzy coalitions. Kluwer Academic Publishers. (1993).
4. Chandra, C., and Kumar, S. Enterprise Architectural Framework for Supply-Chain Integration, International Journal of Logistics: Research and Applications. (1999).
5. Chandra, C., Smirnov, A., and Sheremetov, L., Agent-based Infrastructure of Supply Chain Network Management, In Camarinha-Matos, L.M., Afsarmanesh, H. and Rabelo, R. (Eds.) E-Business and Virtual Enterprises Managing Business-to-Business Cooperation. Kluwer Academic Publishers, (2000), pp. 221-232.
6. Ferber, J. Multi-Agent Systems, Addison-Wesley, Reading, MA, (1999).
7. FIPA FIPA Iterated Contract Net Interaction Protocol Specification, Foundation for Intelligent Physical Agents, URL: http://www.fipa.org.
8. Frayret, J.M., Cloutier, L., Montreuil, B. and D'Amours, S., A distributed framework for collaborative supply network integration. E-Business and Virtual Enterprises: Managing Business-to-Business Cooperation. Kluwer Academic Publishers. (2000).
9. Gasser, L Social conceptions of knowledge and action: DAI foundations and open system semantics, Artificial Intelligence 47 (1--3) (1991) 107--138.
10. Hewitt, C. Open Information System Semantics for Distributed Artificial Intelligence, Artificial Intelligence 47 (1--3) (1991) 79--106.
11. Jennings, N.R. Automated Haggling: Building Artificial Negotiators, URL: http://www.ecs.soton.ac.uk/~nrj/presentations.html
12. Mareš, M., Fuzzy coalition forming. Seventh IFSA World Congress, Prague (1997).
13. Mareš, M., Sharing vague profit in fuzzy cooperation. Springer-Verlag Co. (1998).
14. McKinsey, J. Introduction to the theory of games. The rand series. (1952).
15. Michalewickz, Z. Genetic Algorithms + data structures= evolution programs. Springer-Verlag. Berlin Heidelberg. (1992).
16. Rosenschein, J.S. and G. Zlotkin, Rules of encounter, MIT press, Cambridge, MA, (1998).
17. Sheremetov, L. and Contreras M. Component Agent Platform. In Proc of the Second International Workshop of Central and Eastern Europe on Multi-Agent Systems, CEEMAS'01, Cracow, Poland, pp. 395-402. (2001).
18. Tuomela, R., Cooperation. Kluwer Academic Publishers. (2000).
19. Van den Brink, R. and G. van der Laan. Core Concepts for Share Vectors. Lambda, (1999), URL: http://netec.mimas.ac.uk/WoPEc/data/Papers/dgrkubcen199964.html
20. Wang,J., The theory of games. Oxford Science Publications. (1988).

Learning Collective Behaviour from Local Interactions

Nicolas Sabouret and Jean-Paul Sansonnet

LIMSI-CNRS, BP133
F-91403 Orsay cedex, France
{nico,jps}@limsi.fr

Abstract. In this paper, we propose a reasoning model for extracting collective behaviours in Multi-Agent Systems (MAS) from regularities in interaction streams. Using reflexive structures to describe the actions and knowledge of the system, called *views*, we build chronicles that catch and register the actual situations related to events and actions occurrences. These chronicles are then *intensionalised* in order to extract regularities in a single autonomous agent's behaviour, thus defining a local behaviour. We then propose to extend this model for extracting collective behaviours in MAS using machine learning algorithms. Finally, we try to show that this dynamic analysis of an agent's runtime can lead to organisations in MAS.

1 Context of the Study

1.1 Collective Behaviour's Perception

Organisations appear to be in the centre of Multi-Agent Systems design and development (see [2]). Nowadays, organisations can be either static or dynamic and either defined *a priori* in the system program or emerge during the system execution. However in all cases, the behaviour of an agent in the system is determined by the system organisation.

In this paper, we propose a *bottom-up* approach for organisations detection. If we consider a simple component exposed to an *open context* and provided with interaction capabilities, we can register its effective interactions with its acquaintances to draw a local behaviour. Our proposal is to use these local interactions to define a perceived organisation[1], *i.e.* the representation of a collective behaviour.

The first stage of this modelling is to extract behaviours perceived by a single agent interacting with only one other (1 to 1). We must then extend this study to extract a *collective behaviour* from the interaction of one agent with N others (N to 1). Finally, the principle can be generalised to agents groups (N to N) in order to build dynamic emerging organisations in MAS.

---

[1] This definition is not global like in [6]: it is a model of the world, made by the observer agent. As a consequence, two agents in the same MAS can define different models of organisation.

B. Dunin-Kęplicz and E. Nawarecki (Eds.): CEEMAS 2001, LNAI 2296, pp. 273–282, 2002.

1.2   Learning Behaviour from Interactions

To this purpose, autonomous agents should be provided with "reasoning about actions capabilities". Much work has already been done in this field to extend logic inference mechanisms to active systems (Situation Calculus [12], Dynamic Logic (PDL) [14], ...).

However, in a distributed environment like the Internet, the agents evolve in an *open context* [10]: events may result from external requests that happen during the execution, and the reaction of the agent may depend on its knowledge at that time. In this frame, autonomous agents need to be able to *discover* the behaviour of other agents [11], using the interaction capabilities to determine what are the actions of others.

This requires a *dynamic approach* that consists of *running* the component, like in Evolving Algebras [9]. As a consequence of this constraint, we propose a model for temporal reasoning based on the notion of *chronicles* [4]. For each event that occurs in the system, be it internal or external, we build a model of the situation in which it occurs and memorise it (the situation is stored). This produces the chronicles on which the behaviour extraction will be carried out.

1.3   Intensionalisation of Chronicles

If we consider an active component provided with chronicles, two problems arise:

- On an operational level, the state s_t of the component grows linearly along with the execution steps. We therefore need to represent the chronicles in a compact way, *i.e.* in intension[2].
- On a semantic level, we would like to extract regularities, "behaviours", from event streams. Once again, this requires to build representation in intension of the chronicles.

These chronicles, being *extended runtime traces*, must be built and intensionalised in a dynamic way, *i.e.* during the execution itself. In this article, we propose a dynamic model for building chronicles in intension and we try to show how it can be used to turn a *reactive* component into a *reflexive* agent, like in [8].

Firstly, we briefly present the syntax of the formalism used to describe the components: VDL.

We then propose a structure for the chronicles and a model for building them at execution time. We illustrate this process using a simple example of interaction with a single agent. We show how behaviours can be extracted from chronicles and how this turns a single reactive component into a reflexive agent.

Finally, we propose an extension of this "local" model based on machine learning algorithms to extract collective behaviours in Multi-Agent System (MAS). We illustrate this principle using a simple example of interaction between 1 agent and the whole MAS. We then try to show how this turns *co-active* agents into *cooperative* ones.

---

[2] Note the difference between *intention* (in agents) and *intension* (in mathematics, opposed to *extension*).

2 Introduction to VDL

In the *InterViews* project[3], we deal with *active online components* viewed as Autonomous Agents in the Internet. They are described in a specific language called VDL for **V***iew* **D***esign* **L***anguage*. The component's body is a tree whose nodes are character strings called *concepts*. We call this concept tree a *view*.

A component's runtime is based on rewriting the view at each *step*, like in Evolving Algebras [9]: we defined a function that looks in $view_t$ for specific concepts that are interpreted to build $view_{t+1}$.

In this paper, we will call any view's subtree a *term*. A term whose concept is c and whose attributes are $st_1, ..., st_n$ will be represented using a textual form by $c[st_1, ..., st_n]$. The concepts containing special characters (brackets, commas, spaces) will be written between quotes (e.g. *"greater than"[x,y]*).

We cannot present here all the concepts used to define the views operational semantics. They are presented in [16].

Example. In the next section, we shall use a voluntarily rather simple example, in order to illustrate the chronicle intensionalisation principle.

Let us consider an agent representing a fridge, interacting with both human users and its environment. The environment "heats up" the fridge's contents following a specific law at each execution step[4]. Moreover, a user can open and close the fridge door and when the door is opened, the fridge heats up faster[5]. Finally, the fridge is provided with a cooler that activates when $\theta > 4^\circ$C. It cools down the fridge internal temperature by 0.2°C at each step.

The description of this operating world in VDL is the following, with procedural concepts written in *italics* for easier reading:

```
view[temp[3], factor[1500],
        "open door"[ event[open], put[path[factor], 40] ],
        "close door"[ event[close], put[path[factor], 1500] ],
        "heat up"[ put[path[temp],Δ]] ],
        "cool down"[ guard["greater than"[get[temp],4]],
                put[path[temp],plus[get[temp],-0.2]] ]       ]
```

where Δ is the VDL expression for $e^{-\frac{1}{get[factor]}} \times (get[temp] - 20) + 20$.

The user can interact with the component using the *open* and *close* events to respectively open and close the fridge door.

---

[3] Web page: http://www.limsi.fr/Individu/jps/interviews

[4] If the room temperature is 20°C, we can say that the temperature θ in the fridge increases in function of the time t (given in minutes) following the law: $\theta = 20(1 - e^{(-\frac{t}{T})})$, with $T = 1500$ which makes the temperature in the fridge be 11°C after 24 hours, supposing the fridge is closed and its cooling system is stopped. As a consequence,

$$\theta_{(t+1)} = e^{-\frac{1}{T}} \times (\theta_{(t)} - 20) + 20$$

[5] Say $T = 40$, which makes $\theta = 8^\circ$C after 20 minutes if nothing has been done.

3   Structure of Chronicles

To be able to extract behaviours as regularities within the occurrences of past actions, we need to store the agent's past runtime into chronicles. Our objective is to attach to each VDL term a chronicle which is the representation in a compact form of the operations that were performed upon the component. The chronicles are then intensionalised to study their regularities and to detect behaviours. We define in this section the structure of these chronicles and the way they are built at execution time.

3.1   The Notion of Situation in VDL

Let t be a subterm of the view v and a be an action that will modify t^6. The *situation* in which an action occurred is defined by a 5-tuple:

$$sit(a) = \langle who(a), what(a), why(a), when(a), res(a) \rangle$$

where:

- $who(a) = ref^{-1}(parent(a))$ is the parent term of the operation.
- $what(a) = a$ is the basic action performed.
- $why(a)$ gives the preconditions of the action
  The why criterion will be used to determine the cause of an action and finally the behaviour of the component.
- $when(a)$ recollects the execution step number (the *date*) when the operation was performed.
- $res(a)$ is the new value of the term after the operation.
  The res criterion is what leads to behaviour recognition.

This notion of situation is what makes chronicles be more than simple execution traces, but what we could call *situated* traces.

3.2   Extensional Chronicles

For every term t, we store the situations of actions performed upon t in an *extensional chronicle* Ξ_t. It can be seen as an attribute-value table whose rows are situations and whose columns are the five criteria defining a situation.

Consider the view v defined in section 3 and suppose that the user opens the door at step 3 (event *open*), closes it at step 6 (event *close*), re-opens it at step 10 and forgets to close it again.

The extensional chronicle associated with the term *temp* in the view $\phi^{15}(v)$, *i.e.* at execution step number 15, is given by table 1.

Whereas the modifications of the temperature in the first part of the execution is somehow erratic, the second part appears to be very regular. We will now show how chronicle intensionalisation can bring out this process.

---

[6] In VDL, this means that a *path* subterm of the action a refers to t.

Table 1. The extensional chronicle $\Xi_{temp}(15)$.

who	what	why	when	res	event
$\checkmark$	$\checkmark$	$\checkmark$	0	3	
heat up	put[path[temp],Δ]	$\top$	1	3.011	
heat up	put[path[temp],Δ]	$\top$	2	3.023	
heat up	put[path[temp],Δ]	$\top$	3	3.034	open
heat up	put[path[temp],Δ]	$\top$	4	3.453	
heat up	put[path[temp],Δ]	$\top$	5	3.861	
heat up	put[path[temp],Δ]	$\top$	6	4.260	
cool down	put[path[temp],...]	guard[...]	6	4.060	close
heat up	put[path[temp],Δ]	$\top$	7	4.070	
cool down	put[path[temp],...]	guard[...]	7	3.870	
heat up	put[path[temp],Δ]	$\top$	8	3.881	
heat up	put[path[temp],Δ]	$\top$	9	3.892	
heat up	put[path[temp],Δ]	$\top$	10	3.903	open
heat up	put[path[temp],Δ]	$\top$	11	4.300	
cool down	put[path[temp],...]	guard[...]	11	4.100	close
heat up	put[path[temp],Δ]	$\top$	12	4.493	
cool down	put[path[temp],...]	guard[...]	12	4.293	
heat up	put[path[temp],Δ]	$\top$	13	4.681	
cool down	put[path[temp],...]	guard[...]	13	4.481	
heat up	put[path[temp],Δ]	$\top$	14	4.864	
cool down	put[path[temp],...]	guard[...]	14	4.664	
heat up	put[path[temp],Δ]	$\top$	15	5.042	
cool down	put[path[temp],...]	guard[...]	15	4.842	

3.3 Intensional Chronicles

If two situations s and s' in Ξ_t have the same *who*, *what* and *why* criteria, we say that it is *the same action*.

An action is thus defined by a 5-tuple $\langle who, what, why, W, R \rangle$ where W is the list of its situations' dates $(when(a))$ and R the list of the results $(res(a))$. The *actions* performed upon a term constitute a compacted chronicle Ξ'_t.

We then developed a function ξ to intensionalise *regular* numerical series. ξ transforms a list of numbers L into an ***iterator*** $(L_1, n, |L|, op)$ where:

- L_1 is the first element of L and $|L|$ the size of the list,
- n is the *constant* step between L_i and L_{i+1},
- op is the iteration operator such that $L_{i+n} = op_{(n)}(L_i)$.
  For instance, with $op = \times$, $L_{i+1} = L_i \times n$.

For the purpose of our study, we will use a $\ddagger$ operator such that $\ddagger_{(a,b)}(x) = a.x+b$. We don't give the algorithm that recognises and intensionalises $\ddagger$ series because it is somehow complex. In the iterator with $\ddagger$ operator, we have $n = (a,b)$.

Table 2. The intensional chronicle $\Xi_{temp}(15)$.

who	what	why	when	res
$\checkmark$	$\checkmark$	$\checkmark$	0	3
heat up	put[path[temp],Δ]	$\top$	$(1,1,3,+)$	$(3.011,(0.999,0.013),3,\ddagger)$
heat up	put[path[temp],Δ]	$\top$	$(4,1,3,+)$	$(3.453,(0.975,0.494),3,\ddagger)$
cool down	put[path[temp],...]	guard[...]	$(6,1,2,+)$	$(4.060,(0.975,0.294),2,\ddagger)$
heat up	put[path[temp],Δ]	$\top$	7	4.070
heat up	put[path[temp],Δ]	$\top$	$(8,1,3,+)$	$(3.881,(0.999,0.013),3,\ddagger)$
heat up	put[path[temp],Δ]	$\top$	$(11,1,5,+)$	$(4.300,(0.975,0.494),5,\ddagger)$
cool down	put[path[temp],...]	guard[...]	$(11,1,5,+)$	$(4.100,(0.975,0.294),5,\ddagger)$

This ξ function is always applied in Ξ_t' to the *when* and *res* criteria. This produces an *intensional chronicle* that we note $\Xi_t^{(int)}$. In the *Fridge* example, $\Xi_{temp}^{(int)}(15)$ is given in table 2.[7]

Note that $\Xi_{temp}^{(int)}(1000)$ would be the same chronicle as above, where 5 is replaced by 989 in the last two lines. Generally, the complexity of the intensional chronicle measures the regularity of the view's "behaviour".

Such regular actions (such that when a basic action is performed, it can be added in the same intensional action line in the chronicle) are called *processes*.

We consider that there is a strong relation between building the chronicles and detecting *behaviours*, viewed as processes' regularity.

From reactive components to reflexive agents. In our example, the fridge component will be *aware* of a new behaviour emerging in its environment (see figure 1). It can detect the effective heating process using the regularity that appears in the intensional chronicle, the agent can.

If this behaviour is considered harmful (for any reason), the component can react *at a higher semantic level*, *i.e.* not in response to a single interaction but to a global pattern of past events that was categorised. Consequently, it turns into a *reflexive* agent.

In MAGENTA [17], we proposed a method to look for the causes of a guarded modeless action. However, the model proposed in MAGENTA can't handle the *Fridge* example since there is no direct cause to the heating process, except that the factor is too high. This is a consequence of the ramification problem [7] which asserts that it is impossible to determine all the indirect consequences of an action.

We propose to use *explanatory diagnosis* [13] to determine how the agent can stop the process in our model. At time t_0, the agent will try to virtually perform some actions that stop the process, *i.e.* that can't be inserted into the latest action of the intensional chronicle.

---

[7] Note that $e^{-\frac{1}{1500}} \simeq 0.999$, $20(1 - e^{-\frac{1}{1500}}) \simeq 0.013$, $e^{-\frac{1}{40}} \simeq 0.975$ and $20(1 - e^{-\frac{1}{40}}) \simeq 0.494$.

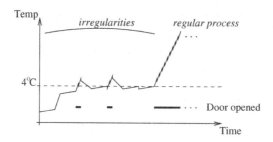

Fig. 1. *Fridge*'s runtime: bringing out regularities

4   Extracting Behaviours in MAS

We will now show that the intensionalisation mechanism can be applied further to discover collective behaviours in Multi-Agent Systems and to characterise the system organisation *a posteriori*, *i.e.* as it is actually emerging.

4.1   The *CoolRoom* Example

In this section, we will consider the following system as an example for organisation emergence with respect to social behaviours in multi-agent systems.

Let us consider the system represented in figure 2. It is made of $n+1$ agents: a room (agent R) provided with a heating process and n agents $(A_1, ..., A_n)$ trying to survive coldness in this room using different behaviours. For instance, when the dangerous cold point is reached ($\theta < 5^{\circ}$C), we have the following behaviours:

- agent A_1, closes the room door in order to limit the room interaction with the rest of the building.[8]
- agent A_2 closes the window for similar reasons (limiting interaction with the outside).
- agent A_3 makes some soup. This action both heats up the room and offers new limited resources to increase all agents' resistances to coldness.
- agent A_4 take a bottle of wine and drinks it.
- *and so on*: we can imagine many other agents.

We don't give the full description of *CoolRoom* $= \{R, A_1, ..., A_n\}$ because it would take too long for this paper, but it is easily representable using the VDL formalism.

In this example, n agents act toward the agent R in order to modify its temperature. Our idea is that agent R should be able to discover this social behaviour and the organisation that emerges from it. This could then be used to propose a solution that would satisfy all agents: agent R should act-back towards the agents A_i in response to their new emergent behaviour.

---

[8] Note that this action might not be a good idea since the temperature may be higher in the corridor than in the room. Agent A_1 is not aware of this.

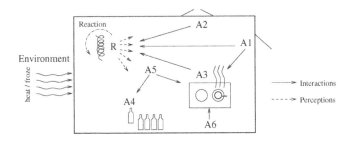

Fig. 2. Interactions in the *CoolRoom* example.

Note that these agents do not cooperate since they have no model of the other agents (see [1]). However, their *co-action* generates a behavioural scheme $\mathcal{B}$ that will be detected by agent R[9] even if this behaviour is not represented *a priori* in the system.

What we intend to do is to extend the behaviour extraction mechanism we proposed for an interaction with *a single agent* into a social behaviour extraction mechanism, *i.e.* for the interaction *with n agents*, in order to discover such collective behaviours.

4.2   The Most Discriminating Criterion

In the chronicle intensionalisation model we proposed in the previous section, only the *when* and *res* criterion are intensionalised. However, in MAS, a process can emerge from the interaction of many agents. For instance, in the *CoolRoom* example, many agents $(A_i)_{i \in [1,n]}$ co-act to solve a temperature problem that they share: all the actions are performed *for the same reason*. We will propose a method based on machine learning techniques to extract this *common* criterion.

Let us consider the intensional chronicle as an attribute-value table. We can then build a decision tree using the machine learning algorithm ID3 [15] to obtain a decision tree with empty leaves (since we don't try to recognise a class).

In this tree, the most discriminating criteria are at upper positions: they are the criteria shared by most actions. This is the reason why the *why* criterion appears on top in the *CoolRoom* example. In case of equality, we take the default order: *who, why, what, res, when*, corresponding to what we consider to be the most discriminating.

The decision trees we obtain for the *Fridge* and *CoolRoom* worlds are given in figure 3. Note how the regularity of processes, linked to behaviour detection, leads to a regular decision tree. In the *CoolRoom* example, the machine learning mechanism puts in evidence a collective intention [5] between the A_i agents.

---

[9] Agent R does not decide whether it is a co-action or a cooperation: it simply detects a collective behaviour.

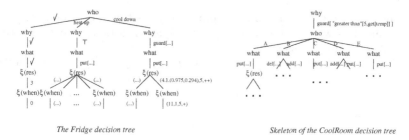

The Fridge decision tree   Skeleton of the CoolRoom decision tree

Fig. 3. Decision trees for behaviour detection in MAS

4.3   From Co-action to Cooperation

Let us consider the A_i social behaviour with respect to the classical distinction between co-action and cooperation in MAS. Agent R detects a *co-active* behaviour, since each agent A_i is not aware of other agents' reactions to coldness.

However, in our example, agent R can extract the common intention of other agents $(A_i)_{i \in [1,n]}$ corresponding to the *higher* criterion in the decision tree. Using causal inference diagnosis like we did in the previous sections, it can then try to satisfy the agents' collective intention by heating up the room.

But furthermore, it can tell the A_i about this social coactive behaviour, thus making them aware of the other agents behaviour, intentions and actions. Extending this principle to a whole MAS and using causal inference on the intentions, the co-active behaviours could be turned into cooperative ones.

5   Conclusion and Discussion

The work presented in this paper is a first attempt for extracting collective behaviours in MAS from N to 1 interaction streams. In our model, the representation of the agent's behaviours (corresponding to regularities in the chronicles) can be used by machine learning algorithms to extract common criteria in the situations and, as a consequence, feature similarities between agents. Each criteria permutation in the tree corresponds to a possible organisation perception.

However, our work is limited to a restricted area and we would like to extend and improve our model in several ways. Concerning the building of decision trees, the method presented here, based on ID3 [15], is not incremental. So we intend to use the ITI algorithm [18] in future work.

The intensionalisation of *res* and *when* is also limited: it should be possible to use many 5-tuples for a single list when needed, *i.e.* when the list is irregular but composed of regular alternative segments. This will result in more "regular" induction trees. Moreover, we should increase the number of operators that the ξ function can process as well as the degree of intensionalisation, in order to detect the regularities of more complex series.

Moreover, we would like to incorporate elements from behavioural logic [3] and to link this work with classical "reasoning about actions" models in order to build real autonomous agents.

Finally, we would like to extend these works to the analysis of interaction streams between agents groups (N to N) in order to build organisations in MAS.

References

1. C. BRASSAC and S. PESTY. De la coaction à la coopération. In *Proc. JFI-ADSMA'96*, pages 251–263. Hermes, 1996.
2. B. CHAIB-DRAA, B. MOULIN, R. MANDIAU, and P. MILLOT. Trends in Distributed Artificial Intelligence. *Artificial Intelligence Review*, 6:35–66, 1992.
3. P.R. COHEN and H.J. LEVESQUE. *Intentions in communication*, chapter Persistence, Intension and Commitment, pages 33–69. MIT Press, 1990.
4. C. DOUSSON, P. GABORIT, and M. GHALLAB. Situation Recognition: representation and algorithms. In *Proc. 13th IJCAI*, pages 166–172, 1993.
5. B. DUNIN-KĘPLICZ and R. VERBRUGGE. Collective intention constitues a group. In Demazeau et al., editor, *Proc. MAAMAW'01*, 2001.
6. J. EPSTEIN and L. AXTELL. *Growing Artificial Societies. Social Science from the Bottom Up*. MIT Press, 1996.
7. J.J. FINGER. *Exploiting Constraints in Design Synthesis*. PhD thesis, Stanford, 1987.
8. Z. GUESSOUM and J.P. BRIOT. From Active Objects to Autonomous Agents. *IEEE Concurrency*, 7(3):68–76, 1999.
9. Y. GUREVICH. Evolving Algebra Lipari Guide. In E. Börger, editor, *Specification and Validation Methods*, pages 9–36. Oxford University Press, 1995.
10. C. HEWITT. The challenge of open systems. Byte, 1985.
11. H. HEXMOOR, J. LAMMENS, G. CAICEDO, and S.C. SHAPIRO. Behaviour based AI, cognitive processes, and emergent behaviors in autonomous agents. In *Applications of Artificial Intelligence in Engineering*, pages 447–461, 1993.
12. J. MCCARTHY and P.J. HAYES. Some philosophical problems from the standpoint of Artificial Intelligence. *Machine Intelligence*, 4:463–502, 1969.
13. S. MCILRAITH. Explanatory Diagnosis: Conjecturing Actions to Explain Observations. In *International Conference on Principles of Knowledge Representation and Reasoning (KR'98)*, pages 167–177, 1998.
14. V.R. PRATT. Semantical considerations on Floyd-Hoare Logic. In *Proc. 17th FOCS*, pages 109–121. IEEE, 1976.
15. J.R. QUINLAN. Induction of decision trees. *Machine Learning*, 1:81–106, 1986.
16. N. SABOURET and J.P. SANSONNET. Automated Answers to Questions about a Running Process. In *Proc. CommonSense 2001*, pages 217–227, 2001.
17. J.P. SANSONNET and E. VALENCIA. An Experimental Framework for Behavior Extraction over Communication Flows in Multi-Agent Sytems. In *Proc. Agent2000 Workshop on Agent Communication*, 2000.
18. P. UTGOFF. An Improved Algorithm for Incremental Induction of Decision Trees. In *Proc. 11th ICML*, pages 318–325. Morgan Kaufmann, 1994.

MAS Oriented Patterns

Sylvain SAUVAGE

GREYC — CNRS UMR 6072, Université de Caen
Département d'Informatique — Campus II
Bd Maréchal Juin — B.P. 5186
F–14032 CAEN CEDEX   (France)
IIUN — Université de Neuchâtel (Suisse)

Sylvain.Sauvage@info.unicaen.fr

Abstract. Multiagent systems (MAS) are spreading, in the academic world as well as in industry. Nevertheless, MAS design is still a problem. The agent community now has some experience. So, we considered existing techniques allowing formalisation and reuse of the experience. We particularly considered object-oriented techniques, for they are close to the MAS paradigm, for they are widely used to implement MAS, and for they are strongly integrated in the computer science world. So we develop – through an example – the idea of using *patterns* to describe the usage of existing models and techniques in MAS domain.

1   Introduction

Analysis and design are becoming an important subject of research in multiagent systems (MAS). Now MAS are more and more used, the need for tools and methods allowing the quick and reliable realisation of MAS is clearly appearing. This need is appearing in the MAS community itself but it's also a necessity to empower a larger community to use the agent paradigm.

Agents, actors and objects are strongly tied [1,2]. They are entities with an internal state and a comportment. Agents and actors also share a notion of action concurrence, and the agent paradigm adds the notions of situation, mobility and, above all, the notions of goal and adaptability. Besides, agents often are implemented with the object-oriented programming paradigm (OOP) or in using the actor paradigm [3].

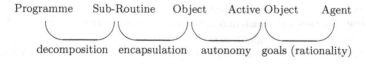

Programme   Sub-Routine   Object   Active Object   Agent

decomposition   encapsulation   autonomy   goals (rationality)

Fig. 1. Links between the different programming paradigms

Present attempts of the community focus on MAS design methodology, [4]. In fact, MAS paradigm development is restricted by the gap between the apparent

B. Dunin-Kęplicz and E. Nawarecki (Eds.): CEEMAS 2001, LNAI 2296, pp. 283–292, 2002.
© Springer-Verlag Berlin Heidelberg 2002

ease to seize the basic concepts (agent, role, organisation and interaction) and the difficulty to create a MAS which resolves or help to resolve a real world problem. Then, to help the MAS designer, we seek a new formalisation.

There are several ways to help the MAS designer. One way is providing tools, *e.g.*, [5,6], another can be giving him a methodology, *e.g.*, [7]. We didn't want to compel the designer with a method or with too much restrictive concepts and models.

On the other hand, as agents are often implemented by the way of object programming, the idea of using object-oriented analysis and design methods is appealing. But those methods are not applicable, simply because objects and agents do not pertain to the same logical and conceptual levels – one can program a MAS in a functional language. Nevertheless, we can draw our inspiration from object methods and from their development to create methods for MAS.

We think that, among the object techniques, the patterns are strongly appropriate to resolve the MAS design problems. In fact, patterns are the perfect means to spread the concepts and the different models used in the MAS design and in their implementation.

In the following sections, we will quickly expose patterns, then – to explain their use in MAS – we will quickly present the *Marks* pattern.

2   Patterns

Definition. *A pattern is a (partial) solution to a contextual problem.*

Patterns have been introduced in 1977 by the architect Ch. Alexander. The matter was to have *recipes* to design good plans: for each problem, its solution. At the beginning of the 90's, [8], the object-oriented community, having then a mature experience of OOP, concerned itself in the patterns to exploit and share this experience. Since then, the use of patterns is only growing, notably with the conferences, [9], and the sustaining of the OMG.

As H.-A. Simon and J.-L. Le Moigne, [10,11], have shown it, the design of complex systems is itself a complex problem. One can't define *the* solution for a set of problems. Nevertheless, because of the object paradigm's modularity, it often happens to the designer or the programmer to find himself in front of a problem he has already met in the past, under the same form or under a lightly different one. Thanks to this sensation of *déjà vu*, he then can try to abstract the solution he had used to reuse it. The abstractions of these already applied solutions are what are called patterns.

By the way they are constructed, patterns are an abstraction, a formalisation of the experience the designers and the programmers acquired.

Patterns also allow documenting the proposed solutions. The designer only has to indicate which patterns he applied for the informed reader to understand the solution, without having to deeply inspect each part to understand the whole.

Presentation

For their presentation, patterns are often described as a tuple whose fields vary with the authors, but among these fields, the main ones are:

- *name:* each pattern has a name (sometimes several, if different authors described it), this name allows to identify the pattern.
- *context:* here, it matters to explicit the situation in which the pattern may be useful;
- *problem(s):* the pattern can resolve one or more problems in its context;
- *solution(s):* the available solution(s) to the problem(s);
- *examples:* they allow better understanding the pattern, a pattern being an empirical creation;
- *directives:* to guide the application of the solution;
- *consequences:* as anybody knows, a solution may imply other problems, the user then need to be warned of their existence;
- *associated patterns:* a list of applicable patterns in similar situations and a list of complementary patterns.

Patterns are often organised in different types, following their abstraction level: analysis, design, implementation (idioms), structure, behaviour, ...

In the following sections, we will present a short version of an agent pattern. The chosen presentation, though lightly different from the object pattern presentation, seems to be appropriate to the agent patterns we have already written.

3   The *Marks* Pattern

Synopsis .... *Short explanation for what the pattern does*

Agents leave marks in the environment in aim to use the environment as an additional, shared, and situated memory.

Forces .... *Contextual constraints summary*[1]

- Agents have limited memory capabilities.
- Agents have limited communication capacities.
- Agents are situated: there are constraints affecting their positions, their moves, there is a *timeness* in the system (evolution).
- There are constraints affecting the resources agents can use: limited speed, energetic autonomy, and time. Agents can't search each other every time to communicate.
- Informations that need to be kept or shared have a spatial characteristic, they are *local* (*i.e.*, they are only locally relevant).

Origins .... *Inspiration sources*

Biology is the main origin of the mark metaphor. This principle is used by several insect species. The most known example is ants: each ant deposits slight

---

[1] There is nor real importance order neither obligation (*i.e.*, your problem may not contain every force hereby presented).

quantities of a chemical matter (called *pheromone*) which enables the agent to make a track of his path (external memory) and to point out his path to his congeners (communication and recruitment medium). Insects are not the only ones to use pheromones; some rodents, some felines, use them to mark their territory and the different functions places can have.

In fact, pheromones directly induce a specific behaviour for the individual perceiving them – it's a *reaction* with the sense used in the *reactive–cognitive* opposition encountered in the agent literature. Pheromones act in the same way the nervous system chemical transmitters, the hormones, do – whence the name *pheromone*.

The marking principle is widely spread out and more used as systems are more organised. As Guy Théraulaz noticed it in [12, p. 41], when there isn't much interaction in a group, qualitatively or quantitatively, there is little coordination between agents, little functional specialisation, and little social integration. The converse is also true: more there are interactions, more the group is a society, more it is organised.

The reader can refer to [12] for an introduction to artificial life and to the biological concepts included in the notion of collective intelligence.

Application to MAS...........................*Using the principle in MAS*

In [13], using the information theory developed by C. Shannon, [14], H. Van Dyke Parunak develops an entropy model for MAS interactions. The main idea is to integrate an entropy leak in the system. Indeed, as stands the Second Law of Thermodynamics, closed systems[2] tends to disorder. But the different natural observed and artificial built MAS examples have an efficient tendency to organise themselves. The explanation therefore is that some energy is added from the outside. Thus, for H. Van Dyke Parunak, agents organise themselves at the macro level because their actions are coupled to dissipation at the micro level. The entropy leak is organised from the macro level – which is the only place where the system's work is realised – to the micro level.

Agents produce energy they dissipate (directly exchanging it to each other or by the medium the environment is). This dissipation creates flow fields agents perceive and reinforce. The agents' behaviour is modified by those flow fields. The agents' actions decrease entropy while dissipation increases it, this leads to equilibrium.

If dissipation happens through the environment (the energy is represented by marks), agents belong to both macro and micro levels on the figure 2. If dissipation happens between agents (the energy is represented by a *currency*), then agents belong to the micro level and only the emergent structures belong to the macro level. H. Van Dyke Parunak gives the example of the economic market in which money benefits those who spend it, and spreads from buyers

---

[2] *I.e.* systems whose energetic cycle is closed, not oppositely to complex systems' openness. Thus, a system can be open – in the way it accepts interactions unknown at design time – and, at the same time, closed in a thermodynamic way, meaning that it evolves in an adiabatic enclosure.

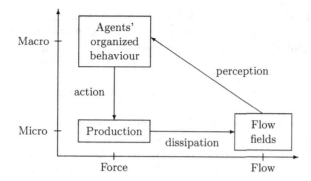

Fig. 2. Macro organisation through micro dissipation, [13, p. 21]

to sellers. Entrepreneurs perceive the money flow fields and orient themselves towards them. The result is self-organising structures such as supply chains and economic centres.

H. Van Dyke Parunak proposes three characteristics to this mechanism:

- It must circulate (either amongst agents, or in the environment), thus creating a gradient.
- Agents must be able to perceive this gradient and orient themselves to it.
- The agents' actions must reinforce the fields (positive feedback).

Usages . . . . *Utilisation examples*

Communication by marks and especially by pheromones has been studied in [15]. The results of a MAS composed by sorting robots communicating by the way of simple pheromones are compared to the same system in which agents can't communicate. The pheromones structure the space and the agents follow this structure to move the pheromones, then appears a virtuous circle that allows the MAS to sort the environment.

The marks model is used in Manta, the simulation of an ant-hill, developed in [16]. Here, the matter is to stick to the insect reality: ants have a reactive behaviour led by external and internal stimuli. External stimuli often are messages sent by other ants, they have a limited range and a strength (a weight) that decreases with the increase of the distance between the sender and the recipient. Those external stimuli represent identifying pheromones for various objects (eggs, larvae, ants, queen) and their states (hungry, full, . . .).

F. Kluegl *et al*, in [17], introducing trophallaxy (energy exchange between two ants) and tank-ants (full of honey ants serving for living tanks and for nodes in the communication and energy dissipation network), demonstrate the utility of introducing the notions of energy and of energy exchange in the system: the simulated ant-hill is more successful and have a more accurate behaviour. As another simulation, we will cite [18] where the introduction of a loss of sensibility in the agents' sensors after those sensors perceived an important pheromonal quantity leads to structuring the MAS simulated harvesting: depending on the used limits, the recruiting and (therefore) the ants' spatial distribution vary.

In [12, p. 216], Hugues Bersini, Pascale Kuntz, and Dominique Snyers develop the use of simple reactive agents using pheromonal marks to resolve a travelling salesman problem. This example shows the utility of the *Marks* pattern and the utility of MAS to resolve problems that have nothing to do with simulation or artificial life.

In [19], John H. Holland describes the tagging mechanism. This mechanism consists in having agents wearing signs provoking attraction or repulsion of other agents. While immunology is the source of his idea, he is here using the pheromonal identification function used by animals. This identification function can be extended to allow an agent to recognise another agent's function inside the group. We can also think about the use of uniforms and badges in human societies.

Pascal Ballet, in [20], uses the *Marks* pattern for its capability to structure the environment. In his application of MAS to edge recognition, each one of his agents increases the image local contrast; that makes, by the successive passing of other agents, the edges of the image appear. Each agent, modifying or not the environment the image is, implies a later modification by other agents; so, this creates a virtuous circle realising the MAS functionality. Pascal Ballet shows that the modification an agent makes must be limited to avoid too much noise.

Ndedi Monekosso and Paolo Remagnino, in [21], use pheromones to enhance the convergence rates of a multi-agent Q-learning algorithm. Using the Marks pattern allows the agents communicating, co-ordinating, and co-operating in learning, without heavy consequences on computational time. The agents have a belief factor for each mark they perceive, allowing them to better tune their reactive behaviour. As in the previous example, Monekosso and Remagnino show that a too low evaporation rate or a too high deposition rate lead to poorer results.

Therefore, we can find different functionalities for the marks used in computer applications. Marks serve to optimise the MAS, either allowing the system to save resources (the environment is used as a shared memory), or allowing the system to structure itself (Jacques Gervet uses the locution: "construction of a signifying structure" in [12, p. 133]).

This structuring can occur in the space: by segregation/identification, with Holland's tagging [19]; by the use of a gradient, in [15]; and by marking (limits and tracks), in [20,12,21,18]. It can also be organisational: by communication, in [16,18]; and, last but not least, by communication and entropy, with [13,17].

Solution .... *How to use this principle in MAS*

The agent deposits marks in the environment. These marks are low granularity objects (*i.e.*, at the implementation level, they are objects with a very simple structure) and with a quantum size: these objects have a minimal size, even no size at all; however, they have some strength (or are found in one place in some quantity) that allows the agent to *sense* their presence at a known distance. Once they are deposited, the environment takes care of their mutation: evaporation, dissemination/propagation, and perception.

Those marks are perceived in a limited zone: there are a perceptibility range and rules controlling the lowering of the perception quality with the distance between the agent and the marks. This range and these rules depend on the pheromone itself and on the environment topology. The perceptibility is, of course, also a matter of capabilities of the agent's sensors: some of these marks may not be accessible in the same way (quantitatively and qualitatively) to all the agents.

Besides, the *marks* allow the agents to communicate without message exchange: depositing some quantity of a known *mark* is a modification of the environment every agent perceives. It must be noticed that *marks* are simple objects, the base pattern does not handle the fact that agents deposit more evolved messages. This can be considered but it then will be a denaturing extension of the *Marks pattern*.

Implementation .... *Some implementation issues*

If the question is to have agents living in the real world (*e.g.* robots), therefore marks are slight quantities of a product that agents are able easily and distinctly to perceive. As Jacques Gervet said in [12, p. 142]: it's unlikely that a chemical matter be used, but one can use marks which will be easy to distinct and which will be persistent to their emission.

If the agents live in a simulated world, therefore the environment has to be pro-active to manage the marks' life-cycle: evaporation, dissemination (due to the wind, other agents' moves), masking (by other marks), disappearance (even removal).

The environment has to take over those marks, as it's the case in reality for the pheromones. A solution would be to simulate the pheromone evaporation by including a date into the structure representing the mark; the agent would use this date to decide if he perceives the pheromone. This solution is not conceptually acceptable because it moves the evaporation activity inside the agent whereas this activity intrinsically belongs to the agent's environment. Other similar solutions (*i.e.* inserting information in the marks' structure to let the agent decide of their perception) are no more acceptable, for the same reasons. The principle is to delegate to the environment all the undertakings of memorisation and life-cycle management of the marks.

Examination .... *Reasons to use this pattern*

There also are problems due to the use of this pattern, Alexis Drogoul, in [22], considers its implementation in a real world (that is, with robots) is not so easy: there are some troubles to find the good *product* – that implies troubles with the sensors, with their sensitivity and preciseness. That's true that sensors as sensitive as insects' ones are not yet available – we can note the innovating approach of Y. Kuwana *et al*, in [23], who successfully uses a butterfly antenna as a pheromone sensor for a little experimental robot. In another hand, as we emphasised it sooner, we don't have to use an as much subtle product as pheromones are, simple visual or magnetic marks suffice.

Concerning the difficulties of the simulation, the required memory and computational resources can't be neglected.

However, this pattern has plenty of advantages, in addition to resolving the constraints exposed in the section **Forces**. Marks are simple messages – as much by their form than by their handling – and the fact that they are deposited allows integrating a locality notion to the information they carry. Moreover, this integration is done in an indirect way for the agent: he does not need a coordinate system, marks are deposited where they have a signification. This lack of requirement for a coordinate system can be primeval for the agent; precise localisation needs complex positioning systems. Besides, the very concept of coordinates – even though it seems simple and *natural* in mathematics – is, at last, fairly complicated.

4   Conclusions

We have just presented a shortened version of the *Marks* pattern, a MAS pattern. This pattern is about a communication model (*without* message, or through the environment). A longer version of the *Marks* pattern can be found in [24] (in French). The agent patterns we are writing are presented and submitted to discussion on `http://www.smile.info.unicaen.fr/` sauvage.

Different works on agent patterns exist; some are interesting, as Kendall's, Deugo's, or Aridor's, [25,26,27,28], but it's a consideration not to limit the MAS application of the pattern technique to the simple use of patterns in a particular domain that MAS are. Indeed, some papers submit patterns presenting agents and agent techniques in an object-oriented way, *i.e.* as object techniques, leaving out the fact that agents are much more than objects – as we pointed out in this paper's introduction.

Indeed, we think that patterns can help to develop MAS, as much in analysis, design or implementation as in teaching and spreading of the agent paradigm.

We think that presenting as patterns the models and concepts of the MAS paradigm, as well as the techniques used to implement them, would enable us to structure, spread and constructively extend the knowledge of the agent paradigm we now have. Indeed, more than their *uniform* structure, patterns allow to understand more easily the concepts – for they emerge from experience and widely use examples, but also for they integrate theory to examples and they explain the conceptual reasons.

With these goals in mind, we are formalising several agent-oriented patterns that take up and expand agent models and techniques. We want to integrate those patterns in what is called a *pattern language* in the purpose of formalising the links that exist between the different patterns: co-operation, use, delegation, conflict, . . .

References

1. Cardon, A.: Modélisation des systèmes adaptatifs par agents : vers une analyse-conception orientée agents. Rapport de recherche, université Paris VI, LIP6 (1998)
2. Stinckwich, S.: Modèles organisationnels et réflexifs des architectures à objets concurrents. Implémentation en Smalltalk-80. Thèse de doctorat (informatique), université de Savoie, Chambéry–Annecy (France) (1994)
3. Agha, G.A., Jamali, N.: Concurrent Programming for DAI. In Weiß, G., ed.: Multiagent Systems — A Modern Approach to Distributed Artificial Intelligence. MIT Press, Cambridge, Massachussets (USA) (1999) 505–537
4. Iglesias, C.A., Garijo, M., González, J.C.: A Survey of Agent-Oriented Methodologies. In: Intelligent Agents V — proceedings of the Fifth International Workshop on Agent Theories, Architectures, and Languages, ATAL'98. Lecture Notes in Artificial Intelligence, Springer-Verlag, Heidelberg (Germany) (1998)
5. Gorodetski, V., Karsayev, O., Kotenko, I., Khabalov, A.: Software Development Kit for Multi-agent Systems Design and Implementation. In Dunin-Kęplicz, B., Nawarecki, E., eds.: Proceedings of the Second International Workshop of Central and Eastern Europe on Multi-Agent Systems, Kraków (Poland) (2001) (in this volume).
6. Oechslein, C., Kluegl, F., Herrler, R., Puppe, F.: UML for Behaviour-Oriented Multi-Agent Simulations. In Dunin-Kęplicz, B., Nawarecki, E., eds.: Proceedings of the Second International Workshop of Central and Eastern Europe on Multi-Agent Systems, Kraków (Poland) (2001) (in this volume).
7. Jennings, N.R.: Agent-Based Computing: Promise and Perils. In: IJCAI'99, Stockholm (Sweden), Springer-Verlag, Heidelberg (Germany) (1999) 1429–1436
8. Gamma, E., Helm, R., Johnson, R., Vlissides, J.: Design Patterns: Abstraction and Reuse of Object-Oriented design. In: Conférence ECOOP'93, Springer-Verlag, Heidelberg (Germany) (1993)
9. PLoP: http://st-www.cs.uiuc.edu/ plop. PLoP (Pattern Languages of Programs) conferences official page (1994–)
10. Simon, H.A.: Sciences des systèmes. Sciences de l'artificiel. Dunod, Paris (France) (1991) French translation by J.-L. Le Moigne.
11. Le Moigne, J.L.: Modélisation des systèmes complexes. Dunod, Paris (France) (1990)
12. Bonabeau, É., Theraulaz, G., eds.: Intelligence collective. Hermès, Paris (France) (1994)
13. Van Dyke Parunak, H.: "Go to the Ant": Engineering Principles from Natural Multi-Agent Systems. Annals of Operations Research (1997) 69–101
14. Shannon, C.E., Weaver, W.: The Mathematical Theory of Communication. University of Illinois Press (1949) Edition of 1998.
15. Booth, M., Stewart, J.: Un modèle de l'émergence de la communication. In: Premières journées francophones IAD & SMA, Hermès, Paris (France) (1993)
16. Drogoul, A.: De la simulation multi-agent à la résolution collective de problèmes. Une étude de l'émergence de structures d'organisation dans les SMA. Thèse de doctorat (informatique), université Paris VI (1993)
17. Kluegl, F., Puppe, F., Raub, U., Tautz, J.: Simulating Multiple Emergent Phenonema — Exemplified in an Ant Colony. In Adami, C., et al., eds.: Artificial Life VI, proceedings of the Sixth International Conference on Artificial Life, UCLA, California (USA) (1998)

18. Nakamura, M., Kurumatani, K.: Formation Mechanism of Pheromone Pattern and Control of Foraging Behavior in an Ant Colony Model. In Langton, C., Shimohara, K., eds.: Artificial Life v, proceedings of the Fifth International Workshop on the Synthesis and Simulation of Living Systems, Nara-Ken New Public Hall, Nara (Japan) (1996)

19. Holland, J.H.: Hidden Order — How Adaptation Builds Complexity. Addison Wesley, Reading, Massachussets (USA) (1995)

20. Ballet, P.: Intérêts mutuels des SMA et de l'immunologie — Application à l'immunologie, l'hématologie et au traitement d'images. Thèse de doctorat (informatique), université de Bretagne occidentale (France) (2000)

21. Monekosso, N., Remagnino, P.: Q-learning augmented with synthetic pheromones. In Dunin-Kęplicz, B., Nawarecki, E., eds.: Proceedings of the Second International Workshop of Central and Eastern Europe on Multi-Agent Systems, Kraków (Poland) (2001) (in this volume).

22. Drogoul, A., Fresneau, D.: Métaphore du fourragement et modèle d'exploitation collective de l'espace sans communication ni interaction pour des colonies de robots autonomes mobiles. In Barthès, J.P., Chevrier, V., Brassac, C., eds.: Systèmes multi-agents, de l'interaction à la socialité, JFIADSMA'98, Pont-à-Mousson (France), LORIA, université de Nancy 2, Hermès, Paris (France) (1998) 99–114

23. Kuwana, Y., Shimoyama, I., Sayama, Y., Miura, H.: A Robot that Behaves like a Solkworm Moth in the Pheromone Stream. In Langton, C., Shimohara, K., eds.: Artificial Life v, proceedings of the Fifth International Workshop on the Synthesis and Simulation of Living Systems, Nara-Ken New Public Hall, Nara (Japan) (1996)

24. Sauvage, S.: Patterns orientés SMA : le *pattern Marques*. In Ghédira, K., ed.: EcoIIA–01, École d'Intelligence Artificielle, Hammamet (Tunisia), URIASIS (2001) 176–187

25. Kendall, E.A., Malkoum, M.T., Jiang, C.H.: The Layered Agent Pattern Language. In: PLoP'97 (Pattern Languages of Programs), Allerton Park, Illinois (USA) (1997)

26. Deugo, D., Oppacher, F., Kuester, J., Von Otte, I.: Patterns as a Means for Intelligent Software Engineering. In: Proceedings of The International Conference on Artificial Intelligence (IC-AI'99), CSREA Press (1999) 605–611

27. Deugo, D., Kendall, E., Weiss, M.: Agent Patterns. http://www.scs.carleton. ca/ deugo/Patterns/Agent/Presentations/AgentPatterns (1999)

28. Aridor, Y., Lange, D.B.: Agent Design Patterns: Elements of Agent Application Design. In: Proceedings of Autonomous Agents'98, ACM Press (1998)

Multi-agent Architecture for Knowledge Fusion from Distributed Sources

Alexander Smirnov, Mikhail Pashkin, Nikolai Chilov, and Tatiana Levashova

St.Petersburg Institute for Informatics and Automation of the Russian Academy of Sciences
39, 14-th Line, 199178, St.-Petersburg, Russia
smir@iias.spb.su

Abstract. Current trends require using a global information environment (infosphere), including end-users and loosely coupled knowledge sources (experts, knowledge bases, repositories, documents, etc.), for decision-making. The vast diversity of the knowledge source management tools has made the problem of knowledge fusion from infosphere's distributed knowledge sources actual. Knowledge logistics as a new direction of knowledge management assumes presence of fusion processes. The paper is devoted to multi-agent architecture organisation principles and properties of the systems dealing with knowledge fusion from distributed knowledge sources.

1 Introduction

Rapid development of Internet has caused the huge amount of information about different problem areas to become available for users. Since the information is represented in various formats and by different tools, the problems of format compatibility, search tools implementation, recognition and fusion of knowledge from distributed sources/resources have become critical. The necessity of knowledge fusion (KF) approach development for global understanding of going on processes and phenomena, dynamic planning and global knowledge exchange has developed. The KF methodology is a new direction of knowledge management in the part of knowledge logistics.

In nowadays conditions knowledge is becoming an important resource. The main characteristics of it are the following: (i) knowledge is a critical source of long-term competitive advantage; (ii) knowledge is more powerful than natural resources; (iii) knowledge resource has cost, location, access time and life-time; (iv) knowledge worker is a owner of knowledge and a member of a team/group.

Related to this, along with development of computing machinery and information technologies, there arose a need of systems working with knowledge, i.e. dealing with knowledge creation, classification, synthesis, analysis, storage, search and mapping.

Intelligent agents are a very hot research topic that significantly changed the way distributed systems are working. An agent must represent its knowledge in the vocabulary of a specified ontology [1]. Multi-agent system technology can be considered as the basis for KF systems.

B. Dunin-Kęplicz and E. Nawarecki (Eds.): CEEMAS 2001, LNAI 2296, pp. 293–302, 2002.

2 Knowledge Fusion in Infosphere

Knowledge can be defined as a set of relations (constraints, functions, rules) by which a user/an expert decides how, why, where and what to do with the information to produce timely adaptive actions meeting a goal or a set of goals. *Knowledge Fusion* can be defined as integration of knowledge from loosely coupled sources into a combined resource in order to complement insufficient knowledge and obtaining new knowledge [2], [3], [4]. In other words, KF is an approach, based on synergistic use of knowledge from different sources. KF is integrated into an information environment for two principal areas: (i) customer KF supports traditional activities with on-line sources and uses a customer profiles, and (ii) KF portals support shared knowledge, an inventory management of the internal and external knowledge sources. The environment includes end-users/customers, loosely coupled knowledge sources /resources, and set of tools and methods for information processing [5], [6]. Network of loosely coupled sources located in the information environment is referred to as "Knowledge Source Network" (KSNet). KSNet life cycle consists of two major phases (Fig. 1): configuration of KSNet (preparation phase of the KF system life cycle) and design of KSFTree[1] (operation phase of the system life-cycle).

As a common model of knowledge representation ontologies [7] based on object-oriented constraint network paradigm are proposed. According to this knowledge can be defined as terms, objects, constraints, and methods that are assumed to exist in some area of interest. Main scheme of ontologies relations within the KSNet system are presented in Fig. 2. It includes the two phases of the system life cycle: (i) preparation phase related to application ontology creation, and (ii) operation phase related to user requests processing. Ontologies are shown as boxes. Top-level ontology defines general notation of knowledge representation (object-oriented constraint networks in KSNet). Constraint networks (shown as double-bordered boxes) are based on ontologies (schematic knowledge flows are shown as narrow arrows) and include some information contents (content knowledge flows are shown as wide arrows).

Since KF is a new research area, few works have been done in methodological aspects of this topic. Holsapple C. V. and Singh M. [8] suggest the most complete sequence of main operations for knowledge integration, referred to as knowledge chain. This offers a base for forming KF operations listed below.

- *Capturing knowledge* from knowledge sources and translation into a form, suitable for supplementary use:
- *Acquisition of knowledge* from external sources;
- *Selection of knowledge* from internal sources (local knowledge bases);
- *Knowledge generation*: producing knowledge by discovering or derivation from existing knowledge;

---

[1] Knowledge Source Fusion Tree. The KF system performs decomposition of the request into its components – subrequests and sends them to processing. During the process of identifying knowledge sources for the subrequests a KSFTree structure is defined. The root of this tree is the user request, the leafs are the knowledge sources and the nodes are the subrequests obtained during decomposition of the user request.

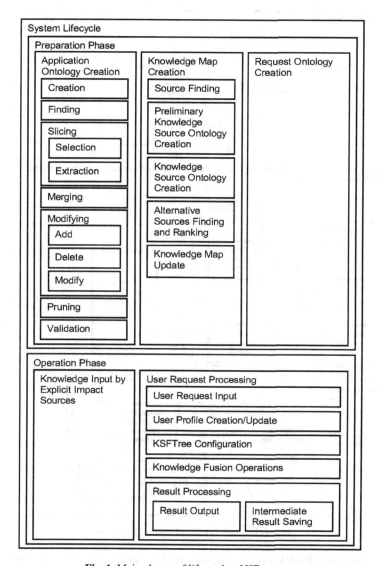

Fig. 1. Main phases of life cycle of KF systems

- *Internalization*: changing system knowledge by saving acquired, selected and generated knowledge;
- *Externalization*: embedding knowledge into system's output for release into the environment;
- *KF Management*: planning, coordination, collaboration, and control of operations constituting the process of KF.

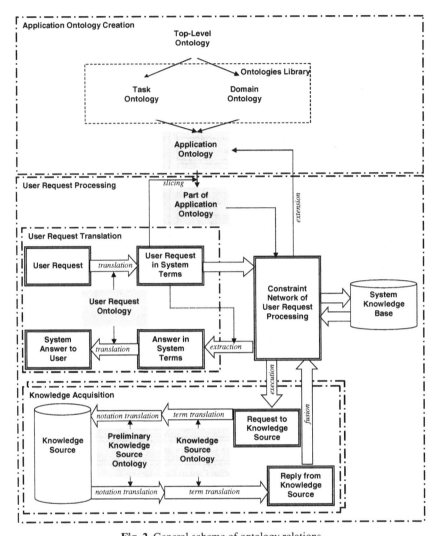

Fig. 2. General scheme of ontology relations

Comparison of the KF system described in the paper (called "KSNet") with some other existing systems/projects oriented on KF is presented in table 1 ([9], [10], [11], [12], [13], [14], [15]). These systems are:

- KRAFT (Knowledge Reuse and Fusion / Transformation) – multi-agent system for integration of heterogeneous information systems. The main aim of this project is to enable sharing and reuse of constraints embedded in heterogeneous databases and knowledge systems. It has hierarchy of shared ontologies for local resource ontology translation.

- InfoSleuth – multi-agent system for retrieving and processing information in a network of heterogeneous information sources.

Table 1. Comparison of some existing information fusion systems

Feature	InfoSleuth	KRAFT	KSNet
Project platforms	OKBC, JDBC. LISP, CLISP, LDL+, Java, C/C++, NetScape	KQML P/FDM, CoLan	RDF, ILOG, C++
Basic ontologies	Depends on application area	WordNet [16]	Depends on application area
User can choose ontology to work with	Yes	No	Yes
Ontology relationship	Meta Level Ontology for other ontologies translation	Hierarchy	Top Level Ontology for other ontologies creation and Application Ontology for other ontologies translation
Ontology-specification language	Initially - KIF and LDL+; currently – OKBC	P/FDM	RDF
Agent coordinator	Broker Agent	Facilitator	Facilitator
Main types of agents	Resource Agent (Wrapper in KRAFT), Broker Agent (Facilitator in KRAFT), TaskExecution Agent (Mediator in KRAFT), User Agent	Wrappers (interaction with sources), Facilitators ("yellow pages" directory service for the agents), Mediators (task execution control), User Agent (interaction with user)	Wrappers, Facilitators, Mediators, User Agent, Translation Agent and KF Agent (provide operation performance for KF), Configuration Agent (provides efficient use of knowledge source network), Ontology Management Agent (ontology operations), Monitoring Agent (knowledge source verifications).

3   Agent-Based Architecture for Knowledge Fusion Technology

The three infosphere components can be selected, for which agent types are to be defined: (i) users - knowledge consumers, (ii) KF system, (iii) knowledge sources.

User Agent is proposed be developed for working with user, knowledge consumer. According FIPA this is an agent interacting with a human being [17].

Knowledge sources can be divided into two groups: (i) *implicit impact sources* (knowledge bases, databases, repositories, etc.), which influence upon knowledge stored in the system indirectly and (ii) *explicit impact sources*, which can make changes to the system knowledge directly (experts, knowledge management tools). For interacting with implicit impact sources it is proposed to use a *Wrapper Agent,* an agent, which provides the FIPA-WRAPPER service to an agent domain on the Internet [17]. *Expert Assistant Agent* is proposed for interacting with experts.

According to FIPA standard it is necessary to develop the technological agents:

- *Facilitator* - Directory Facilitator – is an agent that provides a "yellow pages" directory service for the agents. It stores descriptions of the agents and the services they offer [17].
- *Mediator* – Information Broker Agent, which offers a set of communication facilitation services to other agents using some knowledge about the requirements and capabilities of those agents [17]. Mediator is proposed for task execution tracking inside the system.

Also, KF technologies require additional agents which can be defined as follows:

- *Translation agent* and *Knowledge Fusion Agent* provide operation performance for Knowledge Fusion;
- *Configuration Agent* supports effective use of knowledge sources.
- *Ontology Management Agent* provides ontology operation performance.
- *Monitoring Agent* reduces system failure probability by knowledge source verifications. Life cycle of KF systems consists of forming problem domain (preparation phase) and utilizing it with possible modification (operation phase). During the operation stage KF systems work in real-time mode. Accessibility and consistency of knowledge sources are the critical factors for them.

A major set of agents is represented in Fig. 3 according to described above principles and functions of KF system.

The list of some agent actions during user request processing is given below:

- *Mediator*: tracks out the process of user request processing; performs control for error, malfunction or failure occurrence; stores intermediate results of other agents.
- *Translation Agent*: checks user request for possibility of translation into system's terms, translates it, translates system's result into form, understandable by user.
- *Configuration Agent*: performs decomposition of the request into subrequests and identifies appropriate knowledge sources; configures knowledge sources; configures KSFTree; plans knowledge fusion.
- *Wrapper*: passes the request to the source; receives response from the source.
- *User Agent*: provides user interface; processes user profile.
- *Expert Assistant Agent*: provides user interface for expert knowledge input; performs User Agent's functions; performs actions of narrow-specialized Wrapper.
- *Facilitator*: provides internal system routing.
- *KF Agent*: negotiates with Configuration Agent about possibility of KF and selects fusion patterns; interact with Facilitator – informs it about expected availability/unavailability and possible changes; receives initial request from Mediator and results from different knowledge sources; performs fusion of received knowledge; validates new knowledge and checks it for relevance to the request; passes new knowledge to Monitoring agent for internal processing.

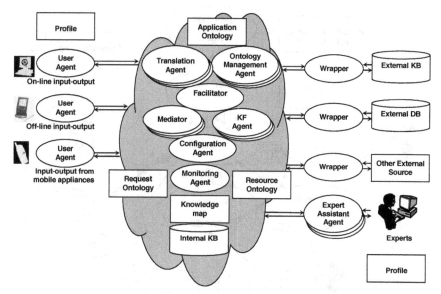

Fig. 3. Basic components of multi-agent environment of knowledge fusion system

- *Monitoring Agent*: updates knowledge map[2]; checks knowledge sources for their availability; checks knowledge sources for changes in their structure and contents; validates stored knowledge, checks it for redundancy; performs knowledge source ranking according to specified criteria.

4   Case Diagram of Major System Scenario

The procedure of user request processing for demonstration of cooperation between agents is described below. After the user has input a request into the system, request ontology is created as a result of translating request into the terms of application ontology. The request is decomposed into an ordered set of subrequests, knowledge for which can be found without any further decomposition. Subrequest processing consists of identifying suitable knowledge sources by the system, querying identified sources, filtering according to user-defined constraints, fusion of knowledge from different sources, validation, check for meeting requirements, presenting results to the user.

Fig. 4 represents Case-diagram of user request processing in the system according to multi-agent architecture. It represents the following scenario: (1) Mediator receives request from User Agent; (2) Mediator passes the request to Translation Agent for processing, Translation Agent and Ontology Management Agent (2.1) check it for possibility of translation into system's terms, translate it, create new request ontology; (3) Translation Agent returns translated request to

---

[2] Includes information about locations of KSNet units utilized during problem solving. It can also include information about alternate sources (KSNet units).

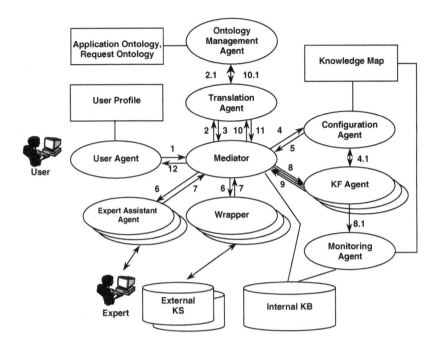

Fig. 4. Case diagram of user request processing

Mediator; (4) Mediator passes the request received from Translation Agent to Configuration Agent. Configuration Agent performs decomposition of the request into subrequests, identifies appropriate knowledge sources, configures KSFTree and plans KF by negotiating price, time, capabilities, etc. (4.1) with KF Agents and Wrappers; (5) Configuration Agent passes results of KSFTree configuration to Mediator; (6) Mediator passes subrequests to Wrappers and Expert Assistant Agents according to the KSFTree, performs control for error, malfunction or failure occurrence; (7) Wrappers translate the request into terms of knowledge sources (KS), pass the request to the KS, receive response from the KS, translate response into system's terms, returns result to Mediator. Expert Assistant Agents perform actions of narrow-specialized Wrapper, facilitates the process of expert knowledge input into the system; (8) Mediator passes results received from Wrappers to KF Agent. KF Agents performs fusion of received knowledge, validates new knowledge and checks it for relevance to the request, passes new knowledge to Monitoring agent (8.1) for internal processing. (9) Mediator receives and stores temporary results of KF. Steps (8) and (9) are repeated several times according to KSFTree structure. (10) Mediator passes result of KF to Translation Agent for processing, Translation Agent and Ontology Management Agent (10.1) translate system's result into form, understandable by user; (11) Translation Agent passes the results to Mediator. (12) Mediator passes the results to User Agent. User agent returns the results to the user, updates user profile.

Monitoring agent performs necessary changes in internal knowledge base[3] and knowledge map.

Mediator used for request processing is cloned when a request comes into the system and exists until the request processing is finished. The number of Mediators simultaneously existing in the system is limited by hardware resources only.

Legend for the case diagrams:
- Lines represent connections between internal information base components and agents.
- Unidirectional arrows marked with numbers represent sequential steps of scenario processing by Mediator and the steps numbers.
- Arrows marked with numbers containing points represent auxiliary operations of scenario processing without mediator. Agents do not wait for a response when arrow is unidirectional and wait for a response when it is bi-directional.
- Bi-directional arrows without numbers and text represent work with external knowledge sources.
- Facilitator is not presented in case-diagrams but it provides a "yellow pages" directory service for the agents.

5 Conclusion

Agent-based technology is the best basis for knowledge fusion since agents can act in distributed environment, independently from the user and use ontologies for knowledge representation and interchange. Utilizing intelligent agents increases system efficiency and interoperability.

Acknowledgements. The paper is due to the research carried out as a part of the Partner Project # 1993P funded by Air Force Research Laboratory at Rome NY, and as a part of the project # 4.4 of the research program # 18 of the Russian Academy of Sciences.

References

1. Huhns M.N., Stephens L.M. Multiagent Systems and Societies of Agents. *Multiagent systems: a Modern Approach to Distributed Artificial Intelligence* (ed. by G.Weiss). The MIT Press, Cambridge, Massachusetts, London, 2000. 79–120.
2. Waterson A., Preece A. Verifying Ontological Commitment in Knowledge-Based Systems. *Knowledge-Based Systems,* 1999. 12. 45–54.

---

[3] Used for storage and verification of knowledge, obtained as a result of knowledge fusion from available sources and/or from expert.

3. Preece F., Hui K., Gray A., Marti P., Bench-Capon T., Jones D., Cui Z. The KRAFT Architecture for Knowledge Fusion and Transformation. *Knowledge*-Based *Systems*, 2000. 13. 113–120.
4. Tsui E., Garner B. J. , Staab S. The Role of Artificial Intelligence in Knowledge Management. *Knowledge-Based Systems*, 2000. 13. 235–239.
5. Smirnov A.V. Rapid Knowledge Fusion into the Scalable Infosphere: A Concept and Possible Manufacturing Applications. *Proceedings of the International NAISO Congress on Information Science Innovations (ISI'2001), Symposium on Intelligent Automated Manufacturing (IAM'2001)*, Dubai, U.A.E., 2001.
6. Smirnov A.V. Knowledge Fusion in the Business Information Environment: Concept and Major Technologies. *The Proceedings of the 7th International Conference on Concurrent Enterprising (ICE'2001)*, Bremen, Germany, June, 2001. 273–276.
7. Smirnov A., Chandra C., Ontology-based Knowledge Management for Co-operative Supply Chain Configuration. *Proceedings of the 2000 AAAI Spring Symposium "Bringing Knowledge to Business Processes"*. Stanford, California: AAAI Press, 2000. 85–92.
8. Holsapple C. V., Singh M. The Knowledge Chain Model: Activities for Competitiveness. *Expert* System *with Applications*, 2001. 20. 77–98.
9. Aguirre J. L., Brena R., Cantu F.J. Multiagent-based Knowledge Networks. *Expert Systems with applications* 2001. 20. 65–75.
10. Gray P.M.D., Hui K., Preece A.D. Finding and Moving Constraints in Cyberspace. *AAAI-99 Spring Symposium on Intelligent Agents in Cyberspace*. Stanford University, California, USA. AAAI Press, 1999. 121–127.
11. Jacobs N., Shea R. The Role of Java in InfoSleuth: Agent-Based Exploitation of Heterogeneous Information Resources. Technical report, Microelectronics and Computer Technology Corporation, 1996.
12. Mena E., Kashyap V., Sheth A., Illarramendi A. Estimating Information Loss for Multi-ontology Based Query Processing. Proceedings of the 13th Biennial European Conference on Artificial Intelligence (ECAI'98), Workshop on Intelligent Information Integration (III98), Brighton, UK, 1998.
13. Nodine M. H., Unruh A. Facilitating Open Communicating in Agent Systems: the InfoSleuth Infrastructure. Technical Report MCC-INSL-056-97, Microelectronics and Computer Technology Corporation, Austin, Texas, 1997. 78759.
14. Tamma V. A. M., Vissler P. R. S. Integration of Heterogeneous Sources: Towards a Framework for Comparing Techniques. *Proceedings of the AI*IA '98 Workshop on Techniques for Organisation and Intelligent Access of Heterogeneous Information*, Padova, Italy, 1998. 89—93.
15. Visser P.R.S., Jones D.M., Beer M.D., Bench-Capon T.J.M., Diaz B.M., Shave M.J.R. Resolving Ontological Heterogeneity in the KRAFT project. *Proceeding of the International Conference On Database and Expert System Applications (DEXA-99)*. Florence, Italy, Springer-Verlag, LNCS, 1999.
16. WordNet - a Lexical Database for English. Princeton University. Princeton, NJ. http://cogsci.princeton.edu/~wn/
17. FIPA 98 Specification. Part 12 - Ontology Service. Geneva, Switzerland, Foundation for Intelligent Physical Agents (FIPA), 1998. Version 1.0. http://www.fipa.org

Universal Formal Model of Collective Intelligence and Its IQ Measure

Tadeusz Szuba

Department of Mathematics and Computer Science, Science College, Kuwait
University, P.O. Box 5969 Safat, 13060 KUWAIT.
szuba@mcs.sci.kuniv.edu.kw

Abstract. This paper presents proposal of a universal computational theory of
Collective Intelligence (CI),. The toll for formalization, analysis, and modeling is
a quasi-chaotic model of computations *RPP*. In the *RPP*, molecules *(CMs)* of
facts, rules, goals, or higher-level logical structures enclosed by membranes,
move quasi-randomly in structured *Computational _Space (CS)*. When *CMs*
rendezvous, an inference process can occur if and only if the logical conditions
are fulfilled. It is proposed that *Collective Intelligence* can be measured as
follows: 1) the mapping is done of a given structure of beings into the *RPP*; 2)
the beings and their behavior are translated into expressions of mathematical
logic, carried by *CMs*; 3) the goal(s) of the social structure is(are) translated into
N-Element Inferences (NEI); 4) the efficiency of the *NEI* is evaluated and given
as the *Intelligence Quotient of a _Social Structure (IQS)* projected onto *NEI*. *IQS*
is computed as a probability function over time, what implies various
possibilities, e.g.: to order social structures according to their *IQS*, to optimize
social structures with *IQS* as a quality measure, or even to compare single beings
with social structures. The use of probability allows estimation of *IQS* either by
simulation, or on the basis of analytical calculations.

1 Basic Concepts of Modeling Collective Intelligence

Formalization and availability of formal definition and computational model of
Collective Intelligence should create a real 'gate to a bonanza' of lucrative
applications, as well as to open new scientific horizons [12]. Just to mention:
optimization of business and commercial social structures, evaluation of collective
intelligence of bacterial colonies against new drugs, formal analysis of intellectual
performance of nations, and so on.

Many people believe that Collective Intelligence a priori represents a higher level
than that of the individual. In addition, in the past some more formal research
considerations have led scientists to this conclusion. An example is the conclusion of
A. Newell considered one of the "founders of Artificial Intelligence", who raised an
objection to the notion of *Collective Intelligence* [6], with the argument:
*"A social system, whether a small group or a large formal organization, ceases to
act, even approximately, as a single rational agent. This failure is guaranteed by the
very small communication bandwidth between humans compared with the large
amount of knowledge available in each human's head. Modeling groups as if they had
a group mind is too far from the truth to be useful scientific approximation very
often."*

B. Dunin-Kęplicz and E. Nawarecki (Eds.): CEEMAS 2001, LNAI 2296, pp. 303–312, 2002.
© Springer-Verlag Berlin Heidelberg 2002

It is a logical result of certain, a pre-assumed model of computations (Deterministic Turing Machine + von Neumann architecture) which can artificially impose such a fear.

It is a paradox that the evaluation of the *Collective Intelligence* of social structures can be easier than the evaluation of the intelligence of a single being.

Individual intelligence has only been evaluated on the basis of external results of behavior during a problem-solving process in real life or during IQ tests. Neuropsychological processes accompanying problem-solving in the brain are still very far from being observable [2]. As a result, it is necessary to create abstract models of brain activity based on neuropsychological hypotheses (e.g. Luria [2]), or to use computer-oriented models like Artificial Intelligence.

In contrast, many more elements of Collectively Intelligent activity can be observed, measured, and evaluated in a social structure. We can observe displacements and resultant actions of beings as well as exchange of information between beings (e.g. human language, the ant's pheromone communication system, the dance of honeybees to direct toward a source of honey, the crossover of genes between bacteria resulting in spreading specific resistance to antibiotics, etc. Individual intelligence and behavior is scaled down as a factor – to accidental, local, and probabilistic processes.

Our fundamental assumption is that <u>Collective Intelligence can be efficiently formalized and evaluated with the help of abstract chaotic models of computations, and statistical evaluation of the global behavior of beings in structured environments</u> [9], [10], [11], [12].

Underlying the design of the Random PROLOG Processor model of computations, and justifying its use for Collective Intelligence formalization and modeling are these basic observations:

- In a socially cooperating structure it is difficult to differentiate thinking from non-thinking beings (abstract logical beings must be introduced, e.g. messages).
- Observing a being's behavior in a social structure, we can sometimes extract, label, and even define rules that signal elements of social behavior, e.g. use of pheromones. However, real goals, methods, and interpretations (from the points of view of a being) are mainly hidden until a detailed research is done in the future. Thus it is convenient to use the mathematical logic of first order predicate calculus with PROLOG as its implementation model, to describe and simulate Collective Intelligence. This allows us to postpone an interpretation of the clauses that label given elements of social behavior. Another advantage is that in the simulation models based on PROLOG, all facts, rules, and goals can easily be run-time manipulated (using assert, retract commands).
- The individuals inside a social structure usually cooperate in chaotic, yet non-continuous ways. Even hostile behavior between some beings can increase, to some extent, the global Collective Intelligence of the social structure to which those hostile beings belong. In the social structure, beings move randomly because needs and opportunities of real life force them to do so. Inference processes are made randomly, most of which are not finished at all. This makes the similarity to Brownian movements almost striking, and suggests using quasi-Brownian movements [14] for modeling social structure behavior. Brownian movements are also fundamental to use as a data storage model in the RPP.
- Individual inferences are also accidental and chaotic.

- Resources for inference are distributed in space, time, and among beings.
- Facts, rules, and goals may create inconsistent interleaving systems. Thus, multiple copies of facts, rules, and goals are allowed.
- The probability of whether the problem will be solved over a certain domain of problems must be used as an IQ measure for the social structure. If we want to evaluate Collective Intelligence, most of the concepts of human IQ tests must be redefined. Usually, they are matched to the human culture, perception, communication, problem solving, and answer synthesis. Thus it is necessary to propose a concept for testing for Collective Intelligence which is absolutely independent from the mental, cultural and perception point of view. This condition fulfills the efficiency of the N-element inference, with separately given interpretations of all formal elements of the test into real inferences or a production process. Precise definition will be given later on, but now we can simply say that it is a net of N-inferences of the form $a_1 \wedge a_2 \wedge ... \wedge a_n \rightarrow b_1 \wedge b_2 \wedge ... \wedge b_m$ with well-defined starting facts and goals. N-element inference can be interpreted as:

  a) any problem-solving process in a social structure, or inside a brain of a single being, where N-inferences are necessary to get a final result, or
  b) any production process, where N-technologies/elements have to be found and unified into one final technology or product.

In the same uniform way with the above concept we can model inferring processes within a social structure, as well as production processes. This is very important because some inference processes can be observed only through resultant production processes, e.g. ants gathering to transport a heavy prey.

Separating N-element inference from interpretation allows us among other things, to test the intelligence of ants through building for them the *test environment* where the sole solution is known to us as a given N-element inference. Observing how ants solve such a problem, we can later on estimate their intelligence. In general, this approach allows us to analyze the intelligence of beings without contacting them, through mapping their behavior into a formal system of logic formulas of facts, rules, goals, and later on through analysis of the dynamics of inference in such a system.

2.1   The Random PROLOG Model of Computations

Upon observing the social structures of humans, it is difficult to separate messages from message-processing agents. The same agent can be the processor, the message carrier, and the message, from the point of view of different parallel-running processes. Thus, as emphasized before, a mathematical logic based representation is necessary for analysis, separate from interpretation. The concept of PROLOG seems to fulfill the requirements. Without changing the PROLOG dialect, it is easy to adopt a molecular model of computations, as has been done in the *RPP*.

2.1.1 Clauses and Computational PROLOG Space in the RPP

The 1st level CS with inside quasi-random traveling CMs of facts, rules, and goals c_i is denoted as the multiset $CS^1 = \{c_1, ..., c_n\}$. The clauses of facts, rules, and goals are themselves 0-level CS. For a given CS, we define a membrane similar to the Chemical Abstract Machine [1] denoted by $|\cdot|$ which encloses inherent facts, rules, and goals. It is obvious that $CS^1 = \{c_1, ..., c_n\} \equiv \{|c_1, ..., c_n|\}$. For a certain kind of membrane $|\cdot|$ its type p_i is given, which will be denoted $|\cdot|_{p_i}$ to define which CMs can pass through it. Such an act is considered Input/Output for the given CS with a given $|\cdot|$. It is also allowable in the RPP to define degenerated membranes marked with $\cdot|$ or $|\cdot$ i.e. the collision-free (with membrane) path can be found going from exterior to interior of an area enclosed by such a membrane, for all types of CMs. The simplest possible application of degenerated membranes is to make, e.g. streets or other boundaries. If the CS contains clauses as well as other CSs, then it is considered a higher order one, depending on the level of internal CS. Such internal CS will be also labeled with $\hat{v}_j$ e.g.

$$CS^2 = \{|c_1, ...CS^1_{\hat{v}_j}, ...c_n|\} \quad iff \quad CS^1_{\hat{v}_j} \equiv \{|b_1, ..., b_n|\}$$

$$where \quad b_i \quad i = 1...m \quad and \quad c_j \quad j = 1...n \quad are \quad clauses$$

Every c_i can be labeled with $\hat{v}_j$ to denote characteristics of its individual quasi-random displacements. The general practice will be that higher level CSs will take fixed positions, i.e. will create structures, and lower level CSs will perform displacements. For a given CS there is a defined position function pos:

$$pos: O_i \rightarrow \langle position\ description \rangle \cup undefined \quad where \quad O_i \in CS$$

If there are any two internal CS objects O_i, O_j in the given CS, then there is a defined distance function $D(pos(O_i), pos(O_j)) \rightarrow \Re$ and a rendezvous distance d. We say that during the computational process, at any time t or time period Δt, two objects O_i, O_j come to rendezvous iff $D(pos(O_i), pos(O_j)) \leq d$. The rendezvous act will be denoted by the rendezvous relation $\circledR$, e.g. $O_i \circledR O_j$ which is reflexive and symmetric, but not transitive. For another definition of rendezvous as the λ-operator, see [3]. The computational PROLOG process for the given CS is defined as the sequence of frames F labeled by t or Δt, interpreted as the time (given in standard time units or simulation cycles) with a well-defined *start* and *end*, e.g. $F_{t_0}, ..., F_{t_e}$. For every frame its multiset $F_j \equiv (|c_1, ..., c_m|)$ is explicitly given, with all related specifications: $pos(.)$, membrane types p, and movement specifications v if available. The simplest case of CS for the RPP used in our simulations is the 3-D cube with randomly traveling clauses of facts, rules, and goals inside. The RPP is initialized to start the inference process after the set of clauses, facts, rules, and goals (defined by the programmer) is injected into this CS. More advanced examples of the CS for the

RPP include a single main CS^2 with a set of internal CS^1 which take fixed positions inside CS^2, and a number of CS^0 who are either local for a given CS^1_i (because the membrane is not transparent for them) or global for any subset of $CS^1_j \in CS^2$.

When modeling the CI of certain closed social structures, interpretations in the structure will be given for all CS^m_n, i.e. "this CS is a message"; "this is a single human"; "this is a village, a city", etc. The importance of properly defining $\hat{v}_j$ for very CS^i_j should be emphasized.

As has been mentioned, the higher level CS^i_j will take a fixed position to model substructures like villages or cities. If we model a single human as CS^1_j, then $\hat{v}_j$ will reflect displacement of the human. Characteristics of the given $\hat{v}_j$ can be purely Brownian or can be quasi-random, e.g. in lattice, but it is profitable to subject it to the present form of CS^i_j. When $\hat{v}_j$ has the proper characteristics, there are the following essential tools:

The goal clause, when it reaches the final form, can migrate toward the defined *Output* location. This can be a membrane of the main CS or even a specific, local CS. Thus the appearance of a solution of a problem in the CS can be observable.

Temporarily, the density of some CMs can be increased in the given area of CS in such a way that after the given low-level CS^i_j reaches the necessary form, it migrates to specific area(s) to increase the speed of selected inferences in some areas.

2.1.2 The Inference Model in the RPP

The pattern of inference in Random PROLOG generalized for any CS has the form:

DEFINITION 1. GENERALIZED INFERENCE IN CS^N

Assuming that $CS = \{...CS^i_j...CS^k_l...\}$, on this basis we can define:

CS^i_j ® CS^k_l and $U(CS^i_j, CS^k_l)$ and C(one or more CS^m_n of conclusions) $\vdash$

───

one or more CS^m_n of conclusions, $R(CS^i_j$ or $CS^k_l)$ ∎

The above description should be interpreted as follows:

CS^i_j ® CS^k_l denotes rendezvous relation

$U(CS^i_j, CS^k_l)$ denotes that unification of the necessary type can be successfully applied;

C(*one or more* CS^m_n *of conclusions*) denotes that CS^m_n are satisfiable;

Notice that the reaction → in *cham* semantics is equivalent to inference • here.

$R(CS^i_j$ or $CS^k_l)$ denotes that any parent CMs are retracted if necessary.

The standard PROLOG inferences are simple cases of the above definition. Later on, when discussing N-element inference, we will be only interested in "constructive" inferences, i.e. when a full chain of inferences exists. Thus the above diagram will be abbreviated as $CS_j^i ; CS_l^k \xrightarrow{RPP} \sum_n CS_n^m$ without mentioning the retracted CMs

given by $R(CS_j^i$ or $CS_l^k)$. In general, successful rendezvous can result in the "birth" of one or more child CMs. All of them must then fulfill a $C(...)$ condition; otherwise, they are aborted. Because our proposed RPP is designed to evaluate the inference power of closed social structures, simplifying assumptions based on real life observation can be made. It is difficult to find cases of direct rendezvous and inference between two CS_i^m and CS_j^n if $m, n \geq 1$ without an intermediary involved

CS_k^0 $k = 1,2...$ (messages, pheromones, observation of behavior, e.g. the bee's dance, etc.). Only if we consider CS^n on the level of whole nations, where mutual exchange (migration) of humans takes place, can such a case be considered an approximation to such higher level rendezvous and inferences. This is, however, just approximation, because finally this exchange is implemented at the level of personal contact of humans, which are just rendezvous and inferences of two CS_i^0 and CS_j^0

with the help of CS_k^0 $k = 1,2...$ In this paper, we only make use of a single CS_{main}^n for $n > 1$ as the main CS. Single beings like humans or ants can be

represented as $CS_{individual}^1$. Such beings perform internal inferences (in their brains), independently of higher level, cooperative inferences inside CS_{main} and exchange of messages of the type CS^0. It will be allowable to have internal CS^k inside the main CS, but only as static ones (taking fixed positions) to define sub-structures such as streets, companies, villages, cities, etc. For simplicity, however, we will try to approximate beings as CS^0; otherwise, even statistical analysis would be too complicated. It is also important to assume that the results of inference are not allowed to infer between themselves after they are created. Products of inference must immediately disperse; however, later, inferences between them are allowed (in [4] is called *refraction*).

2.1.3 Basic Properties of the Random PROLOG Processor

A brief summary of the most important properties of the RPP model of computations includes the following:
- In the *RPP* it is possible to implement more inference patterns than in standard PROLOG, i.e. concurrent forward, backward, and rule-rule inferences.
- Parallel threads of inferences can be run at the same time in the RPP.
- Parallelism of multiple inference diagrams highly compensates for the low efficiency of the random inference process.
- *Information_molecules* infer randomly and are independent, which implies full parallelism.

3   Formal Definition of the Collective Intelligence Measure

The two basic definitions for modeling and evaluating *Collective Intelligence* have
the form:

DEFINITION 2: N-ELEMENT INFERENCE IN CS^N

There is a given *CS* at any level $CS^n = \left\{ CS_1^{a_1}, ...CS_m^{a_m} \right\}$, and an allowed set of

Inferences *SI* of the form $\{$set of premises $CS\} \xrightarrow{\; I_j \;} \{$set of conclusions $CS\}$, and
one or more CS_{goal} of a goal.

We say that $\left\{ I_{a0}, ..., I_{a_{N-1}} \right\} \subseteq SI$ is an N-element inference in CS^n, if for all

$I \in \left\{ I_{a0}, ..., I_{a_{N-1}} \right\}$ the premises $\in$ present state of CS^n at the moment of firing this

inference, all $\left\{ I_{a0}, ..., I_{a_{N-1}} \right\}$ can be connected into one tree by common conclusions and

premises, and $CS_{goal} \in \left\{ set \text{ of conclusions for } I_{a_{N-1}} \right\}$.   ■

DEFINITION 3: *COLLECTIVE INTELLIGENCE* QUOTIENT (IQS)

IQS is measured by the probability *P* that after time *t*, the conclusion CM_{goal} will be
reached from the starting state of CS^n, as a result of the assumed N-element inference.
This is denoted $IQS = P(t, N)$.   ■

The above two definitions fulfill all the basic requirements for evaluating
Collective Intelligence mentioned in our discussion before, requiring that:
N-element inference must be allowed to be interpreted as any problem-solving
process in a social structure or inside a single being, where N inferences are necessary
to get a result, or any production process, where N-technologies/elements have to be
found and unified into one final technology or product.
1. Simulating N-element inference in the *RPP* must allow easily to model the
   distribution of inference resources between individuals, dissipation in space or
   time, or movements (or temporary concentration) in the *CS*.
2. With this benchmark, cases can be simulated very easily, where some elements of
   the inference chain are temporarily not available, e.g. the chain of inference can be
   temporarily broken, but at a certain time *t*, another inference running in the
   background or in parallel will produce the missing components. Such situations
   are well known in human social structures, e.g. when a given research or
   technological discovery is blocked until missing theorems or sub-technology is
   discovered.
3. Humans infer in all directions: forward, backward, and also through
   generalization. The N-element inference simulated in the *RPP* reflects all these
   cases clearly.

The proposed theory of Collective Intelligence allows us surprisingly easily to give
formal definitions of the properties of social structures, which are obvious in real life.
Let's look at some of them:

Let there be given social structures S_a and S_b, which are characterized by IQS expressions $P_{S_a}(t, N)$, $P_{S_b}(t, N)$.

DEFINITION 4: LEVELS OF COLLECTIVE INTELLIGENCE.
Social structure S_a is said to represent a higher level of social intelligence than the compared social structure S_b which is denoted

$$S_a \overset{IQS}{\triangleright} S_b \quad iff \quad \forall_{t,N} \left(P_{S_a}(t, N) \geq P_{S_b}(t, N) \right). \qquad ■$$

DEFINITION 5: SPECIALIZATION OF SOCIAL STRUCTURES.
Social structure S_a is said to represent a higher level of specialization in a given domain D than the compared social structure S_b which is denoted

$$S_a \overset{IQS}{\underset{D}{\triangleright}} S_b \quad iff \quad \forall_{t,N} \left(P_{S_a}(t, N) \geq P_{S_b}(t, N) \right) \ such \quad that \ N - step \text{ inference is taken}$$

from domain D.

$$■$$

Example: A social structure of musicians compared to one of non-musicians.

THEOREM 1. INDIVIDUAL VERSUS SOCIAL STRUCTURE (WITHOUT PROOF).

Let I denote individual, and S denote social structure such that $I \notin S$. The new social structure $S' \equiv \left\{ S \overset{inc+}{\cup} I \right\}$, which emerged after *positive inclusion* (denoted by operator $\overset{inc+}{\cup}$) of I into S, represents a higher level of intelligence than I does i.e. $S' \overset{IQS}{\triangleright} \{I\}$. $\qquad ■$

DEFINITION 6: EQUIVALENCE OF SOCIAL STRUCTURES OVER DOMAIN D.
Social structures S_a and S_b are said to be equivalent in given domain D which is denoted

$$S_a \overset{IQS}{\underset{D}{\equiv}} S_b \quad iff \quad cardinal \text{ numbers } are\ equal\ n(D_a) = n(D_b)$$

$$where\ D_a, D_b \in D$$

$$and\ N - step \text{ inference } belongs\ to\ D_a\ iff\ \forall_{t,N} \left(P_{S_a}(t, N) \geq P_{S_b}(t, N) \right)$$

$$and\ respectively,$$

$$N - step \text{ inference } belongs\ to\ D_b\ iff\ \forall_{t,N} \left(P_{S_a}(t, N) \leq P_{S_b}(t, N) \right)$$

$$■$$

4 Conclusions

The proposed computational model of *Collective Intelligence* based on the chaotic (Brownian) nature of social structures and logic programming, which results in the concept of a *Collective Intelligence* measure (IQS), is developing surprisingly well, both from a theoretical as well as from a practical point of view. It is noted that:

- This proposed model is not contradictory to what are now used in psychometrics as human IQ tests. Our theory assumes that an intelligence measure for a certain problem or class of problems is a probability curve over an assumed time period. Thus human IQ tests should be (theoretically) only repeated more times to estimate probability for a representative number of sample t_i, to generate a proper curve over time. However, for a single human if the same test is repeated many times, to get probability results for different time limits, the test will be seriously affected by the effect of learning, and the human will be seriously exhausted with the test, which also can affect the results.

- The concept of IQS proposed by this theory easily allows comparison of the *Intelligence* of a single being against the *Collective Intelligence* of a social structure. The same problem can be given to the being alone, and later on to the social structure. Finally, only curves $P(t, N)$ are compared, to see who is more intelligent for given time t.

- We can compare different beings, e.g. the *Collective Intelligence* of ants against the intelligence of a single human, under the condition that we manage to find the same problem used to be solved daily by both "species". In the case of ants and humans it is possible, because, e.g. the Hamiltonian Cycle problem can be given to both ants as a foraging problem, as well as to humans as a maze test.

The prevalent theory of group dynamics [5], [7] of humans provides results of experiments and analyses which almost perfectly fit the simulation results of the RPP for analyzing the *Collective Intelligence* problem. For some cases simulations have been done, and the most interesting results are mentioned below. Every such experiment requires a multiprocessor computer, like our 8-processor SGI. For example, the following properties of social structures can be explained as optimization of IQS (see [10]):

PHENOMENON 1: A CITY IN A SOCIAL STRUCTURE OPTIMIZES IQS BY A FACTOR OF NEARLY 10 TIMES !

PHENOMENON 2: AN INCREASE OF ABILITY TO TRAVEL/COMMUNICATE OPTIMIZES IQS LINEARLY

PHENOMENON 3: A SOCIAL STRUCTURE IS ABLE TO INFER EFFICIENTLY IN LOGICALLY INCONSISTENT ENVIRONMENTS WHICH CONFIRMS OBSERVATIONS[1]

It should be mentioned at the end, that the above presented formal theory of *Computational Collective Intelligence* provides not only a clear perspective for *Collective Intelligence Engineering*, which is well presented in the book [12], but also provides some astonishing conclusions in other disciplines, e.g. on relations between Life, Intelligence and Evolution (see [13]).

---

[1] "Small groups produce more and better solutions to a problem than do individuals". (Shaw 1971)

References

1. Berry G., Boudol G.: The chemical abstract machine, Theoretical Computer Science, 217-248, 1992.
2. Das J. P., Naglieri J. A., Kirby J. R.: *Assessment of cognitive processes (the PASS theory of Intelligence),* Allyn and Bacon, 1994.
3. Fontana W., Buss L. W.: The arrival of the fittest. Bull. Math. Biol. 56, 1994
4. Giarratano J., Riley G.: *Expert Systems,* PWS Pub, II ed, 1994.
5. Johnson D.W., Johnson F.P.: *Joining Together – Group theory and group skills,* 7th ed, Allyn and Bacon, 1997.
6. Newell A.: Unified theories of cognition. Harvard University Press. 1990.
7. Shaw M. E.: *Group Dynamics,* IV ed, McGraw-Hill, 1971.
8. Szuba T., Stras R.: Parallel evolutionary computing with the Random PROLOG Processor. Journal on Parallel and Distributed Computing. Special Issue on Parallel Evolutionary Computing, 47, 78-85, 1997
9. Szuba T.: Random parallelisation of computations in the Random PROLOG Processor. Kuwait Journal of Science and Engineering, Topical Issue No 1. 1996.
10. Szuba T., Stras A.: On evaluating the inference power of closed social structures with the help of the Random PROLOG Processor. PAP'97 "Practical Applications of PROLOG", London, April 21-24, 1997.
11. Szuba T., Stras R.: Parallel evolutionary computing with the Random PROLOG Processor, Journal of Parallel and Distributed Computing, 47, 78-85 (1977).
12. Szuba T.: Computational Collective Intelligence. Wiley and Sons NY. 2001, Wiley Book Series on Parallel and Distributed Computing.
13. Szuba T.: "Was there Collective Intelligence Before Life on Earth? (Considerations on the Formal Foundations of Intelligence, Life and Evolution)". Accepted for World Futures - The Journal of General Evolution. Gordon and Breach Publishing.
14. Whitney C. A.: Random processes in physical systems: An introduction to probability-based computer simulations, Wiley & Sons, 1990.

A Programming Language for Coordinating Group Actions

Wieke de Vries[1], Frank S. de Boer[1,4], Koen V. Hindriks[2], Wiebe van der Hoek[1,3], and John-Jules C. Meyer[1]

[1] Utrecht University, Institute of Information and Computing Sciences
P.O. Box 80089, 3508 TB Utrecht, The Netherlands
tel. +31-30-2534432
{wieke, frankb, wiebe, jj}@cs.uu.nl
[2] Accenture, Apollolaan 150
P.O. Box 75797, 1070 AT Amsterdam, The Netherlands
tel. +31-6-22546472
koen.hindriks@accenture.com
[3] Department of Computer Science, University of Liverpool,
Liverpool, United Kingdom
[4] National Research Institute for Mathematics and
Computer Science (CWI), Amsterdam, The Netherlands

Abstract. Coordination and cooperation are crucial notions in multi-agent systems. We provide a constraint programming language called GrAPL, with facilities for group communication, group formation and group collaboration. GrAPL includes three novel statements. Two of these enable groups of agents to communicate about possible constraints on a specific action they might do together. If the demands of the agents are compatible, the group reaches an agreement regarding future executions of the action discussed. The third statement is synchronised action execution. Groups of agents can perform an action together, as long as their constraints on the action are satisfied.

1 Introduction

In this article, we introduce a constraint programming language for multi-agent systems with facilities for group communication, group formation and group collaboration. The language is called GrAPL, which abbreviates Group Agent Programming Language. In GrAPL coordination and cooperation, which are crucial notions in multi-agent systems, are modelled by means of formally defined primitives for dynamic group communication and synchronisation. Existing agent theories logically describe mental attitudes held by groups of agents, like joint beliefs and intentions [8]. Also, theories about commitments are proposed to formalise group agreements on future actions of the agents [4,10]. But in agent-oriented programming languages, formally defined statements for group communication and synchronisation are novel.

The language GrAPL fits in the tradition of the programming languages ACPL [1] and 3APL [6]. Each of these languages focuses on a different aspect of agency: ACPL contains statements for agent communication, 3APL focuses on the internal practical

B. Dunin-Kęplicz and E. Nawarecki (Eds.): CEEMAS 2001, LNAI 2296, pp. 313–321, 2002.
© Springer-Verlag Berlin Heidelberg 2002

reasoning of agents trying to reach their goals, and GrAPL offers primitives for group formation and group action. Though the design of GrAPL is similar to that of the other two languages, GrAPL offers functionality not present in 3APL (which is mainly single-agent oriented) and ACPL (which isn't focused at coordinating actions). GrAPL is not meant to be yet another agent programming language; ultimately, we aim at a language incorporating all aspects of agency. Therefore, we don't devote attention to action effects on the environment and agent beliefs, as this is already covered in 3APL.

GrAPL is based on the paradigm of constraint-based reasoning which enjoys much interest in artificial intelligence because it has proven to be a powerful method for solving complex problems like planning, resource allocation and scheduling. Our language can be implemented on top of a *constraint solver* [13], which finds a consistent assignment of the action parameters satisfying the constraints of the group of agents. GrAPL incorporates ideas from constraint programming [12] to enable agents to produce and query constraints on group actions. While in constraint programming there usually is one global store, in GrAPL each agent has a local constraint store for each action.

Another inspiration for GrAPL comes from synchronisation mechanisms in concurrent programming, more specifically from synchronous communication in CSP [7]. In this language, synchronous communication is used to communicate values. The principles of communication in GrAPL are similar, although communication is not bilateral but multilateral, and formulas are communicated instead of values. By using established ideas from concurrent programming and constraint solving, we hope to prevent reinventing the wheel. Although multi-agent systems have their unique features, many aspects of agents have been studied in other fields of computer science, and results can be adapted to fit multi-agent systems.

In GrAPL, agents synchronously communicate in order to dynamically form groups which synchronise on certain actions. The agents negotiate about constraints on these group actions. The constraints are logical formulas, prescribing properties of the action parameters, e.g., the time and place of a meeting. Subsequently, several agents can synchronously execute the action, obeying the constraints. In this short paper, we present the syntax of GrAPL and demonstrate the usefulness of the new programming constructs. Full formal details, including the operational semantics, can be found in [14].

In Section 2 we introduce the syntax of GrAPL. In Section 3, we illustrate the new features of GrAPL in an extensive example. Section 4 concludes this paper.

2   Syntax

The sets underlying GrAPL are:

- $\mathcal{A}$ = the set of atomic actions. Typical elements are a and b. Each action has an arity, which is the number of parameters it takes.
- $\mathcal{I}$ = the set of agent identities. Typical elements are i and j.
- $\mathcal{V}$ = the set of variables. There are two kinds of variables; $\mathcal{V} = \mathcal{LV} \cup \mathcal{GV}$. Here, $\mathcal{LV}$ are local variables. Each agent has its own local variables. $\mathcal{GV}$ are the global variables, defined as $\mathcal{GV} = \{v_k | k \in \mathbb{N}\} \cup \{g\}$.

Global variables are used in communication and group action, which naturally involve a number of agents, while local variables are used for processing information only relevant to one agent. Above, we attributed disjoint sets of local variables to all agents. This prevents name clashes, which could occur during synchronised action.

$\mathcal{GV}$ is the set of all variables v_i and g. This choice of global variables suffices for GrAPL, because the only global activities, group communication and group action, involve constraints on action parameters. We refer to these parameters in a uniform manner. We call the formal parameters of an action a $v_1, v_2, \ldots, v_k$ if the arity of a is k. The implicit formal parameter for the group performing the action is g. To avoid confusion, global variables are only allowed in constraints, and in no other place in the program. All agents use the same set of global variables to refer to formal parameters of a range of actions. Constraints are always specified relative to an action, so the global variables have an unambiguous meaning. Also, global variables are never bound to values, so there can be no value clashes between agents. Thus, $\mathcal{GV}$ exactly contains the variables needed to work with constraints. We chose to introduce special global constraint variables because it simplifies communicating about action parameters, as all agents always use a fixed variable name to refer to a parameter of an action.

GrAPL makes use of a multi-sorted predicate logical language $\mathcal{L}$. Each agent possesses a *belief base*; this contains closed formulas (no free variables) from $\mathcal{L}$. The constraints on actions are also formulas from $\mathcal{L}$, prescribing properties of action parameters. Each agent locally stores the present constraint for each action. We use φ and ψ to denote arbitrary formulas from $\mathcal{L}$ and $\top$ and $\bot$ to denote the formulas that are always true and false, respectively. We denote the set of variables in an expression w by $var(w)$.

To exemplify the use of $\mathcal{L}$, we give a constraint on the action MoveObject(v_1, v_2, v_3). Here, the first formal parameter is the object to be moved, the second parameter is the original location of the object and the third parameter is its destination location. The constraint distance$(v_2, v_3) \geq 20 \rightarrow (v_2 = \text{Utrecht} \wedge \text{Max} \notin g) \vee \#(g) > 5$ states that when the distance an object has to moved over is 20 or more, the agent having this constraint only agrees to help if there are at least five agents cooperating or if the moving starts in Utrecht and the agent doesn't have to cooperate with Max.

We denote the set of agent programs by $\mathcal{P}$. In order to define this set, we first define the set of *basic statements* $\mathcal{S}$.

DEFINITION 1 (Basic statements)

The set $\mathcal{S}$ of basic statements is the smallest set containing:

- skip
- $?\varphi$, where $\varphi \in \mathcal{L}$ and $var(\varphi) \cap \mathcal{GV} = \varnothing$.
- $?(\varphi, \text{a})$, where $\varphi \in \mathcal{L}$ and $\text{a} \in \mathcal{A}$.
- ins(φ), where $\varphi \in \mathcal{L}$ and $var(\varphi) \cap \mathcal{GV} = \varnothing$.
- CommGroupAdd(φ, a), where $\text{a} \in \mathcal{A}$ and $\varphi \in \mathcal{L}$.
- CommGroupReset(φ, a), where $\text{a} \in \mathcal{A}$ and $\varphi \in \mathcal{L}$.
- $\text{a}(t_1, \ldots, t_k)$, where $\text{a} \in \mathcal{A}$, the arity of a is k and all t_i are terms of $\mathcal{L}$, such that for all $i \in \{1, \ldots, k\} : var(t_i) \cap \mathcal{GV} = \varnothing$.

The language includes a statement for doing nothing, skip. There are two kinds of tests, namely tests of the belief base (simply denoted $?\varphi$) and tests of the constraint on an action (denoted by $?(\varphi, \mathsf{a})$). These tests check whether the formula φ is logically entailed by the belief base or the current constraint on a, respectively. Both tests can yield values for variables. The statement $\mathsf{ins}(\varphi)$ adds the information φ to the belief base, if φ is consistent with the belief base. As global variables are only used in constraint handling, they are forbidden in formulas tested on and inserted into the belief base, and also in actual action parameters. This way, we maintain a clear separation between global and local processing, which adds clarity and elegance. In tests of actions, we do allow global variables, as the constraint on the action can contain global variables. For example, the test $?(v_1 = 10, \mathsf{a})$ tests whether the constraint on a implies that the first parameter of a is 10. The semantics of GrAPL is such that this test doesn't result in a binding to v_1. In case we would perform $?(v_1 = x, \mathsf{a})$, where x is a local variable, and the constraint on a implies $v_1 = 10$, then only the local variable x is bound to 10.

The most innovative statements of the programming language are $\mathsf{CommGroupAdd}(\varphi, \mathsf{a})$ and $\mathsf{CommGroupReset}(\varphi, \mathsf{a})$. Here, a is the action the agent communicates about and φ is a constraint stating demands of the agent on future executions of the action a. Using these statements, agents synchronously communicate about the details of the action and about the group which is going to perform the action. Each agent in a group of communicators executes either a CommGroupAdd-statements or a CommGroupReset-statement. Arbitrary combinations of these two statements are allowed. If an agent executes $\mathsf{CommGroupAdd}(\varphi, \mathsf{a})$, then it proposes its previously accumulated constraint on action a strengthened with φ. If an agent executes $\mathsf{CommGroupReset}(\varphi, \mathsf{a})$, then it erases its present constraint on a and offers φ as a fresh proposal. In both cases, the resulting constraint on a will be the conjunction of the proposals of all communicators. The local bindings of a are updated accordingly. Subsequently, this resulting formula constrains each execution of a for each agent that has participated in the group communication, until the constraint on the action a is changed again. As the constraints are local, it is impossible for one agent to alter the constraints of another agent, without communication with the other agent.

The last basic statement is action execution, denoted by $\mathsf{a}(t_1, \ldots, t_k)$. We use this statement both for individual action and group action. If a group of agents (possibly consisting of only one member) tries to synchronously execute an action, the constraints of the agents on this action have to be consistent with each other and the actual parameters (the terms $t_1, \ldots, t_k$) and group composition have to satisfy all constraints. In implementations of GrAPL, a constraint solver has to be plugged in to check this. Another aspect of action execution is *execution time communication*. If one or more agents use a free variable in an actual parameter, and at least one agent specifies a definite value for this parameter, then the last agent *communicates* the value to the other agent(s). Example 1 below illustrates this. This form of communication generates bindings to the free variables used by the listening agents. In case all agents employ free variables in an actual parameter, a value is randomly picked from the set allowed by the constraints.

The syntax allows free local variables in CommGroupAdd-, CommGroupReset- and ins-statements. These variables act as place-holders, as we assume that these variables are *guarded*. A variable is guarded if there is a statement generating a binding for the variable earlier in the program, such that the free variable lies in the scope of the binding statement. Binding statements are tests and action execution (containing free variables). This implies that at runtime, the local variables are instantiated with ground terms.

The following example illustrates the novel statements.

EXAMPLE 1 (Jogging agents)

Two agents, James and Clare, arrange to go jogging. They discuss and subsequently execute $jog(v_1, v_2)$, where v_1 and v_2 are the formal parameters of the action. The first one is the time at which the agents start jogging, and the second parameter is the distance to be jogged.

Each agent has a constraint it wants to impose on the parameters of jog:

James: $\varphi : v_1 > 19.00 \wedge (v_2 = 7 \vee v_2 = 8) \wedge$ Clare $\in g$
Clare: $\psi : v_1 < 20.00 \wedge (v_2 = 8 \vee v_2 = 9) \wedge (v_1 > 19.00 \rightarrow$ James $\in g)$

So, James wants to start jogging after 19.00 o'clock, he wants to run 7 or 8 km., and he wants Clare to join him. Clare on the other hand only wants James to jog with her when she leaves after 19.00 o'clock, she wants to start before 20.00 o'clock, and she wants to run 8 or 9 km.

They synchronously communicate:

James: CommGroupReset(φ, jog)
Clare: CommGroupReset(ψ, jog)

The result of this synchronous communication is a new constraint, which holds for future executions of jog of both agents:

$$\{19.00 < v_1 < 20.00 \wedge v_2 = 8 \wedge \text{James} \in g \wedge \text{Clare} \in g\}$$

Next, the agents synchronously execute:

James: $jog(19.30, 8)$
Clare: $jog(x, 8)$

Note that James communicates the time 19.30 to Clare; Clare uses a free variable as first actual parameter, thereby indicating she is expecting James to pick the definite time. The constraint solver checks whether the actual parameters satisfy the constraints of James and Clare. This is the case, so the action is successful. In case James had performed $jog(y, 8)$ instead of $jog(19.30, 8)$, there would have been multiple possibilities for the first parameter (namely, every time between 19.00 and 20.00). In this situation, one value is picked.

Having defined the set S of basic statements, we now define the programs of GrAPL.

DEFINITION 2 (Agent programs)

The set P of valid single-agent programs is the smallest set containing:

- α, where $\alpha \in S$.
- if φ then π_1 else π_2, where $\varphi \in L$ and $var(\varphi) \cap GV = \varnothing$.
- if φ for a then π_1 else π_2, where $\varphi \in L$, a $\in A$ and $\pi_1, \pi_2 \in P$.
- $\pi_1; \pi_2$, where $\pi_1, \pi_2 \in P$.
- $\pi_1 + \pi_2$, where $\pi_1, \pi_2 \in P$.

More complex programs are formed using the if-then-else constructs, sequential composition and non-deterministic choice. The composed statement if φ then π_1 else π_2 first checks whether φ can be inferred from the belief base of the agent. If this is the case, π_1 is executed, and if not, π_2. The statement if φ for a then π_1 else π_2 is similar, except that this statement tests the constraint bound to the action a. Inclusion of these statements is useful, because it enables testing whether something *can't* be inferred, which is not possible with the test statements $?\varphi$ and $?(\varphi, a)$. Later on, in Example 2, we will encounter if $\perp$ for a then π_1 else π_2; this checks whether the constraint on a has become inconsistent, and chooses an appropriate course of action. Statements like these allows the programmer to explicitly encode backtracking mechanisms in negotiation.

Repetitive behaviour is not essential for our approach. So, for technical convenience we omitted recursion. GrAPL has a formal operational semantics, which we left out because of space considerations. Details can be found in [14].

3   Illustration

To show the usefulness of our language, we give an example of a multi-agent program.

EXAMPLE 2 (Arranging a dinner date)

Two agents, Martha and Matthew, negotiate the time they will have dinner together. They definitely want to dine with each other, so each of these agents has the constraint that the other agent has to be part of the group performing the dine action. They don't agree yet on the precise time of their dinner. During the negotiation process, the demands of the agents can turn out to be inconsistent. To solve this, at least one of the agents has to weaken its demands. It can also happen that the aggregate constraints are still rather weak and don't fix one specific time for the dinner. Then, the agents can strengthen their demands.

The dine action is unary; its sole explicit argument is the time.

Program of Martha:
01. CommGroupReset($v_1 \leq 19.00 \wedge$ Matthew $\in g$, dine);
02. if $\perp$ for dine
03. then (CommGroupReset($v_1 \leq 20.30 \wedge$ Matthew $\in g$, dine);
04.   if $v_1 = t$ for dine
05.   then dine(t)
06.   else dine(u))
07. else if $v_1 = w$ for dine
08.   then dine(w)
09.   else (CommGroupAdd($v_1 = 19.00$, dine);
10.   dine(19.00))

We number program lines for ease of reference. After the first CommGroup-statement, the program tests whether the resulting constraint set is inconsistent. Inconsistency results if the demand Matthew communicated is irreconcilable with Martha's demand. If so, then Martha weakens her constraints in a new communication attempt (line 03). As the inconsistent constraint has to be overwritten, a CommGroupReset is needed here; a CommGroupAdd would just add constraints to the already inconsistent store. The subprogram of lines 04–06 tests whether $v_1 = t$ can be derived from the result of this communication. If this is the case, the agents agree on *one* precise time, which is bound to the variable t. Then, Martha goes to dinner at time t. If not, she

leaves the choice up to Matthew (through the free variable u). If the outcome of the
first communication action is not inconsistent, the else-branch of line 07 is taken. The
constraint resulting from the first CommGroupReset is tested. If this constraint is not
strong enough to fix one definite time for the dinner, Martha communicates again. Now,
a CommGroupAdd is appropriate, because the earlier constraint on dine has to be kept
and strengthened.

Now, this is the program of Matthew:

```
01. CommGroupReset(v₁ ≥ 18.00 ∧ Martha ∈ g, dine);
02. if ⊥ for dine
03. then (CommGroupReset(v₁ ≥ 18.00 ∧ Martha ∈ g, dine);
04.      ?(v₁ ≤ x ∧ ∄y < x : v₁ ≤ y, dine); dine(x))
05. else if v₁ = y for dine
06.      then dine(y)
07.      else (CommGroupAdd(v₁ ≥ 19.00, dine);
08.           dine(z))
```

Matthew wants to dine after 18.00. If this proposal is not accepted, he tries to persuade
Martha to give in by repeating his proposal of dinner after 18.00. In line 04, Matthew's
constraint on dine is tested in a quite subtle way. We will come to this later. If the first
proposal is accepted, Matthew tests whether one definite time is agreed upon. If not, he
strengthens his constraints.

When these programs are executed, the first CommGroup of the agents yields the
consistent constraint $18.00 \leq v_1 \leq 19.00 \wedge$ Matthew $\in g \wedge$ Martha $\in g$. Martha proceeds
with line 07, and Matthew with line 05, in which they both test their resulting constraints
(stored locally now) for definiteness. Because the constraint still allows a range of times,
the agents communicate again. The constraint resulting from this communication is
$v_1 = 19.00 \wedge$ Matthew $\in g \wedge$ Martha $\in g$. The agents dine at 19.00.

But Martha and Matthew may not be the only agents around. Suppose there is another
agent, Lucy, who would like to join Martha and Matthew. These agents haven't forbidden
other agents to join the dinner; they just demanded that both of them should be present.
Here is Lucy's program:

```
01. CommGroupReset(g = {Matthew, Martha, Lucy} ∧ v₁ ≥ 21.00, dine);
02. if ⊥ for dine
03. then(CommGroupReset(g = {Matthew, Martha, Lucy} ∧ v₁ ≥ 20.00, dine);
04.      dine(s))
05. else dine(21.00)
```

If the agent programs are executed now, then the first lines of the three programs can
synchronise. This results in an inconsistent constraint ($v_1 \leq 19.00 \wedge v_1 \geq 21.00 \vdash \bot$).
So, all programs continue at line 03. Communication of the three agents results in
the constraint $g = \{$Matthew, Martha, Lucy$\} \wedge 20.00 \leq v_1 \leq 20.30$. Lucy then tries
to execute dine(s), but she has to wait for the other two agents to arrive at the dine-
statement. Martha first finds out that the constraint is not yet definite (line 04), and then
proceeds to dine(u). Note that Martha and Lucy both use free variables; this means they
want Matthew to pick the definite time, as long as it is within the constraints they agreed
upon. Matthew picks this time by testing the constraint in line 04. The formula tested
states that x is the smallest upper bound on the time of dinner. The outcome of this test

is that x is bound to 20.30. Matthew then executes dine(20.30) and the dinner party for three takes place.

4   Discussion

We proposed a constraint programming language for agents with novel primitives for group communication and group cooperation. The statements for group communication are very expressive and allow groups of agents to negotiate over the conditions of execution of future group actions. These conditions are constraints on the composition of the group of participants and the parameters of the action. Many coordination problems in agent systems are about finding a solution on which all agents agree in some solution space; constraint solving is especially apt for this. Successful application of constraint-based approaches in artificial intelligence depends on suitably encoding the problems into constraints. But proving that this is possible for all coordination issues agents could encounter doesn't yield a practical coordination language. As we want to focus at applicability, and constraint programming and -solving have proven their practical worth, we believe GrAPL is a significant contribution.

Communication is synchronous, allowing the dynamic formation of groups. In a language with only bilateral communication, programming a negotiation phase would be much more involved than in the language introduced here. If agreement is reached in the negotiation phase, the constraints agreed upon monitor the execution of the action discussed. The agents have to stick to their word; only then, group action can be successful. This way, social cohesion is enforced. Action execution is also synchronous, which is an intuitive manner to implement group actions.

The underlying constraint solver accumulates the constraints of the communicating agents, computes the resulting constraint and delivers this to the communicating agents. The constraint solver makes communication of constraints possible, even if the number of communicating agents is large (imagine going to lunch with eighty agents), as in the implementation of GrAPL the agents send the constraints to the constraint solver, instead of to all other agents involved. One of the benefits of our approach is that we use results from another research area (constraint solving) to construct an agent programming language. In order to implement GrAPL, a suitable constraint solver can be selected and customised to the domain of group action parameters.

Our programming language only provides primitive means for negotiation. More sophisticated negotiation protocols or mechanisms can be programmed in GrAPL.

The gap between theory and practice in agent research is a matter of concern for several authors who contributed to CEEMAS [2,3,5], including ourselves. By providing GrAPL with a formal semantics [14], we have created an agent programming language which is theoretically sound, and which can be implemented to build practical agent applications. GrAPL doesn't feature joint mental attitudes frequently used in logical theories on coordination [4,8], as we didn't focus on the mental aspects of group collaboration. We do think these aspects important, and integration of joint mental attitudes with the programming construct of GrAPL a promising direction for further work.

Coordination and coalition formation are also the subject of [9,11]. In the article of Romero Cortés and Sheremetov [11], a fuzzy game theoretic approach is taken, where vague information on individual agent gains is used for coalition games. A genetic algorithm is used to solve these games. A similarity with our work is that this genetic algorithm is central, like our constraint solver. But the approach we take is more classical in nature and provides a very flexible negotiation space. In GrAPL, an agent could for example negotiate in such a way that its own interest is not served, but that of another agent is, while in [11] the agents seek to maximise their own gains.

Pechoucek, Marik and Barta [9] propose CPlanT, which is a "framework for agents to form coalitions autonomously, collaboratively and without any central facilitating component", to quote the authors. In their framework, agents don't have to disclose all their information about their intentions and resources to their potential coalition partners. This is also true of GrAPL; here, agents only communicate their demands on some action parameters, without disclosing their reasons for this or the goals they have. On the other hand, GrAPL is a programming language, while [9] focuses on an architecture with coalition formation algorithms.

References

1. F.S. de Boer, R.M. van Eijk, W. van der Hoek and J.-J.Ch. Meyer, 'Failure Semantics for the Exchange of Information in Multi-Agent Systems', in: *Proceedings of CONCUR 2000* (C. Palamidessi, ed.), LNCS 1877, Springer, Heidelberg, 2000, pp.214–228.
2. K. Cetnarowicz, P. Gruer, V. Hilaire and A. Koukam, 'A Formal Specification of M-agent Architecture', (in this volume).
3. F. Dignum, D. Kinny and L. Sonenberg, 'Motivational Attitudes of Agents: On Desires, Obligations and Norms', (in this volume).
4. B. Dunin-Kęplicz and R. Verbrugge, 'Collective Commitments', in: *Proceedings of ICMAS 1996*, pp. 56–63.
5. N. Hameurlain, 'Formal Semantics for Behavioural Substitutability of Agent Components: Application to Interaction Protocols', (in this volume).
6. K.V. Hindriks, F.S. de Boer, W. van der Hoek and J.-J.Ch. Meyer, 'Agent Programming in 3APL', *Autonomous Agents and Multi-Agent Systems* 2 1999, pp. 357–401.
7. C.A.R. Hoare, 'Communicating Sequential Processes', *Communications of the ACM* 21(8) 1978, pp. 666–677.
8. H.J. Levesque, P.R. Cohen and J.T. Nunes, 'On Acting Together', in: *Proceedings of the National Conference on Artificial Intelligence*, 1990, pp. 94–99.
9. M. Pechoucek, V. Marik and J. Barta, 'CPlanT: An Acquaintance Model Based Coalition Formation Multi-Agent System', (in this volume).
10. A.S. Rao, M.P. Georgeff and E. Sonenberg, 'Social Plans: a Preliminary Report', in: *Proceedings of the Third European Workshop on Modelling Autonomous Agents in a Multi-Agent World (MAAMAW)*, Elsevier, Amsterdam, 1992, pp. 57–76.
11. J.C. Romero Cortés and L.B. Sheremetov, 'Model of Cooperation in Multi Agent Systems with Fuzzy Coalitions', (in this volume).
12. V.A. Saraswat, *Concurrent Constraint Programming*, The MIT Press, Cambridge, Massachusetts, 1993.
13. E.P.K. Tsang, *Foundations of Constraint Satisfaction*, Academic Press, London and San Diego, 1993, ISBN 0-12-701610-4.
14. W. de Vries, F.S. de Boer, K.V. Hindriks, W. van der Hoek and J.-J.Ch. Meyer, *A Programming Language for Coordinating Group Actions*, Technical report in preparation, Institute of Information and Computing Sciences, Utrecht University.

Optimization of Resource Allocation in Distributed Production Networks

Oleg Zaikin[1], Alexandre Dolgui[2], and Przemyslaw Korytkowski[1]

[1] Technical University of Szczecin,
Faculty of Computer Science and Information Systems,
Zolnierska 49, 71-210, Szczecin, Poland
`ozaikine@wi.ps.pl`
[2] University of Technology of Troyes,
12, rue Marie Curie, 10010, Troyes Cedex, France

Abstract. The development of the stochastic approach, based on queueing models and simulation, to optimize of resources allocation, in distributed production networks (DPN), is examined in the paper. The task of performance optimization of DPN is formulated as a non-linear integer programming problem with stochastic parameters. In our previous works, a branch and bound algorithm based on sequential use of queueing models and simulation is proposed. The analytical models are used for Lower Bound determination and choice of the optimal branching direction. The simulation is used for validation of analytical results and for computation of Upper Bound and stop condition of the algorithm. The developed methods have been used for optimization of corporate computer and telecommunication networks, High-Tech assembly manufacturing, and a printing and publishing company. In this paper, we show a new model and some additional results of simulation study for validation of models used.

1 Introduction

There are three main factors, which affect the development of the new generation of production systems:

- Penetration of information technologies into all levels of production systems,
- Development of telecommunication media for distributed production,
- Customer-oriented and address character of production and distribution.

Information technologies are changing the type of the output of several production systems. During the last decade a new kind of production system has been developed as an independent branch of the industry. The peculiarity of this type of production is that its output is the direct result of information technologies (intelligent products). They are High-Tech electronic production, print media industry, industry of development of databases and software tools, etc.

Production systems for intelligent products are essentially distributed systems for mass production. This type of system can be organized in networks

B. Dunin-Kęplicz and E. Nawarecki (Eds.): CEEMAS 2001, LNAI 2296, pp. 322–331, 2002.
© Springer-Verlag Berlin Heidelberg 2002

with several regional production nodes, which differ geographically as well as functionally.

A typical problem for distributed systems design and planning is the resource reallocation (machines, labor, material) between the central site and some regional sites. This problem appears each time, when the same functions can be performed at the central site and at some of the regional sites.

As a rule exceeding centralization leads to the increase of service costs. Alternatively, high decentralization can provoke the degradation of service quality. Therefore the problem of optimal resource reallocation in intelligent production systems appears. In this paper, a problem of this type is formulated as a performance optimization problem in distributed production networks and is solved by using the queueing models and simulation.

2   An Example of This Type of Problem

We will illustrate this type of problem using an example. In this example, we have a big printing company including several regional (local) factories and a central one (see Fig. 1). The local factories are equipped with offset printing machines, whereas the central one dispose of more sophistic printing machines. As usual, the local factories serve local customer demands. However, when some of them are overcharged, customer demand is transferred to the central factory. The central digital printing is more expensive than the local offset one. On the other side, the lead-time of the central factory is considerably less than the lead-time of the local factories. Note that no customer demand comes directly to the central factory.

Let the rate of the customer's demand for each local factory and the processing time for all equipment be given. It is necessary to find the number of offset machines for each local factory, minimizing the total cost of printing with constraints linked to due dates of the customer's demand.

The studied system can be considered as an open queueing network (QN), which can be represented as an oriented graph. The vertices of the graph are processing nodes and the arcs of the graph are flow processes between them. In the studied case, we examine QN with star configuration, i.e. there is a set of local processing nodes (PN), for serving corresponding local areas and one network center (NC), for serving the global region. Each local PN consists of a number of specialized servers, working in parallel, and an input buffer of given capacity. The NC consists of one or several servers of high productivity and does not need any waiting queue.

It is necessary to find the number of servers and the input buffer capacity at each local PN, taking into account, that the local and the centralized servers have different costs and different productivity rates.

Using the above mentioned properties, we can examine an analytical model of an isolated processing node of DPN. In Fig. 2 the structure of the multi-server queueing system of type $G/G/m/s$ according to the Kendall notation is presented. The incoming job goes to any free server for serving. If all servers are busy, the job goes to the waiting queue. The capacity of the input buffer for waiting queue is limited. If the input buffer is filled up, the incoming job goes to NC.

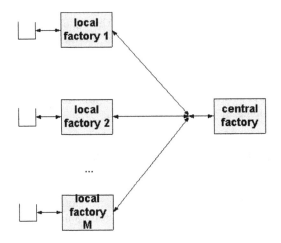

Fig. 1. Graph representation of the studied production system

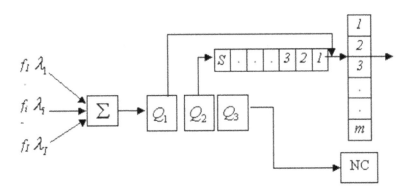

Fig. 2. Structure of the multi-server queueing system

In Fig. 2, the following notations are used:

$f_i, i = 1, 2, ..., I$ is a set of customers,

$\lambda_i, i = 1, 2, ..., I$ is the arrival rate for demand of f_i,

m is the number of identical servers, working in parallel

S is the capacity of input buffer for waiting queue,

$\tau_i^S, i = 1, 2, ..., I$ is the fixed service time for a job from arrival process f_i,
$\tilde{\tau}^W$ is the average waiting time for a job,
$\tilde{N}_i, i = 1, 2, ..., I$ is the average number of jobs 'i' being in the queueing system at any moment,
Q_1 is the probability, that a job arriving goes for service directly (there is an available server at the moment),
Q_2 is the probability, that a job arriving goes to the waiting queue (all the servers are busy),
Q_3 is the probability, that a job arriving go to central node for service (all the servers are busy and the input buffer is filled up)

Using the notation presented above, we can formulate the following optimization problem:
Given:

1. a set of arrival processes $F = \{f_i\}, i = 1, 2, ..., I$,
2. a distribution law $\Psi_i(n, t_i)$ and an arrival rate λ_i of process f_i,
3. a service time $\tau_i^S, i = 1, 2, ..., I$,

Determine:

1. The number of parallel servers m.
2. The waiting queue capacity S.

Provide:
Min of total production costs per time unit

$$C = C_1 + C_2 + C_3 = min,$$

There are three components of the criterion function for an isolated PN:

1. cost of the work-in-process (WIP):

$$C = \sum_{i=1}^{I} \alpha_i \tilde{N}_i = (Q_1 + Q_2) \sum_{i=1}^{I} \alpha_i \lambda_i (\tilde{\tau}^W + \tau_i^S),$$

2. cost of work-time and idle-time of the servers

$$C_2 = C_2^W + C_2^I = m[\beta\rho + \gamma(1 - \rho)] = m[\gamma + (\beta - \gamma)(Q_1 + Q_2) \sum_{i=1}^{I} \lambda\tau_i^S],$$

3. service cost at the central node

$$C_3 = Q_3 \sum_{i=1}^{I} \delta_i \lambda_i.$$

Here, the following notations are used:
α_i is the cost of apart 'i' (semi-finished product),
β is the cost of work-time of a PN server per time-unit,
γ is the cost of idle-time of a PN server per time-unit,
δ_i is the service cost for jobs of type $i \in I$ at the central node,
ρ is the PN server utilization.

The components C_1, C_2, C_3 of the criterion function depend on the control parameters m and S differently. Hence, it is possible to define such values of control parameters, which provide minimum of the criterion function.

Note that this type of problem appears also in several other domains, for example in distribution of multiplex channel in satellite telecommunication systems [13].

3 Solution Method

3.1 Optimization Approach

In our method, to optimize this type of system, we combine analytical methods and simulation. The general schema of our approach consist of the following steps:

- choice of basic queueing network [1], [2], [4], [6] models and their analytical validation,
- incremental construction of the complete model by using the basic models,
- use of simulation techniques for validation of the complete model,
- joint use of simulation and optimization algorithms [5] for optimization of the model, obtained in previous steps.

Some elements of this general approach are given in our previous works [9], [11], [12]. We proposed a basic queueing model, the rules of a complete model design and an algorithm for optimization of the complete model. The proposed algorithm is based on sequential use of analytical calculation and simulation [3], [10]. The algorithm tries to reallocate a part of the resources from NC node to the local PN by [10]:

- choice of a resource quantity to reallocate from NC node to local PN,
- analytical calculation of the criterion value CR, separately for each local PN,
- choice of PN for which the criterion value is minimal; reallocate the resource from NC to the PN,
- simulation for the chosen variant.

If CR value is better, then continue this branch; otherwise return to the previous one. Branching is started from an initial capacity location where all the resources are assigned to NC node.

So, this algorithm applies the main idea of Branch-and-Bound method. The analytical model [3] is used for Lower Bound evaluation and choice of optimal branching direction. The simulation is used for validation of analytical results, for Upper Bound computation and for stop condition of this algorithm. For more details on this algorithm and analysis of its performance, see our works [10]. Here, we present a new analytical model and some recent results, for validation of the analytical models and optimization algorithm.

3.2 Analytical Model

The optimizaion problem does not accept an analytical solution in general case. However, primary evaluation can be obtained on the base of queueing theory [2], [6] using the following assumptions.

1. The total arrival process can be modeled as being Markovian, if the correlation between different input processes, is not present, i.e. an averaging of incoming jobs will assume a new exponential length. It was shown in [8], that merging several processes as input of the queueing system as shown in Fig.1, has similar effect to restoring the independence of inter-arrival times and job service time. Therefore, using the Kleinrock independence approximation and assuming a Poisson total arriving stream, we have

$$\Lambda = \sum_{i \in I} \lambda_i, \widetilde{\mu} = \frac{\sum_{i \in I} \lambda_i}{\sum_{i \in I} \lambda_i t_i},$$

where Λ is the total arrival rate, $\widetilde{\mu}$ is the average service rate.

2. The probability of service for the incoming job Q_1 can be defined from the following reasoning: the queueing system (QS), which comprises m parallel servers and infinite input buffer, can be deemed an Erlang delay system M/M/m according to Kendall notation. The probability of delay Q_D for this kind of QS is given by the following equation

$$Q_D = Q_0 \frac{(a)^m}{m!(1-\rho)},$$

where

$$Q_0 = [\sum_{k=0}^{m-1} \frac{(a)^k}{k!} + \frac{(a)^m}{m!(1-\rho)}]^{-1}$$

is the probability of idle state of QS,
$a = \frac{\Lambda}{\mu}$ and $\rho = \frac{\Lambda}{m\mu}$ are the traffic intensity and the PN server utilization, respectively.
It is obvious that the probability of service for the incoming jobs Q_1 is the following: $Q_1 = 1 - Q_D$.

3. The reject probability for the incoming job Q_3 when no server available and buffer overflow can be considered as the probability of blocking

for M/M/m/S queueing systems. It given by the well-known formula for
M/M/m/S QS:

$$Q_3 = Q_{BL} = \frac{(1-\rho)\rho^S}{1-\rho^{S+1}}.$$

4. The probability of entering the waiting queue for the incoming job Q_2 (all
the servers are busy) is expressed from the normalization condition:

$$Q_2 = 1 - Q_1 - Q_3$$

The average waiting time $\tilde{\tau}^W$ results from the following formula for
M/M/1/S queueing system

$$\tilde{\tau}^W = \frac{\rho}{\tilde{\mu} - \Lambda} - \frac{S\rho^{S+1}}{\tilde{\mu} - \Lambda\rho^{S+1}}$$

Therefore, the average flow-time $\tilde{\tau}_i$ for an incoming job of process $f_i, i =
1, 2, ..., I$ at PN is:

$$\tilde{\tau}_i = \tau_i^S Q_1 + (\tilde{\tau}^W + \tau^S)Q_2)$$

Using Little's theorem, we can get:
  − The average number of jobs 'i' being in PN at any time
    $\tilde{N}_i = \tilde{\tau}_i \lambda_i (1 - Q_3), i = 1, 2, ..., I,$
  − The total number of jobs being in PN at any time $\tilde{N}_\Sigma = \sum_{i=I}^{I} \tilde{N}_i$

The above formulas for an isolated PN can be used for performance optimization
of DPN. However, because of assumptions (1)-(4) from Section 3.2 they have a
restricted utilization. More possibilities for analysis of DPN are provided by
simulation [7], which has no restrictions on dimension, kind of arrival pattern,
discipline and service time. The objective of the simulation experiments is also
verification and validation of the proposed analytical model.

3.3   Validation of Analytical Model by Simulation

In papers [3], [10], we presented another analytical queueing network analysis
method for a simplified case of this type of systems. In this paper, the objectives
of simulation consist in validation of proposed analytical models. The simulation
was performed under ARENA, which is an integrated environment for discrete
event simulation [7].

In this paper we present the simulation model of one node of the proposed
production network. For selected tests, the simulation experiment was conducted
in the following conditions:

1. QN consists of one network-center.
2. The replication length is 1000 tu. Provided simulation experiments show that
   the simulation results become stationary after 500 tu. Warm-up interval is
   200 tu.
3. The-simulation model is realized for three streams of input flows:

- Poisson law of jobs arrival and exponential distribution of service time
- Deterministic law of jobs arrival and deterministic law of service time
- Erlang law of jobs arrival and Erlang law of 2nd degree for service time distribution.

Service discipline is 'First come-First served'. The waiting queue is limited. To find global minimum value of the criterion function we have to examine a three-dimensional space (see Fig. 3). The first dimension is the number of servers in the model, the second is their distribution among locals and central nodes, and finally the third dimension give values of the criterion function.

We examined a model with one PN. The simulation data are the following:

- 1st stream: Poisson law of jobs arrival with $\lambda = 5$ and exponential distribution of service time with $\mu = 0.1$,
- 2nd stream: deterministic law of jobs arrival with $\lambda = 4$ and deterministic law of service time with $\mu = 0.12$,
- 3rd stream: Erlang law of jobs arrival $\lambda = 3$ and Erlang law of 2nd degree for service time distribution with $\mu = 0.08$.

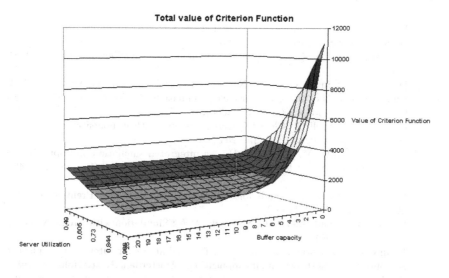

Fig. 3. Search area for optimization

Presented simulation results have proved the adequacy of the proposed analytical models. Conducted simulation experiments have shown that the network configuration obtained by simulation is the same or very close to the optimal configuration computed by using the analytical model.

4   Conclusion

1 The model of a multi-process and multi-server queueing system with limited capacity of waiting queue is examined in the paper. Because of its generality such a model can be basic for analysis of production or corporate or telecommunication networks with studied structures and configuration.

2 In general case there is no analytical solution to obtain the performance measures of this kind of QS. Nevertheless, under certain assumptions on the arrival and service time, an analytical solution can be obtained for primary evaluation of possible decisions.

3 Verification and validation of the proposed analytical solution has been done by stochastic simulation under Arena software. Simulation experiments were performed for different kinds of incoming processes, as well as for different number of servers and utilization rates. Comparisons between simulation and analytical results have shown high adequacy of the proposed analytical method, that allows us to use the obtained analytical results as primary evaluation for decision making and as a Lower Bound in our optimization algorithm.

References

[1] Buzacott, J., Shanthikumar, J.: Modeling and analysis of manufacturing systems. John Wiley & Sons, New York, (1993).

[2] Chee Hock Ng: Queuing Modelling Fundamentals. John Wiley & Sons, New York, (1997).

[3] Dolgui A., Zaikin O.: Queueing Network Models for a Capacity Allocation Problem. Proceedings of the 14th European Simulation Multiconference (ESM'2000), Ghent, Belgium, May 2000, SCS, (2000), p. 315-317.

[4] Gordon W., Newell G.: Closed Queuing Systems with Exponential Servers, Operation Research, v. 15, (1967), p.254-265.

[5] Guariso, G., Hitz, M., Werthner, H.: An integrated simulation and optimization modeling environment for decision support. Decision Support Systems, 1, (1996), 103-117.

[6] Hall, R.W.: Queuing methods for service and manufacturing. Prentice Hall, Englewood Cliffs. N. Y, (1991).

[7] Kelton, W.D., Sadowski, R.P., Sadowski, D.A.: Simulation with Arena. McGraw-Hill, N. Y., (1997).

[8] Kleinrock L.: Performance evaluation of Distributed Computer- Communication Systems. Queuing theory and its applications. Amsterdam. North Holland. (1988).

[9] Zaikin, O., Dolgui, A.: Resource assignment in mass demand HighTec assembly manufacturing based on the queuing modelling. In: Proc. International Conference on Industrial Logistics (ICIL'99), St. Petersburg, 1999, University of Southampton Publication, (1999), 200-209.

[10] Zaikin O., Dolgui, A., Korytkowski, P.: Modeling and Performance Optimization of a Distributed Production System, Preprints of the 10th IFAC Symposium on Information Control Problems in Manufacturing (INCOM'2001), September 20-22, (2001), Vienna, Austria, 6 pages (CD-ROM).

[11] Zaikin, O., Ignatiev, V.: A method of analysis of multi-channel queueing models. Izv. AN SSSR (Technical Cybernetics, Academy of Science of USSR), 6, (1973), 86-88.
[12] Zaikin, O., Korytkowski, P.: Resource assignment and performance optimization in the distributed production network, In Proceedings. of the 7th International Conference 'Regional Informatics 2000' (RI-2000), St. Petersburg , (2000), p. 98-103.
[13] Zaikin O., Kraszewski P., Dolgui, A.: Queuing based approach to resource allocation in the satellite telecommunication networks. Proceedings of the Workshop "Distributed Computer Communication Networks: Architecture, Design and Resource Allocation" (DCCN'98), Moscow, (1998), p. 96-109.

Utility-Based Role Exchange

Xin Zhang and Henry Hexmoor

Computer Science & Computer Engineering Department, Engineering Hall, Room 313,
Fayetteville, AR 72701
{xxz03, hexmoor}@uark.edu

Abstract. In this paper, we examine role exchange in multiagenty. After defining the utility that reflects an agent's orientation toward role exchange, I.e., Role Exchange Value (REV) and the agent's Individual Utility Gain (IUG), we present two theorems and two corollaries that capture properties of proposed utility-based role exchange. Then, we provide an algorithm that predicts IUG for each agent in role exchange. The algorithm is implemented and the results are discussed.

1 Introduction

In multiagent systems, a major issue is for self-interested agents to form coalitions in order to produce the most effective results. Self-interested agents care solely about their own benefits instead of considering the group benefits. Therefore, Pareto-optimality agents [8], which have cooperative characteristics, are preferred. Since "A team in which each boundedly rational player maximizes its individual expected utility does not yield the best possible team" [1], some agents need to sacrifice their individual utility for the sake of the community [6].

The relationship among agents is primarily reflected by their roles [9]. Ferber defines a role as "an abstract representation of an agent function, service or identification" [4]. Role is a common sense notion for agents in communities [5]. Said differently, here the consideration that helps form role selections is synonymous with the consideration that helps form a coalition of agents.

Careful selection of a pattern of roles for adoption is a key point for improving the group performance. We can use the concept of *individual utility* to measure each agent's performance in a specific role and use the *total utility* to represent the team's performance in the formation of roles.

Consider a group of distinct n agents, $A = \{a_1, a_2, ..., a_n\}$, where a_i is the i th agent and a set of distinct n roles, $R = \{r_1, r_2, ..., r_n\}$, where r_i is the i th role, such that $i \neq j \Rightarrow r_i \neq r_j$. For any agent a_i and role r_j, there is a utiltiy $U(a_i, r_j) = u_{ij}$, where u_{ij} stands for the utility of adopting role j by agent i and function $U(a_i, r_j)$ is to get

B. Dunin-Kęplicz and E. Nawarecki (Eds.): CEEMAS 2001, LNAI 2296, pp. 332–340, 2002.

u_{ij}. Any formation F is a set of $\{<a_i,r_j,u_{ij}>\mid where\; i,j \in [1..n]$, for any pair of $<a_i,r_j,u_{ij}>$ and $<a_k,r_l,u_{kl}>$, $a_i \neq a_j \Rightarrow r_k \neq r_l\}$ and each agent is assigned a single distinct role. The cardinality of this set is n. Agent i may adopt any of the other $n-1$ roles and its respective utility. In this model, there are the same number of roles as there are agents [11].

In this paper, we will present an algorithm called "utility-based role exchange". At first we will introduce the related works in the field of formation-based roles in section 2. Then we will provide some assumptions before defining the concept of role exchange value and the concept of utility gain in section 3.1. Then in section 3.2, we will discuss 2 theorems and 2 corollaries for the condition of role exchange. Based on the theorems and corollaries, we will present the utility-based role exchange algorithm in section 4 and the implementation of the algorithm with the results. In section 5, we will provide some concluding remarks.

2 Related Work

Formation as basis of collaboration among agents is introduced in [11]. A formation decomposes the task space into a set of roles. Formations include as many roles as there are agents in the team, so that each role is filled by a single agent. Furthermore, formations can specify sub-formations, or *units*, that do not involve the whole team. A unit consists of a subset of roles from the formation, a *captain*, and intra-unit interactions among those roles.

Formations are commonly found in the game of soccer or Robocup [12]. Agents adopt an initial assignment of roles, but this assignment may need to be revised as the situation changes. Therefore, re-assignment of roles or some role exchanges become necessary [7]. Formation-based role assignment ensures flexibility of role exchange, which was beneficial to the FC Portugal team [10]. In this team, each player exchanges not only its position (place in the formation), but also its assigned role in the current formation. After the exchange, the agent will be instantiated with a new role and corresponding new abilities and goals. Therefore, the team completely loses properties of its old roles. To our knowledge, beyond the game of Robocup, role exchange has not been explicitly addressed in the literature. Work on coalitions is related but the agent and its roles are not differentiated.

Role adoption is the initial state before role exchange takes place. Cavedon and Sonenberg introduced the notion that role adoption results in goal adoption to different degrees [2]. Fosli discussed the relationships among agents, roles, commitments, and obligations: an agent adopts a role, this role is associated with one or more social commitments, and obligations result from the adoption of roles ([3] in this volume).

3   The Assumptions and Properties for Role Exchange

Let's assume the agent is Pareto-optimality agent. In order to get the optimized *total utility*, some agents have to sacrifice their benefits to exchange roles. In order to determine which agent needs to sacrifice its benefit, we need to define a *Role Exchange Value* (REV) for the computation. From this value we present another concept of *Individual Utility Gain* (IUG) for each agent when considering role exchange in an agent pair. If IUG of each agent in the pair increases, role exchange will benefit the group. In some cases, the IUG of the agent may increase, while its individual utility after role exchange may decrease. At this time, we can say that the agent sacrifices its own benefit to maximize the pair utility.

Before presenting the detail of the algorithm of role exchange, we make the following assumptions:

1.   With N agent and N roles, there is a one to one assignment of roles to agents.
2.   Each agent has a unique utility per role. I.e., $V(A,R)$ is agent A's unique utility in role R.
3.   An agent's adoption of a role will not affect the utility of another agent adopting another role.
4.   The *total utility* of a number of agents is equal to the sum utilities from each of these agents. I.e. *Total Utility* $= \sum_{i=0}^{i=n} V(A_i, R_i)$ [1].
5.   The role exchange process takes place only between a pair of roles at one time.
6.   If the margin of gain from a hypothetical role exchange is positive for a pair of agents, they are obliged to exchange. This is due to the Pareto-optimality cooperative agents.
7.   The time consumption or utility loss due to the process of role exchange is assumed negligible and will not be considered.

3.1   Role Exchange Value and Utility Gain

REV involves a pair of agents and a pair of roles, i.e., agent A, agent B and role R1 and role R2. We will introduce the following concepts here:

1. $V(A, R1)$ represents the unique utility of agent A taking role R1.

---

[1] We do not consider varying degrees of contribution. We consider uniform contribution by each agent. This means that we do not consider a weighted generalizing of this formula. Furthermore, individual agents do not have access to this total utility.

2. $V(A, R1, B, R2)$ represents the sum utility of agent A taking role R1 and agent B taking role R2.   I.e., based on assumption 3 and 4, $V(A, R1, B, R2) = V(A, R1) + V(B, R2)$.

3. $REV_A(A, R1, B, R2)$ represents the role exchange value of agent A in the formation that agent A taking role R1 while agent B taking role R2. $REV_A(A, R1, B, R2)$ for role exchange involves $V(A, R1)$, $V(B, R2)$, $V(A, R2)$, and $V(B, R1)$.

We can assume that $V(A, R1)$ is the utility of agent A takes role R1 before role exchange, and $V(B, R2)$ is the utility of agent B takes role R2 before role exchange. The total utility of agent A and B before role exchange is $V(A, R1, B, R2)$. $V(A, R2, B, R1)$ is the total utility of agent A and agent B after role exchange. In role exchange for agent pair (A, B), we define the REV of agent A in the formation that agent A taking role R2 while agent B taking role R2 as equation (1):

$$REV_A(A, R1, B, R2) = 0.5 * \{V(A, R1) + V(A, R2, B, R1) - V(B, R2)\} (1)$$

The origin of this equation lies in the game theory where rewards are divided according to the relative contributions of each member. Here we have two agents and we adopt the Shapley value in the degenerate case of two agents. Since agents map one to one to roles, all exchanges are between pairs of agents and all concurrent exchanges can be pair-wise decomposed. This implies that no complex equation beyond (1) is needed for multiple exchanges. For agent A, the formula captures ½ the marginal gain A would contribute to working with B and ½ the gain it would make by itself. The multiplier 1/2 is used to divide the utility gain equally between two agents.

The *individual utility gain* for agent A in this role exchange formation is as equation (2):

$$IUG_A(A, R1, B, R2) = REV_A(A, R1, B, R2) - V(A, R1) (2)$$

If REV is the gain after exchange, the agent must compare that to the gain when working alone. This will be basis of simple exchange. Based on equations (1) and (2), we use the following 3 conditions to check if role exchange is needed.

1. If $IUG_A(A, R1, B, R2) < 0$, role exchange will degrade to total utility for the entire group and original role formation is better.

2. If $IUG_A(A, R1, B, R2) = 0$, role exchange is not necessary. There is no difference between before and after role exchange.

3. If $IUG_A(A, R1, B, R2) > 0$, role exchange will be beneficial to the entire group.

Conditions for Role Exchange

3.2 Theorems

The following 2 theorems and 2 corollaries present the main properties of the utility-based role exchange using REV and IUG.

Theorem 1: Gains and losses of two agents in a role exchange are the same for either agent.

$\forall i, j \; \forall k, l \; agent(i) \wedge agent(j) \wedge i \neq j \wedge role(k) \wedge role(l) \wedge k \neq l \Rightarrow$

$IUG_i(i, k, j, l) = IUG_j(i, k, j, l)$.

The predicate "agent" picks out agents whereas predicate "role" picks out roles.

Proof. For agent pair A and B, agent A takes role R1, and agent B takes role R2. Let's calculate the gain for agent A and B respectively after role exchange.

$IUG_A(A, R1, B, R2) = REV_A(A, R1, B, R2) - V(A, R1) =$
$0.5 * \{V(A, R1) + [V(A, R2, B, R1) - V(B, R2)]\} - V(A, R1) =$
$0.5 * [V(A, R2, B, R1) - V(A, R1) - V(B, R2)]$ and

$IUG_B(A, R1, B, R2) = REV_B(A, R1, B, R2) - V(B, R2) =$
$0.5 * \{V(B, R2) + [V(A, R2, B, R1) - V(A, R1)]\} - V(B, R2) =$
$0.5 * [V(A, R2, B, R1) - V(A, R1) - V(B, R2)]$.

From above equations, we can see that the utility gain of agent A is equal to utility gain of agent B.

The utility gain after each role exchange for each agent is the mutual gain for the pair of agent.

Corollary 1: If role exchange benefits either agent in a pair, it will also benefit the other agent.

$\forall i, j \; \forall k, l \; agent(i) \wedge agent(j) \wedge i \neq j \wedge role(k) \wedge role(l) \wedge k \neq l \wedge IUG_i(i, k, j, l) > 0 \Rightarrow$

$IUG_j(i, k, j, l) > 0.$

Proof. Using Theorem 1.

Before role exchange, we calculate the utility gain of one agent in the agent pair, if its utility gain is positive, the other agent's utility gain will also be positive. Therefore, role exchange will increase the total utility of the group.

Corollary 2: If role exchange does not benefit either agent in a pair, it will not benefit the other agent either.

$\forall i, j \; \forall k, l \; agent(i) \wedge agent(j) \wedge i \neq j \wedge role(k) \wedge role(l) \wedge k \neq l \wedge IUG_i(i, k, j, l) < 0 \Rightarrow$

$IUG_j(i, k, j, l) < 0.$

Proof. Using Theorem 1.

Before role exchange, we calculate the utility gain of one agent in the agent pair, if its utility gain is negative, the other agent's utility gain will also be negative. Therefore, role exchange will not be performed.

Theorem 2: The marginal utility gain for the agent pair equals twice the IUG for one agent.

$$\forall i,j \; \forall k,l \; agent(i) \wedge agent(j) \wedge i \neq j \wedge role(k) \wedge role(l) \wedge k \neq l \Rightarrow$$
$$IUG_i(i,k,j,l) + IUG_j(i,k,j,l) = 2 * IUG_i(i,k,j,l).$$

Proof. Using Theorem 1.

From the IUG of one agent in a pair, we can simply calculate the total utility gain for the whole group. Since IUG is the mutual gain for both agents, therefore, the utility gain for the whole group during the current role exchange is twice IUG.

4   The Algorithm for Role Exchange

The algorithm for utility-based role exchange takes the following steps. In our algorithm, t is the time index. For instance, $t = 0$ is the time before any role exchange. $t = 1$ is the time at the 1st exchange. Function $add(< x,y,z >, S)$ adds the triple $< x,y,z >$ to set S. Function $delete(< x,y,z >, S)$ deletes the triple $< x,y,z >$ from set S. $stop$ stands for termination of the algorithm. Predicate "formation" picks out a specific formation, e.g., F.

---

1. There is no role adoption for any agent at the very beginning. $t = 0 \Rightarrow F = \varnothing$.

2. When role adoption starts, each agent adopts a role randomly, which means that the agent may adopt any role at first. $t = 1 \Rightarrow \forall i \exists j, agent(i) \wedge role(j) \wedge U(i,j) = u_{ij} \wedge add(< i,j,u_{ij} >, F)$.

3. Search the agent pairs from the first agent for role exchange. If the IUG of the given pair of agents is positive, the agent pair will make role exchange; otherwise search the next agent pair for role exchange. $\forall i, j \forall k, l \forall F, agent(i) \wedge agent(j) \wedge role(k) \wedge role(l) \wedge formation(F) \wedge < i,j,u_{ik} >\in F \wedge < i,j,u_{il} >\in F \wedge$
$IUG_i(i,k,j,l) > 0 \Rightarrow add(< i,l,u_{il} >, F) \wedge add(< j,k,u_{jk} >, F) \wedge delete(< i,k,u_{ik} >, F) \wedge delete(< j,l,u_{jl} >, F$

4. Role exchanges will stop when the utility gain of any agent pair is no more than zero.
$\forall i, j \forall k, l \; agent(i) \wedge agent(j) \wedge role(k) \wedge role(l) \wedge \sum_{i=1}^{n} IUG_i(i,k,j,l) \leq 0 \Rightarrow stop.$

The Algorithm for Role Exchange

Consider the following example involving role exchanges with 2 agents and 2 roles, which are adopted by those 2 agents. We can use a matrix to model this problem. Based on assumption 1 and 2, suppose there are N agents and N roles, we can use N*N matrix to represent the relationship between agents and roles. The rows represent agents such as agent A0 and columns represent roles, such as role R0. The value at the intersection of an agent row and a role column, such as element (i, j), represents the utility that agent i adopting role j. In an implementation of this algorithm, we use a 10*10 matrix shown in Table 1, whose utilities are randomly generated.

According to the algorithm we discussed in above, no role has been adopted at first. So we may just assign each agent A_i with role R_i, as the entities highlighted in the table. Based on assumption 3 and 4, at this time, the initial total utility of the group is $\sum_{i=0}^{i=9} V(Ai, Ri) = 71$. Then based on assumption 5, 6 and 7, we will check each agent pair to decide if role exchange is necessary or not based on conditions we discussed in 2.1. The agent pair of role exchange and the exchange sequence is shown in Table 2.

Table 1. Agent-Role Table

	R0	R1	R2	R3	R4	R5	R6	R7	R8	R9
A0	1	7	14	0	9	4	18	18	2	4
A1	5	5	1	7	1	11	15	2	7	16
A2	11	4	2	13	12	2	1	16	18	15
A3	7	6	11	1	8	9	12	7	19	15
A4	14	3	11	2	13	13	4	1	11	13
A5	8	7	4	2	17	17	19	3	1	9
A6	18	16	15	10	2	8	6	0	2	4
A7	8	6	5	10	9	10	10	6	1	13
A8	8	9	3	4	14	16	0	6	16	11
A9	8	4	19	6	3	17	18	18	2	9

Table 2. Role Exchange Pairs

Agent Pair	PairUtility Gain
A0, A1	6
A0, A2	9
A0, A6	14
A0, A7	5
A0, A2	1
A0, A6	12
A0, A7	8
A0, A9	3
A0, A1	12
A0, A2	12
A2, A8	5

The result for role exchange is shown in Figure 1. From the chart we can see that role exchange increases the total utility of the whole group from 71 to 154.

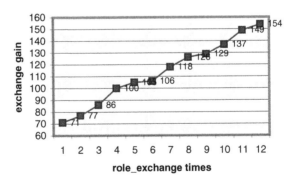

Figure 1. Utility Gain of Role Exchange

5   Ongoing Work

There are a number of possible avenues for future development related to utility-based role exchange. First, since in real world agents' role adoption is influenced by many factors, such as goals, abilities, commitments and etc, we can extend our considerations to other kinds of agent-role mapping relationships. For example, agents and roles are not mapped one by one. The algorithm for this example will be more complicated, i.e., one agent can take two or more roles at the same time. This aspect is not present in the current formalism. Second, in this paper, utility gains or losses are equally divided by a pair of agents since we assumed that every agent has the same priority toward the others. In the condition that agent's priority is not reciprocal, the gains and losses from role exchange will not be linear. Another issue is that when we make role exchanges, we consider all the other agents before making the decision. But some time, the agents do not have enough time to make full consideration, so partial consideration maybe "good enough". Based on the theorems and equations presented in this paper, elsewhere we have reported on two alternative algorithms for role exchange [13].

6   Conclusion

We examined role exchanges in general and suggested utility-based role exchange. We applied role exchange value to compute the utility gain for each agent in an agent pair. We also presented two theorem and two corollaries for utility-based role exchange and the method of computation for mutual gain. We provided the algorithm and conditions for role exchange based on the group utility gain. Finally, we discussed the implementation of the algorithm and analyzed that utility-based role exchange can benefit the group of agents.

Acknowledgement. We wish to thank anonymous reviewers for constructing comments that helped improve our paper.

References

1. Boman, M., Kummeneje, J., Lyback, D., Younes, H. L.: UBU Team. *RoboCup-99 Team Descriptions Simulation League*, pp. 133-138, (1999).
2. Cavedon, L., Sonenberg, L.: On Social Commitments, Roles and Preferred Goals. In Proceedings of the 3rd Int. Conference on Multi-Agent Systems, *ICMAS-98*, pp. 278-289, (1998).

3. Fasli, M.: On Commitments, Roles and Obligations. Pre-proceedings of the Second International Workshop of Central and Eastern Europe on Multi-Agent Systems, *CEEMAS*, pp. 71-80, (2001).

4. Ferber, J., Gutknecht, O.: Admission of agents in groups as a normative and organizational problem. *Workshop on Norms and Institutions in Multi-agent systems at Normative agent*, ACM press June (2000).

5. Hexmoor, H., Zhang, X.: Norms, Roles and Simulated RoboCup. 2nd workshop on norms and institutions in multiagent systems *(Agents 2001)*, Montreal, CA, ACM press, (2001).

6. Ketchpel, S. P.: Coalition Formation Among Autonomous Agents. Fifth European Workshop on Modelling Autonomous Agents in a Multi-Agent World, *MAAMAW-93* (LNAI Volume 957), (1993).

7. Marsella, S., Adibi, J., Al-Onaizau, Y., Kaminka, G., Musela, I., Tambe, M.: Experiences acquired in the design of Robocup teams: A comparison of two fielded teams, *JAAMAS*, special issue on "Best of Agents'99", (2000).

8. Myerson, R. B.: Game Theory: Analysis of conflict. Harvard University Press, London, Cambridge, (1991).

9. Panzarasa, P., Norman, T. J., Jennings, N. R.: Modeling sociality in the BDI framework. In J. Lui and N. Zhong, editors, Proceedings of the First Asia-Pacific Conference on Intelligent Agent Technology. *World Scientific*, (1999).

10. Reis, L. P., Lau, N.: FC Portugal Team Description: RoboCup 2000 Simulation League Champion. RoboCup 2000: *Robot Soccer World Cup IV*, Berlin, (2001).

11. Stone, P., Veloso, M.: Task Decomposition, Dynamic Role Assignment, and Low-Bandwidth communication for Real-Time Strategic Teamwork. Artificial Intelligence *(AIJ)*, Volume 100, number 2, June (1999).

12. Veloso, M., Pagello, E., Kitano, H.: RoboCup-99: Robot Soccer World Cup III. *RoboCup*, (1999).

13. Zhang, X., Hexmoor, H.: Algorithms for Utility-based Role Exchange. (2002 submitted).

Author Index

Lecture Notes in Artificial Intelligence (LNAI)

Lecture Notes in Computer Science